RONALD STEVENSON
The Man and his Music

RONALD STEVENSON
The Man and his Music

**A Symposium
edited by
COLIN SCOTT-SUTHERLAND**

**With a Foreword by
LORD MENUHIN**

TOCCATA
PRESS

First published in 2005 by Toccata Press

Music examples set by Jiří Kub.

British Library Cataloguing in Information Data

Ronald Stevenson: The Man and His Music –
A Symposium
  I. Scott-Sutherland, Colin
  780.92
  ISBN 0–907689–40–X (hd)
  ISBN 0–907689–41–8 (pb)

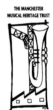

THE MANCHESTER
MUSICAL HERITAGE TRUST

This book is published with the assistance
of a grant from the Ida Carroll Trust and
The Manchester Musical Heritage Trust.

Typeset in 11/12pt Baskerville
by YHT Ltd., London
Printed by Athenaeum Press Ltd., Gateshead, Tyne & Wear

Contents

List of Illustrations

Foreword
LORD MENUHIN

Ronald Stevenson, with whom I share an admiration for my great teacher, George Enescu, is one of the most original minds in the world of the composition of music. His works always seem dedicated to an object beyond the music – a humane impulse, reminding me of Mozart, that makes his music particularly attractive to a wide audience. I found enormous pleasure in conducting his concerto for violin solo and orchestra, which he had written for me many years before and which I had never played, despite my gnawing conscience over all that time. Finally, I performed the work with Hu Kun, one of my Chinese students. I admired in particular the inventive way Stevenson turned the tunes into their various incarnations. The attention of the audience was unflagging, and their enjoyment patent.

Ronald Stevenson has a particularly wonderful gift of conversation. I have rarely enjoyed talking about music – or about humanity, for that matter – as much as with him. His thoughts are obviously the produce of meditation, and the opportunity to dream and to think. I know that he will enjoy increasing popularity and that his music will be appreciated more and more. I am an admirer of the man and his music.

Ronald Stevenson around 1975 (photograph by Helmut Petzsch)

The Editor

Colin Scott-Sutherland is the author of *Arnold Bax* (Dent, London, 1973) and *John Ireland* (Triad Press, Rickmansworth, 1980). He has contributed several articles on Ronald Stevenson's work to various journals, and a chapter on his music to *British Music Now* (ed. Lewis Foreman, Paul Elek, London, 1975). He has recently completed a study of the Glasgow artist Elizabeth Mary Watt (Patten Press, Penzance, 1995) and *Ideala*, an edition of the poetry of Arnold Bax (Dermot O'Byrne) (Fand Music Press, Petersfield, 2001).

The Contributors

Martin Anderson, born in 1955 in Perth, grew up nearby (in Crieff) and graduated from St Andrew's University in mediaeval French and German, although he soon found himself working in economics. He has been editor of *Economic Affairs* for the Institute of Economic Affairs in London and of *The OECD Observer* for the Organisation for Economic Co-operation and Development in Paris. He writes on music and economics for a necessarily wide range of publications, including *The Independent, International Piano* and *Tempo* in the United Kingdom and *Fanfare* in the United States, and runs Toccata Press.

Jamie Reid Baxter, born in Buckie in 1954 and educated in Macduff, Banff and Aberdeen, wrote his PhD thesis on the Cuban novelist and musician Alejo Carpentier. In 1974, with Martin Grossel, he founded the Havergal Brian Society, and subsequently organised many concerts at Aberdeen University. With D. James Ross, from 1982 onwards, he helped launch the rediscovery of Robert Carver. Several of his Scots-language poems have been set to music, including *Domino Roberto Carwor* which Ronald Stevenson set in 1988. His *Passioun o Sanct Andraa* (1986), set to music in 1991 by Dafydd Bullock, was performed in tribute to MacDiarmid's centenary in Edinburgh, 1992. He continues to be involved as best he can in Scottish life, despite having been exiled to Luxembourg in 1987 after five years' unemployment. He works as a translator for the European Parliament and since 1996 has been an honorary research fellow at the Glasgow University School of Scottish Studies.

Alan Bold was born in 1943 in Edinburgh where he attended university and trained as a journalist. From 1966 he was a full-time writer and visual artist and from 1975 lived in rural Fife. He contributed regularly to *The Glasgow Herald, The Sunday Times* and occasionally to *The Scotsman, The New Statesman*

11

and *The Times Literary Supplement*. He published many books of poetry,
including *To Find the New*, *The State of the Nation*, a selection in *Penguin
Modern Poets 15* and *In This Corner: Selected Poems 1963–83*. With the artist
John Bellany he collaborated on *A Celtic Quintet*, *Haven* and *Homage to
MacDiarmid*. He edited many anthologies, including *The Penguin Book of
Socialist Verse*, *The Marital Muse*, *The Cambridge Book of English Verse 1939–75*,
Making Love, *The Bawdy Beautiful*, *Mounts of Venus*, *Drink To Me Only* and *The
Poetry of Motion*. He also wrote critical books on Thom Gunn, Ted Hughes,
George Mackay Brown, the ballad, modern Scottish literature and Muriel
Spark. His biography *MacDiarmid* won him the McVitie Prize as 1989
Scottish writer of the year. He exhibited his Illuminated Poems (pictures
combining an original poetic manuscript with an illustrative composition)
in venues as varied as Boston University and the National Library of
Scotland. His last book was a novel, *East is West*; a biography of Burns was
unfinished at the time of his death in 1998.

Alastair Chisholm is Head of Music at Largs Academy and author of *Bernard
van Dieren – An Introduction* (Thames Publishing, London, 1984), various
articles and radio programmes, and of the Introduction to *Eight Songs* by
Norman Peterkin (Thames Publishing, London, 1983: British Heritage
Series, No. 6). He is the organist of The Cathedral of the Isles (Cumbrae).

Manfred Gordon held chairs of Chemistry at the Universities of Strathclyde
and of Essex. He worked at the Statistical Laboratory of the University of
Cambridge and was a member of Churchill College. As an international
authority on high polymers, he was a Centennial Scholar of the Case
Institute of Technology in the United States and a Heyrovský medallist of
the Czechoslovak Academy of Science. He was also a lover of Dante.

John Guthrie was a New Zealand-born doctor of medicine and Scottish song
composer. He was founder of the first hospital in Kuwait. A Blackwoods
short-story prize-winner, Dr Guthrie died in 1986.

Walter S. Hartley is Professor Emeritus of Music and Composer in
Residence at the State University College, Fredonia, in western New York
State. He is a prominent American composer (of Stirlingshire and
Lancashire heritage), primarily identified with music for wind instruments,
with many publications and recordings to his credit.

Malcolm MacDonald was born in Nairn in 1948. He read English and Music
(in which he is otherwise self-taught) at Downing College, Cambridge. He
lives in Gloucestershire and works as a freelance writer on music. He has
published a three-volume study of the Symphonies of Havergal Brian
(whose writings he is editing in a six-volume series for Toccata Press), as well
as books on Brahms, Schoenberg and John Foulds; his study of Varèse was
published in 2003 (Kahn & Averill, London). He is Editor of *Tempo* and is
also a composer. In 1989 he published a study of Ronald Stevenson for the
National Library of Scotland.

John Ogdon was a giant among musicians. Born in Mansfield in 1937, he was already a fine pianist by the age of five; from eight, at the Royal Northern College of Music in Manchester, he studied with Richard Hall and Claude Biggs and, from 1945, with Ronald Stevenson's former teacher, Iso Elinson. He began composing when he was ten, and in 1953, when he was sixteen and a full-time student, he started composition lessons with Thomas Pitfield; at the same time he took piano lessons with Gordon Green. In 1957 he studied with the Busoni pupil Egon Petri and a year later with Denis Matthews. In 1960 he won the Busoni Prize and made his first appearance at the Royal Festival Hall; the next year he won the Franz Liszt Competition and played at the opening night of the Henry Wood Proms, and in 1963 he won first prize at the Tchaikovsky Competition in Moscow, jointly with Vladimir Ashkenazy. The next years were filled with a breathless mix of touring and recording, encompassing a staggering range of repertoire, mainstream and unfamiliar. In the early 1970s the schizophrenia he had inherited from his father began to manifest itself and in 1973 he disappeared from public view while he underwent treatment. Thereafter he resumed his concertising, though at a less frantic pace, and took up a teaching appointment at Indiana University (1976–80). He returned to the stage with a triumphal concert in the Queen Elizabeth Hall in 1984, and in the five years preceding his tragically early death – on 1 August 1989 – he resumed his career on the platform and in the studio, adding Sorabji's monumental *Opus Clavicembalisticum* to his many recordings.

Ateş Orga, formerly with the BBC Music Division and later (1975–90) Lecturer in Music at the University of Surrey, is a composer, writer and record producer. He is the author of several books, including biographies of Beethoven and Chopin and has written widely on the music of Gerhard, Penderecki, Shostakovich and Camilleri; in 1981 he was a contributor to Ronald Stevenson's Alan Bush symposium, *Time Remembered* (Bravura Publications, Kidderminster). He writes regularly for *International Piano*, *BBC Music Magazine* and *Literary Review*. For his 1993 Wigmore Hall conspectus 'Piano Masterworks', created for Nikolai Demidenko, he received a Royal Philharmonic Society Award.

Harold Taylor studied the piano at the Royal Manchester College of Music with Iso Elinson and Gordon Green, at the Institut Pédagogique de Paris with Raymond Thiberge, and privately with Alfred Cortot and Louis Kentner. He was the Artistic Director of the Bromsgrove Festival from 1966 until 1980 and Head of Music at North Worcestershire College until 1982. Harold Taylor is the author of *The Pianist's Talent* (Kahn & Averill, London, and Taplinger, New York, 1979) and editor of *Kentner: A Symposium* (Kahn & Averill, London, and Pro/Am Music Resources, White Plains, N.Y., 1987) and *Ravel according to Ravel* (Kahn & Averill, London, and Pro/Am Music Resources, White Plains, N.Y., 1988).

Colin Wilson is a leading British existentialist philosopher. Author of *The Outsider* (Gollancz, London, 1956) and many other books of philosophy, criminology and the occult. Author of *The Brandy of the Damned* (Baker, London, 1964 – subsequently issued by Pan Books in 1967 under the title *Colin Wilson on Music*), he has also written several novels. His interest in the psychology of violence led to *The Encyclopaedia of Murder*, written with Patricia Pitman (Pan, London, 1984).

Derek Watson is a composer, pianist and author of volumes on *Bruckner* (1976) and *Liszt* (1988) in 'The Master Musicians' series (Dent, London) and biographer of *Richard Wagner* (Dent, 1979). He gives frequent talks on BBC Radio 3 and edited *Chamber's Music Quotations* (Chambers, Edinburgh, 1991).

Harry Winstanley is the author of a forthcoming study of George Gershwin (Toccata Press) and the editor of *The Godowsky Society Newsletter*. A self-taught pianist, he was until recently employed as a civil servant and lives in Edinburgh.

Albert Wullschleger was born in Switzerland. After qualifying and practising as an architect he has pursued a career as a teacher, and, to a limited extent, a concert promoter. He has taught in the Steiner School in Edinburgh and now resides near Basel.

Acknowledgements

I wish to thank the contributors to this volume who, without fee, have given valuable time and thought to its subject. As editor, I am especially grateful to Martin Anderson of Toccata Press whose helpful suggestions (couched, more often than not, in language that forestalled argument!) have made my task one of much ease and pleasure. Lastly – but with considerable warmth – I wish to thank Marjorie Stevenson for joining in our discussions, and for providing the sustenance necessary to sustain the marathon sessions I have enjoyed at West Linton with Ronald – who knows the extent of my debt of gratitude to him.

Acknowledgement is also due to: Schott Frères of Brussels for the quotation from Ysãye's Fourth Sonata for solo violin; to Novello & Co., Ltd., for the references to the *Prelude, Fugue and Fantasy* and excerpts therefrom; to the Scottish Academic Press for the extracts from *Sorley MacLean – Critical Essays*; to Macmillan and Co. for the extract from Pau Casals' Foreword to Max Pirani's *Emanuel Moór*; to Faber & Faber for the extracts from Mitchell and Keller's *Benjamin Britten*, from *Music Ho!* by Constant Lambert, from *Composers on Music* edited by Sam Morgenstern, and from John Bird's *Percy Grainger*; to *The Musical Times* for Frank Dawes' review of the *Passacaglia on DSCH*; to B. T. Batsford for quotation from 'The Islands of Scotland' by Hugh MacDiarmid – and to the late Mrs Valda Grieve for references and quotations from the *Collected Poems of Hugh MacDiarmid*; to Dover Publications for quotations from *Three Classics in the Aesthetic of Music*; to Lawrence & Wishart for quotation from *Shostakovich*; and to Boosey & Hawkes for quotations from the following: Benjamin Britten's *Peter Grimes*, copyright 1945 by Boosey & Hawkes Music Publishers Ltd., reprinted by permission; and Béla Bartók's *Mikrokosmos*, copyright 1940 by Hawkes & Son (London) Ltd.; corrected edition copyright 1987 by Hawkes & Son (London) Ltd., reprinted by permission of Boosey & Hawkes Music Publishers, Ltd. Acknowledgement is also made to Kahn & Averill for extracts from Stevenson's *Western Music – An Introduction*.

Thanks also to Judith Barnes and Mavis Hammond-Brake at The National Sound Archive of The British Library for help with the discography, and to Pete Caleb of New York Public Library for assistance with some obscure bibliographical references.

Grateful acknowledgement is also made to the various photographers, whose work is acknowledged as it appears. The photographs introducing each chapter were taken by Chris Rice; that on the title page is reproduced courtesy of *The Birmingham Post*. Rob Barnett's offer to help with the proof-reading was gratefully accepted.

Much of Ronald Stevenson's music is published by the Ronald Stevenson Society (*cf.* p. 509); other works are obtainable from the Scottish Music

Centre, 1 Bowmont Gardens, Glasgow G12 9LR; tel: +44/0 141 334 6393; fax +44/0 141 337 1161; e-mail: info@scottishmusiccentre.com; website: http://www.scottishmusic.centre.com. Stevenson's original holograph manuscripts may be consulted in the National Library of Scotland, George IV Bridge, Edinburgh.

COLIN SCOTT-SUTHERLAND

I
RONALD STEVENSON:
AN INTRODUCTION
Colin Scott-Sutherland

The merits and virtues of 'originality' and 'innovation' have been trumpeted near and far, forgetting for the most part that originality is above all a natural gift and that innovations that express no feeling, that use an incomprehensible language and that finally lead to chaos, respond to no requirement of artistic creation. Composers, even great composers, who have refused to follow this road and have struggled to produce not 'modern' music but simply 'music', have almost disappeared from concert programmes and risk sinking into oblivion.[1]

How often today has the new nothing more to commend it than mere novelty? Novelty is not originality: originality is not primarily a way of doing something new, but a new way of doing, a new way of seeing – for there is nothing truly new under the sun. The rules are old – and the strictures, however conventional, are those that bind human expression into the order that articulates the original idea. The articulation presupposes the creative faculty – and the ability to communicate the idea in terms intelligible to the participants. This faculty is shared by a few great men in all ages – and one of those few in our time is Ronald Stevenson.

When I first met Ronald Stevenson he did not presume to show me something new. Our first musical encounter was his playing of Paderewski's Op. 8, No. 3 – most appropriately, a *chant du voyageur*. But he did show me that I could look with new eyes on something old – an identity of vision demonstrated in his recreations of Purcell (for example, *The Queen's Dolour*[2]) and of Bach. His concern and enthusiasm were boundless – and I began to see music with new eyes, and to hear with new ears.

The great musical prophets of the past were those Janus-headed giants of music, the composer-pianists who had, literally within their grasp, the expression of a total concept of music – creation, expression and communication. Such is Ronald Stevenson. For him communication is an art by which his art is divulged – and he is

---

[1] Pau Casals, Foreword to Max Pirani, *Emanuel Moór*, Macmillan, London, 1959, p. 9.

[2] *Cf.* Reproduced in Appendix Five: Some Stevenson Minatures, p. 333. Stevenson's transcriptions include works by composers as diverse as Purcell and Berg, Mozart and van Dieren, Shield and Francis George Scott, Chopin and Kilpinen – *cf.* Appendix Seven: List of Works, pp. 433–47.

Stevenson at home at his piano, February 1989
(photograph courtesy of Scotland on Sunday*)*

better equipped than most to divulge that art and its secrets: he is a master of the keyboard. This implies not merely an impressive technique – which he possesses; he has a depth of insight into the problems of the employment of technique in communication and expression. I have listened on innumerable occasions to his playing of passages that, even when not of any particular technical difficulty, yield in his hands profound secrets. These secrets are, without exception, of deep beauty and meaning, calculated to reveal the musical idea. His own performing editions of such works as the Bach-Busoni Chaconne bear tribute to this – with fingerings, over-writings and altered scoring that, like shafts of light, illumine the darkest corners. To re-write Rachmaninov's E flat Prelude (Op. 23, No. 6) for left hand alone is not an impertinence; nor is it merely a virtuosic *tour de force* – no more so than Godowsky's profound re-creations of Bach or Chopin. And in Stevenson's playing of the Godowsky transcription of the *Sarabanda* from Bach's Cello Suite No. 5 in C minor, the listener seems to hear only the cello line of melody – the harmonic adumbrations, perceived rather than heard, echo like the harmonic haze that surrounds the solo voice of the cello as if in the centre of some immense stone cathedral.

Stevenson is also a born teacher. He has no concern for the acclaim that attends the fashionable: his interests are catholic, his enthusiasms all-encompassing. In his music room (his 'den of musiquity', as he calls it) Busoni, Paderewski, Grainger, Godowsky, F. G. Scott, Brian, Foulds, Medtner and Szymanowski loom large on the musical horizon as seminal influences, so persuasive is his advocacy of their music. This championing of composers all too often considered as peripheral contributors to musical development is not confined to mere prose or verbal argument – it is demonstrated in vital and compelling performance.

Ronald Stevenson was born in Blackburn, Lancashire, on 6 March 1928, the son of a working-class Kilmarnock family whose ancestry was both Scottish and Welsh. These origins bred within him a social conscience that is expressed in his creative work (from *Anger Dance* for guitar, to *The Continents*, his Second Piano Concerto). His earliest musical experiences were of the singing of his father – a fine amateur tenor – and of his Welsh grandmother. Steeped in that most unfashionable of commodities today – melody – his musical development began early.

He took piano lessons at the age of eight with a Miss Ethel Pratt of Blackburn. Above Miss Pratt's boudoir grand piano (at which he

The nine-year-old Ronald Stevenson, 1937

studied the *Andante* of Beethoven's Op. 14, No. 2[3]) hung a
reproduction of the Pre-Raphaelite painting of Dante observing
Beatrice and her lady companion on a Florentine bridge. (Many
years were to elapse before he, too, stood upon that bridge.)
Accompanying his father in Irish and Scots songs and in the
popular operatic gems of the day (by composers such as Vincent
Wallace and Balfe) led him to composition – and at the age of
fourteen he had begun to set the words of Moore, Scott and Byron,
a choice already significantly unusual.

His next piano teacher was Dorothea Fraser May, a refugee
German-Jewish pianist in Darwen, Lancashire, who lived on a hill
overlooking the beautiful Sunnyhurst woods, and who the sixteen-
year-old Stevenson thought always used to smell of apples. A
wholesome lady, she taught him how to play a true legato which he
has ever remembered. Mrs May was on friendly terms with Iso
Elinson, the Russian-Jewish émigré virtuoso, who became Stevenson's next piano teacher, at the Royal Manchester College of Music
(to which, at the age of seventeen, Stevenson won an open
scholarship). Though Elinson actually taught Stevenson little – his
method of teaching being to 'bounce' the student off the piano
stool and demonstrate – his pupil learnt much from him, especially
the stroking touch, not hitting the keys. Elinson had been a

---

[3] Stevenson was intrigued not only by the reprises in variation form but by the strong
and masculine bass line which provided his first introduction to counterpoint.

Blumenfeld pupil in Moscow (as later was Horowitz in Kiev) and looked the part of an old-world virtuoso – a bit Pachmannesque, short, sturdy, with a mane of grizzled hair, a lovely Schubertian smiling expression on his round face. Of both Elinson and his wife, Hedwig Stein, Stevenson has warm memories. As well as the great E flat Sonata of Haydn and Beethoven's Third Concerto – which remained in his repertoire for decades – one of the principal works Stevenson studied with Iso Elinson, and one of the most formative, was the Bax Fourth Sonata: its dark Celtic colour considerably influenced the young Stevenson (and was to have an echo in the *Passacaglia on DSCH* of 1960–62).

Early in his student days Stevenson encountered the music of Busoni. He was fascinated by the cultural lineage implicit in the composer's full name – Ferruccio Dante Michelangelo Benvenuto Busoni – and devoured the vocal score of *Doktor Faust* (in a railway carriage, in a fog-bound and Dickensian Manchester station[4]). Busoni, on whose work he later wrote a deeply penetrating study (as yet unpublished[5]), became a formative influence on Stevenson's music and on his thought.

Stevenson's path was therefore, from the outset, an original one, although he was fully aware of the great classical heritage in music. His book *Western Music*[6] makes this abundantly (if sometimes idiosyncratically) clear. The blurb on the jacket encapsulates his views: 'Man is the core of this book'. And Man's feelings and emotions are the subject of all art and of its expression:

> in art, feeling is held to be the highest moral qualification.
>   In music, however, feeling requires two consorts, taste and style. Now, in life, one encounters real taste as seldom as deep and true feeling: as for style, it is a province of art [. . .]. Feeling is generally understood to mean tenderness, pathos and extravagance of expression. But how much more does the marvellous flower 'Emotion' unfold! Restraint and forbearance, renunciation, power,

---

[4] Later, exploring on the keyboard the intricacies of Busoni's enormous Piano Concerto, he was disturbed by the enquiring entry to the studio of the nine-year-old John Ogdon.

[5] In spite of the written advocacy of various important and influential figures (Bliss, Walton and Lord Harewood amongst them), this volume has not yet appeared, although many of Stevenson's essays and radio talks on Busoni are to be published in his *Busoni – Aspects of a Genius*, Volume One of *Ronald Stevenson on Music* (Toccata Press, London, forthcoming).

[6] Kahn & Averill, London, 1971; a second edition is in preparation.

activity, patience, magnanimity, joyousness, and that all-controlling intelligence from which feeling actually has its source.[7]

Blake became another very important influence. His imaginative power, both as designer and as writer, was one of fiery genius. His precept, 'We are led to believe a lie/when we see with, not thro', the eye', is echoed in Stevenson's work. By 1940 Stevenson had completed nineteen settings of Blake's *Songs of Innocence,* and his first recital (at Blackburn in December 1947 at the age of nineteen)[8] contained, as well as the classics (Bach, Haydn, Mozart and Beethoven), Grünfeld's arrangement of Strauss' *Die Fledermaus* (on which in 1966 he wrote his own *Canonic Caprice,* dedicating it to the memory of Moritz Rosenthal) and his own striking First Sonatina.

He gained considerable youthful experience as accompanist to the Blackburn Ballet Club, not only playing but also composing and editing music. This workmanlike apprenticeship, as well as broadening his knowledge of the more practical aspects of music, in its functional sense, allowed him free rein for the lyrical impulse which drew from him often improvised music of real charm. (All this music, of which there was a considerable amount, is now lost.)

The authorities provided him with his first 'grand tour' – the prisons of Preston, Liverpool, Birmingham and Wormwood Scrubs where, as a pacifist (like Britten, Tippett and William Wordsworth), he was forcibly detained. The alternative of directed labour, after a tribunal, proved an important release – and in 1951–52 he spent first a year-and-a-half in agricultural work (taking private pupils in the meantime) and eventually, after applying for some 32 posts, was offered work by Durham County at Boldon Colliery School as a musician. This congenial post, in which he made many close friends, involved the training of brass players and of singers and was another valuable apprenticeship for later years.

In 1952 Stevenson began teaching in Edinburgh where, as in his later Workers' Educational Association (WEA) classes in musical appreciation, he engaged the interest and affections of a considerable number of avid music-lovers – lovers, not merely students.

---

[7] Ferruccio Busoni, *Sketch of a New Aesthetic of Music,* first published in Trieste in 1907; an English translation appeared from G. Schirmer, New York, 1911, republished by Dover, New York, 1962, in *Three Classics in the Aesthetic of Music.* The quotation (slightly adapted) is from pp. 97–98 of this edition.

[8] *Cf.* pp. 26–27.

February 1943: the fourteen-year-old Stevenson rehearses with the Blackburn Ballet Club

In 1953 he began a correspondence with Edward Gordon Craig, another artist of vision and humanity, who had heard Liszt play and whose understanding of humanity and its theatrical artifice parallelled that of Blake and Busoni. This correspondence lasted until Craig's death in 1966.

In 1955, under the auspices of an Italian government scholarship he went for six months to Italy where, living in Rome and in Florence, he pursued his researches into Busoni and studied orchestration with Guido Guerrini at the Conservatorio di Santa Cecilia in Rome. He revisited Italy on several occasions – in 1958 addressing the First International Busoni Festival at Empoli where he met the great violinist Joseph Szigeti, there as soloist in Busoni's Violin Concerto which he had studied with the composer.

At the Empoli Busoni Festival in 1958 Joseph Szigeti performed the master's Violin Concerto. Afterwards in the Green Room Szigeti's and my mutual friend Frau Gisella Selden-Goth, a former student of Busoni (and of Bartók), introduced me to the veteran violinist. Szigeti discussed the work with me for fifteen minutes – he was still living it – and, incidentally kept a horde of autograph-hunters waiting with Italian impatience! Szigeti temporarily terminated our conversation

PIANOFORTE RECITAL

by

Ronald Stevenson

aet. 19

Lecture Hall
King Georges Hall
BLACKBURN
Lancs.
3 Dec. 1947

Stevenson's first full-length recital programme,
given at Blackburn in December 1947

Programme

Prelude and Fugue in D.	*Bach*
Sonata in E flat	*Haydn*
Fantasia in D minor	*Mozart*
Moonlight Sonata	*Beethoven*

INTERVAL

Invitation to the Dance	*Weber*
Impromptu	*Schubert*
1st Ballade	*Chopin*
Novellette	*Schumann*
Polonaise, in E	*Liszt*
Waltzes, from "The Bat" ... ... *Johann Strauss* (arr. *Grunfeld*)	
Claire de Lune	*Debussy*
Sonatina	*Ronald Stevenson*

This Sonatina was awarded 1st Prize in this year's
Blackburn Music Festival.

("Manchester Guardian" criticism: "It is promising music; it
may in places proclaim its modernity with the defiance of youth,
but it has shape, no undue waste of notes, immense vigour, and
moments of beauty.")

Bechstein Pianoforte by Pickering & Sons, Darwen St., Blackburn.

(mainly his soliloquy), by inviting me to continue it in his hotel room in Florence the next day.

When I arrived for the appointment he greeted me at his room door with his shirt sleeves rolled up and his violin under his arm. He thrust into my hands, as a gift, a sheet of paper on which he had written his reflections on the Busoni Violin Concerto, adding that he couldn't sleep after the performance and had stayed up writing till 4 a.m.[9]

There, too, he met Roman Vlad who, in 1957, dedicated his *4 Studi Dodecafonici* to Stevenson – a work near to Stevenson's own aesthetic. One of the most important compositions of this period was the *Prelude, Fugue and Fantasy on Busoni's 'Faust'.*[10] The work was premiered in London in 1959 by John Ogdon, who later wrote:[11]

> [Stevenson] demonstrates Busoni's concept of the essential oneness of music by unifying apparently diverse strands of his musical thought. Busoni's musical philosophy was sometimes ambivalent since he combined respect for tradition with interest in experiment. Mr Stevenson directs his own thought into classically-orientated forms, as if to prove that the future of music lies in the transformation of the past [. . .]. Its pianism is brilliant and sensitive, and its counterpoint holds one with a glittering eye. The work is conceptually felt, yet its impulse is controlled analytically and its music symphonically organised.

Busonian concerns and ideals occupied him in his early years outside Edinburgh – he and his wife, Marjorie, whom he had married in 1952, settled in West Linton, south of the city, in November of that year – and they are reflected in the principal compositions of these years: the *Prelude, Fugue and Fantasy* and *A 20th Century Music Diary.* An important set of orchestral *Waltzes* was completed – and some idea of the labours which employed his non-teaching hours can be gleaned from the fact that not only the score but also all the orchestral parts[12] are in the composer's own hand.

In 1957 Stevenson had his first encounter – on an Edinburgh bus – with Hugh MacDiarmid (whose real name was Christopher Murray Grieve). Regular, if infrequent, visits to the poet's home at Brownsbank, in Biggar – returned by the poet to Stevenson's West

---

[9] Ronald Stevenson, 'Notes on the Violin Concerto', in *Busoni – Aspects of a Genius, op. cit.*

[10] Published in Novello's 'Virtuoso Series', ed. John Ogdon, London, 1968.

[11] In the Foreword to the published edition.

[12] These still languish in the composer's study, unused.

Linton home – ended usually in all-night discussions (one of which is reproduced in MacDiarmid's *The Company I've Kept*; the subject of the conversation was Sorabji, and the third member of the group was John Ogdon[13]). MacDiarmid encouraged Stevenson to work in, and for, Scotland; and in the poet's work Stevenson found, despite the poet's claim to be tone-deaf, more suggestions of musical ideas (not only sounds but structures[14]) than in any other writer.

In September 1962 MacDiarmid suggested that Stevenson write a large-scale symphonic work of epic proportions based on the long poem by the Gaelic poet Duncan Ban McIntyre – *Ben Dorain* – with the chorus parts to be set in the original Gaelic.[15] The nationalistic impulse thus engendered proved no limiting force but a liberating and expansive inspiration that was to flower when he returned to Scotland after a brief spell overseas.

In 1963 Stevenson was appointed Senior Lecturer in Music at the University of Cape Town – whose Principal of Music was then that adventurous pioneer of Glasgow music-making in the 1930s, Erik Chisholm. With his young family he set out for South Africa:

> I went ashore wearing my black sombrero and white mac – I don't know what that means in terms of apartheid. I was also carrying (in its canvas case) my small harpsichord.[16] Dr Chisholm spotted that – the same evening I was in the orchestra pit in Cape Town Little Theatre playing the continuo recitative in the University production of *Don Giovanni* – I was there every night for three weeks.[17]

While teaching and recitals took up much time the principal occupation of 1963 was the completion of the vast *Passacaglia on DSCH* which had its first performance (by the composer) on 10 December 1963 in Cape Town. Characteristically, two pages of the

---

[13] Hutchinson, London, 1966, pp. 38–70.

[14] In the song *The Skeleton of the Future* Stevenson relates the four chords of traditional harmony – major, minor, diminished and augmented – to the four colours mentioned in the poet's description of Lenin's tomb:
Red granite and *black* diorite
With the *blue* of the labradorite crystals
Gleaming like precious stones
In the *light* reflected from the snow [my italics].
i.e., white (light) – major; black – minor; red – augmented; blue – diminished.

[15] In fact Stevenson used MacDiarmid's own translation in the work, which is still incomplete. *Cf.* pp. 273–74 and 294–95.

[16] The soundboard illuminated for him by Mabel Dolmetsch.

[17] Letter to the author, dated 13 June 1963.

Stages of a friendship: John Ogdon, Christopher Grieve (Hugh MacDiarmid) and Stevenson examine a score by Busoni, West Linton, 1959 (photograph by Helmut Petzsch); and, opposite, with John Ogdon, backstage at the Wigmore Hall, 1985 (photograph by Chris Rice)

work were composed that afternoon – a 'Lament for the Children' based on the seventeenth-century pibroch of Patrick Mor Mac-Crimmon.

The *Passacaglia on DSCH* was begun at West Linton (on Christmas Eve, 1960), when the four-note fragment (Ex. 1) representing the initials of Shostakovich[18] had inspired two pages of variations, away from the keyboard, at one sitting, reminiscent of the plethora of rivers that commingle in Joyce's 'Anna Livia Plurabelle'; it provided a turning point in Stevenson's work – and bridged the transition from South Africa and his return to Scotland in 1965.

[18] To whom the score is dedicated and to whom a copy of the autograph score was presented in Edinburgh in 1962 – *cf.* pp. 98–99. This score omitted the 'pibroch' section and also that marked 'To emergent Africa', which had yet to be composed.

The DSCH motif, with its mirror-like reflection of the rising and falling semitone, like the keystone of a bridge, provided an important symbology which, with the Busonian tritone (FB) and its hegemony of the intervallic second, led – on his return to Scotland, and the completion of the choral cycle (to texts of Whitman), *Songs into Space* (echoing the unusual term 'Gagarin-esco'[19] employed in one passage in the *Passacaglia*) – to the adventurous expansion of the Second Piano Concerto, entitled *The Continents*.

Ex. 1

Stevenson's return to West Linton in the Scottish Border country focussed again his creative activities and energies on the strong nationalist element in Scottish music. In William Sterling's *Cantus*

[19] Yuri Gagarin was the first Russian cosmonaut and the first man to orbit the Earth, on Wednesday, 12 April 1961.

*Stevenson studies in West Linton, late 1950s, with quill, pipe and a
photograph of Edward Gordon Craig on the desk before him
(photograph by Helmut Petzsch)*

Part Book of 1639 he chanced upon a melody that contained yet another quasi-symbolic motif which, with its expressive upward leap of a seventh, formed the perfect foil to the semitonal motif of the *Passacaglia* and, as if echoing the deliverance of the choral cycle, acted like a catalyst in the release of pent-up creative energy that was to surge into numerous large-scale and expressive works, culminating (to date) in the work-in-progress of *Ben Dorain*. First embodied in *Ne'erday Sang* the melodic fragment shown in Ex. 2 became the motivic germ for a work for full orchestra, *Keening Sang for a Makar*, in memoriam Francis George Scott,[20] whose initials the fragment delineates.

Ex. 2

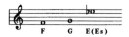

Originally scored for piano, this was followed by two companion pieces forming a kind of Scottish Trilogy – *Keening Sang, Heroic Song for Hugh MacDiarmid* and the *Chorale Pibroch for Sorley Maclean* (the Gaelic poet).

Ronald Stevenson's Scottish music – the epithet implies no parochial narrowness but the expression, in characteristic terms and national accents, of universal thought – includes such pieces as the *Scots Dance Toccata* where several dance tunes are adumbrated in an opening haar[21] and then drawn out into a complex polytonal

[20] 'Makar' is the Lowland Scots for a master poet. Francis George Scott (1880–1958), a lecturer in music at Jordanhill Training College, Glasgow, was in every sense a 'makar' of the Scottish Renaissance. He is noted for his very individual corpus of songs, many of them settings of his one-time pupil at Langholm, Christopher Grieve (Hugh MacDiarmid); *cf.* Maurice Lindsay, *Francis George Scott and the Scottish Renaissance*, Paul Harris, Edinburgh, 1980. In a letter to the author, dated 24 September 1963, Stevenson comments:

> A curious link between Scott and me is that, like me, he had a connection with Lancashire – his maternal grandfather was a Lancastrian with the typically North Country name of Luke Grimshaw. Such a detail is not merely a biographical footnote. Place affects speech and speech affects the composer's approach to melodic inflexion. F G's daughter Lillias sang to me the other day some of her father's early Blake settings – for choir, not like mine for solo voice. I noted with especial interest that his treatment of Blake's words was inflected in a very similar way to mine. He set the words 'Little lamb' on a monotone for the first word followed by an upward leap of a third – as I did without knowing Scott's Blake settings. 'Sweet Dreams' he set as a monotone – and so on.

Cf. also p. 177.

[21] *Collins's Dictionary* defines *haar* (eastern Brit.) as 'a cold sea mist or fog off the North Sea' (related to the Dutch *harig*, damp).

reel; and also the *Young Scotland Suite* – which includes four sets of bagpipes playing together in harmony and also admitted the clarsach, the Celtic harp, to the orchestra.[22] In unrecognised folk origins (so different from the artistically deplorable tartan trimmings that emasculate so much of Scottish origin) Stevenson found an expressive poetic language that derived from a virtuosic instrumental tradition. This music with its gapped scales and microtonal colour shows links with other musics of Europe and the East.

In 1966 Stevenson travelled again, to Halle for the Handel Festival where, on 6 June, he gave the European public premiere of the *Passacaglia on DSCH* in the Great Hall of the Martin Luther University. During this visit one of the deepest impressions made upon him was not Halle, not the sacred Thomaskirche of Leipzig, nor even Weimar where he played on Liszt's piano. It was Buchenwald concentration camp, near Weimar:

'For this I have no words.'[23]

The Busoni centenary that year took him again to Italy – where he met Dallapiccola and Guido Agosti – and attended the Italian premiere of Busoni's *Die Brautwahl*.[24] In March 1966 Stevenson was awarded an Arts Council grant of £750 under the scheme of awards

---

[22] In a letter to the author, dated 19 September 1976, he wrote that:
> I'm in the final throes of my *Young Scotland Suite*. The last two movements are away to the copyist. I'm now occupied with the first movement in which I introduce 4 bagpipes playing in harmony, which hasn't been done before, as far as I know – and in the context of a piece for symphony orchestra. Clarsachs are introduced in the middle movement. This use of indigenous instruments relates to a recrudescence of interest in them and (for instance) their admittance (at last! – only comparatively recently) into the official educational curriculum.

The three-movement work was first performed by Lothian Region Schools Orchestra, conducted by Roderick Brydon, in the Music Hall, Edinburgh, on 23 October 1976. In a letter to the author, dated 21 October 1970, Leopold Stokowski, then 88, wrote to ask for the score of the *Scots Dance Toccata*. Unfortunately his interest never resulted in a performance (Stokowski's copy of the score was lost at sea). *Cf.* also pp. 139–42.

[23] Letter to the author, dated 11 July 1966.

[24] In *ibid.*, he wrote that 'The music has pages of visionary lyricism; but its avoidance of the platitudinously operatic baffled the Italian audience'.

for living artists. While the cash was useful, it is characteristic of Ronald Stevenson that, from the letter accompanying the award, he could single out, with enthusiasm, the phrase 'to enable artists to pursue, or *to meditate upon,* their art' (my italics).

John Ogdon broadcast the *Passacaglia on DSCH* on 22 May 1966 and played the work again at Cheltenham and Aldeburgh. It was at Aldeburgh that, after years of correspondence with Percy Grainger (until his death in 1961), Stevenson finally met Ella Grainger. He was asked then to compile a volume of Percy's works for children (a project that had been considered before by D. C. Parker, a friend of the Graingers and author of a study of Bizet[25]). *The Young Person's Grainger* was the outcome, published by Schott in the following year. Stevenson had demonstrated not only his love for Grainger's music (having arranged *Hill Song* No. 1 for piano, and playing the *Ramble on Love,* Percy's arrangement of the last love-duet from *Der Rosenkavalier,* better than anyone I have ever heard, with crystal clarity in the articulation of the *chiaroscuro*-like piano decoration), but also in this volume a rare and captivating ability to teach – not purely a didactic function but a tender charm and infectious enthusiasm, an enthusiasm not so much to teach as to share and impart. He was delighted to have his children choose the cover portrait of Grainger who, they said, looked like a fairy prince. His final notes on the pieces are an exemplar of clarity for young people.[26] Stevenson subsequently visited White Plains, giving recitals (on Ella Grainger's birthday, 1 May 1967) and also visited Australia. Also in 1967 he was awarded a Harriet Cohen international award – the medal for musicology – presented to him by Jennie Lee (then Minister for the Arts) on 4 December.

A visit to Switzerland in 1979 was followed by the composition of the Violin Concerto for Yehudi Menuhin, to whom Stevenson played the work in Edinburgh:

---

[25] *Georges Bizet: His Life and Works,* Kegan Paul, Trench Trubner/J. Curwen & Sons, London, 1926.

[26] Reviewed by the author, in *Music Review,* Vol. 31, No. 2, May 1970, pp. 172–73.

Of 'Now O Now I needs must part' Stevenson wrote, in the notes, 'Percy was fond of playing this piece at the end of a day, before retiring for the night'. And he illustrated the characteristic rhythm of some Grainger pieces with the words 'beautiful pancakes'.

Stevenson's concern for the child was expressed also in his care for the handicapped child. For the children in need of special care at Garvald School, Dolphinton, near his home, he has arranged music for the local players and set (amongst others) the song *One and All* to words of Christian Morgenstern – which became the school song.

Cf. also Appendix Four, 'Stevenson and the Child', pp. 321–25.

The Stevenson family (Gerda, Ronald, Gordon, Marjorie and Savourna)
with the composer Norman Peterkin in the summer of 1967

At first I gave a running commentary, but soon realised that his acuity
was such that he began to anticipate my remarks; so I continued
playing and refrained from explanations.[27]

That same year he was asked to do a very substantial series of
programmes on Busoni for BBC Radio 3.[28]

In the early 1970s the Stevenson family were introduced to the
island of Tiree in the Hebrides where they were to go on holiday for

---

[27] Letter to the author, dated 25 April 1980. *Cf.* also p. 154.

[28] In Autumn 1970 Stevenson had played the entire *36 Fugues*, Op. 36, of Antonín
Rejcha (Anton or Antoine Reicha) for a broadcast on Radio 3. Twelve programmes
on the work of Busoni – also for Radio 3 – began weekly from 9 October 1972,
complemented by a further series, in 1977. Fourteen hour-long programmes
devoted to Busoni's piano music were broadcast beginning in April 1980. Earlier, in
1974, a television film was broadcast on Stevenson's own work and composition, and
in the same year a television film, *Harlequin and Faust – A Study of the Music of Ferruccio
Busoni*, was given on BBC 2 in the series 'Workshop'.

a number of years. The solace and peace of this 'land beneath the waves' prompted not only renewed musical activity but also a kind of 'taking stock' – musical stock, expressed in his music as a concern for melody that, in innumerable songs, continued to pour from his pen. The island retreat produced not only the third movement of the *Scottish Triptych* (the *Chorale Pibroch for Sorley Maclean*) but also continuing inspiration for his Second Piano Concerto:

> On holiday on the Hebridean Isle of Tiree a few years ago, I met a piper, Calum MacLean of Salum Bay (locally known as 'Calum Salum') who fetched the seals out of the water by playing slow airs on his bagpipes on the shore. Returning to the mainland on the boat, another piper, Kenneth MacDonald, played a 'farewell to the land'. I wrote a pibroch for pipes, entitled *Calum Salum's Salute to the Seals* and Kenneth MacDonald played it for me. Later I turned this into a piano piece, *Chorale-Pibroch for Sorley Maclean.* In 1972 I utilised this pibroch in my Second Piano Concerto, commissioned by the BBC and premiered by myself and the NPO under Del Mar in the London Proms. I introduce the pibroch by a Hindu raga with a passage in which the piano imitates the sitar by plucking the strings inside the piano. I was delighted when one critic wrote that my music sounded 'like the Indian Ocean lapping the shores of the Hebrides'.[29]

Commissions from Aldeburgh (*Border Boyhood*, a cycle to poems and prose of Hugh MacDiarmid), from the harpist Ann Griffiths (the *Duo Sonata* for harp and piano), and from Alan Cuckston (the Harpsichord Sonata[30]) followed. And in December 1978 Stevenson was invited as guest speaker to the Fourth Congress of Soviet Composers in Moscow.

I first encountered Ronald Stevenson in the early 1960s in an Edinburgh public house where, with John Ogdon, Alan Anderson and a few others, we had repaired after a concert (in which Ogdon had played an entire Chopin concerto without letting his eyes light upon the keyboard, constantly watching the erratic conductor). Garbed in coat of black, with a wide-brimmed, jesuitical black velvet hat, Stevenson's Mephisthophelean appearance was complemented by an ancient courtesy of manner. The surroundings were conducive to the generation of heated discussion on topics of art,

---

[29] Ronald Stevenson, 'The Composer and Scottish Folk Music', *Scottish International,* April 1973, p. 14.

[30] Alan Cuckston's own description of the work and its origin forms Appendix Two on pp. 307–10.

and in subsequent months we met, most frequently in the tiled, august and austere – but still fragrantly alcoholic – surroundings of the Café Royal, off Princes Street, in Edinburgh. It might have been Vienna, Helsingfors or Padua, for the topics ranged as widely: from Purcell to Gordon Craig, from Rudolf Steiner to Francis George Scott, from William Soutar to Medtner. But it was Scotland. And the Scottish border country at West Linton, where Stevenson still has his home, is a setting peculiarly appropriate. For from this border landscape – cradled on the south flank of the Pentland hills, where winter's skeletal boughs are decked with green in spring (just as harmony cloaks the bones of melody) and where waters chill from the slopes ripple in a sun-flecked stream through the village – Ronald Stevenson has drawn something of the dour MacDiarmidian strength that is the sinew of his work.

Yet from this quiet retreat his expression embraces elements of cultures far-flung from these borders. Writing in 1969 of his *Passacaglia on DSCH*,[31] he points out that the interwoven nationalist elements present in that enormous work were not the result of intellectual manipulation, but the expression of physical experience:

> I absorbed the pibroch from the performance of Highland pipers heard in Scottish crofts; the Russian revolutionary march from the movement of crowd scenes in Eisenstein films; Spanish dancing from observations made in Las Palmas; the African drumming from a performance by a Bantu tribal virtuoso in the location of Nyanga, just outside Cape Town; the Bachian fugue style from practising and memorising the 48 Preludes and Fugues at the piano [. . .].

Stevenson's working methods show the acute receptivity with which he reacts to the many and varied sources of his inspiration. The supposed myth that inspiration produces a white heat of creativity is borne out in the sketches from which he works. His focus, once realised, begets a generative urge of expansion that is little short of frenetic. His energies are dynamic, and, in his 'Den of Musiquity' I have often seen how he has littered the piano with pages of ink and pencil manuscripts, playing and linking the pages – in a flurry of turns and searches – interspersed with moments of hectic vocal improvisation, demonstrating an astonishing compositional intensity. It is often surprising how closely the finished creation follows the original invention. The demonstration of his idea is utterly

---

[31] 'Passacaglia on DSCH', *The Listener*, Vol. 82, No. 2115, 9 October 1969, p. 494.

With Andrey Petrov (left), his wife (right) and Leonid Balay (second right), Moscow, December 1968, as a guest of the Fourth Congress of the Union of Soviet Composers

convincing, readily translatable into keyboard terms, whatever the medium involved; and his unique understanding of the piano is exemplified nowhere more than in pertinent 'asides' in discussion or in correspondence, where his understanding of musical orthography has the justification of absolute and demonstrable conviction. Mutual enthusiasm for all things musical has introduced me, at his instigation, to such musical treasures as Tagliapietra's *Per la Gioventù*, Paderewski's *Cracovienne Fantastique*, Godowsky's transcriptions of Bach's cello works, the Foulds Cello Sonata, Dett's *Juba Dance*, Busoni's *Indian Diary*, Sandby's *Autumn Mood at the Coast*, Czesław Marek's *Triptychon*, and very many others.

My interest in British composers for the piano[32] led me to send him on separate occasions *A Bach Book for Harriet Cohen* and a number of Bach transcriptions by Herbert Fryer. His comments are brilliant and illuminating.[33]

His knowledge of music is encyclopaedic, and his love of it is

---

[32] *Cf.* Colin Scott-Sutherland, 'British Piano Music of the Georgian Era 1910–1936', *British Music Society Journal*, Vol. 4, 1982, pp. 19–55.

[33] The letters are reproduced as Appendix Three: Stevenson on Writing for the Piano, pp. 311–15.

Thirty-seven years of marriage: Ronald and Marjorie Stevenson in 1989

all-embracing. In the midst of creative compulsion he will digress, often at length, upon some page turned by chance – upon some byway of musical experience which arises fortuitously in conversation – and turn the digression to account in the main impulse of his thought with an impressive grasp of structure and form.

But in the end his convictions are enshrined in his music – before everything else, that universality of expression must come through personal experience. Constant Lambert would have agreed:[34]

> The artist who is one of a group writes for that group alone, whereas the artist who expresses personal experience may in the end reach universal experience. He must not mind if for the moment he appears to be without an audience. He has no right to complain if Cleopatra prefers billiards. There is always the chance that she may become bored with billiards also, and when she returns to the musician his song will be all the more moving for having been written to please not her but himself.

[34] *Music Ho!*, Faber & Faber, London, 1934, p. 234.

II
THE PIANO MUSIC
Ateş Orga

Preludio

> The piano was the Romantic instrument *par excellence.* It still is. Art is Romantic when it suggests a reality larger than itself. That is why the piano is *the* Romantic instrument; for it suggests the orchestra. It is the only instrument that can [. . .].[1]

The piano is Stevenson's instrument as performer. It is also his instrument as a composer. To it he has confessed his most intimate and his most public thoughts. Through it he has remembered nineteenth-century gods; he has suggested the symphonic, imagined the orchestral, essayed the abstract, the descriptive, the worldly; he has dreamt dreams, miniature and monumental. For it, out of pillars of tradition, out of the scaffolding of innovation, he has fashioned a legacy of expression richly new, he has conceived a volume of literature in whose pages can be found past, present and future at once mirrored and illuminated.

Stevenson identifies most closely with Bach and Beethoven, with the Romantic and Russian schools, with Busoni. The dramatic and the visionary, extreme lyricism, extreme tension, the conflict, the resolution of diametric opposites, are what stimulates him. Spiritually, one feels, he is happiest when questing after the post-*Sturm und Drang* Mozart of the D minor and C minor Concertos (for both of which he has written cadenzas), the F minor *Fantasie*, the A minor Rondo; the Beethoven of the Third Concerto, the Fifth Symphony, the 'Hammerklavier', the late quartets; the Chopin of the C sharp minor Scherzo, the *Polonaise-Fantaisie*, the 'Funeral March' Sonata, the F minor *Ballade;* the Liszt of the *Faust-Symphonie*, the Second *Ballade*, the *Mephisto Waltzes;* the grotesquerie, the satanism of Alkan; the duality of Schumann; the *Pathétique* tragedy of Tchaikovsky;[2] the mysticism of Scriabin; the Szymanowski of the B flat minor Study no less than the Third Symphony; the elegant, disciplined lace-work, the alpine thunder of Thalberg; the sun-and-

---

[1] Stevenson, *Western Music*, p. 143.

[2] The *Pathétique* is a work that has always held special emotional significance for Stevenson: in 1972, coincidentally, it made up the second half of the New Philharmonia Prom concert (17 August) which included the premiere of the Second Piano Concerto.

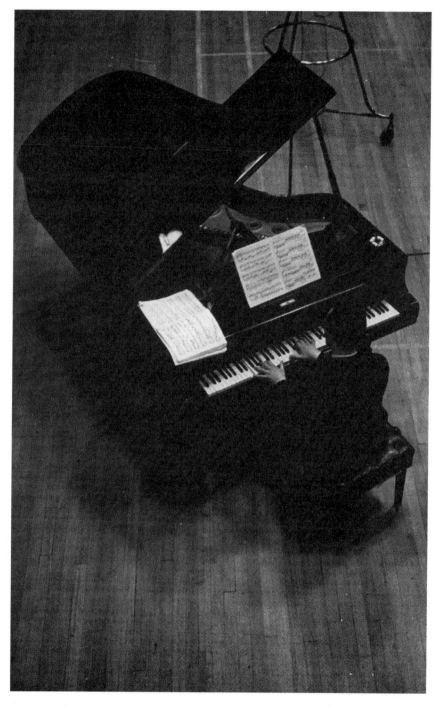

Recording for the BBC, mid-1960s (photograph by Helmut Petzsch)

rain athleticism of Grainger; the prophetic, northern musings of late Grieg; the 'lightning' of Shostakovich; the wit of Prokofiev; the Golden Age perfume of Paderewski (whose Concerto was in Stevenson's repetoire in the 1960s); or when he is glorying in the lofty, German intellectualism, the physical, Latin contact of Busoni.

As a performer, Stevenson values most the artist who is also a creator. In *Western Music,* unfashionably for some, he praises Bernstein as an 'outstanding' conductor 'because like most of those of the older generation, he is also a composer and performer of formidable and versatile talent whose conducting is *informed with creativity*' (my italics).[3] That he consciously seems to have modelled himself as a pianist on the Rachmaninovs, Medtners and Godowskys of this world – grand men all, of big personality and individual distinction, in whom the creative instinct and re-creative act were as one – is no accident.

As a composer, Stevenson's aesthetic is clear-cut:

> If progress towards more human awareness is to be made it can only be made by continuing the tradition of what is good in the past. Wholesale jettisoning of past culture is unproductive and merely a histrionic gesture of futility. The seeds of our age were sown in the 19th century [. . .].[4]

He would find much to agree with in Sorabji's self-assessment:

> I am not a 'modern' composer in the inverted commas sense. I utterly and indignantly repudiate the epithet as being in any way applicable to me. I write very long, very elaborate works that are entirely alien and antipathetic to the fashionable tendencies prompted, publicised and plugged by the various 'establishments' revolving around this or that modern composer.[5]

Is such a philosophy anachronistic at the dawn of the 21st century? Are we wasting our time praising Stevenson? Should we dismiss him instead as simply a throwback, a man born half-a-century too late with nothing of contemporary relevance to say? In the 1950s and '60s, critical opinion – young critical opinion excited by the audacity, the revolution, the fist-shaking Young Turks of post-War Darmstadt and Princeton, of Paris and Warsaw – tended largely to do so. But today the tide has turned. The *volte face* in the past twenty

---

[3] P. 193.

[4] *Ibid.,* p. 194.

[5] Quoted by Stevenson, *ibid.,* p. 203, from Hugh MacDiarmid, *The Company I've Kept, op cit.,* pp. 38–39.

years of so many of his formerly 'progressive' contemporaries
(Penderecki and Maxwell Davies among them), the evidence of a
majority again intent on celebrating tonality and tonal forms, of so
many prepared to learn from the schooled craftsmanship of earlier
masters, have made for a climate in the West altogether freer, less
cliquish, more receptive, less selectively restrictive, more open. The
current of our present age is a mainstream where we accept that
new ideas are not necessarily better than old ones, where Sibelian
'profound logic'[6] as a creative dynamic can flourish equally
alongside the indeterminism, the collective intuitivity of Stockhausen or the mantras of India, where different schools of thought
are not played off against one another but, rather, are accepted for
what they are. Experiment is a life-blood for the future; but so, too,
is consolidation and the recognition of one's heritage. Fusion not
fission, stylistic democracy not sectarianism, eclecticism not
specialisation is the banner of the day. Given such drift, Stevenson
patently *is* a man of his time in whom the tongues of our era find
eloquent and natural voice. If sometimes he seems to be spiritually
stronger than most, that is because when others allowed themselves
to be swayed by the transient fashions, the trends once believed to
be permanent, of two or three decades ago, he had the courage to
resist. For fifty years, weathering all adversity, he has stood firm by
his principles. That speaks of a tough character.

Apprenticeship

> In the arts [. . .] credentials don't matter. Nothing in the arts can be
> taught anyway. Everything has to be *learnt*. And doing is learning. One
> so often hears the question: who was his teacher? – as if teachers are
> the '*open sesame*'! It is the *spiritual* masters who matter; the affinities
> that a composer discovers for himself.[7]

The earliest piano works of significance are the three Sonatinas,
dating from between 1945 and 1948. The first of these was
performed by the composer in 1946 while still a student at the
Royal Manchester College of Music – under Richard Hall for
composition (whose style, however, left no measurable influence)
and the Russian Iso Elinson, a Blumenfeld disciple, for piano. The

---

[6] *Cf.* Lionel Pike, *Beethoven, Sibelius and 'the Profound Logic'*, Athlone Press, London,
1978.

[7] Stevenson, *Western Music*, p. 133.

then *Manchester Guardian* was moved to say that 'it may in places proclaim its modernity with the defiance of youth, but it has shape, no undue waste of notes, immense vigour and moments of beauty'.[8] These three Sonatinas are interesting for many reasons, not least for showing the seeds of Stevenson's art in embryonic form. Their strong linearity (as a student, Stevenson recalls, he 'used to get up at 6 a.m. and do a regular stint of a solid hour's counterpoint exercises every day'[9]), their harmonic idiom, their pre-occupation, vertically and horizontally, with semitonal intervals of decided acidity, their chromatic and diatonic contrasts, their sudden flashes of sweetness and consonance, of bitterness and dissonance, their resolution of ideas over a potentially spacious time-scale – such incident is prophetic. A more sophisticated development of their world can be found in the *Chorale Prelude for Jean Sibelius* (1948, written in Wormwood Scrubs where he was confined as a conscientious objector) – for the old master a 'beautiful composition'.[10]

Two vernal essays, the *Fantasy on Doktor Faust* (1949) and the *Fugue on 'Clavis Astartis Magica'* (1950), are the earliest direct references to Busoni in the Stevenson catalogue. Together, at John Ogdon's suggestion, they were to become, in their revised form (1959), the basis for the *Prelude, Fugue and Fantasy on Busoni's 'Faust'*,[11] a magisterial opus where all the promise of Stevenson's youthful effort was to find its first properly mature flowering.

Variation and/or fantasia form, with its element of continuous development, has always been attractive to Stevenson, a fact evinced as early as the *18 Variations on a Bach Chorale* and the *Fantasia* (or *Fantasy*) for piano and strings (both from 1946). A late apprentice example is provided by the *Variations on a Theme of Pizzetti* (1955), which dates from the period of Stevenson's studies in orchestration with the Busoni pupil, Guido Guerrini, at the Conservatorio di Santa Cecilia, Rome. The theme – the plaintive sarabande from

---

[8] Quoted in Ateş Orga, 'The Piano Music of Ronald Stevenson', *Musical Opinion*, Vol. 92, No. 1098, March 1969, p. 292. The First Sonatina is recorded by John Ogdon on Altarus AIR-CD-9063.

[9] Quoted in Ateş Orga, 'Ronald Stevenson', *Music and Musicians*, Vol. XVII, No. 2, October 1968, p. 27.

[10] From a letter to Stevenson, dated 16 January 1949, quoted in Barry Peter Ould, *Ronald Stevenson – A 50th Birthday Tribute*, New 57 Gallery catalogue, Edinburgh, 29 July–10 August 1978, p. 5.

[11] Stevenson's manuscript gives the title as *Prelude, Fugue and Fantasy on Busoni's 'Doktor Faust'*; the printed score drops the *Doktor*. Cf. also pp. 67–76.

Stevenson at the age of nineteen,
around the time of the composition of the Second Sonatina

Pizzetti's incidental music to d'Annunzio's drama *La Pisanella* (Paris, 1913) – is subject to all kinds of transformation, at one point combining with the BACH motif. In 1961 Stevenson re-addressed himself to another set of variations on the same tune for solo violin. In this manifestation the BACH reference disappears, to be replaced by a quotation from the 24th *Caprice* of Paganini, a satanic stroke of high Romanticism.

A 20th Century Music Diary

Every composer, even the greatest, must start from something that already exists, perhaps one kind of thing, perhaps several related ones. From such foundation, one composer – the innovator – gradually reaches new points, from which it is hardly possible to remember the start. Another composer – the great traditionalist – develops what already exists to a stage never foreseen, and into a unity never imagined.[12]

[12] Béla Bartók, 'Liszt problemák', *Nyugat*, Vol. XXIX, No. 3, Budapest, March 1936, pp. 171–79; quoted in Sam Morgenstern (ed.), *Composers on Music*, Pantheon Books, New York, 1956/Faber & Faber, London, 1958, p. 418 (alternative translation and complete text in Benjamin Suchoff (ed.), *Béla Bartók Essays*, University of Nebraska Press, Lincoln and London, 1976, pp. 501–10).

> I acknowledge artistic traditionalism – what I call 'a good musical education' – as a point of departure, but [. . .] our aim is not 'yesterday' but 'today' and 'tomorrow': creativity is the word, and not a retreat to achievements already exhausted.[13]

A 20th Century Music Diary (1956–59) is rather like a sketchbook full of all kinds of workshop chips, of techniques in stages of evolution, some essential to Stevenson's future development, others not. Each of its sixteen aphoristic movements is terse in statement, concentrated in structure; many are richly chromatic, articulately polyphonic; all are strong in identity, in personal signature, in pianistic effectiveness. Motivated in part by original rather than borrowed ideas – unlike the *Prelude, Fugue and Fantasy* (Busoni), the *Passacaglia on DSCH* (Shostakovich), or the *Peter Grimes Fantasy* (Britten), its indebtedness to the music of others is minimal – it is, one feels, Stevenson's most private, inward work for the piano, as significant in implication, as creatively revealing, as anything larger-scale.

Tonally, the predominant orientation of the collection is either modal, diatonic (in the usual major/minor sense), or (to use a Slonimskyism) pan-diatonic: in other words, whatever else might happen, the music *always* acknowledges the supremacy of one key-note as a central reference point above all others. In *Western Music*, Stevenson talks about classical tonality as '*gravity in sound*'.[14] Such a notion is critical to his thinking. When he serialises – Nos. 9–15; the passacaglia third movement of the early Violin Sonata (1947, rev. 1952); the *Prelude and Fugue on a 12-note Theme from Liszt's 'Faust-Symphonie'* for organ, after No. 14 (August 1961–February 1962, based on the opening augmented triads of Liszt's work[15]); the finale of the Harpsichord Sonata; *Dodecaphonic Bonfire* (1988 Edinburgh Festival) – he does so quite differently from Schoenberg. What matters to him is not the (weightless, anti-gravitational) equality of unrelated notes, but the (weighted, gravitational) inequality of related ones. When he uses familiar serial devices – retrograde motion, inversion, retrograde inversion, transposition –

---

[13] Karol Szymanowski, interviewed in *Kurier Czerwony*, Warsaw, 24 February 1927; reproduced in Alistair Wightman (ed.), *Szymanowski on Music*, Toccata Press, London, 1999, p. 252.

[14] P. 100 (my italics).

[15] For the late Humphrey Searle, 'the first conscious twelve-note theme ever written' (in Alan Walker (ed.), *Franz Liszt: The Man and his Music*, Barrie and Jenkins, London, 1970, p. 305).

With Eduard Weiss, then one of Busoni's last surviving pupils,
touring the two-piano version of his Fantasia Contrappuntistica, *1984*

he does so in ways that emphasise their ancient model rather than
modern revival. He celebrates recurrent metric pulse, he makes a
virtue of repetitive rhythm. He accepts associations of idea or
sound, alignments of pitch, that Schoenberg or Webern would have
rejected. His concern is to reconcile dodecatony with diatony, to
combine, if he can, expressive means that are fundamentally
opposite in polarity, and to use that element of opposition as a
creative spur: 'opposites', he says, 'imply contradiction and contradiction implies relative unity and absolute conflict. It is this law that
transforms the old into the new [. . .]'.[16] Selective, not total, pitch
organisation is the flag under which Stevenson sails. It is a flag that
recognises all those things which for him matter most in music –
things like freedom, reflection, the transformation of reality, the
ability to express emotional states, to convey a sense of human
destiny. Like Busoni he believes that humanity, not technical
dogma, is what makes music endure beyond its time: 'because
humanity is the one factor common to all ages'.[17]

Harmonically, the world of *A 20th Century Music Diary* is both
simple and complex – simple in its primary and secondary diatonic
colour, its direct, public statement; complex in its chromatic

[16] *Western Music*, pp. 7–8.

[17] *Ibid.*, p. 15.

irridescence, its indirect, private confession. Its chromaticism –
manifest most often as an outcome of superimposed voices reacting
variously on each other in the course of either free or strict
contrapuntal movement – remains perhaps its most striking
expressive dimension.

Superficially, Stevenson's chromatic style derives from Hindemith – 'one of the key figures of 20th century music and one of the
few masters in a chaotic era characterised by lack of mastery and
even the lack of any wish for mastery'.[18] Fundamentally, I suggest, it
originates with Bernhard Ziehn (1845–1912) – today an almost
forgotten name, but in his time a provocative thinker famous for his
ideas about symmetrical inversion and the functional equality of
chords. It was of Ziehn that Busoni once remarked: 'He is a
theoretician who points to the possibilities of undiscovered lands –
a prophet through logic. As a master of harmony he stands
alone'.[19] Stevenson's documented interest in him can be traced
back to the mid-1950s at least. In 1975–76 he arranged for a new
edition (the first reprint, in fact) of the important *Canonical Studies:
A New Technic in Composition* – Ziehn's last book, published
posthumously.[20] What Stevenson has to say in his Introduction to
this edition[21] about Ziehn's work and his attitude towards harmony
and canonic counterpoint is valuable. It might almost be taken as
an exposition in part of his own creative rationale:

> Ziehn accepted a tempered chromatic-enharmonic basis for his
> system of harmony and developed Kirnberger's theory that all
> possible chords are reducible to the theory of adjacent thirds. In this
> way, Ziehn indicated connections between triadic and quartal
> harmony, whereas other theorists have regarded the two methods
> of chord construction as mutually exclusive. That is, harmony built
> on thirds has been regarded as traditional and harmony built on
> fourths as 'modern'.

[18] *Ibid.*, p. 180.

[19] 'Die "Gotiker" von Chicago, Illinois', *Signale für die musikalische Welt*, Vol. LXVIII,
No. 5, Berlin, 2 February 1910; reprinted in Busoni's *Von der Einheit der Musik*, Max
Hesses Verlag, Berlin, 1922 (rev. edn., *Wesen und Einheit der Musik*, Max Hesses
Verlag, Berlin-Halensee, 1956), the translation of which (*The Essence of Music, and
Other Papers*, Rockliff, London, 1957) omits this and several other essays.

[20] Kaun Music Co./Kaun Musikverlag, Milwaukee and Berlin, 1912; republished in
Stevenson's edition as *Canonic Studies*, Kahn & Averill, London, 1976.

[21] *Ibid.*, pp. 10–18; the passages quoted here are not in their original order.

Canon [. . .] is the most essential form of contrapuntal composition
[. . .]. Canonic imitation is the common factor in counterpoint of
different periods and styles, from the canons of the Netherlands
School, to the Palestrinian motet, the Purcellian fantasy, the Bachian
or Handelian invention and fugue, or the fugues of Haydn, Mozart,
Beethoven, Reicha, Mendelssohn, Schumann, Brahms, Reger,
Busoni, Hindemith, Shostakovich or Britten.

[. . .] canonic writing need not be limited to simple diatonic
harmony, but may, and – for its complete development – indeed
must, entail a chromatic-enharmonic system of harmonisation
transcending classical concepts of tonality.

The principle [*sic*] innovation of *Canonic Studies* is the theory and
practice of symmetrical inversion. This concept, first formulated by
Ziehn in 1876, postulates a chromatic application of the old
contrarium reversum.

Symmetrical inversion produces harmony through counterpoint
[Busoni's 'second way' in pursuit of a 'New Harmony'].

[Ziehn's] tables of modes [. . .] invite comparison with the [113]
unusual modes suggested by Busoni in his *New Aesthetic* (1906) [*cf.*
Messiaen].

[Progressive tonality, beginning in one key, ending in another] is
endorsed, as it were, by many of Ziehn's examples.

Ziehn's theories are applied in several movements of *A 20th
Century Music Diary.* Stevenson himself singles out No. 1 (the
Preludio al corale) in demonstration of 'the enharmonic unity of
triadic and quartal harmony', explaining that 'the first and third
chords' of his given extract (Ex. 3) 'are identical but the first is
notated as being built in thirds and the third chord as being built in
fourths. The notation, with its enharmonic differences, indicates
the resolution in each case'.[22] Ex. 4(a) gives the six-part conclusion
of this movement, together with an alternative reading (Ex. 4(b))
that clarifies not only its essentially stepwise motion, its linearity,
but also its inherent sense of the need for either 'sharps' to rise or
'flats' to fall. The use of pivotal linking is worth noting.
    No. 5 provides an apposite illustration (Ex. 5(a)) of symmetrical
inversion: in procedure it can be compared with the mirror
inversions (Ex. 5(b)) of Bartók's 'Dragon Dance' (*Mikrokosmos,*

----

[22] *Ibid.*, p. 11.

Ex. 3

Ex. 4

(a)

(b)

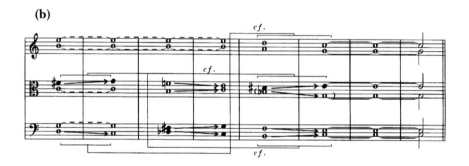

Ex. 5

(a) Stevenson

(b) Bartók

No. 72, Book III) – a piece Stevenson cites in his Introduction as being actually modelled in technique after Ziehn.[23]

For Busoni, 'Ziehn indicates the existence of undiscovered territory and trains young Columbuses'; for Stevenson, he quite simply and comprehensively 'demonstrates how an extensive harmonic vocabulary, embracing every kind of chord structure, may result from the control of contrapuntal lines'.[24] In Ziehn, we can acknowledge an important stimulus in Stevenson's early development.

To summarise and recapitulate points of basic interest in *A 20th Century Music Diary*, consideration of the following may be helpful:

No. 1: enharmonic unity of triadic and quartal harmony (after Ziehn).

Nos. 2–4: scale studies – respectively Indian/Arabic, natural pentatonic/synthetic whole-tone, double thirds.

Nos. 5 and 6: symmetrical inversion (after Ziehn); studies in variable metre and non-retrogradable rhythm.

No. 7: confluence of major and minor.

No. 8: polytonality. Here Stevenson emphasises keys a major third apart – 'black' E flat minor lower stave/'white' G major upper stave (*cf.* the Busoni Piano Concerto, and also No. 9).

No. 9: *Canon in Memoriam Bernard van Dieren*.[25] On his death, van Dieren (1884–1936), once described by Cecil Gray as 'perhaps only the first representative [of Busoni's New Classicism]',[26] left an unfinished treatise on fugue as well as (coincidentally, in the light of the comments above) a sketch for a book about harmony *polyphonically derived.* As early as 1951, Stevenson had made two transcriptions of his song *Weep you no more, Sad Fountains* – for piano, and for small orchestra (there is also an arrangement of the Fifth String Quartet, from 1987). The present Canon confines the

---

[23] *Ibid.*, p. 17; *cf.* also the *Prelude, Fugue and Fantasy*, p. 6, second system, bar 2, and the *Peter Grimes Fantasy*, p. 11, first two systems, outer parts.

[24] *Ibid.*, jacket blurb.

[25] Reproduced in Appendix Five: Some Stevenson Miniatures, pp. 367–68.

[26] *A Survey of Contemporary Music*, Oxford University Press, London, 1924, p. 238.

tonal activity of its four parts within a tritonal orbit, each entry separated by the distance of a tone – C, B flat, A flat, G flat.[27]

No. 10: motif development – BACH. A Lisztian paraphrase using all 24 possible permutations of the cipher (reworked 1987–88, as *Motus Perpetuus (?) Temporibus Fatalibus*).

No. 11 (likewise variously Nos. 9, 10 and 12–15): serial organisation. Here (Ex. 6) Stevenson uses a twelve-note row derived by Milhaud[28] from the Statue Scene in *Don Giovanni*, for Stevenson a derivation symbolic of Mozart's ability to foreshadow the future: he refers to it conspicuously in *Western Music*.[29]

Ex. 6

R.S.:	1	2	3	4	5	6	7	8	9	10	11	12
Pitch-class set:	9	6	2	10	3	7	1	5	11	8	4	0

No. 12: motif development. A set of seven variations, this movement is based on Berlioz's 'Evocation of Mephistopheles' from *The Damnation of Faust* – a theme underlined by prominent and disruptive tritone references (*cf.* the 'Dante' Sonata of Liszt; Busoni).

No. 13: Fugue. A two-part exercise founded on a twelve-note subject drawn from Busoni's overture to *Arlecchino*. Characteristically for Stevenson, the tonality of the music is governed by a scheme latent

---

[27] *Cf.* Ziehn, *op. cit.*, p. 106, Canon A.

[28] In 'Lettre Ouverte à Luigi Dallapiccola', *La Rassegna musicale*, Vol. XXIII, No. 1, Turin, January 1953; *cf.* Luigi Dallapiccola, 'Notes on the Statue Scene in Don Giovanni', *Dallapiccola on Opera*, ed. Rudy Shackelford, Toccata Press, London, 1987, p. 211.

[29] P. 129.

*Stevenson's sketch for the motivic study of BACH that formed
the tenth part of* A 20th Century Music Diary *and was later expanded
to provide the basis of* Motus Perpetuus (?) Temporibus Fatalibus

in the triad cells of the subject – A, B flat, B, C. These pitches form respectively the tonal centres for successive entries of subject and answer, a plan which not only ensures strong organic unity but also makes eventually for *one* complete statement of the subject established across the span of the whole by the different polarities of each new tonal zone. The result is intriguing: the fugue, as it were, becomes simultaneously both a traditionally argued texture and a single thematic intonation – microcosm within macrocosm; as Stevenson once put it in conversation, 'the modulation scheme of the little fugue is governed by the subject. When the scheme is fully stated, the fugue is finished' – a method sharing something with Alan Bush's technique of total thematisation.[30] Stevenson applies it in less advanced form in the early fugue from the *Prelude, Fugue and Fantasy on Busoni's 'Faust'* (1949–59) and in more sophisticated guise in the later fughetta that makes up the fifth of the solo-violin *Variations on a Theme of Pizzetti* (1961). Does the practice have its roots in a chance remark of Busoni's to Mario Corti in 1911 concerning the possibilities of keeping voices 'independent of each other in polyphonic composition'? – 'I have, as an experiment, constructed a five-part fugue in which every voice is in a different key so that the harmony flows in quite new chord successions'.[31] Perhaps.

No. 14: fugato on the opening theme of Liszt's *Faust-Symphonie* – 'Faust the Thinker' (reworked 1961–62 as an organ Prelude and Fugue).

No. 15: serialisation of pitch and duration.

---

[30] *Cf.* Ronald Stevenson, 'Alan Bush: Committed Composer', *Music Review*, Vol. XXV, 30, No. 4, November 1964; also Ronald Stevenson (ed.), *Time Remembered*, Bravura Publications, Kidderminster, 1981.

[31] From 'The New Harmony', written in Chicago in January 1911 for the Berlin periodical *Signale für die musikalische Welt*, Vol. LXIX, No. 7; translated Rosamund Ley, in *The Essence of Music and Other Papers*, Rockliff, London, 1957, p. 24; reprinted Dover, New York, 1964.
   Cf. also Roberto Gerhard, 'Developments in Twelve-tone Technique', *The Score*, No. 17, September 1956, pp. 61–72:
   In composition I use now the complete serial field. The field order is based on the model of the original series, the sequence of transpositions following (so to speak) an acrostic-pattern which reproduces at superordinate time levels the interval structure of the original series.
During the mid-1950s Stevenson was a regular subscriber and contributor to *The Score*.

No. 16: summation – Busoni's 'fifth way', 'the birth of a new key system'.[32]

The Celtic Aesthetic

> I think all great art aspires beyond nationalism, as an exploration of occult regions of experience. But I am convinced that a people's culture cannot get beyond nationalism until it has *realised* it. Scotland hasn't.[33]

Stevenson's 'Scottish' works are significant for many reasons. They range across the larger part of his development. They provide in their commonness of modal, intervallically expansive language and cadence a thread of stylistic continuity between periods of creative thought often otherwise apparently unrelated. Like the Hungarian essays of Bartók, the Spanish ones of Falla, the late Norwegian and Moravian explorations of Grieg and Janáček, they are concerned to reflect the voice, the step, the imagery of a people by a vocabulary of grass-root origin, of authentic rather than borrowed inflexion.[34] They celebrate, passionately and eloquently, Stevenson's birthright, his Scottish-Welsh kinship, his Celtic inheritance. Works of today coloured by ancient time, they are unique.

In his search for an indigenous Scottish music, the example of Francis George Scott has been a source of particular stimulus for Stevenson. Scott (1880–1958) was a true nationalist, a man whose five books of *Scottish Lyrics* (1922–39) and *Thirty-Five Scottish Lyrics* (1949)[35] are deservedly famous, a teacher who wrote an essay on *piobaireachd*, a composer who believed 'that a distinctly Scottish idiom [...] can be created only through a knowledge and appreciation of the speech-rhythm and inflexion of Scottish folk poetry',[36] a *litterato* disposed towards the work of Burns, Dunbar

---

[32] 'The New Harmony', *loc. cit.*

[33] Ronald Stevenson, letter to the author, dated 30 April 1968.

[34] *Cf.* Ronald Stevenson, 'Alan Bush: Committed Composer', *loc. cit.*; also Ateş Orga, 'Ronald Stevenson', *loc. cit.*, p. 31. 'I have learned, and I imbibed very early on, the Scottish language of music, and that is all that matters to me', quoted in Malcolm MacDonald, *Ronald Stevenson: A Musical Biography*, National Library of Scotland, Edinburgh, 1989, p. 108.

[35] Hereafter *SL* and *35SL* respectively; published by Bayley & Ferguson, Glasgow, from 1922 onwards (*35SL* published for The Saltire Society).

[36] From Maurice Lindsay's entry on Scott in *Grove's Dictionary of Music and Musicians*, 5th edn., Macmillan, London, 1954, Vol. VII, p. 669. *Cf.* also p. 34, note 20, above.

and C. M. Grieve ('Hugh MacDiarmid') – who had been his pupil. Writing about the twentieth century in *Western Music*,[37] Stevenson says of Scott that 'it may come as a surprise to people who enjoy the traditional national music of Scotland – the fiddle music and the pipe music' to realise that he is, categorically, her 'only one composer of European stature'. Single-handed, he claims, Scott 'created a tradition, compound of *pibroch*, folk-song, ballads (Border, bawdy and drawing-room), pub songs and an awareness of Central European techniques. [...] No British music from the Twenties is nearer in idiom to middle-period Schoenberg than certain passages in Scott's MacDiarmid songs [...]'. The best of his output 'is precious in the best sense. He never did anything to further his cause: a man of dour integrity'.

The initials of Scott's name, FGS, spell out (in German nomenclature) a modal Gaelic cipher (Ex. 7), and Stevenson uses it as a motto theme in *Keening Sang for a Makar* (1958–59), a majestic, uncompromising paean to mark his passing. Derived from an earlier sketch, *Ne'erday Sang*, one of the later *Scottish Folk-Music Settings*, based on a pentatonic melody (incorporating FGS) found in William Sterling's *Cantus Part Book* of 1639, this work poignantly quotes from Scott's 'St Brendan's Graveyard: Isle of Barra' (*SL* III/8, 1934).[38]

Ex. 7

Early in 1963 Stevenson transcribed seven of Scott's songs for piano (later supplemented):

1. 'There's news, lasses, news'
   (Burns)   *35SL* 20   (1949)
2. 'Ay waulkin, O' (Burns)   *SL*   I/1   (1922)
3. 'O were my love yon lilac fair'
   (Burns)   *SL*   II/6   (1922)
4. 'Wee Willie Gray' (Burns)   *SL*   V/3   (1939)
5. 'Wha is that at my bower-door?'
   (Burns)   *SL*   V/6   (1939)

---

[37] P. 178.

[38] *Cf.* also p. 34, above.

6. 'Milkwort and Bog-cotton'
   (MacDiarmid)   *SL*   III/11   (1934)
7. 'Crowdieknowe' (MacDiarmid)   *SL*   III/6   (1934).

The nine *Scottish Folk-Music Settings* for piano (variously written between 1959 and 1965, and subsequently added to),[39] belong in spirit with the Scott transcriptions. The original version of the fourth (No. 5 in manuscript) 'Lang Hae We Pairted Been' for baritone and piano, is the earliest apparent example of a declared 'Scottish' work in the Stevenson catalogue.

Ronald Stevenson's feeling for Scottish ethno-music proper, with its unmistakable sound, its pagan memories, its quasi-microtonality, its broadly pentatonic or modal (Dorian, Aeolian, Mixolydian) scale-structure, its peculiar instrumental timbre, is best shown (like that of Scott) by his study and assimilation of pibroch. The tradition of pibroch (after the Gaelic *piobaireachd*, 'pipe tune'), the 'Great Music' (*Ceòl Mór*) of the Highland clans, is an old one, reaching back to the late fifteenth century when the MacCrimmons of Boreraig, Skye, hereditary pipers to the Macleods of Dunvegan, founded a school of piping that was to survive uninterrupted until 1840, its principles handed down the generations by either word of mouth or a complex kind of syllabic notation (*canntaireachd*). Confined in pitch to the natural nine-note scale of the *piob mor* or the Highland warpipe – a scale of quasi-Mixolydian, unequally tempered formation (g′–a″) built on A as a tonic drone, with the C and F each about a quarter-tone sharp – the form of a *piobaireachd* approximates most closely that of variation (attractively for Stevenson, given his interest in variation procedure). Classically, the theme or *ùrlar*, of heroic or lamenting character, functions as a recurrent ground: each variation is predominantly rhythmic. Several hundred examples of pibroch exist, mostly dating from before the 1745 Rebellion; the Victorian age helped preserve them through the collections of, notably, Angus Mackay (1838), William Ross, the Queen's piper (1869, rev. 1876, 1896), and Major General C. S. Thomson (*Ceòl Mór*, 1900). In 1980 Stevenson presented six programmes on pibroch for Radio Scotland.

Stevenson's pibroch music (the 'gigantic' conception of *Ben Dorain* besides) includes *Calum Salum's Salute to the Seals* (1967) for pipes, later reworked for piano as *Chorale Pibroch for Sorley MacLean* – a haunting lament of brushed, hammered and plucked strings; and

---

[39] Discussed, with other Celtic aestheticisms, under 'Graingeries', pp. 76–80; *cf.* also pp. 448–49.

Cumha na Cloinne (*Lament for the Children*), interpolated in Part I of the *Passacaglia on DSCH* (following the *Polonaise*). Added as an afterthought in 1963, on the day of the premiere of the *Passacaglia* (10 December), *Cumha na Cloinne* paraphrases a seventeenth-century *ùrlar* by Patrick Mór MacCrimmon composed as a lament on the deaths (all within a year) of seven of his eight sons. 'I recast his melody', Stevenson says, 'thinking of all the child victims of Nazism' (Ex. 8).[40] Its stylisation of drones, frequent minor/major

Ex. 8

[40] In 'Reflections after a Premiere', *Musica Viva*, Cape Town, December 1963; *cf.* also pp. 323 and 325.

third (F/F sharp) clashes suggestive of pipe tuning, and expressive translation of the 'warbler' or grace-notes typical of good pibroch playing, tell something of the extent of Stevenson's perception of his model. A tableau of atmosphere and sadness, of ghostly shadow, of intonationally acid dialect.

Other 'Scottish' works for piano include, at a simple level, examples like *A Wheen Tunes for Bairns tae Spiel* ('four Scottish pieces').[41] More complex is *Heroic Song* (1967), commissioned by the BBC to mark the 75th birthday of Hugh MacDiarmid. Conceived within a concentrated structure that brings together facets of variations and 'telescoped' sonata form ('The Poet Speaks', 'The Poet Laughs', 'The Poet Dreams'), this hybrid piece combines echoing nationalist elements (a Scots New Year's Day pentatonic song from 1639 offset by an imaginative wash of piano harmonics in the bass swelled through artificial reverberation, plus pibroch warbles) with an earlier, Busoni-influenced manner (a *maestoso* motif). Stevenson, writing in 1990, called it 'a song of the high hills, of space and solitude', remembering Ruskin's words, 'these great cathedrals of the earth, with their gates of rock, pavements of cloud, traversed by the continual stars'.[42]

Of the *Three Scottish Ballads* (1973), No. 2, 'The Dowie Dens of Yarrow' (dedicated to the composer's elder daughter, Gerda), less complicated harmonically and pianistically than its companions, must be mentioned for the particular beauty of its keyboard *voicing*, its triadic modality, and its easy handling of variation method. Ex. 9 shows how the nine-bar theme is given new perspective homophonically (Var. ii: Ex. 9(b)) and polyphonically (Var. iii, a three-part canon of wonderfully natural suppleness: Ex. 9(c)).

A gentle enshrinement of the Celtic aesthetic is found in *The Water of Tyne* (dated, according to the manuscript, 6 March 1982, the composer's 54th birthday) – a slow *lontano* dreamscape in D flat, invocative of some mystical union between Scriabin and Rachmaninov presided over by John Ireland in council with William Baines: very romantic, very tender, very intimate, a lovely study in melody 'floating'.

In language Stevenson's 'European' music is dense and semitone-concentrated. His 'Scottish' essays, by comparison, are 'open'

---

[41] *Cf.* p. 396.

[42] Notes to the recording on Altarus AIR-CD-9043. Perfectly formed, tragically hypnotic masterpieces, *Keening Sang, Heroic Song* and *Chorale Pibroch* together comprise *A Scottish Triptych* (1968), recorded by Joseph Banowetz on Altarus AIR-CD-9089.

Ex. 9

(a) Theme

(b) Var. ii

and tone-focussed.[43] The harmonic simplification, the clarity of *The Water of Tyne* and 'The Dowie Dens of Yarrow', is the norm, not the exception. Nowhere is such fact better demonstrated than in the *Barra Flyting Toccata* (April 1980), a bagatelle of much virtuosity depicting, the composer tells us, 'a scolding-match from the Isle of Barra', the southernmost main island of the Outer Hebrides. This is predominantly a black-note piece in F sharp major, relieved by just one twelve-bar episode in E flat affected by an enharmonic pivot (A sharp = B flat; *cf.* the key change from A to A flat Aeolian *via* B = C flat in Var. iv of 'The Dowie Dens of Yarrow'). The rhythmically fertile melodic line (Ex. 10), spanning a major ninth (the range of

[43] *Cf.* Colin Scott-Sutherland, 'The Music of Ronald Stevenson', *Music Review*, Vol. 26, No. 2, May 1965, pp. 118–28.

the Highland bagpipe), is fundamentally pentatonic; precisely, it is compounded of two dovetailed gapped tetrachords, each encompassing a fifth – a sequence Stevenson identifies as 'the essential motif of Scottish music'[44] (Ex. 11).

Ex. 10

Ex. 11

This scale-structure is preserved intact virtually throughout: the only foreign note admitted (B) is initially harmonic rather than melodic. (The bass D flat, five bars into the E flat section, is a departure not found in the F sharp major paragraphs where there are no leading notes at all, flattened or otherwise.) With its triplet and semiquaver movement, its dotted figures and 'Scotch' snaps, this is an exhilarating exercise redolent in many ways of Gottschalk (most obviously the Negritic *Bamboula*).

The *Fugue, Variations and Epilogue on a Theme of Bax* (1982–83), based on the melody of the second movement of the Second Symphony, with the theme quoted at the end rather than the beginning, remains unfinalised. Intended to play for about twenty minutes, Stevenson conceived/conceives it to crystallise all his 'devotion to a Celtic aesthetic'.[45]

Prelude, Fugue and Fantasy on Busoni's 'Faust'

One cannot apply to *Doktor Faust* the ordinary standards of operatic criticism. It moves on a plane of spiritual experience far beyond that

---

[44] In conversation with Malcolm MacDonald, West Linton, December 1988, quoted in MacDonald, *op. cit.*, p. 108. Transposed, the same four notes generate Stevenson's twelve-part motet *In Memoriam Robert Carver* (1987).

[45] Letter to the author, dated 20 May 1982. [Too late to allow the Bax Variations to be examined in this essay, the news came that Stevenson, on a request from the Finnish pianist Matti Raekallio, had resumed work on this score, finishing it in January 2003. –ED.]

of even the greatest of musical works for the stage [...]. It is the summing-up of [Busoni's] life's works and experience [...].[46]

Busoni in his twin-souled breast was a Mefausto. His devil, unlike others, is a high tenor whose spirit cry pierces the world of sensory perception. Busoni's Faust is creative will personified [...]. Busoni's opera polarises fear and peace; the world's present dilemma [...].[47]

She whose hair is plaited
Like the generations of men,
And for whom my heart has waited
Time out of ken.[48]

The *Prelude, Fugue and Fantasy on Busoni's 'Faust'* and the *Passacaglia on DSCH* mark respectively the beginning and culmination of Stevenson's so-called 'Busoni' period. They are imagined on the grandest scale: inevitably perhaps – 'my main interest in music is in the epic. This is an epic age, it seems to me, and only epic forms can fully express its aspirations'.[49]

Writing of the *Prelude, Fugue and Fantasy* in his Editorial Note to the published score,[50] John Ogdon had some pertinent things to say. In it, he argued, Stevenson

demonstrates Busoni's concept of the essential oneness of music by unifying apparently diverse strands of his musical thought. Busoni's musical philosophy was sometimes ambivalent since he combined respect for tradition with interest in experiment. Mr Stevenson directs his own thought into classically-orientated forms, as if to prove that the future of music lies in the transformation of its past.

Busoni, he concluded,

---

[46] E. J. Dent, *Ferruccio Busoni*, Oxford University Press, London, 1933 (reprinted Eulenberg, London, 1974) pp. 304–5.

[47] Ronald Stevenson, 'Mefausto', *Radio Times*, Vol. 89, No. 2284, 4 January 1973,

[48] Hugh MacDiarmid, 'The Gaelic Muse', *Collected Poems of Hugh MacDiarmid*, MacMillan, New York, 1962, pp. 362–67.

[49] Ronald Stevenson, *Composer's Portrait*, BBC Third Programme, 18 January 1967 – a transcript is quoted selectively in Ateş Orga, 'Ronald Stevenson', *loc. cit.* Stevenson has recorded the *Prelude, Fugue and Fantasy* on Altarus AIR-CD-9042, also re-issued – *cf.* Appendix Nine, Discography, p. 474. *Cf.* also his notes to Altarus AIR-CD-9044 (Busoni: Music for Two Pianos and Piano Duet) for an overview of Busoni 'as a Renaissance man of the 20th century. He was a passionate intellectual whose personal philosophy tempered an early commitment to dialectical materialism by a later enquiry into the possibility of spiritual science'.

[50] *Cf.* note 10, p. 28.

felt his Second Violin Sonata to be his masterpiece, in the medieval meaning of marking his emergence from apprenticeship to maturity as a composer, and in this sense the *Prelude, Fugue and Fantasy* is Mr Stevenson's. Its pianism is brilliant and sensitive, and its counterpoint holds one with a glittering eye. The work is conceptually felt, yet its impulse is controlled analytically and its music symphonically organised [. . .].

The *Prelude, Fugue and Fantasy*, a triptych of chronologically distinct movements, ten years in the making (1949–59), consists of around a dozen or so Faust or Faust/Busoni-associated ideas. Each the subject of continuing variation, transformation or cyclic cross-reference, these, in descending order of importance, can be divided into four main groups:

(a) *Doktor Faust*, primary material:
   (i) *Vorspiel II*, opening
   (ii) Duchess of Parma's Aria, 'he [Faust] calls me with a thousand voices' (based by Busoni on the tenor line from Bach's chorale, *Christ lag in Todes Banden*, Terry edition No. 38)
   (iii) '*Clavis Astartis Magica*' (the motif associated with Faust the magician, the theme of the book *The Key to Stellar Magic*, given to him in the opening scene of the opera);
(b) *Doktor Faust*, secondary material:
   (i) *Mephistopheles' Lied*
   (ii) *Sarabande*
   (iii) Credo (*a cappella* choir);
(c) Other Busoni works:
   (i) *Sonatina Seconda*
   (ii) Piano Concerto
   (iii) Violin Sonata No. 2 (three quotations)
   (iv) F minor *Fantasia after Bach, PAX EJ!* (composed in memory of Busoni's father, 1909)
      (Additionally, Bach's chorale, *Christ lag in Todes Banden*, quoted by Busoni in *Vorspiel II*; cf. Duchess of Parma's Aria, (a)(ii) above);
(d) Ciphers:
   (i) BACH (cf. the *Fantasia Contrappuntistica* and, in unordered form, Duchess of Parma's Aria, Ex. 12(b))
   (ii) FB: the opera's tritonic symbol of fear; 'Ferruccio Busoni'.

Last in order of composition (1959), the Prelude is based largely on the source material of the first group (Ex. 12), introduced at first embryonically, then more directly.

Ex. 12

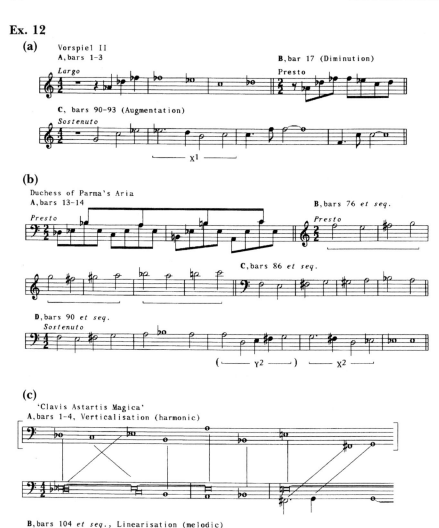

Additionally, it is concerned with another idea (*sonoro*) that seems to be unrelated but which on examination can be shown to be the fruit of an interesting organic cross-fertilisation between the music of the Duchess and Faust – a fusion, if you will, of their opposed identities, the one diatonic and restful, the other chromatic and restless (Ex. 13).

A mutation of strangely frozen rhythm, of fleeting identity, does this theme portray symbolically the dead child of their union in

Ex. 13

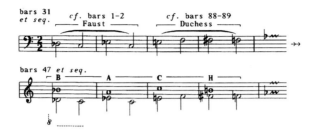

whom Faust will find his eventual 'earthly resurrection'?[51] Emotionally, the tension of the whole is extreme, and nowhere more so than in the *sostenuto: mesto e lontano* passage (bars 90 *et seq.*) immediately before Cadenza I with its quotation from the *Sonatina Seconda*: how Aria, '*Clavis Astartis Magica*', Vorspiel II and BACH combine here to produce a musically and dramatically interlocked moment of powerfully moving expressive intensity (Ex. 14) is noteworthy.

Ex. 14

The three-voice Fugue (conceived originally in 1950, the year following the extraordinarily imagined 'free fantasy' *Fugue on a Fragment of Chopin*, after the Fourth *Ballade*) – full of muscular linear perspective, rich in feeling for a contrapuntal intensity and progression born as much out of Busoni, Liszt, Brahms and Reicha as the teachings of Ziehn – takes for its subject Faust's '*Clavis*

---

[51] 'Earthly Resurrection' – Anatoli Lunacharski's interpretation in his play, *Faust and the City*, 1916; from *Faust and Other Plays*, trans. L. A. Magnus and K. Walter, Routledge, London, 1923.

Astartis Magica'. Its most progressive technical device is the use of the nine pitches of this theme broadly to govern the tonal centres of successive entries of subject and answer, a procedure that makes not only for much organic cohesion but also of course for a macrostructure the foundational pillars of which can be nothing else but one single, grand statement of the subject itself adumbrated across the time-span of the whole in vastly augmented form (*cf. A 20th Century Music Diary*, No. 13[52]).

First in order of composition (1949), the Fantasy is rooted broadly in E: its mediant relationship with the C modality of the Prelude and Fugue compares generally with the arrangement of keys in the Busoni Piano Concerto and especially the internal tonal scheme of that work's first movement.[53] A telescoped sonata-form structure in which complete movements are compressed into subject groups (a Busonian procedure of Lisztian precedent), its six sections comprise:

(i)   Introduction (based on *Vorspiel II*); 'philosophic' in nature;
(ii) Duchess of Parma's Aria (a decorative version); 'lyrical' in style;
(iii) *Tempo di Minuetto* (B flat) ⎫ 'each combined with the
(iv) *Allegretto vivo quasi Ballata* ⎬ fugal subject';
      (*Mephistopheles' Lied*, G minor) ⎭
(v)   Cadenza II ('*Clavis Astartis Magica*'); '*non brillante* – reflecting on all the themes of the work';
(vi) Recapitulations/retrospection (reference to the F minor *Fantasia*, FB cipher, etc.).

My division follows John Ogdon,[54] with the composer's remarks in quotation; in Stevenson's analysis,[55] the sixth section sub-divides into two:

(a) Scherzo: 'recapitulating and combining the Fantasy's two opening themes in metamorphosis';
(b) Coda: 'a final meditation on the fugal subject'.[56]

---

[52] *Cf.* pp. 57 and 59.

[53] Revisiting – paying homage to – the precedent of the C/E, a major third apart, familiar from Beethoven (Piano Sonata Op. 2, No.3, Third Piano Concerto, the 'Waldstein' Sonata), Schubert (the 'Wanderer' Fantasy), Liszt (*Faust-Symphonie*), and Brahms (the Op. 1 Piano Sonata and First Symphony).

[54] *Loc. cit.*

[55] Composer's programme note, Purcell Room, London, 11 March 1969.

[56] Stevenson's 1985 notes for Altarus AIR-CD-9044 define vi (b) further as 'a meditative coda, bearing the superscription PAX EJ! *in memoriam* Busoni'.

Ex. 15

The *Prelude, Fugue and Fantasy* is a work of splendid pianism, whose effects – white-and-black note *glissandi* in the Prelude (more abrasively arresting, it must be said, than Ogdon's fingered pentatonic *alternativi*), stereophonic 'scoring' (principally in the combination of the Credo and Faust's music, Ex. 15), laced terraces of filigree decoration (the Duchess of Parma's Aria in the Fantasy) – make for a banquet of keyboard invention and sonority veritably without compare.

Expressively, its ebony and ivory world is one provocative

panorama of old and modern: modern synthesis, old ancestry. Within pages of mightily extended digital vision, brave new dreams, ghosts of another time – the aristocratic Liszt of the *Réminiscences de Don Juan*, of the Verdi and Wagner paraphrases, of the Beethoven and Berlioz transcriptions, the apocalyptic Alkan of the solo Concerto from the Op. 39 Studies, of the 'Quasi-Faust' tableau from the *Grande Sonate*, Op. 33 – stand in living, haunting confrontation.

In its solo form (premiered by Ogdon at the 1959 Manchester Arts Festival) and its 1960 orchestral reincarnation (Piano Concerto No. 1, *Faust Triptych*), this cycle stands unique: as a homage to Busoni ('a philosophical eclectic [...,] a musical genius [...,] a neo-Renaissance figure',[57] 'my master *in absentia*'[58]) and as a celebration of *Doktor Faust* ('a 20th century masterwork'[59]). It was the first of Stevenson's compositions to gain him wider public and critical recognition.

When one thinks of Faust and Stevenson, it is invariably in connection with Busoni. Yet the Fausts of Liszt and Schumann have also had their part to play, the former most substantially in the (organ) *Prelude and Fugue on a 12-note Theme from Liszt's 'Faust-Symphonie'* (1961–62), the latter in the (piano) *Chorale and Fugue in Reverse* (November 1979).

Written in memory of Stephen Glover, the son of the late Ulster pianist Lawrence Glover (a sometime fellow-student of Stevenson's in Manchester), the *Chorale and Fugue in Reverse* is described as being based 'on themes by Robert and Clara Schumann': respectively, Robert's metaphysically profound choral setting of Goethe's *Chorus mysticus* (Ex. 16(b)) from the end of Part III of *Scenes from Goethe's Faust* (taken by Stevenson from a manuscript variant of bars 5–7 presented by Schumann to Hans Christian Andersen in 1849 – Ex. 16(a), (c)), and Clara's song, '*Geheimes Flüstern*', Op. 23, No. 3 (10 June 1853). The Faust quotation preserves Schumann's original rhythmic shape but distorts the melody (through clef displacement – Ex. 16(d), (e)) so as to be able to accommodate an FB/ 'Ferruccio Busoni' symbol – a very Stevensonian change of focus.

Both the Chorale, *moderato grave*, and the four-part Fugue, *allegro moderato*, are concerned with manifestations of the Faust motif: it appears in prime, inverted, retrograde inverted and retrograde

[57] *Western Music*, p. 170. *Cf.* also Stevenson's recording and notes, *The Essence of Busoni*, Altarus AIR-CD-9041, the title of which is a quiet hommage to Robert Simpson's book *The Essence of Bruckner* (Gollancz, London, 1967).

[58] Quoted in Ateş Orga, 'Ronald Stevenson', *loc. cit.*, p. 27.

[59] *Western Music*, p. 170.

Ex. 16

(a) Manuscript variant

(b) Published text

(c) Schumann: MS pitch variants

(d) Stevenson: Chorale metamorphoses

(e) Stevenson: Fugue subject

profile in the former, and is the issue of rhythmic diminution in the latter. Technically, the exposition of the Fugue (not unlike a canon at one beat's distance: there is no counter-subject) is interesting for providing a mature example of Stevenson's contrapuntal style: its wiry, tough, sinewy gesture is unmistakable (Ex. 17).

Ex. 17

The final Coda, prefaced by a brief *Cadenza lirica* (incorporating the Clara quotation), is remarkable – not least for a cadential resolution where superimposed diatonic F *major* and enharmonic B *major* triads (the FB idea again[60]) not only encapsulate vertically the linear tritone cell of the metamorphosed *Chorus mysticus* itself but also enshrine an originally imagined *tierce de picardie* realisation of the music's opening F minor/B minor harmony (Ex. 18 (a) and (b)).

Ex. 18

(a) conclusion

(b) opening

Graingeries

I am not making out a case for [Grainger] as an 'important figure': fortunately he avoided the bane of the 'important' – especially in the Teutonic sense. But the present century has had no greater indicator of future possibilities in music. If he 'cocks a snook' at tradition, and bids a merry farewell to the past, with the other hand he indicates the future. [...] Grainger was a true democrat in music who broke with the

[60] *Cf.* bar 95 of the *Prelude on Busoni's 'Faust'*.

European cult of the aristocratic artist and who went out among people to make his music [...].[61]

Of all the fellow-travellers who have given Stevenson courage on his journey – Busoni, Grainger, Emmanuel, Paderewski, Hába, Szymanowski, Godowsky, Sorabji, Scott, Delius, Enescu, Tagore, MacDiarmid, Bush, Bernard Stevens – one stands out above all others for having shown him at a stroke how to be free and spontaneous, how to explore the open spaces, how to make a tired sensibility fresh, how to care nothing for what society expects, how to portray tragedy in a clown's mask, joy through profundity: Grainger – a man of vision, a seeker after truth, a lover of the vulgar no less than an admirer of the serious, a collector of songs and dances from the world over, an experimenter of boldness, 'a Kiplingesque "Mowgli of Music": a Siegfried whose anvil was the piano keyboard'.[62]

Grainger and Stevenson got to know each other during the late 1950s. Old master and young aspirer had much to say. Grainger ('one of the most gifted pianists of the century'[63]) applauded Stevenson's playing: 'What an exquisite pianist! Your tone-differentiation (bringing out middle-melodies) is superb'.[64] And Stevenson (in retrospect, something like a decade before the Grainger 'revival' proper, before it became 'respectable' to play his music) showed his admiration by writing 'dished-up' works like the piano transcription of the first *Hill Song* (1960), a piece once held in high regard by Busoni and Delius, the *Jamboree for Grainger* for two pianos (1960, orchestrated the following year[65]), and the exhilarating arrangement for solo piano of the orchestral passacaglia, *Green Bushes* (1963); and by editing, for Schott in 1966, a commemorative volume of Grainger's music (*The Young Pianist's Grainger*) – music that for him, as he says in his Introduction, seems to be like 'a reflection of the nature [Grainger] so passionately

---

[61] *Western Music*, p. 199.

[62] From a programme note by Stevenson, Rudolf Steiner School Hall recital, Edinburgh, 12 March 1980 (*cf.* p. 302). Likening the piano keyboard to an anvil is a favourite Stevenson simile – borrowed from Paderewski (Ignacy Jan Paderewski and Mary Lawton, *The Paderewski Memoirs*, Collins, London, 1939, p. 172) misquoting Shaw (*The Star*, 16 May 1890); *cf.* also pp. 98 and 207–8.

[63] Harold C. Schonberg, *The Great Pianists*, Gollancz, London/New York, 1963, p. 327.

[64] In a letter dated 6 May 1959.

[65] *Cf.* pp. 137–38.

loved: wild, free, and as open as the road over the moors'. Of the *Hill Song*, Grainger wrote to Stevenson:[66]

> I was looking at your piano solo transcription [...] this morning and admiring it. You are a splendid craftsman, indeed. [...] I feel *greatly* honoured that you should wish to investigate my music so thoroughly, and I congratulate you on your mastery of graceful details – in wording, in your handwriting, in your transcribing [...].

Stevenson's folk-song arrangements and his piano music for children, pure and delightful stuff, pay a different kind of homage to Grainger. A charming anthology of pointed educational value, *A Wheen Tunes for Bairns tae Spiel* (1964), written for Stevenson's youngest daughter, Savourna, to play, is one example, for instance, that combines facets of Scottish music in the last two movements ('Reel', and a pentatonic 'Spiel' composed on the black notes) with Grainger in the first two ('Croon' and 'Drone') in a manner that would surely have delighted the old man. In 1965 Stevenson composed two further children's pieces, *Valse Charlot* and *Valse Garbo* – 'like cigarette-cards of famous film-stars'[67] – by way of light relief between the *Passacaglia* and *Peter Grimes Fantasy*.

The following examples, variously mirroring the Grainger spirit, should also be considered:

(a) *Scottish Folk-Music Settings*[68]
    'Waly, Waly' (1959)
    'A Rosebud by my Early Walk' (1961)
    'John Anderson, my Jo' (1961)
    'Lang hae we pairted been' (1961)
    'Ne'er Day Song' (1963)
    'From an old Pibroch' (1965)
    'Ca' the Yowes' (1965)

---

[66] In a letter dated 20 June 1960, quoted in Barry Peter Ould, *op. cit.*, p. 4. Stevenson has recorded his transcription on Altarus AIR-CD-9040. In his notes (1985) to this recording Stevenson quotes Grainger to provide a useful reminder of the original intention behind the *Hill Song*, written in 1901–2: 'What I wanted to convey [. . .] was *the nature of the hills themselves* – as if the hills themselves were telling of themselves through my music, rather than that I, an onlooker, were recording my "impressions" of the hills'. The same recording, an enduring 'Scottish' tribute to Grainger, also includes the fourteen *Songs of the North* together with the *Three Scotch Folksongs* in Stevenson's pianistified, re-ordered arrangement from 1983.

[67] Marginal note on the score.

[68] It is impossible to number these in strict order as several versions for varying instrumental combinations were composed at different times. There are also several other settings, such as *Willie's rare and Willie's fair*. –ED.

'Hielan' Lament' (1965)
'The Birks o' Aberfeldy' (1965)
'Jock o' Hazeldean'
'Hard is My Fate' (1980)[69]
'Wo betyd thy Wearie Body'
'The Queen's Maries'
The Graingeresque title is instructive: Stevenson dedicated the set 'lovingly and reverently' to Grainger's memory;

(b) *Nine Children's Pieces*, 'simply arranged and abridged from the music of Delius' (1962);

(c) *Simple* [jazz] *Variations on Purcell's 'New Scotch Tune'* (Cape Town, 1964). Theme from *Musick's Handmaid*, Part II (Playford, London, 1689), its flattened seventh providing Stevenson with an inflexion applicable as much to Scottish folk music as to the blues. A work of direct expression – *cf.* Grainger's *Walking Tune*;

(d) *Irish Folk-Song Suite* (1965; solo or duet), four movements;

(e) *Chinese Folk-Song Suite* (1965), five movements;

(f) *Ghanaian Folk-Song Suite* (1965), three movements;

(g) *South-Uist (Hebridean) Folk-Song Suite* (1969), seven movements;

(h) *Sounding Strings*: fourteen 'settings of folk music from the six Celtic countries' (Ireland, Wales, Scotland – the Hebrides, Brittany, Cornwall, the Isle of Man), for clarsach, pedal-harp, or piano, dedicated to Savourna Stevenson (published by United Music Publishers in 1979).

Norse Elegy for Ella Nygaard (8 July 1976–1979), the fair copy of which, the manuscript confirms, was 'completed on the veranda of the Grainger House, White Plains, N.Y., June 15, 1979', is a curious late Graingery. Ella Nygaard, who died in 1976, was the wife of Grainger's distinguished Norwegian-American surgeon, Kaare K. Nygaard. A family friend for years (and an outstanding sculptor), it was he who wrote of Grainger during his final illness (1960–61):[70]

> Of course he was a genius – whatever that actually means. Among many other things, he also impressed me as being almost a human Saint. [...] When it came to thinking, Percy was able to refer to that inner light which shone with a clarity dimmed only by the last year of his suffering. And even then he was a Saint.

Evidence of Stevenson's Schumannesque partiality for cipher

---

[69] Reproduced in Appendix Five: Some Stevenson Miniatures, pp. 362–63.

[70] In a letter to John Bird, dated 9 September 1975, quoted in Bird's *Percy Grainger*, Elek, London, 1976 (reprinted by Faber, London, 1982), p. 249.

and monogram abounds in his work. In the *Norse Elegy* he takes an idea based on the musically convenient letters of Ella's name (Ex. 19) and uses this, in bass and registrally transferred form, as a recurrent ostinato ground.

Ex. 19

The *cantabile* middle section (Ex. 20) shares with the *Scottish Ballad* No. 2[71] a harmonic directness and plastic sense of canonic imitation in marked contrast with the chromaticism, parallel chordal movement, and ornate inner textural detail of the flanking episodes.

Ex. 20

The way the music cadences tritonally on the dominant, minor to major, is distinctive (Ex. 21).[72]

Ex. 21

---

[71] *Cf.* pp. 64–66.

[72] *Cf.* an identical procedure in the *Scottish Ballad* No. 2, discussed on p. 64. The *Norse Elegy* is recorded by Donna Amato on Altarus AIR-CD-9021.

Passacaglia on DSCH

> It is really tremendous – magnificent. I cannot remember having been
> so excited by a new work for a very long time.[73]

> [...] one of the great piano works of this century [...].[74]

> [a] monumental work of great mastery and power.[75]

> [...] the plenitude of your obsessive urge to communicate. [...] This is
> something very impressive [...].[76]

Easily Ronald Stevenson's most important work, *Ben Dorain*
notwithstanding, the *Passacaglia on DSCH* (24 December 1960–
18 May 1962) not only marks the high point of his Busoni-
influenced years, it also stands arguably as the most concentrated
example of motif development in the history of western music. In
scope its dimension encompasses the colossal, in spirit its vision
embraces the cosmic. It is a unique tribute to Shostakovich. And it
is a powerful celebration of 'world music':

> I [...] absorb in my music elements from the East and from Africa, as
> well as from Western culture. In my future work I hope to find points
> of coalescence in world musics: there are musical forms which are
> common to all nations [variation, rondo], and although there are
> many nations there is only one human race.[77] I'll use any techniques
> which will enable me to achieve these objectives. My aim is to base my
> music in reality and to allow it to tend towards abstraction but never
> to take abstraction as a premise and so lose all connection with life
> which is much larger than the musical world.[78]

[73] Sir William Walton, in a letter to the composer, dated 18 December 1964 and
reproduced on pp. 96–97.

[74] Robert Simpson, in a letter to the composer, dated 6 November 1973.

[75] Kaikhosru Sorabji, in a letter to the composer, dated 24 May 1966.

[76] Joseph Szigeti, in a letter to the composer, dated 20 November 1964.

[77] A sentiment paraphrased from Paul Robeson, quoted in *Western Music*, p. 197:
'There are many nations, but there is only one race: the human race'.

[78] *Composer's Portrait, loc. cit.* The concept of 'world music' that is the theme of the
final chapter of *Western Music*, the Mahlerian-like desire to create a 'complete music
of mankind' that like 'the whole being of an individual's life' is a sum of 'qualities
physical, spiritual, emotional and intellectual' (*Western Music*, p. 208), has pre-
occupied Stevenson for years. 'Goethe spoke of "world citizenship"', he writes on the
last page of his book: 'Such a concept implies the necessity of world music. No
"world citizen" can go on thinking that the Viennese classics of the 18th century
reflect his world view'. In his search for an expressive key, he has come to realise,
analogously, that 'music has lost its primeval freedom because man has lost his', that

A supranational 'world language of Music', Stevenson has proposed, should combine the predominant features of Africa, Asia and Europe – respectively, rhythm, melody and homophony/polyphony: 'if such a point of fusion is held to be fictitious, the criticism is tantamount to claiming that different peoples – no less than different musics – are incurably incompatible'.[79] Like the related Second Piano Concerto, *The Continents*, of a decade later (incorporating both DSCH and '*Clavis Astartis Magica*' locked together), as well as the Violin Concerto, the *Passacaglia on DSCH*, in part at least, shows such theory put to the test.

The creation of the *Passacaglia* was stimulated by a study of Shostakovich's works incorporating the DSCH motto (the notes D, E flat, C and B in German nomenclature, implicit also in unordered form in '*Clavis Astartis Magica*'[80]) – chiefly the autobiographical Eighth String Quartet, the Tenth Symphony and the First Violin Concerto, and, secondarily, the Eleventh Symphony and the First Cello Concerto. Stevenson described the genesis and early history of the work shortly after its first performance:[81]

> The later works of Shostakovich [...] had begun to interest me. As I studied them more deeply, I felt a sense of gratitude to this great Soviet master. This expressed itself, when, on Christmas Eve 1960, I began, late at night, to conceive a Passacaglia based on Shostakovich's initials. I wrote two pages of music at one sitting, away from the piano. What I had written pleased me, but I could not foresee the continuation. It was a tentative measuring of myself against the nature of the musical material. I was living in Scotland. The ground was covered in snow. Everything was silenced in the little village of West Linton (18 miles southwest of Edinburgh). On Christmas Day I sat before a bright fire and sipped a sherry. The music began to flow. Nearly every day for more than a year, I wrote steadily at my Passacaglia. As much of the work is contrapuntal, I generally worked away from the piano; for I find I cannot think about contrapuntal possibilities with my fingers on the keys. But when the element of pianistic virtuosity succeeded the contrapuntal element [for example, the paragraphs between the Waltz and the Suite in Part I, or

---

'music is like a bastard child who is free to laugh and play until it is old enough to hear what bastardy is'.

[79] *Gambit* (University review), Edinburgh, Spring 1964, pp. 31–32; *cf.* also *Western Music*, pp. 207–8.

[80] *Cf.* Ex. 12(c) on p. 70; also *Vorspiel II*, Ex. 12(a), fig. x[1].

[81] 'Reflections after a Premiere', *loc. cit.*

the set of *études* which form the penultimate section of Part II], I often worked at the keyboard. Experience has shown that pianistic passages composed away from the piano sometimes have to be modified when tried out; the flitting pen, in trying to keep pace with the brain, skips over pianistic problems without taking account of the geometry of the keyboard.

James Joyce, writing the section 'Anna Livia Plurabelle' in his *Finnegans Wake*, began with weaving a few names of rivers into his prose-poem, but went on adding until the text became a torrent of no less than 500 names of rivers. Speaking only of the *method* of composition, and exercising care to make no other comparison, that is the kind of way in which I wrote my Passacaglia. That is to say, I went on piling up the variations until they grew into hundreds. I don't know precisely how many hundreds: I have never counted them. I did not 'through compose' the work: I mean I did not compose the pages in their final order. If one set of variations got 'stuck', I began another set. When I had composed about 15 minutes music, the overall form began to suggest itself.

I felt, after the first two pages, that the nature of the work was 'aqueous' – it must flow. Therefore it should be one long movement. To facilitate the flow, I wrote on large sheets of orchestral MS paper [...].

[...] I completed the work in rough copy on May 18th, 1962. It took about a month to make a clean copy. There were 191 pages. I was greatly honoured on September 5th, 1962, to present a bound [photostat] copy of my composition to its dedicatee, Shostakovich, who was at that time guest of honour at the Edinburgh Festival. The little ceremony took place in the composer's suite in the George Hotel, Edinburgh. There was a small gathering of friends of both composers [...] The chairman was the Scottish poet Hugh MacDiarmid. In handing over my manuscript I told Shostakovich in a brief speech[82] that, in this age of fragmentation, younger composers looked to him with gratitude as a composer who had preserved the lineage of the great masters. He graciously accepted the work, praising it, as he said, 'for its own merits and as a symbol of friendship between Britain and the U.S.S.R.' [...].

[...] I cannot conceive that a work lasting [80 minutes] will ever find a publisher. But I am glad to have completed it, for I have put into it everything I know about the piano.

Commenting on the structure of the piece,[83] Stevenson says:

This composition is a strict Passacaglia because it is based on a constantly repeated theme [the opening seven-bar, 3 + 3 + 1 ground

---

[82] The text is reproduced in the notes with Altarus AIR-CD-9091(2).

[83] 'Reflections after a Premiere', *loc. cit.*

on DSCH] around which variations are woven. It is not a strict Passacaglia in that it does not keep to one key or one mood. It is probably the longest single movement in piano literature [...]. The length has no virtue, except that it allows the work to unfold in a kind of musical fresco. Though the work is sometimes motivated by extra-musical ideas, these are not essential to its appreciation as a piece of music; and it is not intended to be listened to as programme music. It owes allegiance to those contemporary composers (particularly Busoni and Sorabji) who have composed in monumental forms in an age [the early 1960s] when such an attitude is grossly unfashionable (except in the growing appreciation of the Mahler symphonies).

The pitch of the DSCH motto, notwithstanding registral transfer, is constant: it remains unchanged throughout its 645 repetitions, whatever the tonal or harmonic context. But this does not prevent Stevenson, as he says, from creating a tapestry of texture around it that is infinitely free-ranging and tireless in key and mode. It does not stop him (in the manner of Bach in the C minor organ Passacaglia, or Brahms in the finale of the Fourth Symphony) from using it melodically as a *cantus* for middle or upper parts. And, as the broader architectural design of the whole shows, it does not hinder him either from indulging in more extended, independent structural thought as and when he desires; a case clearly (in the tradition of the Diabelli Variations) where economy and simplicity of idea has had the effect of encouraging rather than limiting invention.

The *Passacaglia* is divided into three parts. Conceptually, this would seem to suggest a link with Sorabji's *Opus Clavicembalisticum,* itself modelled after Busoni's *Fantasia Contrappuntistica,* although it is not until Part III that any real resemblance can be properly traced. In the following tabulation (which follows the published plan of the work, roman numeration excepted) the composer's elucidatory remarks[84] are given in quotation:

Pars prima
  (i) Sonata allegro. [A 'telescoped' structure *alla* Busoni, the first movement/subject, *Allegro moderato,* the second *Andantino*];
  (ii) Waltz in rondo-form. 'The ground bass is now the melody. The rondo is unusual because the episodes repeat the rondo theme but achieve contrast through key changes';

[84] *Ibid.*

  (iii) *Episode* [I]: 'An improvisatory-like passage' [composer's italics, here and below];

  (iv) Suite [based on Baroque dance forms]:
- (a) Prelude
- (b) Sarabande
- (c) Jig
- (d) Minuet
- (e) Jig
- (f) Gavotte (polymetric: $\frac{2}{2}$ against $\frac{3}{4}$)
- (g) Polonaise [reminiscent in style of the E major *Polonaise* of Liszt and of Chopin's in A flat, Op. 53];

  (v) Pibroch (Lament for the Children[85]) [added on the afternoon of the premiere];

  (vi) *Episode* [II]: *arabesque variations*;

 (vii) Nocturne [containing 'bitonal elements'].

Pars altera

 (viii) Reverie-Fantasy. 'A fantastic passage of syrinx-like glissandi. The arpeggio glissando is a pianistic innovation (achieved by glissando between and over silently depressed superimposed thirds). The glissandi become arpeggi';

  (ix) Fanfare – Forebodings: Alarm – Glimpse of a War-Vision [*cf.* Sonatina No. 3, first movement: 'War-Vision' corresponds temporally to the Golden Section of the work *in reverso*; *cf.* p. 109, note 114]. 'The reverie is rudely interrupted [...] The harshness gradually sweetens into a peaceful mood'
    [The opening six bars of 'Glimpse of a War-Vision' (Ex. 22), *Allegro senz' allegrezza; con diableria meccanistica; con brutalità*, survive in a sketch, dated 23 February 1962, 8 pm, together with a superimposed photograph of explicit caption:[86]

> Near Smolensk, an old woman weeps over the charred corpse of her husband, burned alive by the Nazis merely because his two sons were serving in the Soviet army. Maria Skvortsova and millions of other Soviet men and women will never forget the vicious reprisals, the appalling atrocities the German fascists carried out against the civilian population. They remember the 1,710 Soviet towns and 70,000 Soviet villages annihilated, the 31,850 factories demolished, the 100,000 farms laid waste, the more than 40,000 miles of railway track destroyed. More

---

[85] *Cf.* pp. 63–64.

[86] Reproduced in Ould, *op. cit.*, p. 8.

important, they remember the millions of men and women and children who died, the 25 million [ringed around by Stevenson] more who were left without roofs over their heads. It isn't strange that the Soviet people are grimly determined: Never again!

Ex. 22

Above the right-hand part (in $\frac{3}{4}$) Stevenson re-interprets the DSCH motif to now read as 'USSR/CCCP'. The clashing left-hand minor seconds (in $\frac{4}{4}$) are given representational significance: 'The Soviet hammer beats the Nazi swastika into a sycle [*sic*]'. 'And the sword shall be wrought into a ploughshare... [Isaiah ii:4]'; 'Is this UGLY enough??' he wonders in the right margin. Scribbled at the bottom of the page is: 'Note for later composition: the 4-square "swastika" *motif* in 𝄢 – will become straightened out into one graceful line – not a zig-zag – later. R.S.' The single side is inscribed 'In memoriam the 25m' (Ex. 23).];

Ex. 23

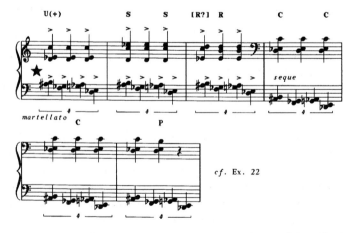

cf. Ex. 22

(x) Variations on [the rhythmic stresses of the Bolshevik slogan] 'Peace, Bread and the Land' (1917) [*Mir, Khleb i Zemlya*, later used in the Second Piano Concerto, fourth section];

(xi) Symphonic March [*cf.* the Shostakovich model – the great march scenes of the Fourth, Fifth, Seventh and Eighth Symphonies];

(xii) *Episode* [III]: 'A *volante* variation';

(xiii) Fandango;

(xiv) Pedal-point: 'To emergent Africa'. [A tenebrous picture of brilliantly imagined colour, of grotesquely primaeval force, dominated by DSCH, intoned 'ostinato fashion, against deep, pulsating bass washes of sound'.] '"To emergent Africa" is based on drum rhythms, beginning in ruthless primitivism and becoming progressively complex [...] on the day of the [first performance] I reworked the [...] music, deciding to use the palm of my [left] hand to strike the [bass] strings inside the piano, to produce a more "African" sound.[87] In Cape Town I had heard Mr Hugh Tracey lecture on native African music and was surprised and delighted when he declared that the passacaglia form was basic to most African drum music. I hadn't dreamt this in Scotland, yet must have had some kind of intuition';

(xv) *Central Episode* [IV]: *études*. 'The excitement [of 'To emergent Africa'] is maintained by a group of central variations, all *fortissimo* and exploiting a quasi-orchestral treatment of the piano. The extremes of the keyboard are used and the fists and palms are employed for explosive *sforzandi*';

(xvi) Variations in C minor. 'An expansive set [...] with a hunting-horn "refrain"'.

Pars tertia

(xvii) *Adagio*: tribute to Bach [temporally, the Golden-Section point of the whole];

(xviii) Triple Fugue over ground-bass (Ex. 24)
Subject I: *andamento*
Subject II: BACH
Subject III: *Dies irae*. 'In memoriam the six million Jews';

(xix) Final variations on theme derived from ground (*adagissimo barocco*). 'The work concludes with an extended set of variations [...]. A grand crescendo leads to the coda which presents the initial theme [DSCH] in block chords. The peroration is broken off and the work ends in quiet

[87] *Cf. Composer's Anthology 3: Ronald Stevenson*, British Institute of Recorded Sound, London, 6 March 1969; *Recorded Sound*, Nos. 42–43, 1971, pp. 749–50.

reflection.' 'In one passage of this section [p. 130] I have used the expression "con un senso di spazio quasi gagarin-esco" (as though with Gagarin's perception of space).'[88]

Viewed globally, Stevenson's pre-occupations in the *Passacaglia on DSCH* are not difficult to trace: classico-romantic structure in Part I; 'world music' and social conscience in Part II; the contrapuntalism of Bach (the Goldberg Variations, *The Art of Fugue*), Beethoven (the *Eroica* and Diabelli Variations), Brahms (the Handel Variations), Reger (the Telemann Variations) and Busoni (the *Fantasia Contra-ppuntistica*) in Part III. The highly original triple fugue of Part III has been generally acclaimed. It is an awesome feat that in intellectual span and technical procedure can only properly be compared with the last-period fugues of Beethoven – the 'Hammerklavier', Op. 110, the C sharp minor Quartet, the *Missa Solemnis*, the *Grosse Fuge*. A real triple fugue insofar as the structure is built around three clearly contrasted subjects (pp. 88 *et seq.*, 99 *et seq.* and 113 *et seq.*), each the basis of independent development and combination, its climactic conclusion, when all three subjects are interlocked with the DSCH ground, is a phenomenal moment (Ex. 24). How Stevenson relishes his polyphonic mastery! In lesser hands, much of this *Passacaglia* might seem pretentious and affected. In his it is a grittily riveting experience, a statement of blazingly honest commitment.

Ex. 24

In some unpublished notes on the *Passacaglia* sent to me in September 1969, Stevenson claimed that 'demonstrably the work

---

[88] In the notes with Altarus AIR-CD-9091(2). For Yuri Gagarin *cf.* note 19 on p. 31, above.

has a more varied range of rhythmic and melodic intonations, harmonic and contrapuntal structures, piano technique and complexes of form than any other single movement in piano literature'. He then went on to list what he felt to be some of its more striking features, together with examples. I quote verbatim, in the order given (page numbers refer to the Oxford University Press edition of 1967):

Rhythm
    (i)   primitive 'African' evocation (p. 67)
    (ii)   'Afro-American' jazz elements (pp. 107–8)
    (iii) 'a-rhythmic' pibroch (pp. 39–40) – properly conceived without barlines [*sic*: in fact, the entire work is metrically barred; there are no *senza misura* passages]
    (iv) barlines displaced by syncopated dissonance
    (v)   polyrhythm: Gavotte (pp. 31–35) – $\frac{2.3}{2\cdot4}$ [Symphonic] March (pp. 57 *et seq.*) – $\frac{6.3}{8\cdot4}$

Melody [*Mode*] (i) ground bass motif [DSCH]: Phrygian [nullified, however, by the Dorian B natural ('H'). The polarity of the ground is elusive, its alternative C minor habitat negated by a D tonicisation suggesting a heptatonic source-set (DE flat-BC) genetically more oriental than occidental in feature – of the 72 Carnatic 'parent-scales' of Southern India, six share the same relatively placed intervals: *Vanaspati* (4) *Natakapriya* (10), *Chakravakam* (16), *Navaneetam* (40), *Shadviamargini* (46), *Ramapriya* (52)]
    (ii) major/minor scale (p. 1)
    (iii) Innovation [I]: multiple scale (*presto scorrevolmente*, pp. 16 *et seq.*) – Indian raga-type [corresponding to a transposed inversion of the second descending scale, bars 5–7, of the Liszt Sonata]/whole-tone/chromatic [combined: Ex. 25]

Ex. 25

    (iv) heptatonic/pentatonic [scales combined] (p. 41) [Ex. 26]
    (v)   [studies] in different national intonations

Ex. 26

(Scottish, Spanish, French, German,
Russian, Indian, [Polish,] etc.)

	(vi)	quasi-serialistic melody: Fugue [I] (p. 88)
Harmony	(i)	chords of seconds (p. 24, line 2, etc.; pp. 50–51)
	(ii)	chords of thirds (pp. 22, last bar–23, last line)
	(iii)	chords of fourths (pp. 124, bars 9–125)
	(iv)	chords of fifths (p. 126, last line)
	(v)	chords of sixths (p. 23, last line–p. 24, top line)
	(vi)	chords of sevenths (p. 7, line 2, etc.)
	(vii)	every combination of these intervals, climaxing in the 12-note cluster (p. 77, last line) [Ex. 27]

Ex. 27

	(viii)	bitonality (pp. 5, 29, line 3) [Minuet]
	(ix)	polytonality (p. 30, top) [Minuet]
Counterpoint	(i)	Innovation [II]: triple fugue over ground bass
Piano technique	(i)	fingers on keys
	(ii)	nails on keys [single- and double-note *glissandi*]
	(iii)	nails on strings (glissando, p. 45 [Reverie-Fantasy])
	(iv)	fist on keys (p. 77)
	(v)	palms on keys (p. 77) [Central Episode]

(vi)   palms on strings (p. 67 ['To emergent
         Africa'])
(vii)   Innovation [III]: glissando arpeggio (p. 45
         [Reverie-Fantasy: Ex. 28 – where the score
         bears the indication 'fingers on tips of
         keys'])

Ex. 28

[Other devices called for include (in the
Reverie-Fantasy) the use of 'knuckles
pressed against piano lid', and the
physically impossible *crescendo* and
diminuendo of silently-depressed chord
harmonics (p. 46): 'in radio performance
[studio recording]', a note in the score says,
'the <> on the harmonics may be obtained
by electronic volume control'; *cf.* the
reverberation of harmonics in *Heroic Song*]

Form   (i)   superstructure of multiple forms (sonata/
                         suite/triple fugue/variations) over
                         passacaglia ground bass [*cf.* the finales of
                         Beethoven's *Eroica* and Tchaikovsky's
                         Fourth Symphony – both similarly
                         composite structural hybrids]
Tonality   (i)   main tonal centre: D
                         shifting to
                (ii)   G (pp. 11–12)
                (iii)   A flat (pp. 12–13, etc.)
                (iv)   B flat (p. 13)
                (v)   A (p. 14)
                (vi)   F sharp (p. 41)
                (vii)   C (pp. 82–86)
                (viii)   G sharp (p. 108)
                         [As Table I (not durationally
                         proportionate) shows, this scheme is
                         tensioned variably across the entire sharp/
                         flat spectrum. Two points deserve attention:
                         (a) the marginally flat bias of the whole;
                         and (b) the two particularly interesting
                         excursions of tritonal orientation –
                         downwards to A flat, upwards to G sharp –
                         placed at either end of the structure. That
                         Stevenson does not specify the mode of his
                         key centres is characteristic: throughout he

thinks of major and minor interchangeably,
an approach nowhere more succinctly
expressed than in the D major/D minor/D
unison cadence of the very last four bars].

Table I

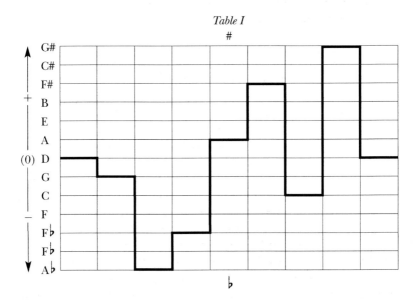

It is noteworthy that these observations resist any attempt to
programmatise or provide a poetic underlay (a favourite Stevenson
resort) – rightly so, given the work's musical self-sufficiency. As Sir
William Walton wrote:[89]

> [On] subsequent hearings I dispensed with the programme notes and
> enjoyed it more without following the various African! etc sections – it
> seems to me to stand on its own feet and has no need of a propaganda
> background. I enjoy its uninhibited exuberance and originality, and
> the absence of [...] fashionable 'isms' appeals to me [...].

The premiere of the *Passacaglia* was given by the composer before
a small audience at the Hiddingh Hall, Cape Town, on 10
December 1963. *The Cape Argus* reported the following day:

> One of the most incredible first performances that Cape Town has
> ever witnessed took place with little fuss or publicity at the Hiddingh
> Hall last night. This was Ronald Stevenson's *Passacaglia* on the initials

---

[89] *Loc. cit*; the first two pages of his letter are reproduced on pp. 96–97.

of Dmitri Shostakovich played by the composer for the University
Music Society's last 1963 concert. The performance was incredible in
every way. The piece itself was a *tour de force* of the first order. Its
uninterrupted one hour twenty five minutes duration [*sic*: the score
advises 80 minutes; Stevenson's Altarus recording takes 83' 07"]
makes demands on the performer far greater than the most arduous
cross-country. And perhaps most incredible of all was that after a
whole evening of one man at one piano with a work containing such
technicalities as a triple fugue over a ground bass, the audience could
break into such prolonged and enthusiastic applause [...].

The European premiere, again played by Stevenson, took place
on 6 June 1966 in the Great Hall of the University of Halle, as part
of the 1966 Halle Handel Festival. In Britain John Ogdon gave the
first BBC broadcast on 22 May 1966, subsequently playing it in
public on 14 June 1966 at the Aldeburgh Festival, before
introducing it to Cheltenham. In 1964, with help from the
University of Cape Town, Stevenson recorded the work on two
LPs – a limited edition of 100 signed copies. Ogdon's commercial
EMI recording, made under the auspices of the British Council in
August 1966, followed in September the next year.[90] And 21 years
on, Stevenson's second (digital) recording was released.[91]
    In 1967, partly at the instigation of Sir William Walton, Oxford
University Press published the score, in an edition engraved by

---

[90] HMV ASP 2321-220.

[91] Subsidised by the Scottish Arts Council and issued on Altarus AIR-CD-9091. The
accompanying notes (by 'C.H.R.' = Chris Rice) confirm that this studio version,
using a Bösendorfer instrument,

> differs in a number of details – some of them far from unimportant [for
> instance, the realisation of note repetitions, p. 66] – from the published score
> and the composer's own earlier performances and recording. Stevenson
> explains this continuing process of re-creation as reflecting his attitude to
> performance in general. As he discovers new technical and expressive
> possibilities in the piano, he incorporates them into his playing, and where
> appropriate, writes them into his existing works.

'A footnote (a pedal-point-in-prose) by the composer' (1988) reads:

> Consider the work as a map in music. The terrain: a life-span. The scale: one
> minute = one year. The duration: 80 minutes. There is a physical climax after
> 35 minutes [corresponding to the Variations of Part II], as there is in life
> about 35 years of age. The final climax is psychical, not physical: psychical in
> the Greek sense – of the mind, not the body.
>   This conception was not premeditated. I became aware of it only after
> performing the work some 20 times over 20 years [across five continents].

Polskie Wydawnictwo Muzyczne of Warsaw. Frank Dawes reviewed it
in *The Musical Times*:[92]

> the Passacaglia is a massive tribute to the greatest of Soviet composers
> and an equally massive assertion of the viability of tonality [...]. In this
> work Stevenson has probably outsoared his influences, but they can be
> detected nevertheless. Liszt pre-eminently: the eloquent, expansive
> Liszt of the B minor Sonata in particular. In the Sonata allegro alone
> one can find many Lisztian elements: Mephistophelean venom (p. 3),
> romantic lyricism (p. 4), brilliant display and panache in the coda (p.
> 12). Then Busoni: not quite the same thing, despite his Lisztian
> leanings, as Liszt at second hand. The wraithlike arpeggios of pp. 1–2
> have, like similar things in Busoni, a visionary quality that comes
> largely from an avoidance of tonal commonplace. The BACH subject,
> too, initiates some grave, awesome fugal writing comparable to the
> parallel passage in the triple fugue of the *Fantasia contrappuntistica* [...].
> One is reminded, too, of Mahler's philosophy of the all-embracing
> symphony. The idea that a great work should draw on all that the
> world has to offer is given new force by the broad time-space range of
> Stevenson's subject matter – its Russian and African episodes, its
> Scottish lament, and its short excursion to Andalusia as well as its
> revivification of old classical and pre-classical forms within the huge
> framework of one of them. Mahler gave everything he touched, even
> in parody, the unmistakable stamp of his own personality. Whether
> Stevenson has been as successful in this respect is a point for posterity.
> I rather think he has, though I harbour a suspicion that if cracks begin
> to appear in the fabric they will be found in the 'geographical'
> episodes. But episodes they are, after all, and there is no doubt that
> the work in its totality is vastly, perhaps uniquely, impressive.

Composer's postscripts are always fascinating. In the case of the
Passacaglia, its footnote is to be found in a *Recitative and Air* written in
1974 and first published in Moscow in 1976 as part of a
commemorative Shostakovich Festschrift edited by Grigori
Schneerson. Based 'exclusively' on the DSCH motto, this work is

[92] Vol. cix, No. 1504, June 1968, p. 565. In the same issue Stevenson contributed an
article on his friend Bernard Stevens. In it can be found this quintessential
declaration (p. 525):
> At a time of extirpation of human content in some Western music, other
> composers – Stevens among them – have remained unshakeable at the
> fulcrum of an artistic creed which attests to the continuing validity of
> embodying human thought in sound. Stevens's music is ratiocinative: it has
> premisses and conclusion; it doesn't merely start and stop. It finds its impulse
> in an awareness of music's past achievements and present problems and finds
> its goal in awakening like awareness in others.
Stevenson might almost have been writing about himself.

as expressively concentrated as anything in the *Passacaglia*: the *Recitative* in particular, aphoristic and delicately sonorous, explores common regions of eloquence (Ex. 29). Texturally and pianistically, however, it is simpler and more direct. The coda to the *Air* – itself practically a valedictory Shostakovich prelude – essays a 'fade-out' twilight world that seems to remember Schumann. That does not lessen its poetry: it is dreamily magical. Note the 'new' tonic – C rather than D – but 'old' major/minor/unison sign-off. (Ex. 30).

Ex. 29

Ex. 30

[...] lightning is the symbol of Shostakovich's music: it has the power to strike tragedy and the ability to etch a gothic grotesquerie across the heavens in its witty, zig-zag calligraphy [...]. Liszt was both Abbé and Mephisto; Busoni, both Faust and Arlecchino. But there are worlds of difference between Liszt's polarisation of religious aspiration and diablerie, Busoni's philosophy and elegant irony,

18. 12. 64

Dear Ronald Stevenson,

Very many thanks indeed for the records of your Passacaglia. I have now played it through for the 4ᵗʰ time. It is really tremendous – magnificent. I cannot remember having been so excited by a new work for a very long time. It is in the line of such great, but comparatively neglected works as Busoni's *Fanto Cont.* & he I am certain would have been among the first to acclaim this work.

Admittedly I was slightly put off by the sleeve & began to listen with a certain amount of trepidation (how is anyone to write 80 mins music on 4 notes, & by a composer, forgive my saying so, who I had never heard of, except by letter?) & was quite prepared to switch it off at the first signs of boredom. But far from it, I was gripped at once & became more & more enthralled as the work unfolded itself. It never lets one down, always at the critical moment,

Part of a letter from Sir William Walton, giving his reaction to Stevenson's private recording of the Passacaglia in DSCH

some new invention, either musical or pianistic, carries one on &
in spite of its ~~intellectual~~ intellectual & emotionally controlled complexities, to
me, even at the first hearing, it was clear, lucid & comparatively
easy to follow. In subsequent hearings I dispensed with the programme notes & enjoyed it more without following the various
African etc sections — it seems to me to stand on its own feet & has
no need of a propaganda background. I enjoy its uninhibited
exuberance & originality, & the absence of the fashionable "isms"
appeals to me. And I must incidentally congratulate you
on your very considerable powers as a pianist & for the excellent
performance on this record.

Presumably no publisher has as yet been enterprising enough to
print it, but if it is available in any form I would willingly
buy a copy so as to follow by eye as well as ear.

I have written to Alan Frank of O.U.P about the work in the
hope that he may be interested by it & some of your other works.
And I should like to think that pianists, such as Glenn Gould,
who I feel sure would be highly interested in it & John Ogdon
might take it up.

Hugh MacDiarmid (right) opening the ceremony at the Edinburgh Festival in 1962
at which Stevenson presented Shostakovich with a facsimile manuscript
of the Passacaglia on DSCH *(photographs by Paul Schilabeer)*

and Shostakovich's tragedy and satire. Liszt's and Busoni's dualism
was the outcome of national and cultural cross-currents: in Liszt's
case, Hungarian and cosmopolitan; in Busoni's, Italian and German.
Shostakovich manifested no such cross-currents; his dualism was
rather the result of his coalescing of twin Russian souls. In one
creative character he combined a Dostoevskian capacity for tragedy
and a Gogolian capacity for satire. Dostoevsky's genius no more
embraced satire than Gogol's encompassed tragedy. Shostakovich's
genius fused both. That is part of his unique achievement. It was only
natural that his wide-ranging style should find expression in the
symphony; but it was also hammered out on the anvil of the piano –
the hammer-blows of tragedy emitting the very sparks of satire.[93]

[93] 'The Piano Music', in Christopher Norris (ed.), *Shostakovich: The Man and his
Music*, Lawrence and Wishart, London, 1982, pp. 82–83. Stevenson's recording of
the *Recitative and Air* accompanies the *Prelude, Fugue and Fantasy* and the *Passacaglia
on DSCH* on Altarus AIR-CD-9091(2).

Transcriptions, Paraphrases, Arrangements

In *Western Music*[94] Stevenson encapsulates the essence for him of transcription and paraphrase by reference, interestingly, not to Liszt or Busoni but to Peter Philips – specifically his arrangement

---

[94] Pp. 84–85; and also in the 1985 sleeve notes to his album, *Twentieth Century Operatic Fantasias*, Altarus AIR-CD-2–9042.

(found in the Fitzwilliam Virginal Book, Vol. I, No. 82) of Caccini's *Amarilli mia bella* (Ex. 31(a) and (b)):

Ex. 31

  (a) **Caccini (Florence, 1602)**

  (b) **Philips (London, 1603)**

A comparison [...] will reveal how free Philip's transcription is; which may come as a surprise to people who regard transcription as a form of 19th century aberration or sacrilege practised by one composer on the music of another. The truth is that this sense of property and propriety has nothing to do with music, and transcription is an art long practised by composers and, at its best, a genre of variation form. The work of a transcriber of originality can sometimes be more creative than the material on which it is based.

Stevenson's thoughts on transcription are also Busoni's. In the autumn of 1910 Busoni wrote in a programme note for a Nikisch concert:[95]

in the virtuoso sense transcriptions are suiting another's ideas to the personality of the performer. [...] From [Bach] I learnt to recognise the truth that *good and great 'universal' music remains the same through whatever medium it is sounded.* [...]. For some curious reason variation form is held in high esteem by serious musicians. This is odd, because if the variation form is built up on a borrowed theme, it produces *a whole series of transcriptions* and the more regardless of the theme they

---

[95] The concert on 7 November 1910, with the Berlin Philharmonic Orchestra, included Busoni's *concertante* arrangement of Liszt's *Rhapsodie Espagnole*. Busoni's programme note, 'Wert der Bearbeitung', appears in *The Essence of Music*, pp. 86–88 (the translation here has been slightly adapted).

are, the more ingenious is the type of variation. Thus, *arrangements* are not permitted because they change the original whereas the *variation* is permitted although it *does change* the original [Busoni's italics].

Subsequently, in a letter to his wife:[96]

> Transcription occupies an important place in the literature of the piano. [...] transcription has become an independent art; no matter whether the starting-point of a composition is original or unoriginal. Bach, Beethoven, Liszt and Brahms were evidently all of the opinion that there is artistic value concealed in a pure transcription, for they all cultivated the art themselves, seriously and lovingly. [...] the art of transcription has made it possible for the piano to take possession of the entire literature of music.

Stevenson's transcriptions are as serious as they are many – and they constitute nearly 40% of his output. They are brilliant studies in paraphrase, inventive recastings that sample freely from all periods and all styles in music, deriving inspiration as much from the Classical example of the seventeenth and eighteenth centuries as from the pianism of the great keyboard eagles of the nineteenth and twentieth. In them the voice, the strength, and the soul of the modern concert grand find expressive celebration.

Early examples range, on the one part, from various *étude*-elaborations on waltzes and fragments by Chopin – singly or in combination, for hands together or separately, for one or two pianos – to the *Six Pensées sur des Préludes de Chopin* (1959), a sequence in some ways reminiscent of Busoni's *Variations and Fugue on a Theme of Chopin* (the 1922 version[97]). And on the other from the *Two Eclogues* (1951/56), based respectively on the thirteenth-century *Sumer is icumen in* and William Shield's *The Ploughboy* – to Mozart's F minor Fantasy (1952) and the *Wiegenlied from Berg's Wozzeck* (1953) dedicated to Dallapiccola.[98]

Stevenson's interest in the music of the English Renaissance, Restoration and Baroque, often finds voice through the medium:

Pavan, Galliard and Jig	Bull	(1950)
Toccata	Purcell	(1955)
Ground in C minor	Purcell	(1955)

---

[96] Dated 22 July 1913; published in Ferruccio Busoni, *Letters to his Wife*, transl. Rosamund Ley, Edward Arnold, London, 1938, pp. 228–29.

[97] Stevenson's recording (Altarus AIR-CD-9041) accords with the altered manuscript in his possession.

[98] Recorded by Stevenson on Altarus AIR-CD-9042.

Ground in E minor (transposed to E flat minor)	Purcell	(1957)
Ground in D minor (transposed to C minor)	Purcell	(1958)
The Queen's Dolour, for harpsichord or piano[99]	Purcell	(1958).

So, too, does his passion for Grainger (himself, of course, an eloquent exponent of the art) and the Celtic aesthetic.[100] Among the Grainger transcriptions, the *Hill Song* No. 1 (1960), played by Ogdon at the 1966 Aldeburgh Festival, is easily Stevenson's finest early achievement in the field, an intricate labour of love that deserves to stand alongside any of his own bigger works.[101]

Stevenson feels his 'free piano transcriptions' (November 1981– January 1982) of Ysaÿe's Six Sonatas, Op. 27, for unaccompanied violin to be a benchmark without comparison in his development. A note at the end of the Fugato of the G minor First Sonata reads: 'This is the proof of what I have learned from Bach, Busoni and Godowsky'. In a letter to me,[102] he wrote that 'the only comparison is with Bach-Godowsky [...]. That is *fact*'.[103] How, in direct reversal of the usual processes of selection and de-instrumentation/ orchestration associated with transcription, he enriches texture and harmony, he adds to the music, the whole within a pianistic concept of singular grandeur and nobility, can be gathered from Ex. 32 (pp. 104–5) – the *Preludio* of the First Sonata, dedicated by Ysaÿe to Szigeti ('West Linton 29.XII.81').

If Liszt was the greatest creative transcriber of the nineteenth century, Sigismond Thalberg was its most elegantly inventive, an aristocrat of classical leaning, 'the only man', Liszt once claimed admiringly, who could 'play the violin on the piano'. His *L'Art du Chant appliqué au piano*, Op. 70, published in 1853, is a work of seminal importance, its Preface concerned with parameters as critical to a knowledge of nineteenth-century performance practice

[99] Reproduced in Appendix Five: Some Stevenson Miniatures, p. 333.

[100] *Cf.* pp. 60–67.

[101] Recorded by Stevenson on Altarus AIR-CD-9040 – *Grainger: Salute to Scotland*; *cf.* p. 00.

[102] Dated 20 May 1982.

[103] *Cf.* the author's notes to the Bach-Godowsky Violin Sonatas, Marco Polo 8.223794 (1997).

as to an understanding of what matters to Stevenson as a player of, and a writer for, the instrument:

> It was once observed, by a celebrated woman, that the art of singing is the same on every instrument. This remark is perfectly true; and, in fact, no concession should be made to the particular mechanism of any instrument; for it is required of every performer to accommodate the mechanism to the demands of the art. As the pianoforte has not the power of sustaining the sound, and cannot therefore be made to sing, in the perfect acceptation of the term, this imperfection must be overcome by artifice and skilful contrivance, and we must obtain the illusion, not only of prolonging the sounds, but even of swelling them. Genius and sentiment induce invention, and, through a desire of expressing what they feel, create resources that escape the mere mechanist.
>
> [...] The prevailing feature of [our] transcriptions lies in the singing part, the *melody*, to which we have paid a special attention. It is by the force of melody, and not of harmony, that a work endures successfully through all ages [...].
>
> [...] the best advice we can give to those who are seriously occupying themselves with the pianoforte, is to study and understand the art of singing. They should never lose an opportunity of hearing great vocalists, and distinguished artists, whatever be their instrument. In every period of their study, and during the development of their talent, the best models should be constantly present to them. [...] the author can say that he studied singing for five years, under the guidance of one of the most eminent professors of the Italian school.

General Rules

1 [Avoid all stiffness, aim for suppleness of wrist, elasticity of fingers]
2 Broad, noble, dramatic melodies should be delivered in *chest notes* (the full tone of the instrument)
3 When the melody is of a tender and graceful character, the notes should be kneaded, the keys being pressed as though with a soft hand (*main désosseé*) and fingers of velvet [...]
4 The melody (*la partie chantante*) should always be clearly and distinctly enunciated, like the tones of a beautiful voice above the subdued accompaniment of an orchestra
5 Avoid the affectation and bad taste of constantly retarding the notes of the melody after those of the accompaniment, thus producing the effect of a continuous syncopation
6 [Hold notes to full value]
7 We recommend artists a severe study of fugues
8 [Observe dynamics, marks of expression, gradations of tone]
9 [Pedals] should not be employed habitually, but occasionally and with much judgement

Ex. 32

(a) Ysaÿe, bars 11 *et seq.*

10 To play too fast is a palpable defect [...]. To avoid hurrying
   and playing over fast is much more difficult than is generally
   imagined
11 [Self-listen, self-question, severely self-judge].[104]

Contemporary with the Ysaÿe transcriptions, Stevenson's *L'Art
Nouveau du Chant Appliqué au piano* ('an appendix to Thalberg',
March 1980–1986), dedicated to the memory of his father, is a
collection based on songs from the Victorian and Edwardian era.
Ranging from Vincent Wallace (for left hand solo), Stephen Foster,
Coleridge-Taylor, Hamilton Harty, Balfe, Bridge, Maude Valérie
White to Leoncavallo and Rachmaninov, the settings (currently 25
in number, though the series is still expanding) are seen by
Stevenson as 'études in the art of *bel canto* piano playing' – *bel canto*

---

[104] Thalberg, Preface to *L'Art du Chant appliqué au piano*, 22 transcriptions, Op. 70 –
from the English edition (Cramer Beale & Co., London, 1853), pp. i–ii (British
Library Shelfmark h.689(2)).

(b) Stevenson, bars 11 et seq.

being 'my main interest in piano playing'.[105] No. 13, *In the Silent Night* ('For M. on 18 V 1982 from the transcriber', after Rachmaninov's early Op. 4, No. 3), a jewel of exquisite nostalgia, of layered tracery, strikingly illustrates of how well the Thalberg model seems to have been absorbed and re-interpreted. 'With *L'Art nouveau du chant*', Malcolm MacDonald suggests, Stevenson

> has in a sense returned to his roots, to the parlour in Blackburn, to that childhood fusion of piano tone and tenor voice as the cardinal symbol of music that reaches the heart [...]. One wonders if there is another composer living who would be able to adorn, en-halo, en-flower this particular repertoire as Stevenson has done, wholly without satirical intent, even apparently without irony [...]. It is the very *unblushingness* of Stevenson's delight in unwrapping these melodic sweetmeats of yesteryear that undermines our own attempts at sophistication.[106]

The Harpsichord Sonata

The Harpsichord Sonata was commissioned by Alan Cuckston[107] for the 1968 Harrogate Festival. Ranging stylistically from Baroque idiom (the first movement) to serial reference (the last), it offers a perfected concept of that historical traversal of time previously attempted in the *Prelude, Fugue and Fantasy*. There Stevenson relied on quotations from Busoni's Second Violin Sonata which, in the words of John Ogdon, 'symbolise the movement of *time* from the

---

[105] In conversation with the author. *Cf.* Ateş Orga, 'Master of Invention', *International Piano Quarterly*, Vol. 1, No. 4 (Summer 1998), p. 76, for a discussion of Stevenson's pianism [and pp. 205–15 –ED.]. His wife, Marjorie, believes that it is through song that Stevenson the man and musician may best be understood (in conversation with the author, September 1988) – an insight supported by the fact that 35% of Stevenson's catalogue is voice-based and that a high proportion of the piano works are song- or opera-derived. In an interview with Harriet Smith (Summer 1997: *International Piano Quarterly*, Vol. 1, No. 4 (Summer 1998), p. 72), Stevenson said that:

> I personally would rather have been a poet than a composer. [...] I'm [...] interested in songs because writing miniatures is much more difficult than writing something huge. To compose a miniature is to attempt the perfect, but to compose an epic means that one is prepared to look imperfection in the face.

The full list of transcriptions in *L'Art Nouveau* can be found in note 28, p. 434.

[106] *Op. cit.*, pp. 92–93. Stevenson's old-world handling of Grainger's *Songs of the North* (Altarus AIR-CD-9040) offers 'unblushingness of delight' of another kind.

[107] Alan Cuckston's essay on the work appears as Appendix Two, pp. 307–10.

past, through the present, to the future'.[108] In the Harpsichord
Sonata he uses original invention to replace direct quotation – with
consequences more far-reaching than anything tried earlier. That
Stevenson should embrace both the old and the new in this work is
not surprising. In the 1950s and '60s he was a man concerned to
transform tradition, to develop rather than reject it, a stand in its
day contrary to that of many of his contemporaries. He has always
desired to evolve tradition: the big triple fugue over a ground bass
in the *Passacaglia* is only one example among many.

Laced by a French double-dotted *ritornello*, the first movement,
'In the heroic style', combines fugue and sonata-form, procedures
for the composer 'effected by their common tripartite structure': a
valid enough option (think of Mozart or Beethoven) weakened only
perhaps by too 'closed' a textbook design for the fugue[109] – by
precedent, after all, a *texture*, 'the rules of which do not suffice to
determine the shape of the composition as a whole'.[110] The second
movement, 'Dirge', is an elegy paraphrasing pibroch elements (*cf.*
the *Passacaglia*): its reappearance towards the end of the work
symbolises a conviction that 'music must and shall again voice
humanity in an age of inhumanity'.[111] The finale, a motoric
statement, brings together parameters of fugue and rondo: in
bridging two such disciplines, its use of episode, the one feature
common outwardly to the structural realisation of both, is not
without ingenuity.

Peter Grimes Fantasy

Peter Grimes is the living conflict. His pride, ambition, and urge for
independence fight with his need for love; his self-love battles against
his self-hate. Others, too, he can (sometimes) love as intensely as he
can despise them, but he cannot show, let alone prove his tenderness
as easily as his wrath [...]. Thus he is destined to seem worse than he is,
and not to be as good as he feels.[112]

[108] *Loc. cit.*

[109] *Cf.* Stevenson's definition in *Western Music*, p. 113: 'There are three sections to a
fugue: the exposition of the subject in all the voices; the middle section or
development; and the final section'.

[110] Donald Francis Tovey, *The Forms of Music* (from articles contributed originally to
the *Encyclopaedia Britannica*), Oxford University Press, London, 1944, p. 360.

[111] Composer's programme note for the premiere, 17 August 1968.

[112] Hans Keller, in Donald Mitchell and Hans Keller (eds.), *Benjamin Britten*, Faber,
London, 1952, p. 111.

This *Fantasy*, commissioned by BBC Television and dedicated to 'my young comrade-in-art', the pianist Graham Johnson, dates from 1971 – the period of the Second Piano Concerto. A quintessential product of Stevenson's mature mind notable for its brevity (less than seven minutes compared with the 29 of the *Prelude, Fugue and Fantasy* or the 80 of the *Passacaglia*), it is an important piece, a provocative opus at many levels of experience that in its incident and relationships can tell us much about the way he thinks, the way he works with material, with medium. Its re-interpretation of Britten's music, its alchemic transmutation of one man's language into another's, its grasp of advanced Lisztian thematic metamorphosis and cyclic organisation, its unique fusion of original composition, poetic paraphrase and inventive transcription are compelling. Its concern with the monumental and the epigrammatic, with epic statement as a consequence of concise speech, is fascinating: large-scale thought tersely expressed is a temporal phenomenon rare with Stevenson.

For him, the essence, emotionally and dramatically, of Britten's tragedy is to be found in its two 'human' elements (the rise of the mob, the fall of Grimes), and its one 'natural' one (the sea in storm and at dawn). The *Peter Grimes Fantasy* uses themes of distinctive cast associated with each:

(a) The rise of the mob – 'accusative music'
    (i) the opening motif of the opera, subsequently the basis of Swallow's pompous 'Tell the court the story in your own words';
(b) The fall of Grimes
    (i) 'Now the Great Bear and Pleiades where earth moves are drawing up the clouds of human grief' (Act I, sc. ii)
    (ii) 'What harbour shelters peace' (Act I, sc. i)
    (iii) 'We strained into the wind' (Act I, sc. i);
(c) The sea
    (i) Interlude II (storm) – 'storm music'
    (ii) Interlude I (dawn).

Additionally, reference is made to the wistful descending scalic theme ('Let her among you without fault cast the first stone') of Ellen Orford – for Stevenson 'but a transient figure in Peter's life'[113] (Act I, sc. i); to Grimes' jaggedly contoured phrase, 'Wrong to plan! Wrong to try! Wrong to live! Right to die' (Act II, sc. i); and

---

[113] In conversation with the author.

to his final 'weary and demented' outcry, with its lonely, rootless *corno da nebbia* E flat (Act III, sc. ii).

Architecturally, these ideas are channelled within a quasi-sonata 132-bar structure, the blueprint of which might be interpreted freely as in Table II (the descriptive labels, the 'recitativo' aside, are mine, not the composer's). Within this plan various sub-structures can be found, several of close or quasi Golden-Section proportion;[114] acknowledging that their presence may well be more instinctive than deliberate (a fact revealing of the composer), or that I may have wishfully contrived some where none is intended (a fact revealing of the analyst), Table III considers eight possible examples, suggested either by placement or aural association. Taking as a common reference point the quaver as the only constantly recurrent durational unit of the work (there are 978 in all from start to finish), my indicated degrees of tolerance show how near (likely) or far (unlikely) each is in Golden-Section terms – a productive exercise. Viewed as a sonata design, the interlocking of subject groups in the 'exposition' and the telescoped/developmental nature of the 'recapitulation' are features especially worth noting, as is the new thematic material of the 'coda'.[115]

Tonally, the progression of the music can be seen in different ways. Generally, it traverses a path from B flat Locrian to B flat minor/major, via, chiefly, E major ('Now the Great Bear'), A major ('What harbour shelters peace') – a long paragraph – and E flat Phrygian/minor (the storm). Particularly, it explores a world of myriad keys in succession; it contemplates the bitonality of Ellen's and Peter's duologue; it essays, more abrasively, the latent polymodality of Grimes' music that for Britten is symbolic of his instability.

Bitonality, a pungent agent, has always been important to

---

[114] Golden Section may be defined as an irrational proportion, thought to possess in itself some aesthetic or mystic virtue, used (knowingly) from ancient times as a means of structural organisation and balance in architecture, sculpture and painting. It can be explained strictly as the division of a fixed length in such a way that the ratio of the smaller part to the larger corresponds with the ratio of the larger to the whole (irrationally, 0.618). In his book *Debussy in Proportion* (Cambridge University Press, Cambridge and London, 1983, p. 9) Roy Howat claims significantly that 'Golden Section is a natural principle like the harmonic series, whose physical existence antedates mankind'. – ED.

[115] In the notes to his 1985 recording of this piece (Altarus AIR-CD-9042), coupled with the *Prelude, Fugue and Fantasy* and other transcriptions) Stevenson identifies its macro-form as a 'fantasy-fugue, preceded by a brief introduction and followed by a recitative-like cadenza and an epilogue'.

Table II

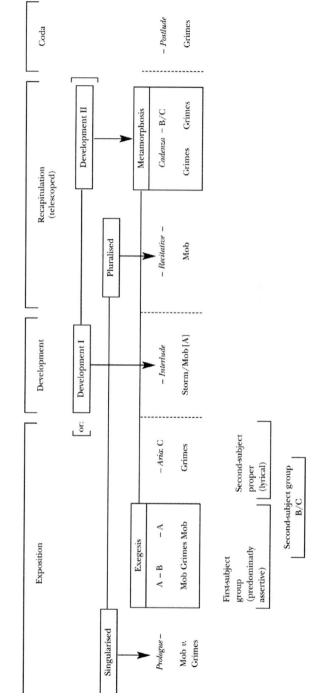

Table III

Formal complex	Bars	Quavers	Predicted GS point (× 0.618)		Actual point of event	Tolerance − = before GS + = after GS	%
			Quaver	Incident	Quaver		
Macro-structure	1–132	1–978	604	Recapitulation (Recitative)	587	−17	1.73
(1) Exposition	3–55	17–316	210	Second subject (Aria)	191	−10	3.33
(2) Development, 'Storm' music	56–73	317–408	373	Grimes' 'We strained into the wind', $\frac{3}{4}$ metamorphosis	386	+13	14.13
(3) Development 'Mob' music	74–97	409–586	528	Swallow's theme, transmoded, augmented	509	−9	5.05
(4) Recitative	97...	587–628	612	Grimes' 'Wrong to plan!'	619	+7	16.66
(5) Cadenza	...97	629–71	655	'Grimes! Peter Grimes', quasi violoncello	655	0	0.00
(6) Recapitulation – Postlude	97–114	587–824	733	'We strained into the wind', symmetrical inversion	744	+11	4.62
(7) Recapitulation – conclusion	97–132	587–978	828	Postlude	825	−3	0.76
(8) Postlude	114–32	825–978	919	B flat major, terminal cadence	917	−2	1.29

Stevenson. In the *Fantasy,* its manifestation is striking, dramatic. It intensifies the first reference to 'Now the Great Bear' (bars 11 *et seq.*: Ex. 33; *cf.* also Exx. 37 and 39), a passage where Britten's E major tonality is retained but against a disorientating minor-third B flat/D flat undulation – a fascinating tritonic inference as much suggested by Britten's (milder) harmonisation as by the Locrian distortion of the 'accusative' music, bars 2 *et seq.*, or the augmented fourth cipher (F/B) of Ferruccio Busoni's name (the fear symbol of his *Doktor Faust*) found so many places elsewhere in Stevenson's *œuvre.*

Ex. 33

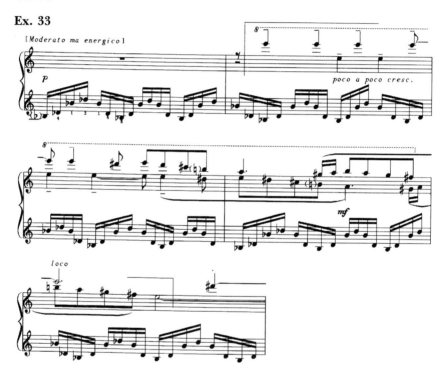

It charges the 'storm' section. It colours the concluding reprise of Grimes' music – especially the 'shadowy' recall of 'What harbour shelters peace', where the bass mirrors the top line in symmetrical inversion against a now new harmonic backcloth compounded, on the one hand, of an inner diadic elaboration notable for the 'Bax-like multiplicity of its accidents' (the description is Stevenson's[116]) and, on the other, of the oscillating minor thirds of 'Now the Great Bear' (Ex. 34).

---

[116] In conversation with the author.

Ex. 34

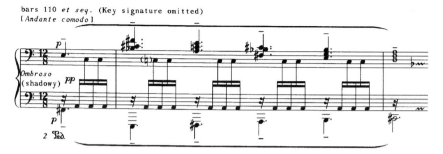

bars 110 *et seq.* (Key signature omitted)
[*Andante comodo*]

And it unsettles, disturbingly, the very last bar, where a high 'open' B flat major triad (spanning an *unbroken* D/B flat/F tenth in each hand – a luminous, silvern sonority) is suspended above a low 'closed' B flat *minor* chord, a major/minor clash with origins as early as the fateful second full-score page of the opera ('Peter Grimes, we are here to investigate the cause of death of your apprentice William Spode').

As is obvious from the Busoni and Shostakovich homages, in writing music based on the work or idea of others, Stevenson's creative rationale has always been to favour a technique founded on developmental rather than quotative reference. In this way genuinely new invention, disciplined by a pre-determined framework, yet at the same time at liberty to glimpse fresh horizons, is encouraged to evolve naturally and without contrivance. The *Peter Grimes Fantasy* applies such method at length, with Britten's themes, singularly, in harness, or in conflict, being used as starting points for a host of new imaginings.

Selectively, Stevenson's practice can be summarised as follows:
(a) Suggestively imitative reference. Coupled with the urgency of its ascending minor-second and minor-third inflexion, the speech rhythm of Grimes' name from the final scene of the opera (Ex. 35) is made much of by Britten. Through diminution and augmentation, and by changes of pitch, Stevenson gives it altered perspective, now more pressing, now more reflective. In the course of the *Fantasy* it acts as an organically important link.
(b) Modal re-orientation: chiefly Swallow's 'accusative' music (Ex. 36). Britten makes a passing minor key reference to this idea towards the end of the Prologue; generally, however, he prefers to keep it in the major. Stevenson acknowledges its major hue once only – at the canonic climax of the 'storm' section in the Interlude/ 'development' (Ex. 36(c)). For the rest he views it, sinisterly, in Locrian, minor, or augmented light – very Lisztian (Ex. 36(b)).

Ex. 35

(a) **Britten, Act III, scene ii, two bars after fig. 48**

MOB: Pe-ter Grimes!

(b) **Stevenson**

(c) Change of original tonal centre. Stevenson retains most of Britten's basic key associations: at the end, however, he alters the tonality of the first Sea Interlude from A minor to B flat minor – a change that helps preserve B flat as the critical gravitational key-note of the work.

(d) Change of metre, rhythm, accent, time-values. Both transformations of 'Now the Great Bear' keep Britten's pitch scheme but change, conspicuously, his rhythm, accent and time values (Ex. 37).

The three-bar continuation of this theme (bars 14 *et seq.*), an allusion to Ellen's 'Let her among you without fault cast the first stone' (Ex. 38(a)) offers further demonstration of re-directioned rhythm, accent, time-values and harmonic underlay.

For an illustration of metric change, the $\frac{3}{4}$ Grimes' 'We strained into the wind' in the 'storm' episode is apposite. When time-values are observed strictly but halved ('What harbour shelters peace', the 'storm' music), it is usually for reasons of practical, visual/sensory convenience: in such places the aural impression is unaffected.

(e) Melodic pitch retention, displacement of original harmonic underlay. The best illustration of this Beethovenian/Brahmsian device is to be found in the expositionary and retrospective treatment of Grimes' music.[117] Ex. 39 details, self-explanatorily, 'Now the Great Bear' as it appears, very differently, at the beginning and end of the *Fantasy*. The treatment of Ellen's theme (Ex. 40), noted already (Ex. 38), must also be mentioned, an elusive example but a significant one for all its brevity.

---

[117] *Cf.* p. 112.

Ex. 36

(a)

(b)

(f) Distillation of linear content through source-set systemisation. Reducing a melodic pattern of disjunct intervals to a scalic succession of conjunct steps so as to generate an organic source-set of variably adjacent pitches is a technique well known to the dodecaphonists. Stevenson, a man of liberated diatonic mind, has long been drawn to the practice: the *Passacaglia* (for instance, thirteen bars before the end, where the DSCH motif is turned into an upwards-rushing scale) is one among several works to demonstrate the device. In the *Grimes Fantasy* the method is used, simply and effectively, for the 'cadenza', a caesura based entirely on a single, climactic bar from Grimes' Mad Scene (Ex. 41).

Ex. 36 (cont.)

(c)

(g) Cross-fertilisation. The welding of elements from disparate ideas can produce syntheses often rich in new imagery or enhanced psychological perspective. One interesting example is the opening treble phrase, Grimes' leitmotif (Ex. 42), where are combined, it seems, in one tightly unified germinal complex, not only, enharmonically, the telling opening major ninth of 'What harbour shelters peace' (in the opera an interval suggestive of isolation and yearning) but also the pathetic dropping-semitone consequence (submediant to dominant) characteristic of both its previous minor form, 'We strained into the wind', and the first Sea Interlude.

When this emotive falling minor second returns cyclically at the end of the work in the Interlude quotation (its tonality, B flat minor, formerly implicit, now explicit), it is for the listener rather like experiencing a journey come satisfyingly full circle, like sensing suddenly that what was once a spring seed has become a harvest

Ex. 37

(a) Britten, Act I, scene ii, fig. 76

(b) Stevenson, bars 11 *et seq.*

PETER: Now the Great Bear and Plei-a-des where earth moves

Breath-ing so-lem-ni-ty in the deep night.

(c) Stevenson, bars 101 *et seq.*

Ex. 38

(a) Britten, Act I, scene i, fig. 28

ELLEN: Let her a-mong you with-out fault cast the first stone –

(b) Stevenson, bars 14–16

Ex. 39

(a) bars 11 *et seq.*

(b) bars 101 *et seq.*

Ex. 40

(a) Britten, Act I, scene i, fig. 28

(b) Stevenson, bars 14–16

fruit. A better example of organic growth within a brief time-scale would be hard to find (Ex. 43, bars 113 *et seq.*). The fusion in bar 7 of the speech rhythms of Grimes' name, as called out by Hobson (solo) at the beginning of the opera and the Mob (chorus) at the end, is the same process in simplified form (Ex. 44; *cf.* Exx. 35 and 36). The origin of such technique in Stevenson's output is difficult to pinpoint: a possible source, however, could be the *Prelude, Fugue and Fantasy* – specifically in the *sonoro* idea, comparably new in life yet old in parentage, introduced at bar 31 of the *Prelude* (*cf.* Ex. 13).

The *Peter Grimes Fantasy* is resourcefully imaginative: its pages abound in symbolism – much of it subtle, some of it defined almost accidentally by the composer in conversation, some of it left open to individual interpretation. Perhaps its most striking example of symbolic theatre is found at the very beginning where in the first two bars there is an uncompromising opposition between low bass (the 'Mob') and high treble ('Grimes') – absolute pitch regions evocative of darkness, heaviness, earthiness and evil, of lightness, rarification, ethereality and transcendence, to quote Deryck Cooke out of context.[118] Metaphorically and literally, the 'malicious mutterings' of the Mob rise, Grimes falls. In the agitated 'storm' music of the central interlude, a fugal texture mindful of Britten's original metric structure (2+2+3+3+2+3+3+2+3), both orbit within

---

[118] *The Language of Music*, Oxford University Press, London, 1959, p. 110.

Ex. 41

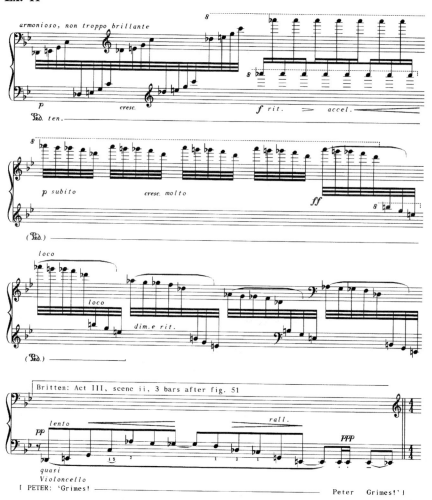

Ex. 42

Ex. 43

Ex. 44

the same tessitura, locked in combat: 'the flight of the fugue, the crowd, from bass to treble, the descent of the lone voice, the individual' is how Stevenson has described it pictorially.[119]

---

[119] In conversation with the author.

Pianistically, the range of the piece is enormous, several important features being:

(a) regular deployment of three pedals;

(b) *pizzicato a corde* – plucking the strings (*cf.* 'Emergent Africa', *Passacaglia*, Part II; *Chorale Pibroch for Sorley MacLean*), a device found, magically, in the postlude quotation from the first Sea Interlude;

(c) harmonics (*cf. Heroic Song*);

(d) notationally, the use of three or four staves for the sake of clarity.

Where he transcribes rather than develops – as, for example, in Grimes' richly spun, tenderly beautiful Aria section, 'What harbour shelters peace', Stevenson's innate feeling for the piano as a virtuoso instrument, a *voix de soupirs*, can be judged by only the highest of Lisztian/Busonian standards. In aspiration, understanding and spirit, it is a truly remarkable thing to experience, given the particular psyche, the antisepticism of the late twentieth century.

The *Peter Grimes Fantasy* was an early sign of Stevenson's regard for Britten. Another can be found in the *Sonatina serenissima: in memoriam Benjamin Britten* (1973/77), where each of the four movements (Barcaroletta on a ground bass, Fughetta, Chorale and Carol – in the French medieval sense of a round dance) refer in some way to *Death in Venice* (except for the Chorale, specific references are found at the end of each section).[120]

The Late Works

Invited in the autumn of 1997 to identify those of his piano works after the *Peter Grimes Fantasy* that he valued the most, Stevenson singled out his *Canto di Compleanno* (1974); *L'Art Nouveau du chant appliqué au piano* (1980–86); the six Ysaÿe transcriptions (November 1981–January 1982); *Le festin d'Alkan* (1988–autumn 1997); *Beltane Bonfire* (early summer 1989) written as a testpiece for the second round of the 1990 Scottish International Piano Competition;[121] and *A Carlyle Suite* (1995). Curiously, he omitted to mention either the implosively concentrated *Symphonic Elegy for Liszt* (1986) or the remarkable *Motus Perpetuus (?) Temporibus Fatalibus* – 'Perpetual (?)

[120] Recorded by Anthony Goldstone on Gamut GAM CD 526.

[121] 'Beltane' from the Scots Gaelic *bealltainn* – an ancient Celtic festival with a sacrificial bonfire on May Day; *cf.* Peter Maxwell Davies' choreographic poem *The Beltane Fire* written subsequently, in 1995.

THE RED HOUSE, ALDEBURGH-ON-SEA, SUFFOLK. IP15 5PZ   December 7ᵉ 1972

My dear Ronald,

Thank you very much for sending the P.G. Fantasy on my birthday — it is fine to have a copy signed by you. I think it is a splendid piece, and are we to have it played by you at the Festival? We all (especially me!) hope so.

I am away from Aldeburgh at the moment, finding piece & quiet (apart from tempestuous rain & gales) to finish the sketches of the new opera. It is a very difficult & tense piece, & has all but killed me!

With thanks once again, & love to all 3,

Yours ever
Ben

A letter from Benjamin Britten;
the opera which 'all but killed' him was Death in Venice

Motion in Fateful Times' — commissioned by Joseph Banowetz (1987–88). The notes which follow are essentially Stevenson's own[122] – adaptations and clarifications notwithstanding.

---

[122] Communicated in a letter to the author from Michael Lister, 17 December 1997.

Canto di Compleanno (*Birthday Song*)

A transcription of Bernard Stevens' *Birthday Song*, originally a piano duet written in 1963 for his friends the pianists Mary and Geraldine Peppin. From this I made a solo piano version in discussion with the composer. To differentiate between the two versions, I chose the Italian translation for my setting – *Canto di Compleanno* – dedicating it to Bertha Stevens, the composer's widow.

[In 1989 Stevenson wrote:

This transcription was made in close consultation with, and was approved by, the composer. He felt the opening accompaniment figure was in homage to Fauré. I feel the main melody has a directness of appeal and a plasticity of contour such as could ensure it the kind of success that Villa-Lobos's *Bachianas Brasileiras* No. 5 has enjoyed, if only it were given the opportunity. The association of the names Fauré and Villa-Lobos is not as curious as it may seem: like Stevens, they both admired Bach; Villa-Lobos's admiration is implicit in the title quoted, and Fauré (with Joseph Bonnet) published an edition of Bach's organ works. The Stevens *Birthday Song* is dedicated to Mary and Geraldine Peppin, who first names are contained in main theme's [thirteen-white-note] cryptogram [the pitches F–A–D–D–G–E–D–A–E–D–B–G–E]. Bernard had a wonderful smile [...]. A genuine smile, in our troubled times, is worth something.[123]]

Le festin d'Alkan

It is unnecessary to explain the title of *Le festin d'Alkan* to those who know that composer's music, as it is a paraphrase of one of Alkan's [the variation cycle *Le festin d'Esope*, last of the *Douze études dans tous les tons mineurs*, Op. 39, published in 1857]. It is a three-movement 'petit concert' for piano solo without orchestra. The sub-title 'petit concert' is again unnecessary to explain to those who know Alkan [his 'petits concerts de musique classique' were given in the Salle Érard from 1873 onwards].

The first movement is a concerto for solo piano *sans orchestre* [*cf.* Alkan's *three*-movement Concerto without orchestra, Op. 39, Nos. 8–10; likewise Schumann's earlier F minor Sonata – *Concert sans orchestre*], the piano texture distinguishing between 'solo' and 'tutti'. This movement [in Stevenson's words] contains the most difficult piano music in the entire Stevenson canon – one passage in particular, lasting about two minutes, exhausting the composer to such an extent as to prevent further performance.

---

[123] 'Music for Solo Piano', in Bertha Stevens (ed.), *Bernard Stevens and his Music*, Kahn & Averill, London, 1989, pp. 124 and 126.

The second movement is a very free and mainly canonic transcription of Alkan's *Barcarolle* in G minor [*Chants*, Book III, Op. 65, No. 6 – 'the piece of Mendelssohn that Gershwin forgot to write'[124]]. Two quotationary trio sections added by Stevenson transcribe music by Scarlatti and Paganini that Alkan used to play. The Barcarolle is repeated *da capo* but in [Ziehnesque] symmetrical inversion, so that it sounds like totally new material.

The third movement freely varies a number of Alkan themes [most movingly, perhaps, 'La Chanson de la folle au bord de la plage', No. 8 of the *Vingt-cinq Préludes*, Op. 31]. Only here is the celebrated *Festin d'Esope* melody quoted – cryptically in inverted, retrograde inverted and canonic presentations. There are three cadenzas: one for left hand alone, one for right, and one for hands combined [*cf.* Alkan's *Grandes études*, Op. 76]. In content, this finale [Romantic style] bears the greater weight of the whole, thereby reversing the honoured [Classical, pre-'Prague'/'Jupiter'/Beethoven C minor] practice of making the opening movement of a symphonic work the weightiest. I also used this procedure in the *Prelude, Fugue and Fantasy*. *Le festin d'Alkan* encapsulates an aesthetic philosophy, and embodies the composer's conviction that there is no fundamental difference between the forms of original composition, free transcription and free variation. This argues for the unity of the work, which may not otherwise be perceived.

Completed in the autumn of 1997, *Le festin d'Alkan* was commissioned in 1988 (the centenary of Alkan's death) by Peter Hick, pianophile extraordinaire, responsible also for commissioning the *Symphonic Elegy for Liszt* [similarly, a centenary tribute]. The manuscript is almost a graveyard of memorial inscriptions – to John Ogdon, Egon Petri, Busoni....

A Carlyle Suite

This 35-minute suite was commissioned by Dumfries & Galloway Arts Association to commemorate the bicentenary of the birth of Thomas Carlyle (1795):

Aubade – 'So here has been dawning/Another blue day' (quoting from one of the few poems by Carlyle – *To-day*).
Variations on Frederick the Great's Theme (as used by Bach in the *Musical Offering*, 1747).
  (i)   Baroque
  (ii) Rococo, with Alberti bass
  (iii) 'Chopin plays for Jane Carlyle' (He did! [in 1848: 'I never heard the piano played before – could not have believed the capabilities

[124] Ronald Smith, *Alkan*, Volume Two: *The Music*, Kahn & Averill, London, 1987, p. 61.

that be in it', she reported]). This variation comprises newly-composed Polish dances and an old Polish carol which combine with the old Scottish psalm-tune to Psalm 23 (Martyrs)

(iv) Jane Carlyle's Fun (scherzo[125])

(v) Serenade (referring to the Aubade)

I am not opposed to the notion of programme music, except when a composer (Richard Strauss, for instance) intends a work to follow a detailed scenario. I believe music can be programmatic in a general, not a specific way. I do not consider the present work to be programmatic at all, more (in the variations) a miniature history of music: even var iii, despite its apparently programmatic title, derives from [absolute] music forms - (a) recitative, (b) Polish and Scottish dances, (c) Scottish psalm.

Joseph Banowetz has described Stevenson as 'not always an "easy" composer for either performer or listener, yet he is one of the few in whose music there can always be felt a personal integrity and a profound emotional message. This makes him very precious indeed'.[126] The following unsigned notes preface Banowetz's 1993 Altarus recording[127] of the *Symphonic Elegy* and *Motus Perpetuus (?) Temporibus Fatalibus* – elevated late examples of *hommage* as a peculiarly Stevensonian genre, 'northern [and] tough-textured'.[128]

Symphonic Elegy for Liszt

A cycle of the seasons, representing the life cycle of a man for all seasons [*cf.* the Alkan *Grande Sonate*, Op. 33, *Les quatre âges*], *Symphonic Elegy for Liszt* is, necessarily, an epic work – epic in conception, not duration [*cf.* the *Grimes Fantasy*]. The monodic opening recalls the late music of Liszt, and the whole work has a sombre, brooding atmosphere; a life seen in retrospect, its passions viewed from afar, not directly experienced. The first section is a gentle, nostalgic barcarolle, a memory of Italy, beloved of both Liszt and Stevenson. An energetic *volante scherzoso* follows, marked *primaverile* – springlike. After a slow section with the characteristic 'Scots snap' [short-long] rhythm – which is also typically Hungarian[129] – in evidence, there occurs the

---

[125] In the manuscript it is labelled a 'Scherzino-Schottische'.

[126] Booklet notes, Altarus AIR-CD-9089.

[127] *Ibid.*

[128] *Composer's Anthology 3: Ronald Stevenson, loc. cit.*, p. 752.

[129] Malcolm MacDonald, *op. cit.*, p. 103, note 5, identifying the work as 'an inspired osmosis of Liszt's and Stevenson's characteristic idioms', perceives 'a kind of "Scoto-Hungarian Rhapsody"'.

work's only direct quotation from Liszt; the [enigmatic] opening descending scale from the B minor Sonata, used first in canon, then harmonised in sixths, then as the counterpoint to another melody, marked *gridante* – clamant [*cf.* Liszt's procedure at bars 105 *et seq.*/600 *et seq.*, the *Grandioso* subject]. Then comes the music of summer, *Romanticamente, con ampiezza estiva* – with a full-blown summer air – but even here the mood is elegiac. The composer refers to the *Ruba'iyat* of Omar Khayyam [Rubat 22, translated by Edward Fitzgerald]: 'And we, that now make merry in the room/They left, and summer dresses in new bloom/Ourselves, must we beneath the couch of earth/Descend, ourselves to make a couch – for whom?' This is swept aside abruptly by the *perpetuum mobile, presto fantastico* which carries a resonance of 'the wind over the graves' [alluding to Anton Rubinstein's description of the monodic finale of Chopin's 'Funeral March' Sonata]. Autumn is ushered in on this first chill harbinger of winter in a sad reminiscence of the barcarolle, combined with the 'summer' music, and then, *avec un frisson*, the summer music is introduced again, now diminished by one beat, in 5/8 instead of 6/8 as before. A climax in orchestral sonority, on the theme from the Liszt Sonata in symmetrical inversion [*cf.* Ziehn, *A 20th Century Music Diary*, *Le festin d'Alkan*, etc.], with *quasi corno* brass interjections, leads to the final icy onset of the winter of old age, the metre 4/8, shorter of breath now, the texture as bare and unadorned as winter branches before the inescapable erosion of time. If this mood of passionate melancholy speaks an appropriate and eloquent *requiescat in pace* for Liszt, it is also archetypally Scottish, and places this work among the great nationalist statements in music – a sentiment with which Liszt himself would surely have profoundly concurred.

Motus Perpetuus (?) Temporibus Fatalibus

The title [...] is derived from Stevenson's concern for humanity in the modern age. In a recent interview (1992) the composer was asked whether he sees the human race as fundamentally self-destructive: 'Yes, I think so, yes. Of course, as a pacifist, I'm deeply concerned with the possibility of nuclear warfare. The question is, is the seemingly perpetual motion of the globe going to go on forever? Perpetual motion has never been possible in physics, why should it be for the human race? It's very difficult to stay optimistic as time goes on. In Walt Whitman's *Song of the Broad-axe* we find these lines: "I see the European headsman,/He stands mask'd, clothes in red, with huge legs and strong naked arms,/And leans on a ponderous axe./(Whom have you slaughter'd lately European headsman?/Whose is that blood upon you, so wet and sticky?)/I see the clear sunsets of the martyrs,/I see from the scaffolds the descending ghosts,/Ghosts of dead lords, uncrown'd ladies, impeach'd ministers, rejected kings,/Rivals, traitors, poisoners, disgraced chieftains and the rest./I see those who in any land have died for the good cause,/The seed is spare, nevertheless the crop shall never run out,/(Mind you O foreign kings, O foreign priest, the crop shall never run out.)" Now this particular passage, these last three lines mean so much to me, and I think this is the best answer I can give to the question "Is the human race self-destructive?"; this is what Whitman says, and I echo these words: "I see those who in any land have died for the good cause,/The seed is spare, nevertheless the crop shall never run out,/(Mind you O foreign kings, O foreign priest, the crop shall never run out.)" If I didn't believe that, I don't think I could go on composing'.

Motus Perpetuus (?) Temporibus Fatalibus ['Omaggi a Bach Shostakovich Busoni Schoenberg ... Dies illa, dies irae, calamitatis et miseriae'] is based on thematic material derived from cryptograms of the names of Busoni [FB], Shostakovich [DSCH], Bach [BACH – drawing on No. 10 of *A 20th Century Music Diary*] and Schoenberg [AS], as well as the 'Dies irae', the latter relating it to the Totentanz in Stevenson's [dance-poem for free-bass accordion, timpani and percussion] *The Harlot's House* (after Wilde), written in [June 1988]. [These cryptograms – including, though he is too modest to say so, his own Schumannesque RS (D–E flat) – form part of a twelve-note row, divided into three four-note groups, each narrower then wider in intervallic profile: B flat–D–A–E flat/C–F–B–F sharp/E–G–D flat– A flat.] After a performance of the *Passacaglia on DSCH* given by the composer in New York [Juilliard School, spring 1987[130]], the American composer Otto Luening, a former student of Busoni, remarked that the work seemed to him to be philosophically in the nature of a continuation of Busoni's *Doktor Faust*. In a manner of speaking, *Motus Perpetuus (?) Temporibus Fatalibus* is even more closely related to Busoni's opera, but exploring the darker, Mephistophelean side of the creative soul, as Busoni himself did in his Toccata [*Preludio–Fantasia–Ciacona*, 1920], which is based on material from *Doktor Faust*. Stevenson refers to 'a fear motif. Music plays more directly on the emotions than any other art. And man's deepest and most primitive emotion is fear. Perhaps fear of the human psyche – one's own. The Busonian influence in my work is associated with explorations of semitones, a symbol of Faust's studies, very introverted

---

[130] For Stevenson – among the most responsibly industrious, stimulating and accessible of presenters – 1987 was a year of vintage pedagogic address, not only with seminars on the repertory of the piano at the Juilliard, but also with a course on 'The Political Piano: 1789–1976' as part of an autumn residency as composer-pianist at the University of York. *Cf.*, besides books, symposia, essays and articles, his 26 BBC Radio 3 programmes on Busoni (1970–80); his 1974 BBC2 television documentary on Busoni; his 'Transcendental Tradition' (art of transcription) lecture-recital (Aldeburgh Festival, 1973, and elsewhere); his Grainger Memorial Lecture and recitals (University of Melbourne, 1980/82, Aldeburgh Festival 1982 – marking the Grainger centenary); his landmark broadcasts of the Reicha Fugues (1970); and his 22 Radio Scotland programmes on pibroch (1980), the Celtic harp (1982) and the fiddle music of North-East Scotland (1984).

and based on fear. One could relate that to my *Passacaglia*, and beyond that, to this work'. A true *perpetuum mobile, Motus Perpetuus (?) Temporibus Fatalibus* progresses throughout in rapid semiquaver motion, varied in texture, density, dynamics and thematic content. Towards the end there occurs a quotation from [...] *Doktor Faust*: the yearning, searching music which accompanies Faust's despairing philosophic quest makes a brief appearance. This is superseded by a chorale-like statement of the thematic material, the semiquaver movement now suddenly frozen at half tempo, the music transformed in architectonic crystallisation, then swept aside in a moment by the apocalyptic climax of the final page.

Epilogo

Genius for the pianoforte should be – like genius in general – a gift which takes a new road and accomplishes unprecedented things: things which it takes others a little time to learn. Such pianoforte geniuses were Beethoven, Chopin, and Liszt; they perceived new means, solved the problems of new effects, created 'improbable difficulties' and wrote a literature of their own [...]. He who stands alone when he appears in public and is only imitated later on by others, who compels pianoforte builders to consider new principles and creates a new literature in which experienced pianists do not find their way at once, has a lawful right to the title 'pianoforte genius'.[131]

On first hearing the *Passacaglia on DSCH*, privately, Alan Bush was 'so carried away that [he] could scarcely speak at all'.[132] Twenty-five years later, reviewing the same work, Bayan Northcott proposed that in Ronald Stevenson was to be found simply 'our most distinguished representative of what might be called the tradition of Philosophical Virtuosity: a tradition in which transcendental pianism is somehow bound up with stylistic eclecticism. And the highest ethical ideals, running back via Busoni and Liszt ultimately to late Beethoven'.[133]

Stevenson has done much to expand the resources of his instrument, he has discovered new roads, created 'improbable difficulties', pioneered innovative techniques and written music of a complexity and scope others still fight shy of taking into the repertory – although he has had his champions, from John Ogdon

---

[131] Ferruccio Busoni, 'Das Klaviergenie', *Allgemeine Musik-Zeitung*, Vol. 39, No. 10, 8 March 1912; translated in *The Essence of Music and Other Papers, op. cit.*, p. 83.

[132] 'Ronald Stevenson's Passacaglia', *Composer*, xiv, Autumn 1964, p. 17.

[132] *The Independent*, 2 April 1988.

to Marc-André Hamelin and Mark Gasser. He may well be a 'pianoforte genius'. Certainly he is one of the very few composers from the British Isles who *knows* how to write for the instrument idiomatically, in the grand, virtuoso manner of old St Petersburg and Moscow, of the Romantics, of those early twentieth-century emperors of the keyboard he so idolises. His piano music is *real* piano music. It grows out of the instrument, it is not imposed on it.

III
THE ORCHESTRAL MUSIC
Malcolm MacDonald

Barred music – accented music – finds its ultimate form in symphony. Unbarred music – quantity music – expresses itself in pattern repetition: hence the idea that the Celt has no architectonic power, that his art is confined to niggling involutions and intricacies – yet the ultimate form here is not symphony, it is epic.[1]

Music for orchestra does not occupy as central a position in Ronald Stevenson's output as do piano works or songs. His compositions involving orchestra are comparatively few and, with the partial exception of the two Piano Concertos, have remained almost entirely unknown to the general public. Yet they include some of his most important creations, and afford valuable insight into the perennial essential concerns of a composer who has achieved the extraordinary feat of conducting his lifework both *in signo Ferruccii Benvenuti Magni* and under the blithe but wistful gaze of Percy Grainger.

Stevenson's earliest experience in orchestration was probably a by-product of his youthful activities during the Second World War for the Blackburn Ballet Company: these included a 'Dvořákian' Waltz which achieved a concert performance in about 1944. By his late teens, Stevenson had already written two works involving string orchestra, the *18 Variations on a Bach Chorale* (1946) and the *Fantasy* for piano and strings (1947). But his first two scores for full orchestra are works of his early twenties, closely and clearly related to his passion for Busoni, and it is with them that this survey starts.

The *Berceuse Symphonique* (1951) evokes that composer's *Berceuse Élégiaque* and *Nocturne Symphonique*, and Stevenson's work clearly owes much to their example – as also to the great Sarabande from *Doktor Faust*. It is already an achievement to have rendered anew, and so potently, the uncanny crepuscular atmosphere of Busoni's pieces. But Stevenson's methods are entirely his own, and the scale on which he is working is ambitious.

There are three main elements: an uneasy bass figure, rising by thirds to outline three mutually disruptive major triads (Ex. 45(a)); and two principal berceuse-melodies (Ex. 45(b) and (c)), the first

---

[1] Hugh MacDiarmid, *The Islands of Scotland*, Batsford, London, 1939, author's note, p. xiii. [I consider this quotation in the context of Celtic art-forms on p. 286. –ED.]

comparatively diatonic, the second more chromatically involved and clearly coloured by Ex. 45(a).

Ex. 45

(a)

(b)

(c)

Punctuated by dramatic trumpet calls, stern chords on low brass and passionate appeals from a solo violin, the piece proceeds on its way, with unhurried and rather sinister inevitability, through an uncanny region of half lights and shadows. It is 'symphonic' in its amplitude and organic coherence rather than in accepting any sonata-style duality of thematicism or tonality. Ex. 45(b) and (c) provide little contrast of character, and all three elements are developed in such a way that, while finding ever new shapes and contexts (sometimes in combination with one another), the work's enshrouding atmosphere is powerfully maintained. In spite of myriad hallucinatory chromatic alterations and curiously inflected scale-patterns, the tonality drifts and eddies about a dark persistent A flat – though the work attains its moment of maximum ardour with a transformation of Ex. 45(b) in an almost radiant C major.

For a first orchestral work this *Berceuse* is an extremely impressive debut. There is no hint of inexperience in the instrumentation – the effect is rather of a confidence and sureness of aim that invite the adjective 'masterly'. Every plangent or evocative timbre is precisely and expertly judged, and an acute sensitivity to sonority is evident in the biggest tutti as in the sparest writing for a handful of instruments. The work stands alone among British scores of its time, and is a definite achievement; that it should not have been heard in public since 1953 is an insult to the appetites of its potential audience.

In November 1952 Stevenson completed his *Waltzes* for orchestra, a single-movement dance-poem in several sections whose immediate aim is clearly the sheer enjoyment of its artful and insouciant parade of good tunes, cunningly though they are related to one another in the overall scheme. The orchestration is less complex, more purely functional than in the *Berceuse*, as befits the forthrightness of the material; but it displays the same confidence and sure command of effect. From the *Moderato fantastico* introduction, through the first *elegantamente* waltz, cheeky fanfare, *energico* main section and glittering coda, it is clear that we have here a lusty love-child of Busoni's *Tanzwalzer* conceived in entirely Stevensonian terms.

At the time of their composition the aspect of these two pieces which a commentator would probably have found most striking was their closeness to the then sorely neglected precepts and example of Busoni. With hindsight, they now assume lineaments more prophetic of Stevenson's own later development. His choice of forms has bypassed the western symphonic tradition as such, going instead for the ultimate musical activities out of which that tradition arose – song and dance. And in the *Berceuse* especially he shows a readiness to dissolve thematic duality into a single onward-flowing process of variation, elaborating and metamorphosing so as to explore more deeply the essence of his musical ideas.

That the concerns of song and dance might well, in time, lead

him in decidedly unorthodox directions was already suggested
(though not to any audience) by a third work of this youthful
period which has remained unheard because never finished,
although much of it exists in full score – the *Suite for Isadora
Duncan*, for large orchestra. Conceived as a tribute to the great
dancer's memory, it partly evokes (and varies) music with which she
was associated in her career, such as the *Marseillaise* (to which she
danced bare-breasted) and Ethelbert Nevin's *Narcissus*, the very
type of Victorian salon piece which nowadays finds itself exploited
for satire or camp; in Stevenson's hands it is restored to the thing of
beauty which it was thought by listeners of Isadora's time.[2]

In 1955, Stevenson studied orchestration with Guido Guerrini –
himself an orchestration pupil of Busoni – at the Conservatorio di
Santa Cecilia in Rome. Certainly from now on his orchestral style
shows a unique blend of adventurousness in sonority coupled with
an impressive sense of responsibility towards the practicalities of
performance. But the essence of that style is already present in the
Berceuse – good orchestrators, it seems, are born, not made.

It was during his studies with Guerrini that Stevenson wrote a
Pavan for chamber orchestra – a free transcription of John Bull's
Spanish Pavan. This was performed in the early 1960s by the RTE
Orchestra in Dublin under the Italian conductor Francesco
Mander. Since Stevenson had not been able to attend Maurice
Miles' performance of the *Berceuse*, this broadcast was the first
occasion since his childhood on which he was given an opportunity
to hear his own orchestration. Leopold Stokowski expressed an
interest in the *Pavan*; but, by an ironic twist of fate, Stevenson's fair-
copy manuscript was part of a consignment of Stokowski's luggage
which was lost at sea during an Atlantic crossing in the *Queen
Elizabeth* (although the parts and rough-draft score still exist).

It was to be five more years before Stevenson completed another
work with orchestra, in April 1960, but its material is practically
coeval with the *Berceuse*. This is his First Piano Concerto, *Faust
Triptych*, itself a recasting for piano and orchestra of the solo piano
Prelude, Fugue and Fantasy on Busoni's 'Faust'. The Fugue and Fantasy
were originally conceived between 1949 and 1951.[3] In a way,

---

[2] Several of Stevenson's orchestral compositions have remained unfinished or in
sketch form, for reasons discussed below (p. 143); at this point it is appropriate to
mention another work of the early 1950s which remains a sketch – a Concertino for
bassoon and orchestra, possibly conceived as a counterpart to the Flute
Divertimento and Clarinet Concertino of Busoni.

[3] *Cf.* pp. 67–74.

therefore, the Concerto is the final stage in the evolution of the central work in Stevenson's development during the 1950s, the work which gives fullest and most explicit expression to his veneration for Busoni.

The lateral dimensions of the Concerto are essentially those of the *Prelude, Fugue and Fantasy.* The Prelude and the Fugue have both been slightly enlarged by the insertion of new material, and the Fantasy has a new coda, shorter than in the piano work but making more explicit the closing reference to the Sarabande in Busoni's opera. But in re-thinking the music for piano and orchestra Stevenson has expanded it vertically, taking advantage of the increased possibilities for polyphonic presentation; at some points therefore (such as the climax of the Fugue), the counter-point is denser while the instrumentation acts to clarify the individual lines. The *mise-en-scène* of the music, too, is opened up in the orchestral setting with many touches of drama, most strikingly in the thrice-repeated episode, found only in the Concerto, where four off-stage trumpets, in cruciform positioning outside the auditorium, drawing nearer and nearer to the audience, intone '*Clavis Astartis Magica*' as a mysterious and sinister chorale against the bell-like chords from Busoni's *Sonatina in Diem Nativitatis Christi* in piano, woodwind and strings.

The original *Prelude, Fugue and Fantasy* is a work of transcendental virtuosity, not least because so much essential material must be encompassed by the two hands of a single pianist. In one sense, therefore, by re-distributing this material between pianist and orchestra the Concerto reduces the music's purely virtuosic features. Instead, the protagonists probe together into the nature of Busoni's thematic inspiration in a spirit of passionate enquiry. The piano still has plenty of stunning things to do, and enriches the music's fabric with new counterpoints. But one never feels that its activities are prestidigitation for its own sake – rather a vital and disciplined part of the metaphysical quest in which the Concerto is engaged.

There could hardly be a starker contrast in mood, technique and aesthetic outlook than the work which followed the First Piano Concerto in fairly short order[4] – the blithe and breezy *Jamboree for Grainger* (1961), originally (1960) for two pianos, and now for a standard symphony orchestra plus harp, piano, percussion and alto

---

[4] An orchestral *Elegy for Kathleen Ferrier* from about 1960 has remained in rudimentary sketch form.

saxophone (*ad lib.*). This is a short and joyous stramash woven out of favourite Grainger tunes (Stevenson's, yours and mine) into a concise piece in ternary form that would bring the house down at any Prom. Prefaced by a fanfare derived from *Arrival Platform Humlet*, the first section climaxes in a glorious simultaneous combination of *Country Gardens, Shepherd's Hey, Molly on the Shore* and *Mock Morris*; a slower, more romantic middle section reminds us of the *Hill Songs*; while the dancing final portion deliciously combines *Country Gardens* with the Children's March *Over the Hills and Far Away*.[5] Just a bit of fun (and so much the better for that) perhaps; yet in a way the *Jamboree* does continue the line of the *Faust Triptych*, in delving deeply into the nature of tunes, and what can be done with them, while at the same time bringing in the fresh air of folk song and catching sight of the 'tents of the happy tribes' who dwell far from the European concerns of concerto and symphony. For these, too, Stevenson would be writing his music.

In his orchestral music he turned now (as he had already done in his piano works) towards Scotland's musical heritage: 1962 saw the beginning of work on *Ben Dorain*, the epic which has ever since been an unseen counterpoint to all Stevenson's completed works.

Around the same time he produced *Three Scottish Folk-Music Settings* (the title directly recalls Grainger) for string orchestra. And his orchestral tribute to the most important native-born Scottish composer of the first half of the twentieth century, Francis George Scott, appeared in 1963. The *Keening Sang for a Makar*, in memoriam F. G. Scott, is, like the *Faust Triptych*, an orchestral recomposition of a piano work (of 1959). Like the *Triptych* and the *Jamboree* it is a homage to an elder master, partly founded on that master's own tunes (here most evocatively one of the greatest songs composed in the past hundred years, Scott's *St Brendan's Graveyard – Isle of Barra*), and seeking to assimilate his characteristic voice and achievement into Stevenson's overall vision. Shot through with the aspiring, deeply Scottish-sounding FGS motif,[6] in its piano guise the *Keening Sang* was already among Stevenson's most memorably powerful works. The orchestral setting – which adds much in the way of contrapuntal interest as well as extending and intensifying the anguished middle section – turns it into a heroic elegy of

[5] In 1989 Stevenson radically reworked the material of *Jamboree for Grainger* into a totally new conception, *Corroboree for Grainger*, a kind of pocket concerto for piano, wind band and percussion (including boomerangs!)

[6] *Cf.* p. 34.

rugged nobility that shows perhaps his finest command of orchestral colour so far. As yet, this superb piece has never been performed.

There followed in 1965 the *Scots Dance Toccata*, dedicated to the composer's children, Gordon, Gerda and Ella Savourna. Colin Scott-Sutherland has deftly summed it up as a work 'in which several traditional dance tunes from Neil Gow's *Repository* are drawn out of an opening *haar* into a Paganini-like polytonal reel of Ivesian complexity'.[7] Of all Stevenson's orchestral works this is the one whose neglect (before its revival by Garry Walker and the BBC Scottish Symphony Orchestra on 3 May 2002, it had been performed only once, at a Scottish National Orchestra Prom in Glasgow in 1970, in which year the 88-year-old Leopold Stokowski began to show an interest in it) I find incomprehensible. It is his first outstanding orchestral showpiece, a vital and vibrant exhibition of high spirits and sheer joy in music-making, crackling with energy and replete with marvellous tunes. It presents the average listener with no problems whatsoever, while being composed with craftsmanship so lavish in every detail that it makes the earlier *Jamboree* look like an almost casual collage – which it is not. The *Toccata* is a testing showpiece: there is hardly an instrument in the orchestra that is not at some stage a highlighted soloist, and every moment of *tutti* or ensemble work demands whipcrack precision and attack in the playing. It abounds with brilliant and witty orchestral inspirations – for example, when tolling clusters in the lowest depths of the piano, reinforced by bass drum, provide the underpinning for a fugal recall of one of the main themes on sepulchral double-bassoon, bass clarinet and trombones. From the gently pulsating opening to the wild Graingeresque flourish of the final bars, the piece is a stunner, a true original, a gem.

One further orchestral work has been purely Scottish in its inspiration, though it did not follow for over a decade: for sake of neatness I shall deal with it here before going back to the intervening scores. This is the *Young Scotland Suite* of 1976, commissioned by Lothian Regional Council for performance by the Youth Orchestra, a stirring and immediately attractive work which makes few concessions to the limited technique of young players – those techniques are not so limited that they cannot be enjoyably stretched by coming into contact with a meaty and

---

[7] 'Ronald Stevenson', in Lewis Foreman (ed.), *British Music Now*, Elek, London, 1975, p. 38.

challenging score such as Stevenson has written. With its triple woodwind, full brass and batteria requiring five percussion players, the orchestra is actually one of the largest for which Stevenson has written – and there are some unusual 'extras' besides. *Young Scotland* is another showpiece, on a bigger scale than the *Scots Dance Toccata*, and displaying an even more audacious orchestral skill.

There are three big movements, and their thematic materials are closely and resourcefully related. A germinal cell, consisting of two rising major seconds a third (or sometimes a fourth) apart, is omnipresent. The first movement, 'Salute of the Pipers', is a spirited *Allegro* dominated by, though by no means exclusively scored for, wind instruments. Stevenson's brass writing is notable in this movement – especially the extended paragraphs for trumpets, trombones and tuba in richly sonorous polyphony, a feature that may reflect something of his interest in the music of Havergal Brian. I give a taste of this in Ex. 46, which also shows how the FGS motif has, quite rightly, been woven into this exhortation to Scottish youth.

Ex. 46

Shortly after this, one of the movement's few passages weighted towards the strings (marked *camminando accanitamente* – 'trudging doggedly') introduces a peremptory fanfare and . . . the entry (in canon) of four bagpipers! The orchestra falls silent as their sounding reeds and drones vibrate the air, blasting a breath of the old tradition of the Great Music (*Ceòl Mór*) into the ears of 'Young Scotland'. For their contribution Stevenson recasts his material in pibroch-style, with appropriately intricate ornamentation – though true to the tradition, he regards his ornamentations as a mere guideline, to be altered at the discretion of the individual players. The orchestra resumes with a brilliant toccata-like development, which presently dissolves into a light-hearted dance, cheekily begun by solo piccolo and double-basses. The strenuous toccata returns: the pipers take up the dance on their own account; and the movement ends with a hard-bitten gesture of defiance in B flat, a kind of musical 'Wha daur meddle wi' me?'.

'Sounding Strings' is the title of the second movement; *Larghetto cantabile* is the tempo marking, and Stevenson has composed nothing lovelier. The scoring is for stringed instruments only – that is, bowed strings plus a harp and two clarsachs (the smaller Celtic harp – the idea is, as I understand it, that two young pupils of the harpist might take these parts). A long, superbly shaped tune, starting almost like a lullaby but gaining weight and passion as it proceeds, provides the main material. It is presented in string-writing of sustained eloquence. The harp and clarsachs provide a contrasting, ethereal sonority: they decorate the tune, then state it for themselves; the strings claim the tune again, but the movement ends in a chill *sul ponticello* shiver.

The finale is a bracing, confident march – the 'Young Scotland' march – beginning with an impressive fanfare and excited percussion preparation on xylophone, glockenspiel and tubular bells. After these preliminaries the grand march theme (derived by variation from the work's germinal motif and the FGS figure), strides on in full orchestra (Ex. 47).

Ex. 47

The second strain of the tune inverts the first, with a counter-point derived from the slow movement. The orchestration bristles like a schiltron, with barbed and gleaming brass and percussion. The march has two trio-episodes of more lyrical character, though with no slackening of pace. The second of them boasts a tune worthy of Grainger's *Colonial Song* (Ex. 48), given considerably to the *second* violins at its first appearance.

The March returns in vivacious *stretto,* adorned with fanfare-figures; the excitement reaches fever pitch; FGS rears up proudly on heavy brass; then the orchestra falls silent, and the four pipers (playing chanters without drones), the harp and the clarsachs have

Ex. 48

the field to themselves to present Ex. 47 in their own plangent way, before *Young Scotland* scampers to its invigorating conclusion.

I have dealt with *Young Scotland* out of its chronological position in order to highlight more clearly two parallel and indeed interdependent concerns evident in Stevenson's other orchestral works since the *Scots Dance Toccata.* One is a continuing and developing interest in variation forms, in itself doubtless profoundly influenced by the experience of composing that 'ultimate' variation-work, the *Passacaglia on DSCH.* The other is an exploration of the role of soloists in relation to the orchestra as an integral part of the variation-process, and the differing degrees and forms that relationship can take. It follows that these concerns are most fully worked through in Stevenson's three subsequent concertos, but in fact (*Young Scotland* apart) all his orchestral works since the *Scots Dance Toccata* have featured *concertante* elements.

The *Simple Variations on Purcell's 'New Scotch Tune'* for B flat clarinet and string orchestra is so modest in its dimensions that the construction of a score involved no undue expenditure of time. This short work, orchestrated in 1967 from a pre-existent piano piece, is a real charmer. The five easily followed variations hardly stretch the technique either of the clarinettist or of the string player, but there is no reason that difficulty should be the inevitable aim of a composer's every work. Stevenson here provides instead a wholesome and unpretentious piece of music-making for its own sake, designed to explore a little of the potential, rather than conceal the true nature, of Purcell's fine melody. There is nevertheless delightful wit in the Jazz and Blues variations, and some beautifully judged string textures in the slow ones. The 'Scottish' inspiration is still there in the theme, but the jazz elements are prophetic of the coming Second Piano Concerto.[8]

The *Vocalise Variations on Two Themes from The Trojans,* for mezzo-

---

[8] *Cf.* also p. 152.

soprano and orchestra, written in 1969 and gallantly dedicated 'To the shade of Hector and his incomparable Dido Miss Janet Baker', is on a more ambitious scale than the Purcell Variations – but one is struck first of all by the restraint and refinement of Stevenson's conception. The themes are both taken from the 'Royal Hunt and Storm'; the orchestra is a severely classical one of double woodwind, three horns, two trombones, timpani, bass drum and strings, and is deployed throughout with a pellucid clarity worthy of Berlioz himself. The harmony, too, is among Stevenson's most classically conceived. Except in one brief cadenza, the wordless voice-part eschews coloratura virtuosity, remaining nobly thematic and often making very evocative use of the lower register. It engages throughout in a calm dialogue with the orchestra, as one voice among equals; from this point of view the most remarkable section is probably the resourceful fugue, its structured counterpoint intercut by *senza misura* episodes for the soloist alone. Even in its fast sections (such as the exciting finale) the prevailing impression is of something radiant, statuesque, outside the confines of its time.

There are, in fact, further variation works, existing in various stages of realisation. As early as 1965, the year of the *Scots Dance Toccata*, Stevenson had conceived and largely composed in short score a set of orchestral variations on a theme of Carl Nielsen. Though he has done some subsequent work on it, the piece – which he intended to dedicate to his friend, the composer and Nielsen-scholar Robert Simpson – has never been put into full score.

As already noted, Stevenson has begun several orchestral works which he has never brought to a conclusion, or left unscored. What, he presumably thinks after a certain stage, is the point in spending a labour of months on the orchestration, only to have another work to languish unplayed along with his other orchestral compositions? This is surely the main reason for the non-appearance of *Ben Dorain*; and most of the works which *have* been scored since have been the subject of specific commissions. Yet certain important conceptions have been fully realised in his mind and partially in sketch form, and it is entirely proper to mention them to gain a fuller picture of his compositional development.

The *Variations round a Childhood Tune of Carl Nielsen* is inspired by the A major violin polka which was Nielsen's first composition, at the age of ten. As the title implies, the variations are arranged *round* the work's centre, where Nielsen's theme appears, in full, on solo violin. This central statement divides the predominantly slow variations of the first half from the predominantly quick ones of the second: in different ways, they all seize upon the first four notes

The opening of the fugue in the Vocalise Variations,
composed in 1969, in Stevenson's manuscript score

of Nielsen's tune – E, D, B, A, a melodic formation which is the
essence of pibroch. The work in fact begins with a most beautiful
oboe solo (against a pedal A, five octaves deep, on the strings) *nello
stile del Pibroch,* evoking the Scottish Highlands. Thoughts of
mountains continually arise from the basis of this simple tune
from the low-lying Danish islands: a 'Tyrolean' variation conjures
up the Alps, and towards the end of the work there is to be a

'Himalayan' variation. Among the quicker variations are a march, a waltz, and a tarantella, this last inspired by lines of Tagore: 'On the seashore of endless worlds children meet. The infinite sky is motionless overhead and the restless water is boisterous'.[9] In these words we see the whole conception of what would be – if put into shape for performance – a most delightful work.

Two further substantial orchestral variation-works were long planned but have never been committed to paper. Each of these

---

[9] *Gitanjali* (*Song Offerings*), No. 60, Macmillan, London, 1913, pp. 54–55.

projects is inspired by the art of a great Scandinavian sculptor – one Swedish, Carl Milles; the other Norwegian, Gustav Vigeland. Both pieces have taken detailed shape in Stevenson's imagination,[10] and together with the still-unfinished Nielsen Variations could perhaps form a 'Scandinavian triptych' of variation-sets, symbolic of the fascination with the musical expression of northern-ness which he shares with Percy Grainger.

During the same period (the late 1960s), with a certain measure of subsequent work, Stevenson also sketched a three-movement cello concerto, accruing a substantial amount of material for it. This is one project which eventually reached full fruition, since it may be regarded as the initial form of the very different Cello Concerto composed much later, in the early 1990s. But it long lay unrealised; instead, commissions from the BBC and from Yehudi Menuhin ensured that Stevenson's two principal orchestral compositions of the 1970s were concertos for other instruments: the Second Piano Concerto and the Violin Concerto, both large-scale (indeed, epic) designs which in different ways extend and explore the idea of 'world music' first promulgated and demon-strated in the *Passacaglia on DSCH*.

The *Passacaglia* had (along with many other things) incorporated numerous forms with explicit or implicit national associations – waltz, polonaise, *piobearachd*, African drumming, a march based on Russian speech-intonation, a fandango – into its overall structure. An (unstated) theme of the work is (human) unity in diversity; or rather, to put priorities the right way round, the blessed diversity and multifariousness possible within a simple, basic, shared human concept – the urge to make music. This is achieved through continual variation of primal ideas, very strict in the *Passacaglia* and thus easily recognisable. Some of the less intelligent reviews that greeted Stevenson's Piano Concerto No. 2, *The Continents*, at its premiere in the 1972 Proms (for which it was commissioned), represented it as merely a rhapsodic Cook's Tour of the world, a series of picture-postcards. That stemmed from a failure to recognise its true nature as a process of freer but still faithful variation. Indeed, in one sense *The Continents* could claim to be the Passacaglia continued in a different medium and on a different structural level.

The Concerto's imaginative point of departure was a poem, 'Das

[10] The Milles work, provisionally entitled *Orpheus Variations*, would be for tenor and orchestra, with a text by Rilke.

Kind', by the Afrikaans poetess Ingrid Jonker, prophesying that the child-victim of the Sharpeville massacre will become 'a giant without a pass-book', trekking through the world, a symbol of the nations of all humanity. The main materials whose infinite human potentialities are explored on this trek form a double theme, presented at the outset: Stevenson's main thematic obsessions of the 1950s and '60s now locked in vertical combination – DSCH (derived from Shostakovich via the *Passacaglia*) and '*Clavis Astartis Magica*' (from Busoni via the *Faust Triptych*). Ex. 49(a) gives this theme; the rest of Ex. 49 chronicles a little of the ensuing variation-process. Indeed, it will be seen that the two components are themselves so closely related as almost to be variations of one another, by inversion. (There may be a subliminal symbolism here, DSCH standing for the rational and 'Clavis' for the irrational, magical side of man's nature.)

Ex. 49

(a)

(b)

(c)

(d)

(e1)

(e2)

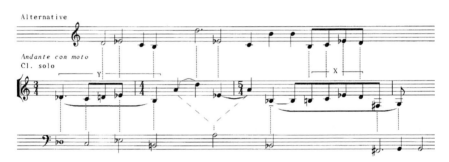

(f)

(g)

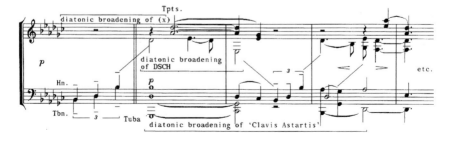

(h)

(i)

(j)

Knowing that Stevenson is one of our finest virtuoso pianists, and that he himself has been the soloist in all the concert performances of *The Continents* to date, one might have expected him to have written a heroic display concerto in the tradition of Liszt and Rachmaninov – piano against orchestra, the piano winning hands down. But this is no more the case than it was in the First Concerto. The piano part is certainly highlighted, and is challenging in technique and brilliant in sound. But its role is always changing with the changing character of the material – sometimes merely accompanying, sometimes reinforcing, sometimes encouraging or exhorting the other instruments in their endeavours. It becomes the main thread of continuity and integrity in a *corporate* effort, developing the subtle and complex *obbligato concertante* piano style adumbrated in the later movements of Busoni's Piano Concerto. (It is instructive that only some of the thematic presentations quoted in Ex. 49 are taken from the piano part.) The orchestra is a full one (though requiring only double woodwind), with a big battery of percussion and two harps.

After a brief introduction in which Ex. 49(a) is introduced mysteriously and quietly, and then suddenly blazoned fiercely by full orchestra complete with gong, bells, and massive piano chords,

Stevenson's Concerto divides into five 'continental' sections, each concentrating one element of music and bringing one orchestral department into prominence. The first two (evoking respectively Africa, and Australia with Polynesia and Asia) are in a sense 'pre-variations' – they revert to a musical culture prior to, though no less highly developed than, that which could produce Ex. 49(a), and must first evolve the raw elements of which Ex. 49(a) is end-point as well as new beginning. 'Africa' finds the piano being used as a drum (as in the 'Emergent Africa' section of the *Passacaglia*), pitted against real drums of several kinds (timpani, bass drum, side drum, bongos and congas), building up to a furious polyrhythmic toccata. Sudden rhythmic unanimity (with tritone chords in timpani) breaks off the section like a succession of gunshots.[11]

The 'Pacific' section features unharmonised or droned pentatonic melody, mainly on the strings, with the piano's strings plucked to give a *pizzicato* effect. An initial melodic idea (Ex. 49(b)) discovers the octave and then a sighing third, an echo of the salient thirds in Ex. 49(a); seconds and semitones follow. The orchestration is Stevenson's lushest: warmly pulsating strings, tintinnabulating piano and harps, lazy woodwind solos – the music seems sunk in some ancient dream. But three times, and with increasing fervour, a more developed idea in canon on piano and wind (Ex. 49(c)) insists *con urgenza* on its right be heard – a Vietnamese popular song, bringing what was then a very contemporary issue into the argument. The relationship to Ex. 49(b), through chromatic twisting, is patent: the cellos' sighing *portamento* tailpiece is also due for much development. The other 'eastern' musics move steadily towards melodic complexity, with a big pentatonic tune for a Chinese section (saved completely from anodyne prettiness by its clacking wood-block accompaniment). An aspiring whole-tone figure, Ex. 49(d), grows from the cellos' sighing figure and steers the music westward, towards polyphony. The piano enunciates a rāga on plucked strings then, skipping continents to the only European folk-music with close similarities to the music of Asia, plays a proud and solemn pibroch – as if the Indian Ocean were

---

[11] An early idea while composing the Concerto was actually to have the DSCH rhythm enunciated in pistol-shots; reasons of practicality led Stevenson to drop it, along with the sitar he once intended to incorporate in the orchestra. One regrets their absence nonetheless, though to be sure the work is cornucopic enough without them.

Stevenson using the piano as a drum, in a photograph taken during the rehearsals
for the Scottish premiere of the Piano Concerto No. 2, The Continents,
at the BBC in Glasgow, 1974 (photograph by W. Gordon Smith)

lapping the shores of the Hebrides. The melody here is Stevenson's
own, taken from his *Chorale-Pibroch for Sorley MacLean.*[12]

Europe, the home of counterpoint, is now represented by two
contrasted fugues and a march, all featuring wind instruments. The
theme of the first fugue, Ex. 49(e)1, sometimes bears the marking
Andante dialettico, and coalesces the DSCH/'*Clavis*' cells into a
single organic chain, using their salient intervals as links rather
than an arbitrary succession of pitches. Ex. 49(e)2 shows a possible
alternative means by which this coalescence is achieved. It also
varies elegantly the contour of Vietnam's song of struggle,
Ex. 49(c). It is one of Stevenson's finest fugues, with a broad,
noble horn counter-melody which is an augmentation and
inversion of Ex. 49(e). This melody forms an 'eastward-looking'
transition to the second fugue, which takes the form of an
enormously exhilarating dance in Bulgarian rhythm, the soloist
accompanying with a toccata-like *perpetuum mobile.* A *stretto* and

---

[12] *Cf.* also p. 62.

cadenzetta lead to a fiery brass-dominated Russian march, a
recomposition and elaboration of the 'Peace, Bread, and the Land'
section of the *Passacaglia* and thus closely related to the DSCH cell
(Ex. 49(f)).

Swirling piano figuration and misty string harmonics waft us
swiftly across the Atlantic, where we are greeted with a languorous
Blues. The page of score reproduced opposite gives the whole tune
and some of the superbly louche jazz-style development to which
Stevenson treats it. Its derivation from Ex. 49(d) and, more
distantly, from the contour of DSCH, is clear. Note also its initial
accompaniment by an ironically lugubrious solo viola, with one of
the most effective examples of quarter-tone writing I know. Soon, a
simple, tender brass music, broad as ten thousand beeves at
pasture, evokes the wide prairie in Ex. 49(g) – a noble diatonic
development of Ex. 49(d). Rushing figuration ushers in the passion
of South America: exotic percussion alternates with urgent episodes
(including warning reminders of the Vietnamese song) until a
sweeping Latin-American waltz carries all before it (Ex. 49(h); the
listener may not immediately realise its derivation from the sighing
cello figure of Ex. 49(b) – but Ex. 49(i), from a little further on,
should make that clear). Another sonorous yet poised brass
transformation of Ex. 49(a) – Ex. 49(j) – gives way to increasing
excitement that bubbles up into the other jazz number, a rollicking
rag – itself a fairly strict fast-tempo variation of the blues. Its
development is the most uproarious orchestral climax in the
Concerto, but it is brutally and suddenly cut short. Fragments of
previously heard 'national' musics from the various continents
begin to return, accumulating for the first time in contrapuntal
combination: practically all the ideas in Ex. 49 are heterophonically
recapitulated in a few short pages of score, a hubbub of many
voices. The unsupported 'voice' of the solo piano wrenches free of
the confusion, with agonised, rapidly throbbing chords and
flashing arpeggios – a lone human spirit. No synthesis, no solution,
is possible in this confrontation. The polarities and problems
remain. But Ex. 49(a) returns calmly in the orchestra, broadened
into a kind of benedictory chorale; and the piano's chords toll like
responses before the final thunderous agreement on an *Eroica*-like
E flat.

It is clear from the foregoing description that, in seeking to
conjure a 'world music' out of national and ethnic diversities,
Stevenson has rejected not just the traditional 'contest' element in
the concerto form, but also the neat oppositions of sonata style and
the idealised 'struggle and victory' format of the Romantic and

The 'Blues' passage from the Second Piano Concerto

post-Romantic symphony. Instead, through metamorphosis and cross-connexion, reflection and resemblance, kinships are continually being recognised and established, and a pattern far more intricate – far more like life as we experience it from day to day – being woven. The Violin Concerto continues and extends this process, dividing into three large, discrete, and progressively longer movements which are related intimately to one another and allow development of basic ideas to be pursued in diverse contexts over even larger time-spans than in *The Continents*.

Stevenson's Violin Concerto, subtitled 'The Gypsy', was completed in 1979 after several years' gestation and was his last substantial orchestral work before the Cello Concerto of 1992–94, although a number of smaller works intervened in the 1980s.[13] The scoring is original: double woodwind, two horns, and strings, but also a substantial percussion battery, and a triumvirate of harp, piano and cimbalom (whose part is cued into the piano, but is highly desirable). It was commissioned by Yehudi Menuhin, and Stevenson dedicated the work to the memory of the great Romanian composer, conductor, and violinist George Enescu, who had been Menuhin's teacher. Here at last the soloist boldly and deliberately steps into the limelight. A 'gypsy' quality, celebrated in some of Enescu's own compositions – such as his superb Third Violin Sonata – is often hinted at in Stevenson's Concerto (the cimbalom may be one element in it); and here again we seem to journey from East to West, taking in on the way several folk cultures which have especially prized the music of the violin. But the structure of the Concerto is such that every fresh vista proves to be a subtle variation of previous matter (its effortless blend of seemingly improvisatory spontaneity with exhaustive thematic working recalls the Violin Concerto of Ernest Bloch); and its tonal argument explores both the light and dark sides of virtuosity, symbolised in so many folk-tales where the violin is the Devil's instrument. The result is a gripping musical experience.

The Violin Concerto does not begin so much as dawn; indeed, *albeggiante* ('dawn-like') is one of the directions at the opening. A tranquil introduction arises from the darkness of a low pedal C sharp and drifts towards thematicism in shimmering waves of colour and hints of birdsong. String chords stack up in fifths, wind instruments breathe thirds and seconds, the strings of harp and piano resound to soft chromatic glissandi. It is like the birth of music from the ultrasonic background noise of nature. And then the soloist enters, giving shape to those primal elements (Ex. 50).

The seeds of the entire Concerto are in this long theme, which at

---

[13] These include a string-orchestra version of the *Recitative and Air* for Shostakovich (*cf.* pp. 94–95); the song-cycle *St Mary's May Songs* for soprano and strings, and whose texts range from Chaucer, through Tennyson and Joyce, to Stevenson's own Italian translation of an English poem by D. G. Rossetti; and a *Rhapsody in memoriam Ernest Bloch* for violin and strings, which has not progressed beyond draft. To this *concertante* work we should also add the 1989 *Corroboree for Grainger* for piano and wind-band previously mentioned (*cf.* pp. 137–38); and in 1990–91 a brass-band piece, the *Stratchclyde's Salute to Mandela*, celebrated the release from imprisonment of Nelson Mandela.

Ex. 50

its outset is virtually a kind of scale or rāga; a scale that changes and inflects itself as it moves to the higher octave. Its various segments, therefore, hint variously at diatonicism, at pentatonicism, at chromaticism, and at oriental gapped modes. The ensuing music will develop in (and combine) all these directions, and play them off against each other, often to dramatic effect.

An ardent development of the motif I have marked *a* leads towards F sharp and the second main idea (Ex. 51), a soulful tune with a hint of a waltz in it, but completely avoiding lachrymosity through its pungent alternation of thirds and seconds; indeed, its effect is rather sinister.

Ex. 51

The soloist immediately gives this a heroic development while the strings take up the 'rāga' in ghostly harmonies. The mood becomes more animated, with a new skirling chromatic figure in the orchestra and 'devilish' tritones in the violin, until we find ourselves launched on a fiery 'Danse Roumaine', its theme developed from the skirling semiquaver turn. Here full-blooded virtuosity emerges, not only in the solo part but throughout the orchestra. The mood, however, remains spectral, Mephistophelean. All the elements heard so far are varied and developed – most recognisably when Ex. 51 returns in a clear *Tempo di Valse*. As the movement proceeds, the violin's pyrotechnics become ever more flamboyant, with a hectic coda still in the spirit of the 'Danse Roumaine'.

Substantial and full of contrasts though it is, this first movement is to some extent merely a prelude. The E minor second movement, marked *Andante elegiaco*, also begins with an atmospheric orchestral introduction, but this now adumbrates the movement's main theme, which reshapes the premises of the Romanian dance into a refined and sombre cantilena dominated by the intervals of seconds, sevenths and ninths. A declamatory secondary theme is related closely to Ex. 51: strings introduce it against a glinting new version of the 'skirling' motif in woodwind, piano, harp and percussion. The soloist develops all of these elements at length and with real passion, while hints of Ex. 51 in its waltz guise, and of the skirling 'Danse Roumaine', intrude like skeletons at the feast. In answer to these sinister forces the soloist finally states a broad, calm tune (Ex. 52).

Ex. 52

Here, surely, is celebrated the richness and spiritual authority of Enescu's Bach playing; here, too, is a recreation of Bach's grand and memorable line in wholly Stevensonian terms. It is elaborated by soloist and orchestra against continuing developments of earlier material, climaxing in a gorgeous *tutti* statement. The waltz, Ex. 51, is again recalled, in a less disruptive harmonic guise, before the heart of the Concerto is reached in an extraordinary '*Cadenza in parte accompagnata*' – a brilliant, and ferociously difficult, review and preview of the whole material of the work, partly accompanied by cimbalom, piano and harp. A transfigured coda is based on the movement's opening theme, on echoes of Ex. 52 and on hints of what is soon to emerge as Ex. 53 – the main theme of the finale, announced at once in a dialogue between soloist and orchestra.

Ex. 53

This pithy idea is clearly derived from previous elements, and in its vaunting fifths, diatonic forthrightness, and sudden chromatic twist it concentrates much of the Concerto's harmonic argument into a single bar. It proves extremely adaptable: it goes equally well in inversion, its fifths can be flattened into tritones, its various elements can be reshuffled within the bar and to a different beat. All these things happen within its first, high-spirited, presentation (whose direction *cavalleresco* recalls Nielsen's Violin Concerto). A strenuous development leads to a Norse episode. This begins with a splendid 'Hardanger Wedding March' – clearly a tribute to those astonishing late pieces by Grieg, the *Slåtter*, and to the Hardanger fiddle music that inspired them. There is an epic nobility as well as a celebratory quality here. To this succeeds a 'Wedding Dance' that works up to a strenuous climax in which elements of the 'Danse Roumaine', the slow movement's main theme, and Ex. 53 are combined. But soon a 'Norse Funeral March' intervenes – a minor-key version of the 'Wedding March', with the soloist adding a new form of Ex. 51 as lugubrious counterpoint. Again a dance follows, but this time it is a 'Dance of Death', dominated by the tritones and skirling chromatics which have dogged the brighter diatonicisms throughout.

This passage unleashes a grimly hectic development which is the

A sketch for the cadenza of the Violin Concerto

Concerto's major confrontation between the light and dark sides of its musical nature. And out of it all emerges another dance – a 'Blue Mountain Dance', transforming Ex. 53 itself with a lazy lilt and deliciously 'blue' harmonics. All passion spent, a *calmo* coda ensues. The original 'rāga' from the work's opening returns; so does Ex. 51, transformed into a resolute march shared between soloist and orchestra; and a final reminder of Ex. 53 brings this hugely eventful concerto to a decisive conclusion.

In spite of its completion in 1979, and in spite of the prestige of Menuhin's commission, the Violin Concerto long remained unperformed. It was only in 1992 that Menuhin – not as soloist but as conductor – was able to direct its premiere, resigning the heroic solo role to his young Chinese pupil, Hu Kun. Only three years later, in December 1995, Edinburgh and Glasgow saw the first performances, on two consecutive nights, of Stevenson's Cello Concerto, *The Solitary Singer.*

The original spur for the substantial sketches of the Cello Concerto that were in the late 1960s[14] was provided by an aphorism of Berthold Brecht, to the effect that 'since Truth is no longer beautiful, Beauty can no longer be true' – a deliberate negation of Keats' famous line in *Ode to a Grecian Urn.* Brecht's thought was anathema to Stevenson, a life-long champion of the beauty to be found in the smallest things, and of musical beauty: beauty of melody in writing, of tone in performance. A saying of Oscar Wilde provided a counter-epigraph: 'There is no progress in art: all beautiful things belong to the same age'.[15] With this as his watchword, Stevenson set out to compose a cello concerto as a riposte to Brecht's pessimism. The original sketches adumbrate a three-movement plan: a stern, impassioned *Allegro impetuoso* first movement; a central scherzo, principally in $\frac{5}{8}$ with a motoric *Allegro telegrafico* main idea; and a deeply expressive *Adagio* finale.

An invitation from BBC Radio Scotland for the 'Musica Nova' festival projected for 1994 sent Stevenson back to this 1968 draft, but in the event the work that he composed in 1992–94 – though still in three movements with a central scherzo, owing an appreciable debt to that earlier conception and sharing some of its material, particularly the main theme of the finale – is very different from it. The circumstances of the first performances, too, were not those first envisaged: the 'Musica Nova' festival was cancelled, and the Concerto was taken up instead by the Royal Scottish National Orchestra. The soloist was Moray Welsh, a close friend and colleague of the late Jacqueline du Pré. The Concerto Stevenson had sketched in 1968 was conceived as a vehicle for

---

[14] *Cf.* p. 146.

[15] Stevenson encountered this quotation in Suzanne Bloch and Irene Heskes (eds.) *Ernest Bloch, Creative Spirit – A Program Source Book,* Jewish Music Council of the National Jewish Welfare Board, New York, 1976, p. 33. Although I have been unable to trace it complete in Wilde's works, the sentence 'All beautiful things belong to the same age' occurs in the essay 'Pen, Pencil and Poison', published in *Intentions* (1891). As Wilde tended to recycle his best phrases, it is probable that the complete quotation may be found elsewhere in his voluminous critical writings.

Hu Kun (the soloist), Geoffrey Trabitchoff (then leader of the BBC Scottish Symphomy
Orchestra), Stevenson and Yehudi Menuhin take a bow after the premiere
of the Violin Concerto, Royal Concert Hall, Glasgow, May 1992
(photographs by Patrick Douglas Hamilton)

du Pré, then at the height of her fame; *The Solitary Singer* that
emerged almost a quarter-century later is a profoundly elegiac work
dedicated to her memory. Its duration is considerably shorter than
that of the Violin Concerto, but the orchestra is now of a more
standard size, enlarged by the presence of harp, piano, celesta and
some unusual percussion. Stevenson's scoring is often almost
chamber-musical in its delicacy, with a wide range of colour.

The passion for beauty which du Pré brought to the bold lyricism
of her unique style of playing, and to the repertoire she
championed in her concert career, chimed with the original idea
of a concerto dedicated to the celebration of musical beauty.
Though the Concerto is in no sense programmatic, the way
du Pré's career was cut short and her fortitude in the face of
progressively crippling illness nonetheless give rise in the outer
movements to a dark colouring against which the beauty appears all
the more precious, because so hard-won. The central scherzo, by
contrast, is unrelated to the more sinister one of the original
conception but seems rather to evoke du Pré's marriage to the
pianist Daniel Barenboim with a specific flavour of Jewish music.

This 'Hebraic' element may reflect an influence of Bloch's *Schelomo*, a favourite work of du Pré, by a composer Stevenson has always honoured. It colours the proceedings elsewhere, even in the first movement's opening bars, where a three-fold reiteration of the dark triad of A flat minor, on low wind and brass, is immediately enveloped in string figuration that stresses 'oriental' augmented seconds and, through them, the ambiguous co-existence of major and minor triads.

The composer sees this three-fold tolling or knocking as a tragic presence throughout the work. So often in this Concerto does major turn to minor, light to dark, allied to the character of a march (in the first movement) and a farewell (in the finale) – allied, too, to a range of material that embraces (in the scherzo) Jewish popular song – that the work strikes me as in some respects Stevenson's most Mahlerian creation. Yet its overall movement is from minor to major, from dark to light and from the depths to the heights – and to the opposite pole of the tritone's *diabolus in musica*: a giant tonal progression from A flat minor to D major, adumbrated already in the D tonality of the first, unaccompanied entry of the cello. After this the movement, which bears the subtitle 'Nocturne héroïque', develops into a slow processional, with a central *Con moto* section propelled by an obsessively repeated march-rhythm. The cello-writing is at first direct and unadorned, but in the transition back to the *Marcia lenta* music Stevenson

A discussion with Moray Welsh after the premiere, in Edinburgh,
of the Cello Concerto, 8 December 1994
(photograph by John Humphreys)

begins to deploy a veritable thesaurus of cello technique: *sautillé*,
double artificial harmonics, triple- and quadruple-stopping, left-
hand pizzicato over a bowed melody in thirds, and so on. All this
display is an index of the expressive intensification that take place
in the latter stages of the movement, climaxing (if that is the right
word for a basically quiet passage) in a flurry of *Quasi chitarra*
strummed chords.

The second movement, designated 'Scherzo with slow trio',
opens with wind instruments imitating the ancient Hebrew *shofar*,
or ram's horn, introducing a festal *Allegro* where the idea of the
three-fold beats is subsumed into a lively alternation of $\frac{3}{4}$ and $\frac{3}{8}$ bars.
The trio proves to be a set of variations on the Hebrew chant *Kol
Nidrei* (which has previously inspired cello works by Bruch and
Bloch). Before returning to the music of the scherzo, in place of a
cadenza Stevenson introduces an unaccompanied cello setting of
Erez Yafa (*What a Beautiful Land*), a hiking song of the Israeli Young

A discussion with Edward McGuire after the Glasgow
performance of the Cello Concerto, 9 December 1994
(photograph by John Humphreys)

Pioneers which dates from the year that Jacqueline du Pré married Daniel Barenboim. This carefree tramping tune (opening with the three repeated tones) then mingles with the return, much transformed, of the scherzo.

The slow finale ('Elegy') is the heart of the Concerto. Heard at the outset is a most beautiful pentatonic melody with a pronounced Celtic tinge. Stevenson associates this theme with memories of Tiree, and here, perhaps, the title of the Concerto, *The Solitary Singer,* most clearly justifies itself: it might be the song of Wordworth's Solitary Reaper, or something heard along the sands of some Hebridean shore.[16] This finale is the most eventful of the three movements, with the widest variety of ideas and textures, though the argument continually circles back to the lyrical *Larghetto* theme. The three-note figure returns with tragic import. There are expansive counter-melodies, richly scored for full strings. Twice the

---

[16] It is heard as a lyric essentialisation of the hearty *Erez Yafa* tune (the accompanying timpani now have the three-fold beat). Yet this *Larghetto* dates back to Stevenson's original sketches of 1968, whereas *Erez Yafa* entered into his conception of the Concerto very much later.

soloist duets with an alto flute. Elements of the first movement
return, and two back-desk cellists echo a phrase from the Cello
Concerto of Schumann. In the final peroration the solo cello
intones the aspiring melody of one of Stevenson's own MacDiarmid
settings, *The Song of the Nightingale*:[17]

> Cares the nightingale
> Who hears it? [...]
> You cannot sing until your flight
> Leaves you no audience but the night [....]
> The fire of your flight in the height of the heavens
> Surprises my eyes like a sight of your song.

The tune rises higher and higher, to the top of the cello's register
until its song is taken over by the keening, tremulous voice of a
flexatone, against an A flat timpani pedal and sinister trumpet
reiterations of the three-note rhythm. Finally a quiet chorale, and a
seraphic cello phrase in harmonics, confirm the final resting place
of the music in D major.

The eventual realisation of the Cello Concerto, over a span of
nearly thirty years, must give cause for hope that the same may be
true of the choral-orchestral *Ben Dorain*. I have purposely refrained
from writing of that work, possibly Stevenson's *summa summorum*, of
which, in any case, I have seen almost nothing.[18] For long,
Stevenson spoke of it (provisionally) as the *Ben Dorain Symphony*,
though of recent years he has tended to reject the 'symphonic'
label altogether, opposing to this the definition 'epic', which – as
the MacDiarmid quotation with which I began this chapter
suggests[19] – is proper to its variation form. Yet perhaps at a deeper
level the terms are not mutually exclusive: Stevenson's variation-
works are his symphonies, in the sense that they occupy the place
which symphonies might hold in the output of a more conventional
composer, as the channels through which his deepest and most
impressive thoughts are directed at the widest possible audience.
But audiences have to be given the chance to hear them.

---

[17] No. 12 of the second numbered sequence with 'To Circumjack Cencrastus, or The
Curly Snake', in Michael Grieve and W. R. Aitken (eds.), *The Collected Poems of Hugh
MacDiarmid*, Martin Brian and O'Keefe, London, 1978, Vol. I, p. 192.

[18] I commend to the reader Jamie Reid Baxter's explication of *Ben Dorain* on
pp. 273–74.

[19] *Cf.* p. 133.

IV
THE CHAMBER MUSIC
Alastair Chisholm

Stevenson's chamber and instrumental music occupies an important place in his *œuvre*. While it is not as powerful as some of the large piano and orchestral works, it does show the development of his music from college days onwards. All his major compositional trends are reflected in it, and many of the works are impressive in their own right. Unlike most of his contemporaries, he felt little empathy with the European tradition as it has been taught, seeking inspiration instead from composers whose importance has been considered merely marginal by many critics. Since the 'marginal' composers whose ideas Stevenson's creative genius has fused into a living tradition are Busoni and Grainger, it was perhaps inevitable that his use of conventional chamber-music forms should have been minimal; there are, for example, only two substantial original works for that touchstone of European chamber music, the string quartet. Most of his chamber music involves an important piano part, and as Stevenson's own capabilities as a performer have always encouraged others to take part in his works, pieces like the *Duo Sonata* for harp and piano and *Variations and Theme* for cello and piano have not lacked performances.

The earliest surviving chamber work is the *Minuet: Homage to Hindemith* for oboe and piano, composed in his nineteenth year. Its assurance and poise are remarkable for such a young composer. Already his fertile imagination was at work, and some features which were to become characteristics of his music can be seen already; not least, his delight in elaborating a repeated melody – in the oboe Minuet following each of the three Trios, the Minuet is decorated differently.

The Sonata for violin and piano (1948), or *Sonatina Concertante*, to give its original Busonian title, is a work of struggle and exploration, rather than of confident achievement. This was written at a period of uncertainty in his life, between the college years in Manchester and his final settling in Scotland. Unusually for Stevenson, it is based on a note-row, though the treatment is tonally based. The Sonata is in a single continuous movement with several sub-sections: *Agitato con fuoco*, Variations, *Passacaglia*, *Fuga*. As well as the emergent interest in variation and fugal forms, other Stevenson finger-prints can be found – for example, the repetition of short phrases with slight chromatic alterations. Ex. 54 compares a passage from the Violin Sonata (a) with another from the first

167

movement of the *Duo Sonata* of 23 years later (Ex. 54(b)).

Ex. 54

This Sonata is the first of a series of violin works which have punctuated his career and of which those who think of him only as a piano composer are perhaps unaware.

In 1958, during a spell of especial interest in the music of Purcell, Stevenson produced three transcriptions for unaccompanied violin of Purcell's keyboard grounds. These transcriptions are of quite unusual skill, maintaining melodies and ground bass simultaneously within the restricted harmonic possibilities of the solo violin.

They seem to have acted as studies for the *Variations on a Theme of Pizzetti* (1961) for solo violin. Dedicated to Szigeti, the eight variations demonstrate many of the techniques of the virtuoso violinist. The theme (the 'Sarabanda' from the orchestral suite from Pizzetti's incidental music to *La Pisanella*, composed in 1913) is in A minor, pithy and full of possibilities, and its harmonic ambiguity appealed to Stevenson's fertile imagination. The variations feature, first, the theme with *tremolando* accompaniment, *pizzicato* triplets, a semiquaver *perpetuo mobile*, a *Fughetta*, and the combination of the Pizzetti theme with the famous theme from the last Paganini's *Twenty-four Caprices*, Op. 1. The concluding *Lento* variation is in the major mode, and the work finishes with an arpeggio flourish.

Following a gap of more than ten years, the next violin work was *Recitative and Air* (1974), an arrangement for violin and piano of a short piano piece dedicated to Shostakovich.[1] It was commissioned by the Union of Soviet Composers for an album planned for Shostakovich's seventieth birthday (1976), although by the time of publication the album had become a memorial tribute. Stevenson's

---

[1] *Cf.* pp. 94–95.

piece consists of a *senza misura* recitative leading to a passionate slow violin melody over a Bachian *pesante* bass. The melody throughout is limited to the four-note motif DSCH. To some extent the *Recitative and Air* is a footnote to the great *Passacaglia on DSCH* of 1962. Interestingly, the final cadence of the *Passacaglia* is on D, while in this later piece the close is on C.

To date, Stevenson's major violin composition is his Concerto of 1979. In some ways all these earlier pieces can be seen as studies leading to this work, although there are close contemporaries of the Concerto in two highly unusual violin solo transcriptions from the piano *Études* of Chopin – the *Studio Lirico* (from Op. 10, No. 3) and *Studio Paganinesco* (Op. 25, No. 4 – Ex. 55). Stevenson, aware that he is heir to the Romantic tradition, realised the significance of these transcriptions. Chopin's original inspiration was partly linked to the violin style of Paganini; how appropriate, in the year before the bicentenary of Paganini's birth, to transcribe these superb piano *Études* for solo violin.

Ex. 55

Stevenson's *Scots Suite* for solo violin is a substantial work – it is some 25 minutes long – which was given a memorable premiere by the late Leonard Friedman at a Festival Fringe concert at the Demarco Gallery in Edinburgh in 1988. Its six movements abound with technical difficulty, but since the origin of the musical idiom is that of the Scots fiddle, the fourth, fifth and sixth movements are respectively a 'Strathspey', 'Reel' and 'Jig'. The second movement offers a novel contrapuntal form: a 'Pibroch-Fugue'.[2]

At an earlier stage in his career, while he was Senior Music Lecturer at the University of Cape Town, Stevenson produced his *Four Meditations* for string quartet (1964). These four short slow movements each centre on one technical feature. The third *Meditation, Andantino lagrimoso* ('in memoriam Bernard van Dieren') – a transcription of Stevenson's piano original, No. 9 of *A Twentieth Century Music Diary*, is particularly revealing.[3] To the listener, it is an exquisite elegy, but it conceals true craftsmanship. It is a real canon in four tonalities at the major second (Ex. 56). The concluding chords (Ex. 57) are formed from the tonal centre of each canonic voice.

Ex. 56

Ex. 57

On his return to Scotland he became deeply involved in the 1966 Busoni centenary celebrations. This influence, ever strong on him, led him to produce the *Quartettino*, a transcription for string quartet from *Sonatina ad usum infantis*, the third of Busoni's six *Sonatinas*

---

[2] Stevenson's own analysis of the *Scots Suite* is reproduced in facsimile as Appendix Six on pp. 370–73. –ED.

[3] *Cf.* pp. 56–57. –ED.

for piano. Another outcome of the celebrations was the *Nocturne* for
clarinet and piano (1965). Stevenson was aware of Busoni's interest
in the piano *Nocturnes* of John Field. In turn, Stevenson's study of
the *Nocturnes* inspired him to begin an *omaggio* whose melody
seemed to suit the clarinet well (such is the empathy between
Stevenson and the Italian master that one wonders if he was
subconsciously writing with the clarinet playing of Busoni's father
in mind). The *barcarolle*-like *Nocturne* uses the ghostly harmonies of
Busoni's later music.

In the later 1960s Stevenson's identification with Scotland and
Scottish culture, especially the Scottish Renaissance of Hugh
MacDiarmid, became an increasingly dominant element in his
creative life. From this time come many of the vocal settings of the
poetry of MacDiarmid, Soutar and Sorley MacLean. Almost alone
among Scots composers, he identified, in his music, with the
nationalist aspirations of a substantial part of the nation at that
time. His attempts to achieve a distinctly Scottish music can be
heard in works as early as the *Keening Sang for a Makar* (1963), and
later his interest in *piobaireachd* and Gaelic culture in general led to
a group of Celtic works, notably the *Duo Sonata* for harp and piano.
This superb two-movement work was written for the Welsh harpist
Ann Griffiths, and premiered by her and the composer at a
memorable recital in the Purcell Room in London in 1971. The
first movement ('Celtic Sunlight') uses harmony based on
pentatonic and hexatonic scales. Both the principal themes have
the wide, sweeping range associated with Scottish folk music. The
form is Stevenson's own version of sonata-form, with a simultaneous
recapitulation of themes, and a coda using each instrument
alternately and contrasting major and minor harmonies. In the
Adagietto opening of the second movement ('Nocturne – the
Midnight Sun') the links with the melodies of John Field are
evident (Ex. 58). This range of melody is maintained in the later
vivace section. *Adagietto* and *vivace* sections alternate until the
opening of the *Duo Sonata* returns to claim its rightful place as the
real kernel of the work.[4]

Stevenson's pre-occupation with the soaring melodies of Scottish
music was again the inspiration for the *Variations and Theme* (1974)
for cello and piano. Written for the young Scots cellist Moray
Welsh, this is a set of variations on one of the loveliest of old Scots
tunes, 'The Bonnie Earl o' Moray' – not the tune Britten used in his

[4] *Cf.* also pp. 271, 272 and 289–90.

Ex. 58

Folk-Song Arrangements, but the more expansive older one. It was published in a harmonisation by Robin Orr in the *Kelvin Series of Scots Songs,*[5] although first printed in *Orpheus Caledonius* in 1725. Comparisons between the 1974 *Variations and Theme* and the 1961 Pizzetti Variations are interesting. Superficially the two have much in common, but the later set has more marked maturity and individuality. The themes are totally different: the Pizzetti is angular and pithy, the folksong lyrical and a marvellous self-contained melody. In his *Variations and Theme* Stevenson chose to unfold the folksong gradually and, indeed, a direct statement of the theme is allowed to become the climax and final section of the work – hence the title.

Following an introduction with falling sevenths and arpeggios for solo cello, Variation I is a setting of the inversion of the tune in canon between cello and piano. In Variation II the tune appears in the form of fantastical distortions, some microtonal. Variation III incorporates into its structure the retuning (*scordatura*) of the two lowest strings. With the lowest strings acting as a C sharp-G sharp drone the theme is picked out as the top note of huge arpeggios. A second section of this variation exploits simultaneous *arco* and *pizzicato* playing. The fourth variation has the air of drunken soldiery about it, while later ones include a *Fughetta,* and the use of cello octaves and artificial harmonies (*Marcia funebre*). At the climax of this overwhelming invention, the theme unadorned is presented by the cello at soprano pitch with a dry chordal accompaniment. The coda allows the piano to support the long-sustained last cello note, and the music fades on the sound of the Scottish flattened seventh.[6]

Between the *Variations and Theme* and the *Fantasy Quartet* of 1985 Stevenson produced no large-scale chamber music. In addition to some occasional pieces like the violin and piano piece, *Prelude for a Centenarian,* for Horace Fellowes (1975), he has written two short works for piano trio. These are designed more for domestic music-

[5] Bayley and Ferguson, Glasgow, 1965.

[6] *Cf.* also p. 272.

making than for the concert platform. The first, *Weihnachts-variationen* (1979) is on a theme from Othmar Schoeck's *a cappella* motet, *Agnes*. The second, *Ländler* (1980), is a series of characterful settings of dance tunes which Schubert had written down unharmonised.

The *Fantasy Quartet*, completed on 3 February 1985, is a further realisation, in contrapuntal terms, of his preoccupation with the national music of Scotland. It is a work overflowing with ideas, all derived from an arresting sequence of chords. The title indicates a continuous single movement work with subsections, but 'Alma Alba', the subtitle, is much more indicative of the work's content. The words are Latin and Gaelic respectively and can be translated as 'Scotland's Soul'. Using no genuine folk music but rather ideas he has developed from his lifelong absorption of the essence of Scotland's national music, Stevenson has produced a most unusual and disturbing piano quartet. Following the dramatic opening with the piano's germinal chords there are three short sections evoking the music of Scotland's folk instruments: the clarsach, the great highland bagpipe and the fiddle. In the first of these a 'prepared' piano sound is used, while in the second the violin uses quarter-tone inflections to simulate the bagpipe scale. The music of the third evocation, the fiddle, leads to a Border 'Ballad' where the piano predominates. A fugue follows and a quodlibet in which each string instrument in turn plays a strathspey, a reel and a jig. These are presented simultaneously in different keys while the piano has a subservient role. The three string instruments create a kind of polytonal Scots invertible counterpoint. The coda shows a return to the germinal chords of the opening. The final cadence moves from pentatonic chords to rest upon an open tonic A.

The *Fantasy Quartet* contains a wealth of interesting contrapuntal detail and repays repeated hearings. Perhaps the intensity he has managed to achieve in this work may have encouraged Stevenson to embark on more chamber music as he moved into his seventies. The completion of his piano transcription of van Dieren's Fifth String Quartet in 1987 may likewise have led him to re-assess the possibility of using the string quartet. Certainly, when the Edinburgh String Quartet commissioned a work for their thirtieth birthday, there was no hesitation on Stevenson's part, and the result is his most important chamber work to date.

The String Quartet of 1990, entitled *Voces Vagabundae*, is a four-movement work lasting a little more than half-an-hour. The tonal plan is an interesting one, with each movement centred on one of the violin's open strings – E, A, D and G (a characteristic

Stevensonian device). The opening movement, marked *Maestoso –
Allegro ardente,* is headed with a quotation from Whitman: 'I take to
the open road – the world before me – leading wherever I choose'.
It begins with a memorable succession of three four-part chords,
each played slowly by two instruments and then repeated *sforzando*
by the other two at pitch. The *Allegro ardente* matches its marking
with a confident melody played in octaves over a chordal
accompaniment. The melody and accompaniment alternate
between the soprano and the bass of the texture, which later thins
out, and the mood becomes slower and less certain. A slow middle
section follows, using a melody, derived from the opening, that
undergoes chromatic alteration. The music regains speed and the
buoyant mood of the opening comes back. After a return to the
three opening chords (now played in reverse order), a succession of
dissonant chords leads to a cadence on E.

The extremely concise scherzo which follows is marked *Volante* –
appropriately, for it is dedicated to Kenneth White, poet of *The Bird
Path.* The swift opening chords and passage-work soon become the
accompaniment for melodies based on the opening of the first
movement. Later, chordal ostinatos centre on tone clusters which
spread outwards and lead to a frenetic canon and then a swift close
on A.

The slow movement, *Adagietto cantabilissimo,* is subtitled (again
from Whitman) 'A backward glance o'er travelled roads'. It is the
emotional heart of this very personal work. Beginning in D, with a
slow-moving tune over rich muted chords, the music seems to turn
first one way and then another. When it settles on a repeated
F sharp, there is a reminder of the scampering passage-work of the
scherzo. Then, as if in a sudden vision, the sweeping melody of
Stevenson's *Calbharaigh* breaks in.[7] The spell is broken, and the
music becomes more disturbed – a passage of clashing bitonal triads
in contrary motion and another of eerie chords in harmonics –
before it moves seamlessly into the fugal last movement.

This is a technical *tour de force,* with a walking fugue, a fugue *à la*
strathspey, one *à la* reel, a double fugue on strathspey and reel, a jig
fugue, and finally a quodlibet in which all the themes meet. Thus
the open road of the first movement eventually leads back to
Scotland, but a Scotland of incredible richness and diversity.
Perhaps this Quartet had to wait all these years to be written, for in
many ways it seems like an allegory of Stevenson's entire musical
life.

---

[7] *Cf.* Ex. 65 on p. 193. –ED.

V
THE SONGS
Derek Watson

The human voice – that is what is lacking in the twentieth century. Even when composers these days write for the human voice they often treat it most inhumanly. I want the direct speech of the human voice – even in instrumental music.[1]

In 1947, aged 19, Ronald Stevenson set these lines of Blake in his cycle *19 Songs of Innocence*:

'Piper sit thee down and write
In a book that all may read.'
So he vanish'd from my sight,
And I pluck'd a hollow reed,

And I made a rural pen,
And I stain'd the water clear,
And I wrote my happy songs
Every child may joy to hear.

They are an apt introduction to a discussion of his songs: for the composer who from his Celtic base reflects, projects and resounds a world ethic, the image of the piper is a happy start.

Not that *Songs of Innocence* is the start of the story of Stevenson as song-maker. Blake's imagery occupied him before 1947 and has since (an early song, *War*, is a powerful pacifist protest). The love of song is in his blood:[2]

My father was an amateur tenor. I owe him practically everything in music. He was a poor man who thrived off thrift – which is, I suppose, a very Scots thing. And I played the piano and accompanied him in the *Irish Melodies* of Thomas Moore and Scottish folk song. When I began to compose at about 13 years of age, my first efforts were settings of Thomas Moore, Sir Walter Scott and Lord Byron – who was, of course, a Scot.

Ex. 59 gives a fragment of a very early song which clearly shows a grasp of Scots idioms, *The Violet* (Sir Walter Scott; set in 1943).[3]

[1] Ronald Stevenson, in conversation with Michael Oliver, *Music Weekly*, BBC Radio 3, 16 December 1979.

[2] *Ibid.*

[3] Jamie Reid Baxter (*cf.* p. 268) cites *The Violet* as evidence of Norwegian allegiance. There is no real incongruity here as the Nordic element is expressed in the piano accompaniment. The Scottish element is related more particularly, in the melody of this setting, to Lowland song rather than to the Hebridean (which features markedly in Stevenson's later work and which has conspicuous points of contact with the East and the oriental). –ED.

Ex. 59

An unexpected delight encountered during a visit to the composer to consult the songs was sharing Ronald's joy in John McCormack's performance of 'Believe me if all those endearing young charms' – a record he remembers first hearing played in his Lancashire childhood by his bargee grandfather. On my way to see him I calculated that I knew (had performed, studied or heard) about seventy of Stevenson's songs. During that visit I was shown, and we discussed, over one hundred more.

Songs therefore are a large and essential part of his creative world. Their range of expression is also very wide. Hugh MacDiarmid's lyrics (mainly the later poems) and Stevenson's close friendship and artistic sympathy with the poet are of supreme importance in his music. *The Rose of all the World* shows him as

master of the miniature. It is a tender and unpretentious setting of
this sweet lyric – the simplicity is thoroughly apt. Here is the
romantic image of the flower of Scotland (as opposed to the fitba'
nationalistic one): sharp and sweet – the microcosmic view. But just
as MacDiarmid contains within himself that small, still reflection
and also the epic, soaring, cosmos-embracing vision, so does
Stevenson in his musical treatments. An example of a complete
contrast to these two short songs is the cycle *The Infernal City* (1968)
which illustrates his mastery of time-scale on an altogether broader
and bolder level. It is to me one of the measures of Stevenson's
greatness as a song writer that the verbal imagery of MacDiarmid is
captured and musically reflected in multiform ways. Indeed, the
composer has consciously striven towards a musical equivalent of
the poet's vision of a world language – beyond the songs and in his
Passacaglia on DSCH and the Concertos in particular.

The Infernal City verbally and musically depicts a macrocosm – as
much Edinburgh as Glasgow; or in its implications as much Moscow
or Calcutta – and in the first song evokes Berlioz's hatred of Paris
and Wagner's of Berlin. Berlioz's *Dies Irae* theme and Wagner's
Fafner motif are quoted and skilfully combined in a thematic
counterpart to the richness of MacDiarmid's poetic references.
'Glasgow', the first song of the cycle, invokes the name of Francis
George Scott whose songs are '*di essenza populare*' but 'Scott popular
in Glasgow? – what a place for bat-folding!'[4] Stevenson has often
gratefully acknowledged his debt to Scott and to the study of his
songs. Scott in turn was MacDiarmid's mentor and together they
spearheaded the musico-literary movement of the 1920s, the
'Scottish Renaissance'. Ronald Stevenson is their heir. In his own
separate MacDiarmid setting *The Last Trump* he outdoes the Scott of
the cantankerous blaspheming bluster (compare Scott's *Crowdieknowe*). *The Last Trump* is a bold tarantella in the mould of
Stevenson's own spiritual mentor, Busoni.

The Infernal City also contains tributes to Charles Rennie
MacIntosh ('Open Glasgow up!') and to the Eric Satie of the *Messe
des Pauvres*. Sorley MacLean, the Gaelic poet, is represented in the
cycle with his 'Calvary' in a metrical Lallans translation by Douglas
Young. Stevenson has also set this poem in the original Gaelic
('Calbharaigh') – an unaccompanied meditation in which the
singer's eyes are not on Calvary or Bethlehem but on Scottish city
slums where growing life decays.[5] Another (separate) Sorley

[4] Grieve and Aitken, *op. cit.*, Vol. I, p. 355.

[5] *Cf.* pp. 192–94. –ED.

The song The Rose of all the World, *composed around 1966,*
in Stevenson's manuscript

MacLean song, *Shores* ('Traighean', 1979) is rich in melodic and harmonic evocation of the wide solitude of the island shore (Ex. 60).

Ex. 60

The natural complement of *The Infernal City* is another Mac-Diarmid cycle, *Border Boyhood* (commissioned by Peter Pears for the Aldeburgh Festival of 1971); again settings of the later poems, here rejoicing in the colours and celebrating the birth and life of things in the countryside which poet and composer shared as home. As in the other cycle, there are seven movements, of which the central one is a piano interlude. The final song, 'The Nook of the Night Paths', is a fugue which uses the voice integrally and I think uniquely: at one point the singer performs in two-part counterpoint with himself, off-setting the normal register and head voice (Ex. 61).

Only a brief glance at the many individual MacDiarmid songs can be given here. Mention must be made of the shorter cycle, *Songs from Factories and Fields* (composed for William McCue in 1977). Of separate settings, note *The Bonnie Broukit Bairn*, a lyric in which MacDiarmid views earth in a space-time context and in which the piano part wonderfully depicts the starry kaleidoscope in a chromatic wheeling; *The Bobbin Winder* with voice and accompani-ment weaving sunlit, elfin threads; *The Barren Fig*, a 'blues écossaise' with a hilarious, improvisatory gusto; and *My love is to the light of lights*, which quotes the opening of the melody 'My luve is like a red, red rose' and treats this phrase canonically in piano strophes between

Ex. 61

vocal verses. In *A'e Gowden Lyric* the width of the vocal intervals should be noted. This is a feature of several of the songs and has a specifically Scottish origin.[6] It is found again in 'Requiem', the last song of the Robert Louis Stevenson cycle, *Hills of Home* (Ex. 62).

Ex. 62

[6] *Cf.*, for example, Francis Collinson, *The Traditional and National Music of Scotland*, Routledge and Kegan Paul, London, 1966, p. 27.

A manuscript copy of Stevenson's song A'e Gowden Lyric

When another R. L. S. cycle, *A Child's Garden of Verses,* was commissioned by the BBC for the 1985 centenary of the publication of the poems it meant much to the composer who, (much like Britten in *his* variety of works concerned with childhood innocence and with childlike imagination) has the ability to write music for children to listen to, for children to play and sing, and music *about* the magic of childhood.[7] Just as the adult R. L. Stevenson remained

[7] *Cf.* Appendix Four, Stevenson and the Child, pp. 321–25. –ED

'Songs are a large and essential part of his creative world':
Stevenson in discussion with the American folksinger Pete Seeger,
New York, 1984

a boy in his imaginative world, the first and last songs of this important cycle frame, from an adult viewpoint, the world of boyhood shot through with sunlight and memories of vivid sounds, sights and scents. But the sorrows and sickness of the poet's early Edinburgh years also cast their very dark shadow across the colour of the music. These 'scenes from childhood', to borrow a Schumannesque phrase, use tenor voice as well as children's solo voices.

Other cycles include *Songs of Quest*, five settings of John Davidson (composed 1974 and premiered that year in Vienna); *The Weyvers of Blegburn*, a significant excursion into the Blackburn poets of Britain's first industrial society in the 1860s, and in which the link between Scots and the Lancashire dialect is manifest; and the *Nine Haiku* (1971), settings of the classical Japanese verse form from the school of Bashō, translated (via an interim French version) by Keith

Bosley, who also wrote one of the poems himself. The *Haiku* (like some other songs, including the *Four Vietnamese Miniatures* of 1960) are for voice and harp, and in this and other works Stevenson proves himself one of the finest contemporary writers for that instrument. Melodically, the structure of the songs parallels the verse structure of the haiku. In the 'Dedication' (Ex. 63), for example, line 1 is of 5 syllables (pentatonic); line 2, seven syllables (heptatonic); and line 3, five syllables (pentatonic again). Here Scottish or Celtic pentatony is extended into Japanese chromatically inflected pentatony. In another example ('Hiroshima') it can be seen that line 3 selectively juxtaposes or coalesces lines 1 and 2 to form dodecaphony (Ex. 64). Other points of tangent with the orient in the songs include settings of Rabindranath Tagore and Mahmood Jamal.

Ex. 63

Ex. 64

The sheer number of Stevenson's songs (there are around 230) precludes examination of them all here, although three very different examples insist on comment. *Eins und Alles* (Christian Morgenstern, translated by the composer) reflects his involvement with children. A commission from Garvald (Rudolf Steiner) School for mentally handicapped children near West Linton, Peeblesshire, it was broadcast on Radio 3 during 1979, the International Year of the Child. *The Moon*, a Sacheverell Sitwell setting, is noteworthy for

*Marjorie and Ronald Stevenson, the soprano Patricia Rosario
and pianist Graham Johnson, backstage at the Wigmore Hall
after Stevenson's sixtieth-birthday concert in 1988; Rosario
and Johnson had performed the* Nine Haiku *of 1971*

its nocturnal filigree Godowskian piano-writing. And of the many
Scottish poets represented other than MacDiarmid, I cite *Voskhod
over Edinburgh* by Alan Bold. This is more of a *scena* than a song and
contains in its contrast of chromatic intensity (the cosmonaut-
apparition) and popular tune (the reflective watchers from the
tenement) a dramatic image of modern man on the threshold of a
new age.

In summary, the songs must be seen in the context of Stevenson's
overall technical working-out of his philosophy. In terms of
structure, many of them could be analysed as multiform workings
of variation techniques. At the simplest level – such as a pentatonic
folk-melody – a varied strophic setting might be the procedure. In
the *Haiku* another, more complex, principle of variation is realised.

In terms of the voice, the directness of speech-melody is never lost. In terms of the piano – and in a sense the songs cannot be viewed independently from the piano works – the directness of speech-melody is also present. In this context it is appropriate to mention the appendix to Thalberg, *L'Art Nouveau du Chant appliqué au Piano*, piano transcriptions of Victorian and Edwardian songs to which the composer's wife Marjorie has added the important suffix 'being études in the art of *bel canto* piano-playing'.[8] (The marriage of vocal and instrumental styles is also seen in *A Rosary of Variations on Seán Ó Riada's Irish Folk Mass* of 1980.)

In an age starved of singable song I would urge young performers to explore Stevenson's work. Publication of his songs is an essential step towards their wider performance and richly deserved recording and the Ronald Stevenson Society is making praiseworthy progress in this direction.[9] A short appraisal such as this can only hint at the variety of expression they contain. There is no doubt that their range and integrity have something to teach us all.

[8] *Cf.* pp. 102–6 and 280–81. –ED.

[9] The first CD of Stevenson songs, recorded by The Artsong Collective, appeared in 1998 and featured *Border Boyhood*, *A Child's Garden of Verses* and the *Nine Haiku* (Musaeus MZCD 100) – *cf.* Discography, p. 476. –ED

VI
THE CHORAL MUSIC
Jamie Reid Baxter

Ronald Stevenson's music springs from the human voice. In a radio interview in 1979, he answered the question 'Why did you become a musician?' with the simple words: 'It was my father's singing'.[1] Stevenson has written an enormous number of solo songs, but there is also a less well known corpus of music for many voices. Yet his choral music is central to his output, as the texts he has chosen to set make unambiguously clear. The quality of the word-setting in these works means that their immediate impact on audiences is guaranteed, but their sound-world is nonetheless a highly individual one – as Michael Tumelty wrote in 1993, 'Stevenson has a quite remarkable flair for capturing a quality of light in sound'.[2] Fortunately, two of these pieces are already available in commercial recordings,[3] and the first of them, 'Calbharaigh', makes a perfect point of entry into Stevenson's choral *œuvre*.

This setting of a short, deeply disturbing lyric sprang directly from the sound of a specific human voice – that of Sorley MacLean (1912–97) himself. It comes at the centre of *Anns an Airde, as an Doimhne* (*In the Heights, From the Depths*), the composer's own title for a choral triptych of MacLean settings commissioned in 1966 by Grant Kidd for the Greenock Gaelic Choir. Stevenson himself explains that he chose

> three poems, *Ceann Loch Aoineart, Calbharaigh,* and *Lìonmhoireachd*: the first sings of nature's majesty in the Scottish Highlands; the second laments human misery in the Lowland slums; and the third contrasts the remote beauty of the cosmos with the only true miracle of human love.[4]

[1] *Cf.* note 1, p. 177. This essay is an expansion of my 'Ronald Stevenson and the Choral Voice', *Chapman*, Nos. 89–90 (double issue), Summer 1998, pp. 40–45.

[2] *The Herald* (Glasgow), 6 June 1993, reviewing the premiere of *Psalm 23*. Tumelty also spoke about light in Stevenson's music in a review (*The Herald*, 25 January 1992) of Stevenson's motet *In memoriam Robert Carver*.

[3] 'Calbharaigh' ('Calvary') in *Eurocantica*, Section Art Vocal du Cercle Culturel des Communautés Européennes à Luxembourg, dir. Dafydd Bullock, SAIN SCD 2047; *In memoriam Robert Carver* in *Twentieth Century Scottish Choral Music*, Cappella Nova, dir. Alan Tavener, Linn Records CKD 014.

[4] In 'MacLean: Musician Manqué (and a Composer's Collaboration)', Raymond J. Ross and Joy Hendry (eds.), *Sorley MacLean – Critical Essays*, Scottish Academic Press, Edinburgh, 1986, p. 178. The texts of the three poems are to be found in Sorley MacLean, *O Choille gu Bearradh/From Wood to Ridge: Collected Poems in Gaelic and*

'Calbharaigh' begins with wordless humming from the full choir, before a solo voice sings 'Chan eil mo shuil air Calbharaigh' – 'my eyes are not on Calvary, nor Bethlehem the blest' – only to give place to the full choir once more. The presence of that murmuring choir, that multiplicity of individual voices speaking 'as one', is essential to Stevenson's conception. He re-used this music to create a solo-voice arrangement of Douglas Young's Scots translation, Stevenson's discussion of which indicates the degree of care that goes into his word-setting:

> The absorption of Gaelic words into Scots is more widespread than is generally realized; likewise Gaelic melodic idioms are frequent in Lowland folksongs; and it was this factor that determined my use of the same melody for both Gaelic and Scots words. Sometimes Gaelic and Scots own a common allegiance, a mutual source in Latin-rooted words, as in the line from 'Calbharaigh'
>> agus air seòmar an Dùn-Éideann
>> seòmar bochdainn 's cràidh.....
> which is translated by Douglas Young as
>> and a stairheid room in an Embro land
>> a chalmer o puirtaith an skaith [poverty and hurt].....
> Here 'seòmar' and 'chalmer' both derive from the French *chambre*. Young's Scots is coarser, cruder than MacLean's Gaelic. For example, MacLean writes
>> ach air cùil ghrod an Glaschu ...
> whereas Young writes
>> but on shitten backlands in Glasga toun.
> 'Cùil ghrod' literally means 'a putrid nook'. 'Shitten' is strong in meaning but fortunately the 'sh' is soft in sound. I say 'fortunately' not out of prudery but out of concern for the hush of the song, its still intensity. I attempted to match the coarser element in the Scots by using a few harsher discords in the harmony of the accompaniment, which I had not done in the original Gaelic setting [Ex. 65].[5]
>
> Another stroke of luck for the composer was that the soft sound of MacLean's ending of 'Calbharaigh' 'gu bhàs' (till death), is translated into Scots also with a hushed sound – 'till daith'. (Here I remember that James Joyce – and no writer has been more concerned with the music of words than he – said somewhere that at the end of his *Ulysses*, and again in the non-end of his *Finnegans*

English, Carcanet Press, Manchester, 1989, pp. 36, 34 and 16. 'Calbharaigh' is also used in the cycle *The Infernal City*, which includes five MacDiarmid poems.

[5] Stevenson has set the poem for a variety of forces: unaccompanied voice, soprano and tenor soloists with unaccompanied SATB chorus, and soprano and clarsach; it also appears, for tenor and piano, in the song-cycle *The Infernal City*.

Ex. 65

Wake, he attempted to take language to the threshold of silence: in
the one the last word is 'yes' (the sibilant approaching a whisper); in
the other the last word was 'the' (without the full stop). Joyce felt the
word 'the' was even nearer to silence that the word 'yes' was).[6]

'Calbharaigh' is a poem of pain, a shocking statement of
unpalatable truths about how 'man's inhumanity to man makes
countless thousands mourn'[7] – but Stevenson's setting is no howl

---

[6] *Ibid.*, p. 179. Also in 'Traighean' ('Shores'), Stevenson notes and prefers
MacLean's translation of 'measuring sand, grain by grain', with its sea-like sibilant,
to Crichton Smith's 'counting the sands grain by grain'. –ED.

[7] Robert Burns, 'Man was made to mourn', *Poems and Songs*, ed. J. Kinsley, Oxford
University Press, Oxford and London, 1969, p. 94.

of protest or anger. Instead, it is perhaps the most beautiful music
he has ever written, and its euphony and glowing loveliness are a
harrowing reminder of what life could be here on Earth.
Stevenson's setting grieves for all of us in our failure to be what we
could be.

The third part of *Anns an Airde, as an Doimhne* sets a love poem, in
which the individual 'I' is expressed by a multiplicity of voices, for it
is not the cold multitude of the distant stars that light the universe
which the human heart inhabits – it is the miracle of that sense of
oneness with another being which we know as love (Ex. 66).

Ex. 66

Stevenson's socialism is a belief in the collective identity of
human individuals, and it is not an adjunct to his music. His own
awareness of the mutual interdependence of all life, of the 'usness'
of all creation, informs all his activity. I believe it to be of real
significance that Stevenson's choral music – by definition 'plural' –
so often sets texts written in the first person singular. 'I' sings as
'we'. This surely constitutes one of the most powerful expressions of
his commitment to all-embracing solidarity – the awareness that
'stars and heart are one with another' spoken of by Busoni, in the
essay turned into verse by Hugh MacDiarmid at the beginning of
the final section of *In Memoriam James Joyce*.[8]

Though Busoni and MacDiarmid (and Percy Grainger) are
widely thought of as Stevenson's principal spiritual mentors, there
is one whose presence is even more fundamental. When the
eighteen-year-old Stevenson was jailed for the crime of refusing to
do national service out of pacifist conviction, he drew much
strength from the wisdom of William Blake's compassionate
critique of human life. In prison, he set many Blake songs,
including a four-voice chorale version of 'On another's sorrow',
which voices solidarity with all creatures in their suffering:

---

[8] Grieve and Aitken, *op. cit.*, Vol. II, p. 881.

Can I see another's woe,
And not be in sorrow too?
Can I see another's grief
And not seek for kind relief?[9]

The music is serene, but the harmonisation is far from conventional, and the work breathes a calm sorrow: we can be fully human
only if we express compassionate solidarity, although the existence
of suffering is not a reason to rejoice. Yet Stevenson's awareness of
suffering is realistic: joy exists, too. And joyous cosmic solidarity, of
a sort that Blake would have applauded, is expressed in Stevenson's
ecstatic (and simple) setting of his own translation of *Frate sole*, the
hymn of praise to all creation written by St Francis of Assisi in the
first quarter of the thirteenth century (Ex. 67).

This feeling for the underpinning harmonious co-existence –
despite all appearances to the contrary – of everything that is finds
overwhelming expression in his largest work of all, the choral and
orchestral epic *The Praise of Beinn Dobhrain*.[10] The entire fabric of
this celebration of life and nature is literally 'grounded' on the idea
that 'light comes pouring' – Brother Sun, indeed. Light that drives

Ex. 67

[9] *Complete Prose and Poetry*, ed. G. Keynes, Nonesuch, London, 1989, p. 63.

[10] *Cf.* pp. 273–74 and 294–95. –ED.

Ex. 67 (cont.)

out darkness also drives out fear, because it lets us see. It gives the unknown a face and an identity; for, as William Soutar wrote, 'in the mood of Blake':

When men bind armour on the breast
They crush the faith they have confessed,

But when they fear no brother's face
Truth walks about the market place.[11]

Stevenson's choral works include delightful settings of Soutar's children's verse in Scots,[12] and also *Amhran Talaidh*, a Gaelic translation of *Day is düne*,[13] a magically rapt lullaby in which men and women sing as parents watching over young life's innocent sleep as darkness falls.

In his setting of Psalm 23, a large-scale choral work of 1993, written for Cappella Nova, Stevenson brings light blazing out of darkness and awestruck mystery in the 'choral recitative' which forms the prelude. The psalm itself is sung in a noble Middle Scots translation by Alexander Montgomerie (c. 1555–98),[14] whereas the prelude sets W. L. Lorimer's modern Scots translation[15] of the opening of St John's Gospel. Stevenson unleashes an explosion of extraordinary brilliance for the words 'Aathing that hes come tae be, he wis the life in it, an that life wis the licht o man; an ey the licht shines in the mirk'. *Psalm 23* is a fascinating work using a variety of compositional techniques, including the quotation of the tune 'Crimond' and the old Scottish practice of singing psalms 'in reports' – a kind of primitive fugue. It even includes spatial effects *à la* Gabrieli, with the 'deadlie way' of death's dark vale represented by a group of singers set apart from the main body, preferably invisible to the audience and if possible singing from the crypt. Michael Tumelty wrote of its 'spellbinding journey through the dark, dense complexities of death to a kind of radiant catharsis'.[16]

Of course, it's when it's dark that we most need a sense of trust. But the fact is that solidarity is most easily perceived when light is pouring forth. As Blake wrote:

[11] *Poems*, ed. W. R. Aitken, Scottish Academic Press, Edinburgh, 1988, p. 22.

[12] *Cf.* Alastair Chisholm, 'Stevenson's Soutar Settings in the Context of Some Personal Memories', *Chapman*, Nos. 89–90 (1998), p. 75.

[13] Soutar, *Poems*, p. 110.

[14] *Collected Poems*, ed. J. Cranstoun, Scottish Text Society, Edinburgh and London, 1887, p. 255. In fact, the poem is almost certainly by the Rev. James Melville, imitating Montgomerie (it was published in Melville's *Fruitful and comfortable exhortation anent death* of 1597).

[15] *The New Testament in Scots*, Lorimer Trust, Edinburgh, 1983.

[16] *The Herald*, 6 January 1993.

God appears, and God is light
To those who dwell in darkest night,
But doth a human form display
To those who dwell in realms of day.[17]

That focus on the divinity of the human individual is given forceful expression in Stevenson's dramatic 1969 setting of Emily Brontë's *No coward soul is mine* for women's voices and harp. A heroic F sharp major opening section, marked *moderato maestoso* leads to a *pp misterioso,* starting in a Phrygian B flat minor:

O God within my breast,
Almighty, ever present deity,
Life that in me hast rest,
As I, undying Life, have power in thee.

The music is now A minorish, and a passage for harp alone heralds the affirmation that 'Vain are the thousand creeds that move the hearts of men' – 'creeds' highlighted by a raised fourth, and the whole line echoing Eastern music. *Allegro moderato e con spirito,* an unaccompanied modal melody from soprano solo declaims, *libero,* that 'Strong I stand', words taken up by the choir in imitative polyphony, and a chordal passage on the harp marks the transition to the final section, in B flat major, which returns to the opening words and melody in expanded form. *No coward soul is mine* explicitly rejects as 'unutterably vain' the thousand creeds that move the hearts of men, but while Stevenson has no time for organised ideologies, he nonetheless suffered imprisonment for the pacifist beliefs he has consistently upheld. Solidarity with all life is inherently and ineluctably pacifist, and Stevenson's vision of reality is that everything forms part of the vast, peaceful circle of being evoked in the 'round dance' (*Reigen*) of the spoken Epilogue to Busoni's *Doktor Faust.*

Stevenson's pacifism has been stated with absolute simplicity in the four *Peace Motets,* premiered in a 'concert for peace' on St Andrew's Day in his sixtieth birthday year. 'Thou shalt not kill' is set as a series of repeated, declamatory injunctions. 'Put up again thy sword into his place, for all they that take the sword shall perish by the sword' is contrastingly lyrical, though still admonitory. 'They shall beat their swords into ploughshares, nation shall not lift sword against nation, neither shall they learn war any more' begins,

[17] 'Auguries of Innocence', in Keynes (ed.), *op. cit.,* p. 121.

fittingly, with a jubilant hammering before ending serenely in preparation for the radiant, almost motionless music which enhaloes the quiet repetition of the Seventh Beatitude, 'Blessed are the peacemakers, for they shall be called the children of God'. These texts are universal in inspiration and in application; hence the setting for multiple voices. But Stevenson has taken care that the multiplicity will in no wise obscure the very clear message. He envisaged this work as being sung by amateur choral groups as well as professional singers. In a radio broadcast in 1979, he spoke about 'the desire for universal peace – man's greatest need', referring to his own wish for a 'music of many musics, a music of oneness – it's like the desire for universal peace, really'.[18] And he went on to quote Paul Robeson: 'There are many nations, but there's only one race – the human race'.

But we should not misunderstand this Stevensonian view of the oneness of humankind. This unity has nothing whatever to do with uniformity. On the contrary, like St Francis in *Frate sole*, Stevenson seeks to express a solidarity with every specific thing. It's a oneness of endless uniquenesses: William Blake with his heaven in a wild flower, universe in a grain of sand, and eternity in an hour. There are indeed many nations, and our own smaller identities – as individuals, groups, cities, nations – are also unique. So the man who wrote the *Peace Motets* is also the composer of the *Mediaeval Scottish Triptych*, which sets extremely patriotic words from the most violent period in Scotland's history – an epoch whose factual history the Hollywood horror of *Braveheart* did nothing whatever to elucidate, but whose violence it did at least faithfully depict.

The *Triptych* begins quietly, *lento, lamentoso e lagrimoso,* with the oldest surviving Scots poetic text, 'Qwhen Alexander our king wes dede', set to quiet, nobly diatonic music that erupts into a *fortissimo* appeal that Christ 'succoure Scotland'. The cycle ends *allegro moderato e maestoso,* with a rather more chromatic setting of John Barbour's great paean of praise to 'Fredome!' from his epic *The Bruce.* The very word is thundered like bells, first tolling (*rintoccante*) and then pealing (*scampanatamente*) in a choral ostinato *alla marcia,* with the text declaimed over it. The harmonic complexities resolve into a quiet blaze of D major, in a coda the organ-like sonorities of which affirm that freedom should be more highly prized than 'al the gold in warld that is'. The most chromatic and technically challenging music comes in the centrepiece, part of

[18] *Cf.* note 1, p. 177.

Blind Harry's epic *Wallace*, namely the eponymous hero's '*Lament for the Graham*'. *Andante doloroso*, the piece is pervaded with ostinato cries of 'Alace!', and at one point Stevenson actually writes that the text is to be sung *con compassione*. The melodies are of clearly Celtic inflection, particularly in the heartshaking central section, beginning with divided tenors and basses, who then fall silent for over 40 bars of women's voices recalling the dead warrior's human qualities. This expression of collective fellow-feeling ends 'Martyr thou art, for Scotlandis richt and me: I sall thee venge, or ellis therefore to de'. The word 'venge' is marked *fff*. Part of a serious pacifism is a love of justice, and the suffering of a tiny free nation at the hands of a huge invading power bent on destroying its identity is something still appallingly familiar at the beginning of this 21st century. The heroic and victorious struggle of mediaeval Scotland to retain its right to be itself – what John Barbour calls 'fre liking', i.e., self-determination – is seen by Stevenson as an inspiration to all minorities, and individuals, everywhere in their fight against oppression which would deny them the right to exist – and which thereby, of course, would diminish the diversity of oneness. And so this *Triptych*, composed in 1967, also received its premiere in that 1988 concert for peace.

   The *Mediaeval Scottish Triptych* spectacularly displays the sheer range of Stevenson's masterly handling of choral sonorities ranging from unison and solo melody through two- and three-part writing to densely clustered six-part *divisi* singing. Stevenson is much liked by singers, because he always writes gratefully – never instrumentally – for the voice. But that does not mean that the results are conventionally 'grateful to the ear'. Stevenson does not limit himself to the diatonic homophony of *Calbharaigh*, the *Christ Child's Lullaby* (another Gaelic work) or the *Peace Motets*. His concern for textual clarity does not mean an absence of polyphony, and his choral writing is often highly chromatic and fiercely dissonant. Much of Stevenson's choral writing requires performers of the highest calibre, for the effect of every chord, consonant or dissonant, is essential to the whole. I was lucky enough to observe the truth of this when working with the singers who premiered the madrigal cycle *Ballattis of Luve* (which deserves a mention in this chapter, since four solo voices – and lute – create a 'choral' sound). Long hours were spent getting all Stevenson's unexpected harmonic shifts to 'come right' – and there was no mistaking the moment when they did so, glowing, gleaming, shimmering, shining.

   Five intricately worked and layered lyrics of Mary Stuart's court poet, Alexander Scott[19] – 'It cumis you luvaris to be laill', 'Luve preysis but comparesone', Lo, quhat it is to lufe!', 'In June the jem of joy and geme' and 'Fra raige of youth the rink hes rune' – are organised as a life-cycle, a typically Stevensonian approach; the last song, celebrating the wisdom of age, recalls elements from its predecessors. The music evinces a detailed, positively loving attention to every nuance of these subtle texts, making the songs a source of constant surprise and delight. Stevenson here eschews polyphony almost entirely, capturing the lyricism of the verse in a melodious homophony that really does sing – appropriately, since most Renaissance lyric poetry was intended to be sung. The melodic lines convey Scott's texts with exemplary clarity; the complexity is in the iridescent harmony, changing from moment to moment, even word to word, quicksilver as the poet's wit. One of Stevenson's most perfectly realised conceptions, *Ballattis of Luve*, written in 1971, remains unheard in Scotland. The cycle was premiered in Luxembourg in March 1993 to mark its composer's 65th birthday.

His sixtieth-birthday year had been marked by the triumphant premiere by Cappella Nova of the most complex and technically challenging of all his unaccompanied vocal works, *In memoriam Robert Carver*, a fifteen-minute-long motet for twelve-part choir to a text by the present writer, inspired by Carver's Mass *Pater Creator omnium*. This is the only choral work other than *Calbharaigh* to be have been recorded, by Cappella Nova.[20] Here Stevenson deploys a dazzling array of choral techniques in music of often wellnigh overwhelming chromatic density and intricacy. In the concert programme I wrote:

> The poem *Domino Roberto Carwor* describes a specific event and my reactions to it. My words were a spontaneous expression of gratitude for the miracle of music, or rather, for the miraculous generosity of one creative artist – an individual who had the courage to share his personal gifts and visions with the rest of us less articulate folk, in what ultimately amounts to an act of solidarity with the future, an act of trust. No artist can know whether his or her work will survive.
>
> Robert Carver's music very nearly did not. The Abbey of Scone was burnt down by the 'rascal multitude' in 1559, quite probably before Carver's very eyes, for he lived on into his eighties, at least until 1568 –

---

[19] The poems can all be found in *Ballattis of Luve: The Scottish Courtly Love Lyric 1400–1570*, ed. J. MacQueen, Edinburgh University Press, Edinburgh, 1970. It was the publication of this book that inspired Stevenson to take up Scott's work.

[20] *Cf.* p. 191, note 3.

long enough to realise that his life's work had been rendered
meaningless. It had no place in the new Reformed Scotland, and
indeed there were no choirs to sing it. Even the choir stalls had been
smashed along with the statues and altars. Yet all this destruction had
happened before. In the 1540s the armies of Henry VIII of England
had annihilated all in their path, towns, villages, men, women and
children, churches, castles and abbeys. But in 1546, amid these
horrors and intimations of the uselessness of all endeavour, Carver
had composed his mass *Pater creator omnium.*

This commitment to meaningfulness and to hope, this refusal to
reject a sense of trust in those yet unborn, was something that over
the years I had found exemplified in Ronald Stevenson's life and
work. And so I sent him a copy of my 'meditation in winter', in
gratitude for all he had taught me about music and its power to heal
and reconcile. The persistence of the evil madness of war is no reason
to abandon a pacifist creed; lack of present recognition for work
achieved is no reason to abandon the generous activity of artistic
creation, and Stevenson has never ceased to create and to share. I was
nonetheless taken by surprise at his reaction to my poem – a twelve
part setting of my text for three choral groups conceived as a
monument to Scotland's greatest composer.

Stevenson had understood far better than their author the
deeper meaning of my words, for I had thought of the poem as a
subjective monologue, obsessively restricted to the first person
singular. But while the poem is certainly about an alienated
individual, 'this lanely saul' is singing the anonymous Gregorian
cantus firmus on which Robert Carver based his mass, while others
are singing around that *cantus firmus.* The poem is about *choral*
singing – communal music-making. What breaks down the barriers
of alienation in the poem is quite as much the shared experience of
singing *with others* as the music itself.

Stevenson begins *andante maestoso e sciomantico,* summoning up
the shade of the dead composer by turning the dative ('for sir
Robert Carver, canon of Scone') of the poem's title into a vocative,
the name 'Robert Carver!' resounding up through the full vocal
range of the three choral groups; and its owner's ecclesiastical
status is turned into a musical pun, in a freely heterophonic canon
that conjures up an image of a whispering crowd invoking the
sixteenth-century master. This is, of course, all very Busonian, in
perfect keeping with a text which itself is haunted by Busoni, who
once wrote that music acknowledges no border posts. For music
also transcends the frontiers of space and time; the crux of the
poem is literally a cross which comes at its centre: '*Roberte, frater mi,*
in thir derk dayis noo/I think on you, *o faber optime*'. The modern

individual breaks through the barriers of the alienated, fear-driven ego and addresses the 'best of craftsmen' across the centuries as Latin and Scots criss-cross in the rhetorical figure of *chiasmus*, and in an echo of the youthful Carver's great contemporary, the poet William Dunbar.[21]

As a poet himself, Stevenson is not one of those who simply put music to whatever is set in front of them. He has given a written account of some of the processes that take place when he sets words,[22] but the results make it quite audible that like Busoni and MacDiarmid, what he is seeking is a fully conscious synthesis of all the aspects of the human spirit. Every nuance and detail of a text elicits a response, and receives due attention. When the Carver poem refers to the speaker 'singing the *cantus firmus*', Stevenson inserts the text '*cantus firmus: PAX*'. And just as the Carver poem itself quotes from St John's Gospel, the text of Carver's mass and William Dunbar's 'Meditation in Winter', so the Carver Motet quotes the opening *symphonia* ('Easter Vespers') of Busoni's *Doktor Faust* (the music being on the word '*pax*'), and half-quotes that great musical statement of alienation and loneliness, Allegri's *Miserere*, a psalm of the winter of the soul. And inspired by the mediaeval practice of 'troping' which features in the text set by Carver in the mass *Pater creator omnium* (tropes cited in the poem), Stevenson added words in Latin to the text,[23] glossing the poem and creating a wondrous vision in sound of a literal 'family of God and man': *pater creator, mater creatrix, filius creator, filia creatrix OMNIS VITAE.*

In such a vision, the fear and alienation of the frightened individual must vanish. The Motet concludes with a rainbow-like chord spanning three-and-a-half octaves on the words 'the soondin colours o eternitie': the male choir sings in fifths, the mixed choir in fourths, and the female choir in thirds, as the music shimmers up from 'from the foundation of foundations in the depths to the dome of all domes in the heights' in a twelve-note chord, so that

[21] The reference is to 'In to thir dirk and drublie dayis', *Poems of William Dunbar*, ed. J. Kinsley, Oxford University Press, Oxford and London, 1958, p. 61.

[22] 'Composing a Song-Cycle', *Chapman*, No. 89–90 (1998), pp. 33–36.

[23] In *Ballattis of Luve*, Stevenson had troped Alexander Scott, pausing in a magical moment of 'Luve preysis but comparesone' to gloss the statement 'men and wemen, less and mair, ar cumd of Adame and of Eve' to ask, *sotto voce*, 'Quhen Adam delvit and Eve span, Quho wes than the gentleman?'

'there is nowhere an end, nowhere a hindrance'.[24] This ending recalls the opening of the work; the great circle of being is affirmed, and conflict and fear are shown to have been an illusion. In his unpublished biography of Busoni, Stevenson has written eloquently of 'The fear which Busoni so palpably expresses [....,] the fear of the destructive force of great knowledge wrongly used. We have all met this fear, between heartbeats, in moments of truth. Busoni's work is pervaded by it'.[25] That great knowledge, it seems to me, is the individual's consciousness of the finitude of his earthly existence. Truly to know that some day, one will no longer exist is to possess a knowledge great indeed, unlocking access to vast reserves of power and energy. What we do with it is up to us. We can use it with ruthless self-interest, desperately trying to squeeze yet more out of our ever-shortening span – or we can let it free us from the demands of finite self, and thus find a voice that can address others in ways that may aid them – and ourselves – to realise that 'stars and heart are one with another'.

Ronald Stevenson's choral voice speaks with magisterial power, and the message it conveys is one of reassurance. The braids *can* be bound together if awareness of mortality leads to the recognition that the one and the many need each other in order to be whole. There is no need to fear our brother's face: singing together in the first person singular is perfectly possible, and endlessly beneficial. All we need to do, of course, is to grow up and be oorsells – as MacDiarmid urged, adding with pragmatic realism that 'nae haurder job tae mortals hes been gien'.[26] Stevenson's superbly crafted choral music, light breaking from every bar and chord, celebrates the fact that humanity does have the spiritual drive to emerge from fear-filled darkness into the dawn.

[24] MacDiarmid's version of Busoni's essay, *Collected Poems*, Vol. ii, p. 874.

[25] An extract containing this excerpt was published in *Chapman*, Nos. 89–90 (1998), p. 85.

[26] *A Drunk Man Looks at the Thistle*, in Grieve and Aitken, *op. cit.*, Vol. I, p. 107.

VII
STEVENSON'S PIANISM
Harold Taylor

At the heart of Ronald Stevenson's pianism, as of all his creative work, lies a compelling urge to communicate, which manifests itself continually through composing, writing, talking or playing. These activities sometimes overlap, as when a recital becomes a lecture-recital or even an illustrated polemic on the decline of melody in the twentieth century, ending with a performance of his latest Edwardian ballad transcription. Ronald could never be accused of lapsing into good taste, nor has he ever belonged to that impotent body of musicians succinctly dismissed by Jorge Bolet as 'the *urtext* crowd', who exalt the letter at the expense of the spirit – if they are able to decide what the letter should be in the first place. I remember a performance given by Ronald of the D minor *Fantasy* of Mozart which had the real ring of truth – not simply 'with ornamentation', but with subtle melodic, rhythmic and even harmonic alterations such as Mozart himself might have improvised in performance. Certainly, Mozart could not have done any better in the little comic-opera finale, where with one single, masterly change of register, a duet was born and Zerlina and Don Giovanni danced momentarily before us. On a less rewarding occasion, Ronald had just discovered the delights of Soler's *Fandango*, which he insisted on sharing with his audience without proper preparation, punctuating the performance with shouts of 'olé!' whenever the going got rough.

Quite early in his career, and not unexpectedly, the passionate communicator fell under the spell of the greatest of all pianistic orators – Ignacy Jan Paderewski. Indeed, 'Paderewski Lives!' might be a good title for this essay, since Ronald has thoroughly assimilated the salient characteristics of Paderewski's playing – his histrionic use of timing and gesture, the rolling of chords, 'breaking' between the hands so that the bass is heard before the treble, and the aristocratic posato coupled with extensive use of the *una corda* pedal in *cantabile* passages. This is not only evident from his performances of the Polish master's own compositions, but also from his declamatory approach to such works as the *Ballade* in G minor of Chopin or Liszt's E major *Polonaise*, and throughout his performances of the Romantic repertoire in general.

To be a disciple of Paderewski in our present streamlined era might appear on the surface to be anachronistic, even obscurantist. Ronald has argued that he is not behind the times but ahead of

Joseph Stones, Harold Taylor and Stevenson
at the Bromsgrove Festival, 1965

them: he believes that those very aspects of Paderewski's art which
modern pianism rejects are part and parcel of the lost tradition of
nineteenth-century piano-playing which the musicologists have yet
to re-discover. He also points out that the 'woolliness' of most
modern grand pianos, to which modern ears are accustomed,
positively encourages the proliferation of characterless performances, to which modern audiences are also unfortunately condi-
tioned. Certainly, the *una corda* tone of most modern pianos leaves
much to be desired compared with that of Paderewski's favourite
hard-hammered Erard.

On 'breaking' between the hands, it is noteworthy that the
greatest Romantic pianist of recent times, Vladimir Horowitz
(whose own piano dated from World War I), often sounded the
treble before the bass in *cantabile* playing. Both pianists are devotees
of *bel canto*, but whereas Ronald finds deep satisfaction in recordings by Caruso and McCormack, Horowitz was known to be more
interested in recordings by the female singers of the Golden Age.
Perhaps these preferences account for the light, 'feminine' quality
of much of Horowitz's lyricism, while to my ear there is always a
strong 'masculine' feeling about Ronald's playing. In any case, to
be a Romantic pianist worthy of the name demands first and
foremost, unswerving dedication to the cause of making the piano
'sing'. For this and other reasons, Ronald was fortunate in having
Iso Elinson as his professor at the Royal Manchester College of

'Paderewski Lives!' – Stevenson (aged 60 in the right-hand photograph)
shares some salient characteristics with Paderewski's playing –
and a striking physical similarity

Music. Moreover, Elinson believed that to train the fingers to 'sing' polyphonically, as in the great fugues from the '48', was the finest technical and musical foundation for any pianist; Ronald's contrapuntal clarity, even in passages of massive sonority, has always been one of his real strengths.

Busoni, whose *Klavierübung* Ronald copied out meticulously by hand as a student, has been another major influence. Busoni widened Ronald's technical horizons in composing as well as playing; I believe that his influence is the main reason that Ronald is as much at home with three pedals, 'six fingers'[1] and 'three hands'[2] as most pianists are with the more usual numbers. He has certainly followed Busoni's precept that 'the acquirement of a technique is nothing else than the fitting of a given difficulty to one's own capacities'.[3] Ronald often re-writes parts of works which he is studying, not simply to make them feel right for his own

[1] Increasing the number of notes available in one hand position by the use of the same finger on adjacent keys.

[2] Dividing melody, bass and accompaniment between the hands, using the sustaining pedal to give the illusion that each part is being played by a separate hand.

[3] *The Essence of Music and Other Papers*, p. 94.

hands, but to improve the 'orchestration'. For instance, he may transfer melody notes from the right hand to the left to give more expressive power, because the thumb and index fingers of the left hand are naturally stronger than the outer fingers of the right hand. Or he may divide a solo passage between the hands so that he can 'point up' its dynamic contours by creating them naturally from his playing gestures.

The finest testament to Ronald's pianism is his own *Passacaglia on DSCH* – a marvellous compendium of all that makes him 'tick'. In spite of the transcendental nature of its material and the vastness of its canvas, the *Passacaglia* is not at all difficult to play for the most part, because it lies so well beneath the hands. Any reasonably fluent pianist who is prepared to liberate himself from conventional finger patterns (Ronald's favourite 12345, 12345 fingering is essential for many passages) and to give some time to the study of 'three-handed' playing, will find it very rewarding to work through and gain a splendid insight into Ronald's pianistic thinking.

Of course there are immense difficulties in actually giving a *performance* of the *Passacaglia* – so immense that to the best of my knowledge, only John Ogdon, Raymond Clarke, Murray McLachlan and Mark Gasser, other than the composer, have so far taken up the

*In over forty years Stevenson's approach to the keyboard has remained
essentially unchanged: left, aged fifteen, when he was répétiteur with the
Blackburn Ballet Company, and above, in 1985, 42 years later,
in rehearsal at the Shanghai Conservatory*

challenge. Consider some of the requirements: uninterrupted
concentration for one-and-a-quarter hours; an enormous dynamic
range; the ability to control gradations of tone over very long spans,
without which the interpretation can never match the size of the
work; a sense of climax, together with the rare quality of a feeling
for narrative; an orchestral range of tone-colour. Above all, the
performer must have the breadth of culture and emotional
response to encompass a myriad of styles – from Schubertian
charm to Shostakovichian irony, from polonaise to pibroch, from
coolly classical to wildly romantic, the list is endless. He must create
a whole world, without the benefit of Mahler's orchestra. Those of
us who have heard this world warmed into life by Ronald's
incandescent playing can never have any doubts about his pianistic
stature – he is a giant.

How does he do it? Physically, he is no giant, being of middling
height, slightly built, with no ox-like shoulders nor keyboard-
swallowing hands. But his hands give an immediate impression of
strength combined with sensitivity. The palms are unusually broad
and muscular; the fingers pale, slightly tapering and well-fleshed
but not chubby. He does not have the advantages of a long thumb

Stevenson at the Shanghai Conservatory in 1985, demonstrating
the importance of having the chord prepared in the fingers
before bringing the hands to the keyboard

or fifth finger, but these are compensated for by the width of the
palms. (I do not wish to suggest that Ronald's strength lies in the
palms of his hands – like that of any other performer, it lies in his
capacity for 'putting his back into it'.)

Does he use bent fingers or flat fingers? Arm-weight? Fore-arm
rotation? Fixation? One can only answer this kind of question by
pointing out that no pianist worth his salt will limit himself to any
single method. He will adopt the gesture which he feels to be right
for himself in response to the demands of the music at any given
moment. Thus Ronald is not averse to playing with his fist if need
be, nor to following Percy Grainger's directive to play with 'stiff
fingers, stiff wrists and stiff elbows' when appropriate, but I have
never seen him go to the other extreme of hyperactive, floppy
playing. Generally he tends to feel his way around the keyboard
with clinging rather than thrusting fingers, with knuckles, wrist and
forearm kept in the same horizontal plane. He is fundamentally the
sort of pianist who could play all his passage work with a coin

balanced on the back of the hand, as some teachers of the 'old school' used to advocate. The lack of 'break' at the wrist arises because Ronald subtends a 'one-piece' arm with no acute angle or 'break' at the elbow. He also uses the arm in one piece for massive chords, rotary movements and shaking octaves 'out of his sleeve' in the time-honoured Lisztian manner. In other words, he gives it to us 'straight from the shoulder', which, knowing Ronald, is exactly what we might expect.

Unfortunately, the outward and visible manifestations of an artist's personal playing style give very little indication of the real, hidden nature of piano technique, which as Busoni rightly says, 'has its seat in the brain, and is composed of geometry – an estimation of distance – and wise co-ordination'.[4] On the subject of geometry, Ronald has one particular stratagem which deserves mention, and which curiously enough, I have not seen used by any other pianist except Horowitz. I can best describe it as the 'bottom shift' technique, whereby the whole body is displaced laterally along the piano bench – albeit only a few inches, but sufficient to remove the awkwardness from certain passages by the simple alteration of the angle of incidence. For an example of 'bottom shift' to the bass side, I think of the march-like section of Chopin's *Impromptu* in F sharp with its leaping left-hand octaves; on the treble side, anyone can discover for themselves how much easier the opening of *La Campanella* becomes after a shift to the right.

Finally, a note on Ronald's programmes and repertoire. As a piano composer himself, who is also a keen explorer of the whole realm of literature for the instrument, he has no time whatsoever for the 'three or four major works' type of programme solemnly paraded by too many of his 'distinguished' contemporaries and those who ape them. When one also considers his passionate interest in the art of transcription – much derided by cultural mandarins and therefore neglected by career-minded concert pianists – it is not surprising that he produces a type of mixed recital programme which can only be described as 'Stevensonian'. He likes best to devise programmes to suit different occasions. I have two in front of me as I write. One is for an intimate lunch-hour recital, beginning with two Schubert *Moments Musicaux* and ending with three *Essays in the Modes* by John Foulds, taking in short pieces by Grieg, Stevenson and Medtner on the way. The other, quite extraordinary, programme is for a full evening's recital devoted to

[4] *Ibid.*, p. 80.

Two piano pioneers: Stevenson in discussion with Peter Jacobs
in the Green Room of the Wigmore Hall, during the recording sessions
for Grainger and Scotland, *1985 (photograph by Chris Rice)*

the theme of 'Faust in Music'. It consists entirely of transcriptions and operatic fantasias.[5]

There are certain composers I always associate with Ronald's recitals: Alan Bush, Percy Grainger, Paderewski, Grieg, Gershwin. Some of their works, such as the splendid Sonata, Op. 71, of Alan Bush, or Grainger's *Rosenkavalier Ramble*, he has made so particularly his own that I never expect them to be better played. Like most other composers in Ronald's repertoire, they not only care for the piano and write for it sympathetically, they are friendly composers; they compose 'with notes related to people', to borrow a phrase from one of Ronald's newspaper articles. This phrase also brings the wheel of this chapter full circle, for 'notes related to people' encapsulates Ronald's own creed as performer and composer. To be a 'passionate communicator' is synonymous with being an educator. During the past forty years, I have learnt so

---

[5] *Cf.* also pp. 248 and 301. –ED.

much from Ronald's playing – about the repertoire, about technical possibilities, about piano tone, of which he is one of the masters – that I cannot imagine my musical life without him. I have also been entertained and occasionally exasperated but, above all, I have often been very much moved. One cannot wish more than that from any artist.

VIII
EIGHT PORTRAITS
Colin Wilson

John Ogdon

Harry Winstanley

Walter Hartley

John Guthrie

Albert Wullschleger

Manfred Gordon

Alan Bold

Colin Wilson

Ronald Stevenson turned up at our house in the summer of 1966. He had read my book on music, *Brandy of the Damned,* and wanted to argue. And that is precisely what he did, almost non-stop, for the next two days. Oddly enough, this was not an exhausting experience, for the vitality of his mind and the astonishing breadth of his knowledge kept me in a permanent state of over-stimulation – a condition we both endeavoured to keep under control through the consumption of large quantities of wine and other soothing beverages. He also played and sang for me – on our out-of-tune piano – two whole song-cycles (of Blake and MacDiarmid), which I recorded on tape.

Talking about it afterwards to another musician friend – Malcolm Arnold – I commented that there is a quality in Stevenson's mind that reminds me of Bernard Shaw. And the more I think about it, the more I feel that the comparison pinpoints some essential quality of Stevenson's volcanic creativity.

To begin with, of course, he *can* be infuriating. Try, for example, opening his *Western Music* at the chapter on the twentieth century,[1] in which he devotes two-and-a-half pages to jazz and half-a-page to Bob Dylan, while most of the major composers – from Sibelius to Stravinsky – are lucky if they get three lines. The unprepared reader will conclude that Stevenson has allowed his Marxism to distort his perspectives, and that he is only interested in composers who can be classified as nationalists or as revolutionaries. Yet if the reader can restrain the impulse to hurl the book across the room, and will turn back to the beginning, he will soon find himself prepared to forgive everything. For Stevenson is obviously a man who knows too much about too many things to be dismissed as a narrow-minded leftist. He is equally at home talking about the troubadors, French mystical sects of the Middle Ages, the bronzework of the Vikings, the difference between St Peter's and York Minster, and the influence of Galileo's cosmology on the music of Monteverdi. His

---

[1] *Op. cit.*, pp. 166–96, esp. pp. 170–73 and 193.

mind darts impatiently from age to age – so that he describes the
quality of Scarlatti's music by referring to Lorca's essay on the
duende – the demon of inspiration. In one of his most provocative
pages[2] he discusses Mozart as a social revolutionary – then disarms
all criticism by quoting E. J. Dent on Mozart to precisely this effect.
Of all my books on music, this is the one I most enjoy browsing
through on a winter evening. And this is because Stevenson's
comments keep me jumping to my feet to put on recordings of the
music. It is the sheer breadth of his sympathy that excites me. In
short, his mind itself has a quality I associate with great music.

This may, of course, be the reason that he is relatively
underestimated at the present. It would be easier if we could pin
him down as a serialist or neo-classicist or social realist or
experimentalist. But his finest works quite simply decline to be
pigeonholed. When I first bought the Ogdon recording of the
Passacaglia on DSCH, my first impression was that it was a rather
'modern' and difficult piece of music. But I found it frustrating
having to get up twice to change sides – since it spread over three
sides of a two-record set. I decided to transfer it on to tape, so I
could play it straight through. And the first time I played the tape, I
realised that I had stumbled on the right way to grasp its essential
quality. It is a single piece of argument, one enormous arch, like
the Sydney harbour bridge. It does not require listening accompanied by the record sleeve to remind us that we are listening to the
'Pibroch', or 'Glimpse of a War Vision' or the 'Tribute to Bach'.
The music says it all; it speaks its own language. It contains some of
the most dramatic and electrifying pages in the literature of the
piano since Liszt; but I would not like to play these in isolation.
They make their effect as a part of the total argument, which
resembles a long, closely reasoned speech. And another great piano
work, the *Prelude, Fugue and Fantasy on Busoni's 'Faust'*, has much the
same effect. I was lucky enough to record this piece from a
broadcast some years ago, together with the *Peter Grimes Fantasy* and
the *Passacaglia* – all played by Stevenson.[3] (I prefer Stevenson's own
playing of the Passacaglia to Ogdon's; the latter is more brilliant,
the former more involved and committed.) The Busoni Fantasy has
become my own favourite of all Stevenson's work.

When I listen to the big piano works – including the Second
Piano Concerto – I suddenly become aware of the problem of an

---

[2] *Ibid.*, p. 130.

[3] Broadcast on BBC Radio 3 on 17 September 1976.

artist of Stevenson's stature in the opening years of the 21st century. His own analysis – in the final chapter of *Western Music* – is that 'Western culture is [...] like a worked mine. Europe is tired'.[4] This is, of course, true, but it is perhaps taking too lofty a view of the situation. What happened is that the art and philosophy of Europe swung from one extreme to another – from a bird's eye view to a worm's eye view. The great Victorians had a breadth and generosity of intellect that Stevenson shares: it is the most obvious quality of Ruskin, Carlyle, Spencer, George Eliot, T. H. Huxley, William Morris. Shaw and Wells possessed it too. The artists and writers of the early twentieth century felt they could no longer compete on this level: it would be difficult to be more brilliant than Shaw, more encyclopaedic than Wells, more comprehensive than Tolstoy, more universal than Wagner. The result was a reaction into experiment-alism, a search for novelty that produced Schoenberg and Picasso, Brancusi and Gertrude Stein, Marinetti and Wittgenstein. It was as if the artists and thinkers had decided they were tired of looking at distant stars through telescopes and preferred to study a piece of cheese through a microscope.

It is easier for a writer or a thinker to keep 'abreast of his times' than for a painter or musician. The writer has only to observe what is going on around him and reflect upon it. If he also has a sense of the past – as both Wells and Eliot had – then he has all the necessary equipment to produce work that will be relevant to his contemporaries. But for the composer it is more difficult. He may possess a firm sense of the past – as Stevenson does – but he cannot use it as a foundation for his own work. He cannot write as though Schoenberg and Stravinsky and Hindemith had never existed. The unfortunate composer of today cannot write as though Boulez, Stockhausen and John Cage had never existed.

I think this helps to explain why Stevenson pays so much attention to 'outsider' figures like Sorabji, Brian and van Dieren, as well as currently unfashionable composers like Busoni and Medtner. They firmly declined to absorb the requisite 'modern influences' and went their own way. The result has been artistic isolation – an isolation that Sorabji accepted as inevitable, and willingly embraced. Stevenson obviously admires their courage and learns from their example; yet he has no desire to retreat into the artistic wilderness. He sees the alternative in another great tradition: of nationalism and 'social realism'. He notes that national

[4] *Op. cit.*, p. 196.

With Alan Bush in 1974 (photograph by John Humphreys)

composers like Szymanowski, Sibelius, Nielsen (whose Fifth Symphony he regards as the greatest of the past century), Janáček and Enescu have been able to create major works without straining to be modernistic (Shostakovich is an even more striking example). This explains why Stevenson has apparently turned his back on his Busoni period,[5] and decided that his destiny as a composer is bound up with Scotland. In an article on Stevenson in 1968,[6] Ateş Orga expressed misgivings, commenting that since other Scottish

[5] It is not strictly correct to suggest that Stevenson turned his back on Busoni. Undoubtedly his contacts with Grainger – himself a Busoni pupil – liberated him from the more intellectual concepts in music born of Busonian ideals (as expressed by Busoni in his *New Aesthetic*, and by Stevenson in *A 20th Century Music Diary*); but one can quite readily draw a parallel between the 'plein air' music of Grainger and the glorious 'Bluebird's Song' in Busoni's *Indian Diary*. The Red Indian was a subject that interested Busoni and Grainger and Stevenson, who kept up a correspondence with the composer Louis Ballard (Hunka No Zhe), whose tribal origins are Sioux and Cherokee. It should be noticed that Stevenson's transcription of Grainger's *Hill Song* No. 1 predates the *Passacaglia*. Busoni himself gave evidence of a nationalistic element in his make-up: the title page of the Piano Concerto is printed in Italian, with Busoni styling himself as 'da Empoli'. –ED.

[6] *Cf.* p. 49, note 9.

composers have adopted more universal means of expression, it seemed possible that Stevenson was fighting a losing battle. But this, surely, depends on Stevenson himself. No artist creates major works out of theories, but out of his own compulsion to express himself. And this, fortunately, is something Stevenson has never found difficult.

It also explains some of the contradictions – or, at least, puzzling inconsistencies – in his outlook. I, for example, find it very odd that he seems to regard Schoenberg with admiration. Schoenberg was *non grata* in Soviet Russia, and his intense subjectivity – at times amounting to downright self-pity – has made him one of the major disintegrative influences on modern music. Ernest Ansermet wrote a book (accompanied by a gramophone record) explaining why he felt that serialism was simply an intellectual and artistic mistake, a creative dead-end.[7] His basic argument was that harmony and melody appeal to an intuitive sense of meaning in the listener, and that to break them up arbitrarily is like jumbling up the words and altering the punctuation in a sentence. Stevenson's own preference for melody makes it clear that he shares this view. Yet he has the intellectual generosity to recognise the daring of Schoenberg's conception and to salute him as a master. Again, I recall Stevenson singing with deep feeling his own setting of MacDiarmid's poem about a 'golden lyric', with its line 'Better a'e gowden lyric, than anything else ava'.[8] In Russia, I suspect that MacDiarmid's highly subjective sentiment would have landed him in the Gulag Archipelago, for no social realist has any doubt that a golden lyric was very low on that society's list of priorities. But MacDiarmid was himself too massive an intellect to be a slave to any 'ism', including Marxism. His *Hymns to Lenin* reveal a mind that belongs to the great humanistic tradition that runs from Rabelais and Montaigne to Ruskin and Morris. (I recall an evening in his cottage in Biggar when there were several other Scots writers present, and the subject of Marxism came up. 'I think it's bloody rubbish', said one well-known bard scornfully. I expected to see MacDiarmid order him out of the house, but he merely smiled sympathetically and refilled his guest's glass. He was too big a man to place political formulae above friendship.) Stevenson himself is as magnificently subjective

---

[7] *Les Fondements de la Musique dans la Conscience Humaine*, La Baconnière, Neuchâtel, 1961; the accompanying record, *What Everyone Should Know about Music*, was issued by Decca in 1967.

[8] Grieve and Aitken, *op. cit.*, Vol. 1, p. 265; *cf.* also p. 183, above.

a composer as any of the nineteenth century. Then how can he accept the cheerless formulae of socialist realism?[9] He would reply – or I will reply for him – with Walt Whitman's 'I contain multitudes'.

Colin Scott-Sutherland has called Stevenson 'an aristocrat of the mind'.[10] The description seems to me accurate. This quality is one he shares with MacDiarmid and James Joyce, and it emerges clearly in the essay he wrote for the MacDiarmid *Festschrift*: 'MacDiarmid, Joyce and Busoni'.[11] Rereading it before I wrote this essay reminds me of something that I tend to forget whenever I am out of Scotland: that the Scots are the 'cleverest' people in the world. I apologise for the adjective, but it is the only one that fits. Again and again I have observed in Scotland this quality of swift, intuitive intelligence, the ability to leap two steps ahead of you in a discussion. Its negative side, unfortunately, is a tendency to lack the sheer persistence required to create works of art or literature, which explains why I have met more unpublished geniuses in Scotland than anywhere else. Again, Stevenson is lucky in having a very English streak of doggedness in his nature, which explains the considerable length of the list of his works. But the sheer breadth of his intellectual sympathies underlines his problem as a Scottish artist. The few years I spent living in London and mixing in 'literary' circles made me aware that a passion for ideas is no longer a characteristic of the British intelligentsia. But it still exists in abundance in Scotland, as it must have done in the London of Ruskin and Carlyle. In this sense, Stevenson is almost a Victorian. Indeed, his qualities are those that would have ensured worldwide celebrity in the age of Liszt and Thalberg – or even of Busoni. He is, as Scott-Sutherland points out,[12] one of the few composer-pianists in Great Britain, and the only one in Scotland. There is a tremendous virtuoso quality in his playing. So he belongs to a broader, greater, more generous tradition than the one that dominated the art and music of the late twentieth century. This

[9] Stevenson would certainly not accept those 'cheerless formulae' if they were limited to a 'kitchen-sink', Zola-esque expression of realism. But he is fully in accord with Maxim Gorki's concept (that of an artist, not a bureaucrat) of socialist realism: *cf.* his *Western Music*, pp. 180–82, and his essay on Shostakovich's piano music in Norris (ed.), *op. cit.*, pp. 97–100. –ED.

[10] In *British Music Now*, p. 40.

[11] K. D. Duval and Sydney Goodsir Smith (eds.), *MacDiarmid: A Festschrift*, Duval, Edinburgh, 1962, pp. 141–54.

[12] In 'The Music of Ronald Stevenson', *loc. cit.*

means that – although it will embarrass him to have it said – he belongs to the tradition of 'outsiders' who are two sizes too big for their own age. Baudelaire describes them in 'The Albatross':

> Le poète est semblable au prince des nuées
> Qui hante la tempête et se rit de l'archer;
> Exilé sur le sol au milieu des huées,
> Ses ailes de géant l'empêchent de marcher.

But to speak of 'giant's wings' that prevent the poet from walking is to put it too pessimistically. He is as well-adapted for survival as anyone. What he cannot hope is to strike that fashionable chord that will convince everyone that this is the art of tomorrow. Sibelius expressed the same feeling when he said gloomily that most modern musicians offered their audience cocktails, and he offered cold water. Stevenson's situation in the second half of the twentieth century and since has much in common with Sibelius' in the first. But Sibelius' tendency to austerity led to *Tapiola* and the Seventh Symphony, then to silence. Stevenson has chosen a solution that is equally honest, and rather more interesting: to attempt to create a music that is connected to the mainsprings of humanity. He has also decided – rather more controversially – that 'Western art must look to the East'.[13] And I find this rather more difficult to accept. The Second Piano Concerto, *The Continents*, strikes me as a moving and exciting piece of music, in the same tradition as the Ravel and Gershwin concertos. But the various Chinese and African sounds do not seem to me to be an essential part of its texture: they seem to be merely a kind of flavouring, like the Chinese chords in Saint-Saëns' *La Princesse jaune* or Puccini's *Turandot*. Neither am I convinced when Stevenson discusses various works showing 'Eastern' influence in the final chapter of *Western Music*.[14] Various *danses orientales* and Indian fantasias do not strike me as being any more 'universal' than Gilbert and Sullivan's *Mikado*. Mozart's Turkish march is certainly no more universal than *The Marriage of Figaro*; and Messaien's *Turangalîla* Symphony will probably strike posterity as far less important than his *Vingt Regards sur l'Enfant Jésus*. This, I suspect, is in Stevenson a false line of reasoning. Yet if false reasoning it is, it has produced a fine piano concerto. On the other hand, the *Passacaglia on DSCH* seems to me to show precisely where Stevenson's strength lies. The very idea of

[13] *Western Music*, p. 197.

[14] *Ibid.*, pp. 198 *et seq.*

Townfoot House
West Linton
Peeblesshire
Scotland
21.9.83

Carissimo Martinus!

Your two mailing-tubes ~ quite apart from their contents (of which more anon) ~ have provided the wherewithal to realise a minor project of mine: namely, to reconstruct Percy Grainger's piano-roller mechanism, for which these artefacts are indispensable. Music is pasted on to huge sheets of brown-paper, rolled round the mailing-tubes inside a shallow wooden box that rests on top of the piano. A cable is attached to a roller-skate which is itself attached to the left pedal. A rapid skating motion of the left foot sets the music rolling. At one fell swoop (or skate) the services of page-turner are rendered redundant! In a letter to me, Grainger claimed "This roller makes the perfect concert. Concerts are attended by music-lovers and snobs and prigs. The music-lovers enjoy the music-making and the snobs and prigs enjoy watching the music-roller."

One day Bob's Sonata for 2 pianos may resound to a reading from the very mailing tubes which brought them here!

In 1983 Martin Anderson sent Stevenson (for performance with his duo-partner Lawrence Glover) a photocopy of Robert Simpson's Sonata for Two Pianos, *each part wrapped in a cardboard tube; this is part of Stevenson's reply.*

creating a work along the lines of Busoni's *Fantasia Contrappuntistica* (and Sorabji's *Opus Clavicembalisticum*) seemed anachronistic in 1960 (when it was begun). Humphrey Searle was an admirer of Liszt; but he never attempted to write Lisztian music. Stevenson took the bit between his teeth and wrote this magnificent Lisztian-Busonian structure, without concerning himself with anything but his own artistic compulsion. The result is a masterpiece. The same is true of his Busoni *Fantasy*. I am reminded of Wagner's favourite story, of how the chapter of Cologne cathedral said to the architect: 'Build me a cathedral so vast that people of the future will say the chapter must have been insane to think of such a thing'. Alan Bush wrote, after hearing the *Passacaglia*: 'I was so carried away that I could scarcely speak at all'.[15] It is a proof that if an artist dares to pour all his energy and conviction into a masterwork, the result will triumph on its own terms. Stevenson is a major composer because he is one of the very few who possesses that kind of courage.

---

[15] In a letter to the composer, quoted in *Composer*, Autumn 1964.

John Ogdon

My first memory of Ronald Stevenson is of hearing him practise the Busoni Piano Concerto at the Royal Manchester College of Music. It was my first acquaintance with this marvellous piece, and Ronald's enthusiasm for Busoni sparked off for me a deep love for the Busoni tradition, including in my case a short period of study with Egon Petri.

As a pianist Ronald at first seemed most akin, among Busoni pupils, to Michael von Zadora,[1] and adopted a piano-playing style of a rather delicate, crystal-like clarity, not unlike Michelangeli's, with a singing, *bel canto* formation of melody. I had the immense pleasure of visiting Ronald many times between 1956 and 1970 for the West Linton Musical Society used to present a charming series of concerts with which Ronald helped, and which I was pleased to attend.

Ronald's enthusiasms at that time included the poetry of Whitman, Thomas Wolfe's *Look Homeward, Angel* and Sir Compton Mackenzie's novel *Sinister Street* (Ronald introduced me to Sir Compton, who founded *Gramophone* magazine and who also introduced Siamese cats into England). He was much helped at this time by Sir Adrian Boult and thoroughly taught by Iso Elinson at the Royal Manchester College, then under the guidance of Robert Forbes, as Principal, who admired Ronald's work very much. Around this time Ronald's excellent *First Sonatina* won a composition prize in his native Blackburn.

Regarding Ronald Stevenson as a composer, I find myself returning with profound admiration to his astonishing mastery of writing for the piano. To have continued the Liszt-Busoni tradition of the operatic fantasia with his *Prelude, Fugue and Fantasy* on Busoni's 'Faust', and his *Peter Grimes Fantasy*, and with such a truly gentle poetry, is really quite wonderful. John K. Boulton, writing in the *Hallé* magazine, found Ronald's monumental *Passacaglia on*

---

[1] Michael von Zadora (1882–1946) was one of Busoni's favourite students; he also composed under the pseudonym Pietro Amadis. –ED.

Thirty years of friendship: John Ogdon with Ronald and Marjorie
Stevenson at home in West Linton in 1959 (photograph
by Helmut Petzsch) and receiving Stevenson's thanks after playing
in his sixtieth-birthday concert at the Wigmore Hall in 1988

DSCH close in idiom to Bartók, and I often feel this to be very true –
also as, for instance, in his *A Wheen Tunes for Bairns tae Spiel.*

I noticed in the *Passacaglia* that he seemed to sketch different
parts separately and I deduced that he might have interleaved them
in a somewhat unexpected order. The triple fugue in the
Passacaglia sparks off with a truly Rachmaninov-like vigour and
incandescence, and Ronald attributes his knowledge of counterpoint to studying the writings of the famous counterpoint teacher
J. J. Fux. Ronald's researches into the music of Busoni and Percy
Grainger have been complemented by his interest in the lesser-
known works of Geirr Tveitt, Anton Rubinstein, and by a keen
interest in jazz idioms, notably those of Gershwin and Charlie
Mingus; and, as a *littérateur,* his keen interest and enthusiasm for
James Joyce and Edward Gordon Craig, frequently held me
spellbound when I was a student. His eclecticism and enthusiasm
can only augur well for his and our musical fibre.

Harry Winstanley

Ronald Stevenson first entered my consciousness during a performance of his First Piano Concerto which was given by John Ogdon with the Scottish National Orchestra. I had not gone to this concert to hear that particular work, but the then rarely heard Ravel left-hand concerto. Such was the impact made on me by Ronald's work that for once the Ravel failed to work its magic on me.

It was a few years later, when I was again settled in Edinburgh, that I heard of the Musical Appreciation Classes which Ronald gave under the auspices of the Workers' Educational Association. These classes, for reasons of space, were restricted to fifty students (auditors might be a better description, for there is little of the pedagogue about the lecturer) and were always heavily over-subscribed; so much so, that to ensure a place, it was essential to arrive early on the first evening of enrolment, and to be quick off the mark on arrival – failure to move with ruthless single-mindedness invariably resulted in learning the class was complete by the time the necessary forms were filled in and presented. This I learned to my cost at my first attempt.

There was no doubt that the popularity of those classes was due to Ronald's brilliance as a communicator and to his generosity with his illustrations at the piano. Ronald did not like *that* piano, which had done yeoman service for generations of piano teachers and pupils, but it did its best for him, and sounded just right on at least one occasion, when he leant inside to play and strum Henry Cowell's weird *Banshee*.

Billed as giving a background to concerts and opera being presented in Edinburgh during the winter season, these talks no more concentrated on the work in question than a symphony concentrates on one theme or remains in one key.

If I may further exploit this analogy, the tuning-up started when the faithful Mr Bathgate removed the cover from the piano. With most of the audience assembled (like a performance of *The Ring*, where by the fourth evening, everyone knows everyone else, their likes and dislikes), Ronald would arrive straight from the West

Linton bus like a breath of fresh country air, heavily coated, scarved, with his Sandeman's black hat, and overloaded briefcase. There would be a brief pause while the outer garments were discarded and the briefcase pitilessly disgorged during which there would be a flurry of conversation, the audience bringing up points which had come up the previous week, and about which they had been thinking, while Ronald would embroider on one or two digressions he had made. The evening would then come to a kind of order and the first theme announced – the subject of the talk; but a second theme would quickly follow and the development section would lead us into exotic keys far removed from the original. Something strange would then happen, for there would be audience participation. And this is what, I think, Ronald loved about these classes, the feed-back: he would make a statement so outrageous that even the douce Edinburgher, that pillar of phlegmatic rectitude and reticence, was sufficiently enlivened to make a rejoinder, whereupon the class became totally involved in the performance. Eventually, Ronald would remember the first statement and introduce the coda to bring the movement to an end.

Like a Mahler symphony, the talks embraced the world: primarily they concerned music, but the sister arts and their practitioners were never ignored; there could be a few words about Whitman on slang, or Gordon Craig's theories on the theatre or perhaps Hugh MacDiarmid's rumbustious disinclination to toe any line (in which Ronald resembles his old friend, though without the aggressiveness).

After the classes, as he stuffed music, books, records and other paraphernalia into that expanding briefcase – hurriedly, for he was ever running late (he must have been the caretaker's least popular lecturer) – he would enlarge on points raised by the handful of his class grouped around him. It was at this time, after the first class I attended, that I asked him a question about Godowsky, whereupon he suggested that he could answer it best if my wife and I would accompany him down to his bus stop. So we walked the path, he staggering under the load of that case, filling and lighting his pipe while he spoke. His conversation was typical, for instead of pontificating (which I later discovered was not his style), he asked in turn of my wife and me if we played the piano, and of me just how I had become interested in Godowsky. In this manner he was able to gauge the nature of my interest and just how technical he could be with his answer. Ever since then (and that was some years ago) there has come my way from him a steady stream of music,

Stevenson in 1989, when he was one of the orchestral pianists
in the 'imaginary ballet' The Warriors *of his pen-friend Percy Grainger*
(photograph courtesy of The Birmingham Post)

cuttings and photocopies on Godowsky. And not only that: he has opened my ears to a new world of music by virtue of his wide-ranging enthusiasms. Paderewski, for instance, is now as dear to me a composer as he is a pianist; the holy trinity of Bach, Beethoven and Brahms has been enlarged by the inclusion of Busoni, and a fresh trinity of Godowsky, Gershwin and Grainger canonised. The world of pianism has had ever fresh aspects imposed on it by his learning, for to him it is a developing art, not something which finished with Liszt, but was developed further by Busoni, Godowsky and Grainger (for whose present renaissance he is largely

With the composer David Dorward and conductor Elgar Howarth,
at the time of Stevenson's performance of Dorward's
Piano Concerto in Glasgow, 1980

responsible), whose ideas and notation he enlarges upon, adding
his own innovations.

It is not only the secret of his pianism which I would like to wrest
from Ronald, but his energy, because, like all artists of stature, he is
a man of prodigious energy. Elsewhere in this volume can be seen
his enormous output: the music written, the occasional writings
(and he writes uncommon well), and his books, *Western Music* and
the staggeringly comprehensive, imaginative study of Busoni, as
yet unpublished.[1] But it does not stop there, for there is his vast
correspondence and his involvement in the projects of friends,
whether they be engaged in research on Van Dieren, Sorabji, Liszt
or Gershwin; his readiness to help and give his time is as generous
as his commitment is absolute. Again, there is his genuine love of
Scotland's indigenous culture: his programmes for the BBC on the
pibroch and the clarsach were so deeply researched and comprehensive that a book on each subject should have resulted. His
efforts on Scottish music have not been confined to folk sources as
his work on behalf of such figures as Francis George Scott, Eugen

---

[1] *Cf.* p. 23; his *Busoni: Aspects of a Genius* (*cf.* p. 23, note 5) is an edited collection of
radio broadcasts, essays, articles and other material.

d'Albert and Ronald Center shows. Living composers, too, have benefited from his advocacy: those who heard his performance of David Dorward's Piano Concerto at one of the Scottish National Orchestra's Musica Nova concerts in 1980 will testify that this was no run-through of the work, but a deeply thought-out performance.

His collection of music is enormous and catholic in its taste (this latter word he himself uses to good effect when he says that 'music is being strangled by good taste'). He has boxes underneath his piano literally stuffed with music and albums where Ethelbert Nevin might be found next to Brahms' transcriptions, Coleridge-Taylor with Scott Joplin (his filing system, as it is somewhat laughingly called, is rather whimsical) or Tcherepnin with York Bowen. Ronald has played them all, with his composer's eyes and ears ever on the alert. Typically, he keeps his criticisms to himself, but is ever ready to praise with his quick enthusiasm.

His literary tastes are equally catholic, and he is as ready to quote Harpo Marx as Karl. But I suspect his deepest affection is reserved for poetry, as might be expected from his large output of songs in which he mirrors words and images so lovingly.

He has a tolerably good conceit of himself but is exceedingly modest – except where his family and their achievements are concerned, and there he is justifiably proud.

He is also very good company.

Walter Hartley

Some of my best friends in music have been so geographically removed that I see them but rarely. One of the most cherished of these has been Ronald Stevenson, whom I met in 1965 by a most strange set of circumstances. In the spring of that year I was living with my family in South-East London, having crossed the Atlantic for the first time on a sabbatical leave from the college in West Virginia where I was then teaching. My musical connections had acquainted me with the magazine *Composer* wherein I had read an appreciative letter from Alan Bush describing Ronald Stevenson's

Stevenson's home: Townfoot House, West Linton
(photograph by Burnett Cross)

Passacaglia on DSCH.[1] Later, visiting another composer friend, Raymond Warren (at that time in Belfast), I came upon Ronald Stevenson's address which I carefully filed away; still later, a month before returning to the States, we had the opportunity to drive to Scotland. I persuaded my wife to make an excursion to West Linton and there we went (in a Volkswagen bus, with two small daughters). Since Ronald at that time had no 'phone, we had no way to warn him of our arrival (and no way of knowing he was even there). But West Linton is a small village and Townfoot House in the very centre thereof, to which we were directed.

I knocked apprehensively and was at once admitted by Ronald himself – thus began a marvellous seven-hour afternoon with Ronald and Marjorie, myself and Sandra, and the children of both families, exchanging performances and copies of one another's music, excellent conversation and tea. There has been much further correspondence and further music exchange since, and meetings in both White Plains, New York (in 1976 and 1978), due to our mutual interest in Percy Grainger's music (and in Busoni, Sorabji and many others) and in West Linton.[2]

Ronald Stevenson is a fabulous pianist and composer and Renaissance man of music whom it has been a pleasure to know – even at a distance: we share a Scottish heritage (my mother was born in Stirling, and my paternal grandfather, like Ronald's father, is a Lancashire man) – and much else.

---

[1] *Composer*, Autumn 1964.

[2] In 1985 Stevenson went to Fredonia as a guest of the Hartleys, to give lectures and recitals; and in 1986 and 1988 they visited the Stevensons again in West Linton. –ED.

John Guthrie

I first met Ronald Stevenson one evening more than twenty years ago at the house of a mutual friend in Edinburgh. It was to be an ordinary enough occasion, I supposed, with no expectations beyond a little music indifferently performed by a few amateurs such as myself, and no doubt some rather ordinary talk over a tankard or two of beer. But when I was told that Ronald was about to join us, my expectations sharply rose. I had heard of him by reputation as a brilliant young musician already on his way to great achievement. What would he be like, I wondered? A leonine figure with a mane of hair, voluble and dominating, or perhaps, on the contrary, reserved and shy as many musicians are?

He was neither. As he entered the room he was relaxed and smiling, with no trace of self-consciousness in his quiet manner. He was of middle height, well built, with a hint of the pianist's strength in his shoulders. Otherwise, at first sight there seemed to be nothing particularly remarkable about his appearance, till you noticed the broad brow, the alert eyes, the firm mouth, and an unmistakable air of easy confidence which aroused expectancy. The evening suddenly promised to be a good deal more than ordinary.

Our host sang some songs, and Ronald, accompanying him at the piano, often had to sight-read roughly scribbled manuscripts bristling with inaccuracies. (I can vouch for this, as some of them were mine!) In spite of the misinformation confronting him, Ronald was cheerfully undismayed. He played unerringly from those rude scribblings, anticipating and correcting wrong notes and forgotten accidentals without any hesitation. And as he played he intuitively expressed the intention of each unfamiliar song.

After a well-earned pause and a little beer to revive him, Ronald was asked to play some other music. He sat down happily and played to us for an hour or so. His playing was eloquent, commanding, faultlessly secure and seemingly quite effortless, whatever the technical difficulties. It was a brilliant and impressive performance, though Ronald himself thought nothing of it.

Later in the evening we talked about music and many other matters. I was again impressed by his range of interests, his general

*The view from Stevenson's piano in 'The Den of Musiquity'
in Townfoot House (photograph by Colin Scott-Sutherland)*

knowledge and sure grasp. He seemed to be at ease with any subject, speaking with enthusiasm, authority and much laughter as our conversation warmed. His response to any new idea was immediate, whether dismissive or in agreement; it fuelled debate or shared enthusiasm with delight. As we talked, I learned that he had already composed a number of large and varied works and written a good few papers.

Here was a man of most unusual gifts, pianistic, intellectual and creative, who also possessed a lively sense of humour and the charm of direct simplicity. Before the end of that evening we had formed a friendship which has never faltered, despite my own long absences in Arabia, where I was working as a doctor, and later in Cyprus, after I had retired from medicine.

It was during those long years that, paradoxically, I came to know Ronald well. He had agreed to tutor me by correspondence in harmony, counterpoint and composition, sending me reams of exercises to grapple with and return to him for correction and advice. Back they came, not only meticulously corrected but accompanied by long letters of general advice and comment, often illustrated with alternative solutions to a problem, written in his beautiful clear script. My early essays in composition were returned with detailed notes emphasising the demands of form and equally, the importance of imaginative thinking, not merely 'correctness'. He was never didactic, always adventurous and encouraging as he led me from necessary disciplines groping towards freedom. I have those letters still. They are more illuminative of Ronald as a friend and teacher than any words of mine. In many of them there is also mention of his current compositions and performances, as with prodigious energy he pursued his rapidly developing career.

Though distance and the lapse of time were bridged by lively letters, the occasions when we met again are, of course, the most vividly remembered. Several pictures come immediately to mind to match and amplify that first indelible impression.

Sometimes we would meet at a bus station in Edinburgh, to go together to Ronald's home. I would be waiting there in good time before the bus was due to leave. But as the minutes ticked away there would be no sign of Ronald. Had he forgotten our appointment? As the driver switched on the engine, Ronald in his black Homburg hat would appear in the distance walking unhurriedly, absorbed in some treatise he was reading. Just as the bus began to move he would step aboard, still deep in thought. Time even to the minute was to be used with concentration. As soon as he was in his seat, he would put away his paper and turn to eager conversation, listening as attentively as, a moment before, he had been reading.

Ronald's innate and highly developed gifts, and his equable unworrying temperament would alone have been enough to account for his relaxed assurance. But it often occurred to me that his power of concentration was at the root of his confidence. I once asked him if he was ever nervous when playing to a large and distinguished audience. With a puzzled look he laughed and said that the larger it was, and the more filled with composers and musicians, the happier he was. There was no hint of boast in that. It was a simple statement of confidence in his abilities and the joy of sharing them.

Townfoot House evokes a score of other pictures, of evenings spent there in Ronald's studio in the little room with shelves crammed to the ceiling with books and manuscripts, a piano at one end and a harpsichord at the other. As we talked and laughed, he would hunt through the crowded bookshelves for some obscure reference, or perhaps a manuscript written in his precise calligraphy, or go to the piano to illustrate a point in our discussion. Sometimes, if it was relevant, he might read some passages from a book or paper he was writing about the work of a

The hut at the back of Townfoot House, where many
of Stevenson's compositions have been written
(photograph by Colin Scott-Sutherland)

composer – great or perhaps still awaiting recognition – whom he
esteemed. At other times he would take a manuscript of my own
and go through it with me, analysing, questioning, suggesting.
Whatever subject might be touched upon, he gave his whole mind
to it with zest and a natural enjoyment. The climax of each evening
would arrive when he was persuaded to play some masterly piano
music of his own.

It would already be growing late when his wife Marjorie would bid
us come and eat our supper. In that happy trinity around the table,
sometimes augmented by the further trinity of their brilliant young
children, Gordon, Gerda and Savourna, the talk would continue
six-fold till it was time to catch the last bus home, Ronald strolling
with me – as usual, just in time.

On the way home in the bus, my mind would be crowded with the
impressions of the evening, especially of Ronald's versatility, to
which there seemed no limits. He was responsive to every thought
and challenge. Once he told me as though it were nothing out of
the way, about a recital he had given in an English country house.

The programme included some Mozart sonatas, one of which lacked its final movement. Settling himself in his seat on the Night Scotsman, he proceeded to supply it. He finished it as the train drew into London, and that afternoon played the completed sonata at his recital![1]

Two further pictures of Ronald are firmly lodged in my memory. One was an embarrassment to me, though not apparently to Ronald. The other shows him in full splendour.

One afternoon we arranged to meet at a BBC studio in London where Ronald was to record a programme of Percy Grainger's piano music. Cheerfully but misguidedly, Ronald insisted that I turn the pages for him. Somehow I managed to keep pace with him in the first two pieces. But the third was my undoing. The pages were black with notes. The pace was frighteningly fast. From the outset Ronald was helping *me*, nodding and surging on ahead as I fumbled half a page behind him. Disaster came when having caught up with him at last, I triumphantly seized a dog-ear on the corner of a page, and ripped it off. The page remained in place! The piece had to be re-recorded, but Ronald merely smiled and murmured that next time all would be well. It was, but I suspect only because he had memorised all the notes and required no further 'help' from me.

The last picture is like a huge enlargement of the very first when we had met one evening many years before. It surely illustrates much that I have dwelt upon in this sketchy portrait.

At short notice Ronald had agreed to give a recital in the Wigmore Hall in aid of a production of the opera *Wat Tyler* by his old friend Alan Bush. The programme consisted of piano music by a number of very eminent British composers, most of whom were present. The music was for the most part unusually difficult and the Hall was filled with an audience of critical musicians – including, as well as Alan Bush, John Ogdon, Louis Kentner, Frank Merrick, Edmund Rubbra, Graham Whettam and Robert Simpson.

Ronald was in his element. He stepped onto the platform relaxed, smiling, and evidently enjoying the formidable prospect ahead of him. Behind him came a young woman (an expert 'turner' this time), carrying the music he would have to read since there had been little time at short notice to practise it. His performance was the most astonishing I have ever witnessed. His

---

[1] The piece in question was not in fact a sonata, but the Minuet in D (к355) which has no trio. –ED.

Benno Schotz's bronze head of Stevenson, 1968

reading of those complex scores seemed as natural to him as reading simple prose. His playing was majestic, in the grand manner. At particularly complicated passages I often noticed that he was serenely smiling. The applause was almost riotous, and afterwards in the Green Room the composers surrounded him to pay their own delighted tributes.

It is not for me but for his peers to assess his achievements. I speak of him in all simplicity as an inspiring teacher and a warm and unfailing friend who has enormously enriched my life. He is a virtuoso in all he does who has never forgotten his humanity. That I believe is what gives depth to all his thought, and that I know is what brings the delight and understanding of his friendship.

Albert Wullschleger

Ronald Stevenson has been a dear friend since 1956. We both had strong connections with Garvald School, a home for mentally handicapped children at Dolphinton, near West Linton. Our friendship deepened in 1966, when my wife and I lost our eight-year-old daughter, Regina. This tragic event linked our two families with unbreakable bonds in a spiritual unity. No words can express what Ronald and Marjorie Stevenson did for us during those days and months of grief and trial. For the funeral of our daughter, Ronald composed and performed a song based on a poem by Christian Morgenstern, 'Reinkarnation'. This song was the beginning of a small cycle called *Liederbüchlein für Regina Beate*. When in 1971 my family moved back to Switzerland it was hard to leave our friends behind, although we were determined to have them with us for a holiday soon. But many years went by until, at last, in 1977 Ronald agreed to visit us on condition that he could give one or two concerts, as he could not accept a 'paid holiday' from us.

I had known Ronald mainly as a warm-hearted friend, a highly gifted person with a tremendously wide range of interests. His study always reminded me a little of the study in Goethe's *Faust* with hundreds of books, documents and photographs reflecting his immense love for and interest in all the great things of this world. I also had known him as a composer whose work always spoke more directly to my heart than I had ever felt with any other contemporary composer – I am deeply moved when I listen to his music. Strangely enough, I had never heard one of his piano recitals although I knew that he was a very fine pianist. It was only during his concert tours in Switzerland that I fully realised his unique gifts as an interpreter.

To be enthusiastic about Ronald and Marjorie Stevenson's visit is one thing, but to be an impresario with no experience whatsoever and to fix dates, places, have programmes printed, amongst many other things, within four months, is quite a different story. But being full of anticipation I was most interested to find out about various possibilities, although I soon had to realise that big places like Basel or Zurich would be out of the question as concerts are usually planned two or three years ahead. Finally I contacted the priest of the small city of Rheinfelden who often arranges organ recitals in his church. He was most helpful in arranging the concert and the church committee spontaneously offered a deficit guarantee. In the end I had fixed three concerts, including one for the students at the school where I teach, so that everything was ready for their arrival.

At last it was 23 February 1978. My wife and I went to meet our long-expected guests at Zurich airport. This reunion was like a dream one had to treasure so that it would not vanish! We had hardly arrived at our house in Magden when Ronald inquired, rather tentatively, if it would be possible to visit the Segantini Museum in St Moritz. What, doesn't he want to spend the time before the concerts practising? How does he know about Segantini, a little-known Swiss painter, and who told him about the museum? (I doubt whether many Swiss people know of the painter, let alone the museum.) I told him that it was quite a strenuous journey across the Alps to the Engadine, with a lot of snow still, taking at least four to five hours each way. But the painter seemed to be of more importance than anything else at that moment. We did visit the museum the following day and what an experience it was to stand together with Ronald, in front of these wonderful light-filled paintings. The famous triptych, *Birth – Life – Death*, three vast paintings, made an unforgettable impression on us.

On Sunday afternoon, 26 February, Ronald's first concert in Switzerland was to take place in the Church of Rheinfelden. On the programme were works by Scarlatti, Mozart, Beethoven (the 'Moonlight' Sonata), Chopin, Stevenson and Grainger. I had never heard a piano recital of Ronald's before, and feeling somehow 'responsible' I was rather nervous. But as soon as he played the first notes every ounce of tension was taken from me. At once I was completely drawn into his playing and felt more strongly than with any other pianist before that he was not just reproducing music but really creating it anew. In familiar pieces notes appeared which one had apparently never heard before – he was opening the ears and hearts of his listeners. After the concert a friend of mine, a connoisseur with a world of experience in organising concerts, approached me spontaneously and said: 'He is one of the very great interpreters; I would travel far to hear him'.

The next tour in Switzerland was planned for September 1979 with concerts in Aarau, Rheinfelden and Kölliken. In the programme were also included two works by Paderewski, and it was Paderewski who was to be of prime importance during Ronald's second stay in Switzerland. The three concerts took place within four days after his arrival and received enthusiastic critiques in the local newspapers. After all this hard work Ronald and Marjorie wanted to spend a few days in the mountains and we found a charming place in Wengen at the foot of the 'Jungfrau'. But before setting out for the Bernese Oberland it was Ronald's wish to visit the famous Paderewski estate on Lake Geneva. It was on a cold and stormy day, with gusts of rain sweeping across the street when we set out on this adventurous journey. In the centre of Morges we found a beautiful bronze statue of Paderewski; after this began what could be called the 'haunting of Morges'.

Paderewski (1860–1941), perhaps the most celebrated pianist of his time, lived for the last 40 years of his life on his sixty-acre estate, 'Riond-Bosson', in a castle-like mansion. Having made a full study of the life and work of Paderewski, Ronald was now anxious to visit his home. We drove to the outskirts of Morges as we were told to do by the local police but could not find the house, which was most peculiar. It was like searching for an enchanted castle. In spite of the terrible weather we continued to look for the park and, after about an hour going round in circles and enquiring many times, we finally were told by someone that Paderewski's villa had been pulled down in 1966. This shattering news came down on us like another thunderstorm. We eventually found what used to be one of the most beautiful parks as well as the site of the house. No ruins were left – just a few bricks lying scattered around. What forty years ago used to be a meeting place of musicians and statesmen was now desolate and neglected. There we stood in silence thinking of the glory of days now dead, unable to grasp what had happened there. Hidden under a bush we found a piece of sandstone from the banister, a witness of the past, nicely worked in the shape of a vase. Ronald took it with him to Scotland – in spite of the weight – in memory of a friend in spirit.

Just as rain is followed by sunshine, so this shattering experience was followed by some unexpected good news. After Ronald had returned to Scotland I wanted to find out more about this mysterious story, and in the course of my investigations I discovered that a 'Société Paderewski' had been founded in 1977; its aims are to revive the memory of the great man, to open a 'Musée Paderewski' and to organise concerts.[1] Now who would be more

[1] Its current address is: Centre culturel, Place du Casino, CH-1110 Morges, Switzerland.

The Villa Riond-Bosson, Paderewski's home, demolished in 1966

suited to give a concert in this society than Ronald, one of the few pianists who still include Paderewski's compositions in their recitals? I contacted the secretary of the society, M. Guex-Joris, and was very warmly received. He was extremely interested to hear about Ronald and his work. As plans were in progress for a third concert tour in 1981, I told the secretary that Ronald would be very pleased to play in memory of the fortieth anniversary of Paderewski's death. M. Guex-Joris brought it before the committee and Ronald was invited to give a recital on 14 May 1981 in Vevey. The concert took place in the old patrician house of a patron of the Society. The drawing room held about a hundred people, and there was a truly special and solemn atmosphere in this exclusive setting. The population of that region of Switzerland is mainly Catholic, and most of the audience were still suffering from the shock of the attempted assassination of the Pope the day before. Ronald began by playing Schubert's *Moment Musical*, D780/Op. 94, No. 2 – Swiss radio had played this piece in announcing Paderewski's death and one really felt that he was celebrating it like a prayer to comfort human hearts. There was a long and intense silence after this piece. The rest of the programme included works by Beethoven, Chopin and, of course, Paderewski. It ended with a suite from Paderewski's opera *Manru*, arranged for the piano by Ronald Stevenson as early as 1948. It was obvious that the audience was deeply impressed by his playing, and a letter

which I later received from the committee stated that they
considered his concert as one of the most important events in
the history of the society. Ronald was asked to give a recital on his
next visit to Switzerland.

The crowning of this third tour was his concert at the
Goetheanum, a huge building situated on a hill in Dornach near
Basel. It is the centre of the anthroposophical movement, founded
by Rudolf Steiner. Ronald's connection to anthroposophy goes
back to his early days, when he and his wife stayed at Garvald School
where the education is based on the principles of Rudolf Steiner. In
his BBC talk on the handicapped child[2] he discussed Rudolf Steiner
and the importance of his indications for curative education.

For many years it had been his wish to give a concert at the
Goetheanum as a tribute to Steiner. Thanks to a friend of mine it
proved possible for Ronald to play there on 17 May 1981. He chose
an entire 'Faust Programme', firstly because this theme has played
an important part in his life, and in his compositions, and secondly
because the Goetheanum is the only place in the world where the
whole of Goethe's *Faust* (Parts I and II) is produced on the stage.

As we walked up towards the huge building that Sunday
afternoon, about two hours before the concert started, one could
feel the tremendous anticipation and the importance which Ronald
attributed to this event. We were led up to the big hall which was
immersed in warm light streaming through the stained glass
windows. Ronald sat down at the grand Steinway and remained in
silent contemplation for a few moments.

Marjorie and myself were the only people present during these
solemn moments. Then gradually sounds began to evolve from the
piano, sounds that filled the room, already bathed with the play of
the coloured light from the windows. It was the Bach-Busoni
Chaconne in D minor, which Ronald played as his personal tribute
to Rudolf Steiner.

After the concert, which included works by Wagner-von Bülow,
Stevenson (*Prelude, Fugue and Fantasy*), Boito-Stevenson, Berlioz-
Liszt and Gounod-Liszt, and which was very well received, Ronald
was deeply moved. He told me: 'This has been one of the most
important concerts I have ever given – if not the most important
one'.

At the end of this compact concert tour with four different
programmes, Ronald and Marjorie wanted to have a few days' peace

---

[2] *Cf.* note 26, p. 36, above, and pp. 323 and 325, below.

*Czesław Marek in his late eighties,
just before his first meeting with Stevenson
(photograph courtesy of the Czesław Marek
Foundation, Zurich)*

in the mountains and it was again Wengen they were drawn to. From Wengen one gets a most spectacular view of the mountains on the other side of the valley with a sheer drop of at least 500 metres. It is from there that the famous 'Staubbachfall' ('water falling in spray') descends. Christian Morgenstern wrote a most beautiful poem on a waterfall, describing the absolute peace of this natural spectacle. During his stay in Wengen Ronald was so much impressed by this sight as well as by the poem that he wrote, high up in the Alps, what is, in my opinion one of his most serene compositions: *Wasserfall bei Nacht*, for voice and piano. This composition may also be a reflection of Ronald's deep spiritual experience in Dornach.

This account of Ronald's connection with Switzerland would be incomplete if I did not mention his memorable encounter with Czesław Marek in Zurich.

In 1981 we visited the Polish Museum in the Schloss Rapperswil investigating the possibility of a future piano recital. The director of the Museum mentioned the name of Marek, then a 90-year-old composer-pianist, suggesting that it might be important for Ronald to visit this famous personality. Ronald, not wanting to miss any opportunity of meeting somebody who had been personally connected with Busoni, set off a few days later. He was received like a friend by Professor Marek who, in spite of his advanced age, still radiated spirituality and warmth of heart; indeed, he taught the piano up to his death in the summer of 1985, at the age of 94. He was born in Poland in 1891, studied piano in Vienna with Paderewski's teacher, Leschetizky, and composition with Pfitzner. What an experience to be received by somebody who had walked the streets of Zurich at the side of Busoni who, by the way, had himself chosen Marek's first grand piano. Busoni's famous piano bench was still to be found in Marek's music study; it is now in

Composers, critics and pianists at the beginning of the Marek revival:
a photograph taken in the British Music Information Centre, London,
in 1982, after Stevenson had given the first public performance
in Britain of Marek's Triptychon *– from left to right,*
Alan Bush, Stephen Johnson, Malcolm MacDonald,
Robert and Angela Simpson, Martin Anderson, Louise Taylor
and Ronald Stevenson

Stevenson's. Ronald and Marek were exchanging ideas about music and soon it became evident how much these two composers have in common. Ronald was presented with a number of Marek's compositions and at once took to his *Triptychon*, Op. 8, which he refers to as 'a resplendent work in the line of César Franck'.[3] On 16 September 1983, on Marek's 92nd birthday, Ronald had included the *Triptychon* in his recital in Rheinfelden. Because of indisposition the composer was prevented from attending the concert but was most anxious that Ronald should play it for him at his home.

And so, on 23 September, I had the privilege of accompanying Ronald, who had just spent a week's holiday in Wengen, to Professor Marek's. We were shown into his music study and Ronald sat down at the Steinway grand, not having touched the keyboard for a whole week, and started to play this twenty-minute work. Marek sat motionless, listening intently to Ronald's playing. Only occasionally he would turn sideways to look at him. Ronald's playing was stirring. He was absorbed by the music and obviously

---

[3] Stevenson has recorded the *Triptychon* for Altarus Records, on AIR-CD-9043. –ED.

deeply inspired by the composer's presence. When the last powerful chords of the final Fugue had faded away there was a deep silence in the room. Then Professor Marek got up and walked slowly towards Ronald who had also risen. The dignified old master opened his arms to embrace Ronald and gave him a kiss on his forehead – all in absolute silence. It was a truly 'holy' kiss, as Ronald put it afterwards. When he asked for criticism Marek said: 'Alles war richtig, alles, alles! You are a great pianist! Not only a great pianist but a great musician!'

In April 1985 Ronald gave an all-Polish concert at the Schloss Rapperswil to mark the tenth anniversary of the Polish Museum. It was a special event: Professor Marek was present. It proved to be his last concert: he died three months later – a dignified farewell to a great man and musician.

Manfred Gordon

Townfoot House, from the outside an unobtrusive Scottish stone cottage, now standing among its sisters near the centre of the main street in the village of West Linton, holds surprises for the visitor. When I enter the first of its rooms, a kind of living-studio which Ronald Stevenson calls his 'den of musiquity', I feel each time transported into a curious world in which past, present, and future are magically blended. The walls and the desk, the grand piano and even the book-shelves are studded with portraits, many of them signed photographs: aspects of Ferruccio Busoni or of Alan Bush, of Hugh MacDiarmid on a Scottish moor or of Dimitrov in his Sunday best, of Tagore, Brahms and Gordon Craig; Lange's portrait of Mozart amid Stevenson family photographs, the gifted Stevenson children, their paternal grandfather with his railwayman's lamp, and their great-aunts portrayed around their loom 'at t'mill' in Blackburn around 1910 – they all look out on a fine portrait that Percy Grainger dedicated to Ronald and on a quite magnificent drawing of Paderewski's head by Burne-Jones. The 'den' is stacked with divers treasures, correspondence and original wood-cuts by Craig, and more correspondence: with Sibelius, Walton, Menuhin and Britten, in files which may one day find their editor.[1] For the present, however, the room in the stone cottage expresses an acknowledgement by an artist of his inspiration, his sources and his roots; and it encircles a wealth of testimonies to his uncommon gift for friendship.

Into that circle I found myself admitted not quite half a century ago. Such lasting friendships are likely to be built on tension, not merely on pure harmony. Ours has been an intense, if intermittent, dialogue; as if we were driven, almost each time we meet, to compare notes. The arid truths in the notes of the natural scientist against the flowing semiquavers of the virtuoso composer? Hardly

---

[1] Stevenson's correspondence has since been deposited in the National Library of Scotland, in Edinburgh; cf. Christopher Lambton, 'Collecting Key Signatures', *The Daily Telegraph*, 2 January 1999, and 'Dear Ronald Stevenson', *BBC Music Magazine*, Vol. 7, No. 5, January 1999, pp. 26–28. –ED.

that – for two cultures there cannot be. What seems to lie behind the illusion of two cultures may be an exchange of traditional roles: today's successors of Prometheus are the artist, the poet and the musician, striving to bring unfamiliar kinds of fire to a shivering generation, while men of science have retreated to fastnesses where they enact the solipsist vision of Narcissus. But this interchange of roles is not complete, and its progress must be resisted. True, the leading scientists of the century have been reluctant to let their physics venture beyond the information which their brains receive of the state of their sense organs, so that they barely managed to save the outer world as an inference, a hunting ground for the empiricist in a framework of relativities.

But it is also true that Einstein played the violin; it was the violin that Professor C. H. Bamford played on one of those musical evenings in Edinburgh in the late 1950s, where a cross-section of Ronald's friends informally met together. 'Bam' was the famous British kineticist – not the kind who habitually juggles fiery colours that might (or, more probably, might not) have made Caravaggio envious, but the juggler of molecules who times their motions and analyses the 'kinetics' of their chemical reactions. Yet that evening, Bam was more concerned with exploring the chromaticism of César Franck's Violin Sonata, his characteristic sensitivity reflected by Ronald Stevenson at the piano. In the audience there were teachers and scientists, and the technologist (or music critic) John Boulton. There were a handful of composers, and a whole thirst of poets. Sydney Goodsir Smith as well as Christopher Grieve have now left us to join the Honour'd Shade. So too has Norman MacCaig whose intellectual power of synthesis, ranging over natural and human history, from worm to angel,[2] held us enthralled so many years ago.

Another literary figure, Marcel Proust, began soon after to dominate our discourse. His quest to analyse the artist's task, the process of raising memories to the conscious surface of the mind, occupied me most. For Ronald, on the other hand, Proust was 'that Spinozan lens-grinder of jewelled prose' in contrast to Joyce, 'who breathed the azure air of Elysium, like Mozart'.[3]

His gift of pairing two seemingly disparate characters (Prometheus embracing Narcissus?), illuminating both, remains one

[2] *Cf.* his poem 'In a level light', in *Honour'd Shade. An Anthology of New Scottish Poetry to mark the Bicentenary of the Birth of Robert Burns,* selected and edited by Norman MacCaig, W. and R. Chambers, Edinburgh and London, 1959.

[3] His thumbnail characterisations are from a letter to the author, dated 1 December 1960.

*1959: Stevenson and MacDiarmid listen as the 22-year-old John Ogdon
plays Sorabji's* Opus Clavicembalisticum, *the only time
MacDiarmid – the dedicatee – ever heard the work
(photographs by Helmut Petzsch)*

characteristic *forte* of Stevenson's prose style. What Ronald meant in
this specific instance is probably that limits must be set, perhaps
unconsciously, to the analysis of his own creative processes, as if
reason might drive them back to unreachable depths, rather than
to raise them into welcoming consciousness. I blush to remember
my unhappy experiment of timing Ronald with a stopwatch (Bam
would have known better!) during a brilliant pianistic *presto* of a
previously unseen score. When I had worked out that, on average,
he had taken from that page of score, and translated into sound,
one item of information every three milliseconds (0.003 seconds!),
he somewhat abruptly closed the score and the lid came down on
the keyboard. The scientist's concept of human response time may
set a limit to virtuosity, but it is a limit better left unexplored in
theory or in measurement in the azure air of Elysium.

Yet Proust's *milieu,* and even the old lens-grinder in his den of
silence himself, exerted their spell strongly enough on Ronald.
Contemporary photographs and paintings that reflect this milieu,

and explain Proust's poetic perception to us so directly – over these Ronald could pore and linger. That complex European age, of Joyce, Proust and Paderewski, and of Busoni proclaiming the dawn of a new aesthetic, remain one of Ronald's lost paradises (for there are several). I shall never hear the waltz from *Der Rosenkavalier* without recalling his sigh: 'there goes the Edwardian era waltzing out of the window for ever ...'.

Earlier in the same year, 1960, Ronald composed his *Epitaph for*

Paderewski.[4] It was the centenary of the Polish hero's birth. But the *Epitaph* was not a *pièce d'occasion*, rather a sign among many of a deep admiration, almost of a friendship, if such a thing were possible. Twenty years later, Ronald was to search in vain for the exiled master's noble residence in Switzerland. At last some local inhabitants could be found who could point out part of the remaining terrain where once a great spirit had honoured their country with his presence and his music. It was there that Ronald discovered part of a stone column that, as a photograph at Townfoot House proved, had belonged to the balustrade of a first-floor balcony of Paderewski's vanished palatial villa.[5] That relic was carefully engraved with the letters IJP by a craftsman, and given a refuge in West Linton. It has a place of honour at Townfoot House, where from time to time it can vibrate again to the sound of Ignacy Jan Paderewski's music.

Such gestures do not, in Ronald Stevenson, reflect any trace of sentimentality. Perhaps a trace of despair to be fought and overcome by defiant gestures does show itself. A significant aside occurs in a chapter which Ronald contributed to MacDiarmid's autobiography[6] in the year after Paderewski's centenary: 'artists, throughout the world, form a race of their own, a race apart, like a lost tribe'. The chapter was in celebration of Sorabji, as living master of long and complex piano compositions, not merely a scion of a lost tribe, but a recluse from the world. Ronald's gift, and his informed enthusiasm for Sorabji's music, had gained him the friendship of this 'outsider', then living entrenched in Corfe Castle in Dorset. When Ronald calls Sorabji the 'Zoroastrian musician', this is not yet another example of his power to pair great spirits: Zoroaster was the founder of Sorabji's religion.

Ronald's empathy with a race of artists whose intellectual complexity sets them apart and can goad them into fierce criticism of a century of decline and decay – MacDiarmid and Sorabji are obvious examples – is balanced by his much wider sympathies. The broad spectrum of his friendships appears to me unprecedented in life or in fiction. Mental handicap, which can isolate human beings as surely as supreme mental creativity, has a poignant relevance to art, and especially to music. Ronald and Marjorie Stevenson, and

---

[4] This work, in the nature of an improvisation, was never written out. Stevenson says that it is now forgotten, 'though I can still remember the opening chord'. –ED.

[5] *Cf.* Albert Wullschleger's essay on pp. 244–51, above. –ED.

[6] *The Company I've Kept, op. cit.*, pp. 38–70.

their children too, have done selfless service for this cause. Ronald has composed songs, which the handicapped children in the Peeblesshire community at Garvald have been singing with enthusiasm, and their performance was taped and broadcast by Ronald in a moving contribution to the Year of the Disabled (1979) in one of Michael Oliver's *Music Weekly* programmes on BBC Radio 3.[7] Words like 'service', 'cause' and 'sympathy' must not be misunderstood here: more than a handful of mentally handicapped youngsters have grown up to enjoy Ronald's friendship, which flows equally naturally, with its tensions as well as its harmonies, across all the human spectrum.

If I had to 'pair' Ronald with a kindred spirit, it would be with Walt Whitman, that generous poet whom he admires above all for his naturalness. In the letter from which I quoted earlier, Ronald proved to me that D. H. Lawrence ('that tortured Beethovenian daemon') had also drawn inspiration from Whitman: he praised 'the *honesty* of his [Whitman's] genius' – the emphasis is Ronald's – and added: 'It had no cleverness'. Trying to defend and to define himself and his artistic task, some six months later, he was to end a letter[8] with a defiant rejection of clever analysis, and of the Proustian introspection: 'no subterranean or aerial escapes, no catacombs or empyreans of flight and fantasy. Reality is needed. If I can't manage it, I'd better be silent'.

It is for others, in this book and beyond it, to say whether Ronald Stevenson's music has 'managed' it. I can only add that his appeal for reality is topical for science, too. This is not to suggest that I immodestly offer myself as his peer and counterpart after all – I stand by my choice of Walt Whitman and content myself with that most generous gift of friendship embodied in Ronald's much-thumbed copy of *Leaves of Grass*. It is already long ago that he took it from behind Whitman's portrait on his bookshelf, and pressed it into my hand.

[7] 'Music and the Handicapped Child', broadcast on 16 December 1979.

[8] Dated 19 May 1961.

Alan Bold

Your inner ear grows sharper. Do you hear
The deep notes and the high notes?
They are immeasurable in space and infinite as to number.[1]

FOR RONALD STEVENSON[2]

Your name, dear friend,
Sets off a melody of memories,
Notes that tick through time
That began for me at Broughton School,
Where you taught music in the classroom
And in yourself pronounced a pantheon:
Busoni, the visionary virtuoso;
Sorabji, the esoteric adventurer;
Chris Grieve, the bard at Biggar,
Sometimes known as MacDiarmid,
The poet who reached out to touch
The universe.
You were mad about music,
Passionate about poetry,
Carrying a briefcase packed
With Pound and Joyce and Whitman.
You embodied enthusiasm and erudition,
Were crazy about culture,
Championed younger men like John Ogdon
'Sixteen stones in his stocking soles
And a heart of gold'.
(My first public house pint
Was with you and Ogdon in Rose Street.)

[1] MacDiarmid, after Busoni, 'In Memoriam James Joyce', in Grieve and Aitken, *op. cit.*, Vol. II, p. 871.

[2] First published in *The Glasgow Herald* ('Weekender', No. 8, Saturday, 16 December 1989, p. 28) to accompany the exhibition of Stevenson's work held in the National Library of Scotland, Edinburgh, from 8 December 1989 to 28 February 1990. –ED

To me you gave your time
In enchanted weekend sessions
At West Linton as Townfoot House
Became a compact concert hall
And you performed for friend and family:
Marjorie, Gerda, Gordon, Savourna.
It all comes back, the sight
And sound of you
Playing your Passacaglia
At the little grand piano,
Four notes multiplying into many,
Intricate strands of sound
Weaving into ingenious patterns
Of rhapsodic rhythm.
Who could be more musical?
You whistled as you spoke
(Those sibilants, the Liszt Sonata,
Sorabji and *Opus Clavicembalisticum*,
The Scottish songs of F. G. Scott,
The birdsong of Messiaen).
You broke into song
When speaking of Pizzetti
And Roman Vlad
(Your Italian interlude).
You soared with Shostakovich
(Begetter of the *Passacaglia*,
Well met in Edinburgh
With MacDiarmid).
And always, always
You sang the praises of
Busoni:
'For achievement, Mozart,' you said,
'For vision, Busoni'.
When I think of you
I see your vision
Of humankind in harmony,
All the colours coalescing
(Your favourite word)
Into a dazzling radiance,
What MacDiarmid called
A 'shining vision of Alba'
(The Scotocentric universe)
In a passage in *Lucky Poet*

Where he cites what Busoni
Said in 1910:
'At last I have learnt
How to get hold of (*anpacken*)
The first movement
Of the Waldstein Sonata,
Which would never unfold
Its full beauty
Just as it should
(*so rechte blüten wollte*)
And I have been playing it
For nearly thirty years'.
For you there are no coincidences,
Only correspondences so Biggar
Gives headroom to Busoni
(Booze-oni, you pronounced it).
And everything under the sun
And beyond the stars
Holds together, the variations
Underpinning a quintessential
Unity expressed in the wordless
Eloquence of music.
'Music needs air,' you said
And you have orchestrated
The atmosphere around you,
Creating a climate
In which every breath
Is an interval
In an endless arpeggio.
Knowing you has often
Compelled me into poetry;
'You ask a poet to sing,'
I wrote in 'Recitative',
Looking for the line
That linked art and political
Affirmation.
And you did:
You asked a poet to sing,
After Hiroshima.
In a *Homage to MacDiarmid*
(A verbal counterpoint
To a visual sequence
By John Bellany)

I remembered my first sight
Of MacDiarmid
Sitting in a bus
In Edinburgh's St Andrew's Square,
Bound for Biggar,
After a day on the town,
Sitting alone,
Smoking a pipe
As I approached with you
And you exclaimed
'That's Chris Grieve'
Who gave a wave
That rippled through my life.
You gave a theme to my life
And I see you now,
Hands caressing the keyboard,
Head back, the motion
Of your mind
Which is both here and there,
Mindful of the craft of art,
As your ears hear airs
From the music of the spheres.
After making music
You told me, once,
Coming back to earth as always:
'I am a manual worker:
I play the piano'.
That's only a part of it,
The physical art of it.
Through the metaphysics of music
You live another life,
Speak a language that persists
(Mystical lament, spiritual song)
By meditating on mystery.
I will always hear your music,
Emotion at the heart of it:
I will always see you
Touching the piano
With passion.

IX
**STEVENSON
AND SCOTLAND**
Jamie Reid Baxter

It is within, and not outside, that we must seek for man: in the very bowels of what is local and lies around us, the universal, and in the depths of the temporal and transient, the eternal.[1]

Stands Scotland where it did?
Alas poor country,
Almost afraid to know itself: it cannot
Be called our mother, but our grave.[2]

Is Ronald Stevenson a Scottish composer? This essay will attempt to answer that question by asking what the word 'Scotland' itself means, and by showing what it means to Stevenson, a man born and brought up furth of Scotland, author of Japanese haiku settings, a piano concerto subtitled *The Continents*, arrangements of folk music from all over the globe, an indefatigable ethnomusicologist who has incorporated elements of Indian, African, Irish, North American, Norwegian, Australian and gypsy music into his own musical language.

There is a Gaelic proverb which says *Tir gun chanain, tir gun anam* – a land without a language is a land without a soul. Perhaps it would be truer to say that a land without a language cannot express its soul. It cannot know itself, and hence cannot be known by others. To the Scots, there is no question that they are Scots. The problem, for themselves, and consequently for others, is that they do not know what that means. Our 'multiform, our infinite Scotland' is a Glen of Silence filled only with the stillness of foetal death, 'the tragedy of an unevolved people', in the words of the poet Hugh MacDiarmid.[3] But – it is important to add – a people nonetheless.

The riches and diversity of Scottish Gaelic culture, still alive to the present day; the variegated wealth of Lowland Scottish folk culture in ballad, song and dance; the masterpieces of mediaeval and Renaissance Scottish civilisation that survived the Reformation – all these are still there for him who seeks the hidden soul of Scotland. But they have to be hunted out; they are anything but to hand for a

---

[1] Miguel de Unamuno, quoted by Alejo Carpentier, 'Música nueva: *Castilla* y el paisaje en la música nueva', *El Diario de la Marina* (Havana), 26 June 1927, p. 33.

[2] Shakespeare, *Macbeth*, Act IV, sc iii.

[3] In Grieve and Aitken, *op. cit.*, Vol. II, pp. 1170 and 1310.

Scottish artist trying to give expression to himself. There is, in a word, no conscious Scottish 'tradition'. Gleams and flickerings amid a murk of grey mediocrity, even the odd volcanic eruption – these do not constitute a tradition. The greatest of these eruptions was Robert Burns whose work, growing directly out of Lowland folksong, proved capable of absorbing many outside influences without losing its individual Scottish identity.

But instead of Burns' achievement being the precedent and foundation of a conscious national cultural voice, Scotland continued to shroud itself in self-perpetuating fog while all over Europe, and then Latin America, national cultures were evolving apace.

The reason for this anomalous situation is to be found in the fear of self-knowledge which is, and has been for four hundred years, a fundamental characteristic of the Scottish establishment. It is derived directly from the loss of a national centre of cultural gravity in the Reformation. Those who control Scottish education, industry, administration, the mass media of every kind in Scotland, have taken their cue from the Scottish Kirk which opted for English as the language of the soul. It was not always so. Under James IV (r. 1488–1513), a Scots- and Gaelic-speaking Renaissance prince, Scotland entered the sixteenth century in a blaze of cultural splendour and vigour, with its perennial divisions into Lowland and Highland, Germanic and Celtic, potentially resolved and poised for cross-fertilisation. National confidence is exemplified in Bishop William Elphinstone's creation of a new Scottish liturgical calendar packed with Celtic saints (1508). But by 1603, when the court left for London, Scotland was more divided than ever. Now it lost its European identity and status, and by the time of the country's self-abolition in 1707, any confidence in its own cultural tradition had long since disappeared.

From the 1920s on, a plethora of men and women have made a determined and consistent effort to give Scotland a universal voice. A glance at the catalogue of Ronald Stevenson's works will give many of their names, chief amongst them the poet, polemicist and socialist Hugh MacDiarmid (1892–1978). This blazing upsurge, the 'Scottish Renaissance', has an aspect of real importance to this investigation of Ronald Stevenson's own Scottishness as a composer. Its greatest figures are geographically and socially marginal. MacDiarmid, of working-class origin, grew up, like his mentor, the composer Francis George Scott (1880–1958), in the rural Border country, not in Edinburgh. Likewise the painter William Johnson. Sydney Goodsir Smith, arguably the finest lyric voice in Scottish

Marjorie and Ronald Stevenson with the poet Sydney Goodsir Smith
around 1958 (photograph by Helmut Petzsch)

poetry, was born in New Zealand and educated in English public schools, coming to live in Scotland only when in his twenties, while Deorsa Mac Iain Deorsa (George Campbell Hay) and Somhairle Mac Gille Eathain (Sorley MacLean) wrote in that Gaelic language and tradition which is less than marginal to the Scottish urban establishment. Malcolm MacDonald, writing on Francis George Scott and his status as a native-born Scots composer of international stature, has drawn attention to the work of the Aberdeenshire composer Ronald Center. Center (1913–73) created his distinctively Scottish musical language in virtual isolation in the remote and rural North East which he never left.[4] Edwin Muir was an Orcadian, Neil Gunn a Caithness Highlander, and Lewis Grassic Gibbon a product of the Mearns farming community.

Though born in Lancashire, Stevenson is a Celt. Such a claim is not romantic nonsense based on the fact that Stevenson's father was a Scoto-Lancastrian: the child Stevenson used to listen to his Welsh grandmother's stories of her life as a child truck-pusher in the coalmines, as well as to her Welsh songs and occasional remarks in the Welsh tongue – a link with part of the experience of the

---

[4] *Cf.* Malcolm MacDonald, record review in *Tempo*, No. 139, December 1981, pp. 56–58, and James Reid Baxter, 'The Music of Ronald Center', *Cencrastus*, No. 5, Edinburgh, 1981.

Celtic-speaking peoples in the British Isles. Furthermore, much of the music made in that working-class home (his father was a railwayman) was 'Celtic' in inflection, since it included not only Moore's *Irish Melodies,* but arias from the operas of Balfe and Wallace. Stevenson's father was a keen amateur tenor and the repertoire included the songs of Burns and of Grieg. Burns was the young Stevenson's companion on his country walks amid the pungent smell of the manure-laden fields of Lancashire – a far cry from the cant of the Scottish 'Burns Cult', but reminiscent of Grieg's love of the stink of fish at Bergen harbour, which the Scoto-Norwegian composer claimed to have written into his music. Metaphorically, Stevenson's spiritual and musical compass was firmly orientated West and North – the Nordic music of Grieg was his first conscious musical influence, as can be seen in Ex. 59,[5] from a song composed when Stevenson was fourteen. The Celtic strain is manifest in the opening of the *Chorale Prelude for Jean Sibelius,* written when Stevenson was eighteen (Ex. 68).

Ex. 68

[5] On p. 178.

The work's dedication reflects Stevenson's intense admiration for the Finnish composer, 'a lighthouse amid the maelstrom' of post-War contemporary music to which he was exposed as a student at the Royal Northern College of Music in Manchester, where he had also encountered the names of F. G. Scott and Hugh Mac-Diarmid in the pages of Sorabji's *Mi Contra Fa*.[6] The *Prelude* was composed at the end of Stevenson's first-ever journey southwards, as he sat in Wormwood Scrubs prison for the crime of being a pacifist. On release he was 'allocated to the agricultural condition' and sent to work on a pacifist farm near Colchester. He found Colchester alien to him and compensated by setting William Blake 'in Celtic mood & mode' (Ex. 69). (He was to find the farm much more alien on the day that the pacifist farmers saw no objections to the use of their lands by the local fox-hunt.)

Ex. 69

Con spirito

mf

When the voi – ces of chil-dren are heard on the green

On his return to the civilian condition Stevenson made 33 unsuccessful applications to Education Committees, which refused to employ conscientious objectors to National Service. Eventually he found a job at Boldon Colliery, between Newcastle and Sunderland. But by now the yen to retrace his father's footsteps and move to Scotland was overpowering, and in 1952 he and his fiancée moved to Edinburgh. Almost at once Stevenson met Hugh MacDiarmid and seized the opportunity of making his acquaintance, sensing a kindred spirit – the start of a friendship which would prove an abiding inspiration. Within the decade the composer had brought out his essay 'MacDiarmid, Joyce and Busoni'.[7] The endless stream of Scots-language poetry settings had begun immediately, for Stevenson, universalist disciple of Busoni and Percy Grainger, had no more intention of being a cosmo-politan purveyor of rootlessness and angst than MacDiarmid had

---

[6] Kaikhosru Shapurji Sorabji, *Mi Contra Fa: The Immoralisings of a Machiavellian Musician*, The Porcupine Press, London, 1937.

[7] *Cf.* note 11 on p. 224.

when he wrote *A Drunk Man Looks at the Thistle*.[8] MacDiarmid had tackled the lack of a Scottish cultural tradition head-on, with an encyclopaedic attempt at naming the unknown Scotland.[9]

With the example of MacDiarmid before him and the poet's personal encouragement, Stevenson commenced the task of exploration and definition in the landscape of Scottish music, studying folk dance and folk song, and above all the Celtic tradition of variation by decoration – the infinitely decorated circle fundamental to Celtic art, the circle of the day, the year, of human life, each day the same and each utterly unique. The most striking result of this approach, always implicit in Stevenson's pacifist beliefs, is the *Passacaglia on DSCH*, but the same principle can be seen in many other pieces (even in the very title *A Rosary of Variations on Seán Ó Riada's Irish Folk Mass*), and not least in the fact that this pianist-composer has never written a piano sonata. The 'conflict-form' of sonata, of comparatively recent Germanic origins and Graeco-Roman classical inspiration, has never attracted Stevenson, whose goal is to reveal the underlying wholeness of diversity.

Alongside his interest in variation form Stevenson's catalogue of works reveals another major pre-occupation – the human voice. And, it should be noted, predominantly a Scottish voice. He has set literally hundreds of Scottish texts, whether for choir, ensemble or solo voice – ranging from the earliest extant Scots poem 'Qwhen Alexander our King' (fourteenth century) in his *Mediaeval Scottish Triptych*,[10] right through the centuries – *Ballattis of Luve* is a large-scale setting for four voices and lute of five lyrics by the mid-sixteenth-century court-poet Alexander Scott – to the myriad MacDiarmid settings, the choral settings of Somhairle Mac Gille Eathain and songs to Gaelic texts written in contemporary Glasgow by his son-in-law Aonghas MacNeacail. Like his systematic study of folk song, this activity reveals Stevenson's concern with air – the old word for melody – which is as necessary to speech as to song. The setting of words in Scots, Gaelic or Scottish-English has ensured that the melodies and airs created by the composer are Scottish in inflection and, by virtue of the texts chosen, in intent. A Scottish voice, then – but above all a human voice.

---

[8] Blackwood, Edinburgh, 1926; *cf.* Grieve and Aitken, *op. cit.*, Vol. I, pp. 83–166.

[9] A close parallel can be found in the work of the Chilean poet Pablo Neruda, and the heart-shaking injunction from the close of his vast *Alturas de Macchu Picchu*: 'Rise to birth with me now, my brother'.

[10] *Cf.* pp. 199–200, above.

Even more universal than song is dance which, free of the specific referentiality of text and language, can appeal directly to the atavistic physical sense of rhythm implicit in the beating of the human heart. Scottish folk dance, therefore, has received Stevenson's attention, not only obviously in such works as his *Scots Dance Toccata* but in a work which reveals most fully his desire to celebrate wholeness, the Violin Concerto. The work sets out *calmo ed albeggiante* with a pentatonic dawn rāga, which enables the composer to unify all the disparate folk elements employed in the course of this 55-minute work. This opening 'song' of the first movement grows into a dance as the violin is brought from India by the gypsies to Romania: the Concerto was commissioned by Yehudi Menuhin and is dedicated to his great teacher, the Rumanian violinist and composer George Enescu. The spirit of the dance is present even in the vast central elegy, which embraces Viennese traditions and Spain, while the finale begins with a 'strath-reel-jig' in which Stevenson combines the rhythms of all three Scots-Irish dances, and the violin continues its journey through space and time in a homage to the Hardanger fiddle which inspired Grieg's *Slåtter*: a Norwegian wedding-march becomes a Norse funeral march. With the *Dies Irae* night begins to fall, but the Atlantic is crossed in a rumbustious square-dance, and the cycle of the day closes with a reference to a new day to come. East and West, dawn and dusk, song and dance, life and death themselves are all shown to be ornamentations on the great circle of being. Even the solo instrument itself, in this concerto, is mainly a participant in the celebration of existence: there are important parts for piano and for cimbalom, and at one point the violin soloist strums an accompaniment while the timpani intone the tune.[11]

This is reminiscent of James Joyce's *Ulysses*: Stevenson as a Scotsman looks both West and North, a point beautifully illustrated in his *Duo Sonata* for harp and piano where the Celtic element, the harp, has Lydian fourths deriving from Scandinavian music – while the Germanic piano has the Scottish dance (Ex. 70).

Stevenson's Scottish spirit, untrammelled by a Scottish upbringing and education, has never been in danger of suffocating in twilit mist, while it is precisely his sense of being rooted in what is Scots that gives his music the confidence to bestride the world. In his search for the unknown Scotland Stevenson has attained the universal in the local and in what lies around him. He knows that

---

[11] *Cf.* pp. 154–59. –ED.

Ex. 70

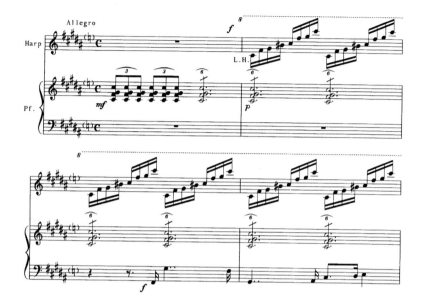

he and his music fit into the decorated circle of mankind, and what his art affirms is the falseness of pessimism and alienated angst. Stevenson's conviction that alienation and separation – disunity, fear and violence – can be overcome is exemplified in his *Variations and Air* for cello and piano (Ex. 71). This cramped and fearful music, crushed and flattened, gradually expands and grows through the variations until at last it blossoms into a quiet rendering of the ancient folk song, 'The Bonny Earl o' Moray' (Ex. 72).[12] Some seem to prefer to call this retrogressive, but the point of the piece is that it works toward the revelation of the song whose simplicity underlies the complexity of the variations.

Ex. 71

---

[12] *Cf.* pp. 171–72. –ED.

Ex. 72

Tema:'The Bonnie Earl o' Moray'

   Since 1962 Ronald Stevenson has been engaged on a vast project, the so-called Symphony, *Ben Dorain*, which I have been able to discuss with its composer and even hear in a fragmentary piano 'realisation'. The origins of this work link it directly with the Celtic-derived variational ideas already seen: after presiding over the presentation in 1962 to Dmitri Shostakovitch of the bound score of the *Passacaglia on DSCH*, Hugh MacDiarmid suggested to Stevenson that he might be able to apply this kind of compositional approach to the poet's own English verse-paraphrase of the *Moladh Beinn Dòbhrain* (*Praise of Ben Dorain*) by the eighteenth-century Scottish poet Donnachadh Bàn Mac an t-Saoir (Duncan Ban McIntyre, 1724–1812). Stevenson began to set the poem at once, for double chorus and large orchestra, but the result was not in fact a 'symphony' in the Central European sense at all. It is a development or extension of *Ceòl Mór*, the 'Great Music' of the Highland Pipes, vulgarly known as pibroch: for Donnachadh Bàn's virtuosic poem is constructed as a pibroch, a set of variations on a basic slow air or 'ground', the variation taking place by ever more complicated ornamentation. In the poem the *ùrlar*, or ground, is the splendour of the mountain itself:[13]

---

[13] In Grieve and Aitken, *op. cit.*, Vol. I, pp. 587–600; *cf.* Stevenson's incipit, Ex. 78, on p. 295.

Over mountains, pride
Of place to Ben Dorain!
I've nowhere espied
A finer to reign.
In her moorbacks wide
Hosts of shy deer bide;
While light comes pouring
Diamond-wise from her side!

In ever more complex variations the poem describes this haunt of the wild deer 'Keenest of careering/Of smelling and hearing', with plentiful and accurate information about the animals. For Donnachadh Bàn was in modern terms a gamekeeper, and his great praise-poem culminates in a wild deer hunt, which Stevenson sets as as a breath-taking and fiercely exultant fugue. Into the work's fabric the composer has woven many of the traditional melodies associated with the mountain, and the singing text employs parts of the Gaelic original as well as MacDiarmid's version. How can a man of Stevenson's convictions set hunting poetry? In *Ben Dorain* the deer are not the prey, but the quarry – from Latin quaerere, 'to seek' (*cf.* Spanish *querer* – to love). What Stevenson's hunters are seeking out, with all their skill, all their love and understanding of the quarry, is the soul of Scotland.

That soul is no illusion, but it is certainly becoming more and more elusive. The very Gaelic language itself is on the knife-edge between extinction and survival, and with it any living Gaelic culture in Scotland, while the rural folk-culture of Lowland Scotland is already extinct, like the society within which it had a genuine folk life. The situation for Scottish music particularly is critical. A poem requires only to be printed; music has to be performed – and performed frequently and performed well. Ronald Stevenson's realism about the Scottish situation has always gone so far as to admit that it might already be too late – too late, that is, for Scotland to be brought face to face with itself, achieve self-knowledge, articulate its soul and live. Although in the spring-summer of 2004, Stevenson is working on completing the orchestration. *Ben Dorain* remains in some sense a vision – and it will be no less a vision even when there is a bound full score. Nobody is clamouring for the honour of giving the first performance; and the most fitting setting for that premiere, the Edinburgh Festival, has never featured a note of Stevenson's music to this day.

Yet Stevenson's ceaseless activity, whether as composer, per-former of the music of F. G. Scott and Ronald Center, broadcaster of radio series on pibroch, the Celtic harp and the fiddle, as well

Stevenson in the Pentland Hills near West Linton, 1965
(photograph by John Ellis)

as Grainger and Busoni, all indicates an indomitable refusal to give in to fashionable pessimism. In 1926 Hugh MacDiarmid asked:[14]

> What are prophets and priests and kings,
> What's ocht tae the people o' Scotland?

In the 21st century the cultural situation in Scotland looks even bleaker than before, despite cosmetic parliamentary changes. The new depths of consumerist materialism and general stultification achieved by the present-day United Kingdom makes it well nigh

---

[14] In *A Drunk Man Looks at the Thistle*, in Grieve and Aitken, *op. cit.*, Vol. 1, p. 108.

impossible for the figures of the twentieth-century renaissance to be other than nocht to the people of Scotland. Yet for Stevenson and his fellow prophets, their quest for ways of understanding and expressing what it means to be Scottish enabled them to voice their own souls in 'a language [that] rings / Wi datchie sesames, and names for nameless things'.[15] Those nameless things are an integral part of the universal heritage of all mankind. Through his self-discovery and self-knowledge as a Scot, Stevenson has found a universal language in which he has created a unique body of work that will enrich future generations. It was Stevenson himself, after all, who wrote of Hugh MacDiarmid that 'we are not his contemporaries. His contemporaries are those unborn'.[16] Scotland's modern renaissance donned the long-discarded mantle of the giants of the Stewart Renaissance – the mantle of Bishop Gavin Douglas, translating Virgil's *Aeneid* into Scots; of George Buchanan, universally acknowledged the greatest Latin poet of his day; of Robert Carver, singing the union of the choirs of heaven with the voices of mankind; of Bishop Elphinstone founding his university in Aberdeen and making that city shine with European light – ferocious patriots all of them, citizens of the known world, hunters of the souls of men and seekers of wholeness, truth and peace. Ronald Stevenson's Scottish vision is a universal vision, the soul of Scotland hunted on Ben Dorain is that Celtic and Germanic heritage of the Scottish nation which is Scotland's unique contribution to the universal spirit of man. Seeking that Scottish soul, Stevenson's work has realised the synthesis of which James IV may, perhaps, have dreamt, and in so doing, has attained the universal in the local, the eternal in the transient – and found Man.

> *S ged a thuirt mi beagan riu*
> *Mu'n insinn uil' an dleasnas orra*
> *Chuireadh iad a'm bhreislich mi*
> *Le deismireachd comraidh!*[17]

---

[15] MacDiarmid, 'Garmscoile', in Grieve and Aitken, *op. cit.*, Vol. I, p. 74. 'Datchie sesames' are secret passwords.

[16] 'MacDiarmid's Muses', in P. H. Scott and A. C. Davis (eds.), *The Age of MacDiarmid*, Mainstream, Edinburgh, 1980, p. 169.

[17] Donnachadh Bàn, *Moladh Beinn Dòbhrain*, final stanza, transl. Hugh MacDiarmid, in Grieve and Aitken, *op. cit.*, Vol. I, p. 600.

> Though I've told a little of Ben Dorain here
> Before I could tell all it deserves, I would be
> In a delirium with the strange prolixity
> Of the talking called for, I fear.

Envoi
WHAT NOW?
Colin Scott-Sutherland

It is tempting, at a vantage point such as a published survey of a man's work, to take a retrospective view. In Ronald Stevenson's case – although this reveals two piano concertos, a violin concerto, most recently a cello concerto, a string quartet, a piano quartet, several major works for harp, harpsichord and for cello, a series of innovative orchestral works, some ten song-cycles, to say nothing of a vast corpus of piano music and songs – it gives only a partial understanding of a complex creative personality. The variety of thought and idea thus demonstrated is perplexing enough: to make any kind of generalisation or pigeon-holing of his versatile spirit is virtually impossible.

After only a few years' acquaintance with him I felt able to write (in 1965):

> It is salutary to reflect that Ronald Stevenson is only thirty-six. And, what particularly prompts this article now, he has recently entered upon a new and vital phase of creativity, significant in that it reflects a deep understanding of a genuine Scottish element in music [...].[1]

This, at a point when the introverted semitonalism of his work to that date – when he had already completed the vast *Passacaglia on DSCH* – had begun to stretch itself into the sixths and sevenths engendered by the ingestion of Scottish song melody into his expression, first enunciated in the FGS motif[2] that appeared in the *Ne'erday Sang* and *Keening Sang for a Makar*. What I saw then as a fresh burgeoning of creative activity has not ceased in the ensuing forty-odd years, and continues today. This energy of creativity ensures that fresh ideas and new stimuli constantly produce new works, varied both in content and medium. A survey of Ronald Stevenson's music thus has to take a Janus-headed view – for the impressive energies that powered the *Passacaglia* and the hectic enthusiasm of the many piano transcriptions spill over into a

---

[1] 'The Music of Ronald Stevenson', *loc. cit.*, p. 118.

[2] *Cf.* p. 34. Stevenson mentions (in 'MacLean: Musician Manqué', *loc. cit.*, p. 177) that his 'initiation into Gaelic Song happened when I was 30. The year – 1958', and he goes on to note that on several occasions it was the complex and intricate rhythms that impressed him at that point.

Stevenson and Colin Scott-Sutherland in 1968
(photography by Marjorie Stevenson)

continuing corpus of recent compositions and works-in-progress that includes not only several large-scale variation structures, but the choral-orchestral epic *Ben Dorain* and innumerable other ideas that demonstrate a marvellous facility as well as a fertile and receptive imagination.

In this book little account has yet been given of the various miscellaneous works which fit into no particular category but demonstrate this variety of idea and purpose. There is a variety of instrumental compositions for harp, organ and less usual media that fit into no suitable chapter. It is with these – as well as, in a measure, with the underlying concepts of his creative imagination – that I wish to deal here.

A number of pre-occupations are realised in such an overview. Stevenson is concerned with melody – specifically with the song, of which he has written well over two hundred. This concern is further demonstrated in many keyboard works, in particular his *L'Art Nouveau du Chant appliqué au piano* – an echo of Thalberg's Op. 70 (a cycle of some two dozen pieces, studies in the art of *bel canto* piano playing) in which he transcribes various Victorian and Edwardian ballads by, among others, Wallace, Balfe, Maude Valérie

White and Coleridge-Taylor (Ex. 73).[3]

Ex. 73

This melodic pre-occupation does not confine him in any way simply to varied arrangements of such tunes, or of Scots folk melodies, for he makes frequent use of fragments of other music (Purcell, Chopin and Berg, among others), such as the twelve-note theme from Liszt's *Faust-Symphonie* which begets the *Prelude and Fugue* for organ; and, of course, themes of his own devising (*Andante Sereno, Norse Elegy, Recitative and Air* and *Song without Words*[4]). These melodic germs lead to the use of harmonic colouring far removed from the common conception of Scots folksong although, having a close relationship with the Gaelic,[5] they

---

[3] It is worth noting that, amongst the many felicities in this set of melodic pieces (which includes several for left hand alone), Stevenson in his transcription of Ivor Novello's *We'll Gather Lilacs* quotes from Rachmaninov's song 'Lilacs' – a quiet demonstration of his wide and catholic knowledge and interests. He once mentioned to me that Coleridge-Taylor, who set his own *Negro Melodies* for piano, was advised by no less a purist than Stanford to send his melodies to Percy Grainger for 'treatment'. *Cf.* p. 434, note 28.

[4] This last is reproduced in Appendix Five: Some Stevenson Miniatures, pp. 364–65.

[5] *Cf.* p. 270.

are frequently related specifically to formal and architectonic constructions – as in the 'Clavis Astarte Magica' theme from Busoni's *Doktor Faust* which he uses in the *Prelude, Fugue and Fantasy*.

A concern with melody is not the only element which emerges. It is immediately apparent that Stevenson is deeply concerned with texture – not only that implied by the scoring for a particular instrument or instruments (witness works for clarsach, bagpipe, guitar duo, and free-bass accordion and percussion) but also as demonstrated in his transcriptions for piano, of which art he is surely the most accomplished practitioner alive today.[6] Here, in transcriptions of works of quite catholic diversity, he voices his concern not only to translate – born of his enthusiasm to communicate and his desire to make all music more accessible – but also to transfigure, in itself a creative activity, either simply as in his editions of Delius, Grainger and Tchaikovsky, or with the musical erudition of a Busoni or a Godowsky in such works as Grainger's *Hill Song No. 1*, the *Canonic Caprice (after Strauss' The Bat)*, or such 'arrangements' as that in 1983 of Boccherini's famous minuet described as being 'in forma di uno studio polifonico' (Ex. 74).

This pre-occupation that the texture should enshrine the musical idea is clearly demonstrated in all his work, not only in the more unusual combinations, such as the *Duo Sonata* for harp and piano, but in his 'arrangements' of the simplest folk melodies. In his transcription of the folk melody *The Water of Tyne* (for piano) he begins with Schubertian 'glass octaves' high on the keyboard register, followed by a clustered chordal variation, rich in dark harmonic foliage. A subsequent variation has the melody in the inner parts under a Palmgren-like filigree arabesque in the upper register. A similarly creative use of texture as an expressive element can be heard in the opening bars of *Heroic Song* which exploits echoing overtones,[7] and there are recurrent instances (in *The Continents* and elsewhere) of his use of the struck or harped strings of the piano, the pianist reaching inside the instrument.

Texture, the canvas of the music, the sound that is produced, is essentially an amalgam of harmony, counterpoint and form – the first being the colour, the second the line-drawing, and the third the structure, into all of which the melodic thread is embedded.

---

[6] Busoni himself suggested (in *Sketch of a New Aesthetic of Music, op. cit.*, p. 85) that notation was the transcription of an idea – and performance a further transcription of the printed note. Stevenson's transcriptions include a number for strings and other solo instruments, as well as for piano. *Cf.* also pp. 98–106 and 433–47.

[7] *Cf.* p. 64.

Ex. 74

Stevenson's use of harmonic resource employs a considerable amount of dissonance (particularly in the early works such as the Violin Sonata, and the first three Sonatinas for piano) – and yet is often limpidly direct (as in the opening song of the cycle *Hills of Home*, quite Quilterian in its direct appeal (Ex. 75). His use is in no way impressionistic; it is closely developed from the interaction and interpenetration of the polyphonic lines of melody – with a marked use of canon.

There are, too, many fugues amongst his compositions and many instances of fugal writing of one sort or another.[8] His approach to fugue is original and unusual. It is noticeable that, unlike classical

---

[8] *Cf.* 'Hard is My Fate', reproduced in Appendix Five: Some Stevenson Miniatures, pp. 362–63.

Ex. 75

procedures, the position of the fugue in a complex Stevenson work is generally at the beginning – 'when' as the composer points out, 'the listener's ear is fresh'[9] – or in the centre. It is noteworthy also from both a harmonic and melodic point of view that the theme of the fugue from the *Prelude and Fugue* for organ is palindromic: it ends with a mirror-image of its opening statement.

This originality extends also to his use of variation form – where the accustomed practice is reversed to forms like variations-and-theme, or the *Fugue, Variations and Epilogue on a Theme of Bax*. The fugue in *Ben Dorain* is, in fact, the scherzo of the symphonic/epic form, and only seldom in Stevenson's *œuvre* does a fugue end a work.

Within the problem of texture, therefore, Stevenson is also deeply concerned with the problems of form. He has expressed the theory that each period in history is encapsulated in a specific form – the age of reason in Bach and his contemporaries (such as Leibnitz, Spinoza and Descartes – and even Linnaeus) in fugue and counterpoint, the age of the enlightenment in sonata-form reaching its apogee in the *Eroica*.[10] In the twentieth century variation techniques culminate in the dodecaphonic procedures of the Second Viennese School – which procedures carry with them their own strict rules. Seán Ó Riada suggested that the trajectory of sonata form, or 'first-movement form', was that of an ascent towards the 'Golden Section' point, its nature angular and aspiring, and contrasts that with Cencrastus, the Celtic snake, its tail in its mouth, the completeness of the circle (total variation).[11] Ronald Stevenson sees in his own work the dual tributaries of the mid- and eastern European (Busoni and Shostakovich) and the Celtic, and asserts that variation form is the form in which much of his own work is cast. In many variation structures the climax comes often in a plain and simple statement – accented and perhaps *allargando* – of the theme itself, a return of the principal idea like the head of the snake. In the pibroch, however, there is no real climax other than that suggested by the *cruanlath* or crowning variation, which is decorated in a multiplicity of ornament – of which MacDiarmid wrote:[12]

[9] In conversation with the author. *Cf.* also, for example, Myaskovsky's Piano Sonata No. 1 in D minor, Op. 6.

[10] *Ibid.*

[11] In Thomas Kinsella (ed.), *Our Musical Heritage*, The Dolmen Press, Dublin, 1982, p. 21.

[12] *The Islands of Scotland, op cit.*, p. xiii.

They [pibrochs] were timeless music – hence their affiliation with plainsong, with the neuma, the song which hangs on to the end of a word without a word, 'uaill-gluth an Aoibhnis' (the exultant note of joy) as O'Heffernan the Irish Gaelic poet called it. Barred music – accented music – finds its ultimate form in symphony. Unbarred music – quantity music – expresses itself in pattern repetition: hence the idea that the Celt has no architectonic power, that his art is confined to niggling involutions and intricacies – yet the ultimate form here is not symphony, it is epic.

In this there is also a strong parallel with the work of Arnold Bax:

It is a curious beauty, eminently sane and yet tinged with a certain wist-fulness wherein resides at once its charm and its paradoxical nature, for to be wistful and at the same time robust is a combination of qualities that falls to few. In his larger works it enables him to allow his ideas to become fluid with the full confidence that they will not lose their plastic shape, and in the smaller compositions, such as his piano-forte pieces, it gives him an unusual degree of liberty in dealing with the background before which the material is presented in motion.[13]

In Bax it is often the second-subject material, the feminine or 'B' element, that is in the end dominant or at least an amalgam of both 'A' and 'B' material.[14]

Consideration of variation form must also involve fugue and canon, where strict imitation must be handled in masterly fashion. If one studies the *Passacaglia on DSCH* – written using surely one of the most severely restrictive and rigid of procedures, relying on the constant repetition of a four-note motif (even if this is, within itself, a three-fold variation cell, shown in Ex. 76) – then the complexity and variety of the processes derived from, and superimposed upon, this fragment can be seen as masterly in their ingenuity.

This work provides a perfect illustration of the marriage of the thematic idea – the endlessly repeated DSCH motif – and the wealth of changing landscape, or tone-scape, which the composer

---

[13] Edwin Evans, 'Modern British Composers, II: Arnold Bax', *The Musical Times*, 1 March 1919. In all this there is a very strong connection with the East. Gaelic songs are markedly oriental in the cast of the melody – and Margaret Hannagan (in *Londubh an Chairn – Being Songs of the Irish Gaels*, Oxford University Press, London, 1927) wrote that 'We are really Orientals in our singing and the gravity of the Gaelic singers is that of the East'.

[14] Grainger once remarked that the satisfaction of sonata form was a kind of intellectual orgasm where the foreplay of development and the climax of resolution were a kind of expression of purely masculine libido. 'Obviously the recurrence [of the statement] would be more effective if delayed for a time' (R. O. Morris, *The Structure of Music*, Oxford University Press, London, 1935, p. 55).

Ex. 76

weaves around it, culminating in a triple fugue, perhaps the most technically and intellectually demanding formal musical construction that could be devised, yet here expressed with the most glorious freedom, a masterpiece of contrapuntal ingenuity, bending the requirements of the strictly formal process to the expressive human need that is, in effect, the burden of the *Passacaglia,* despite its existence as a technical *tour de force.*

Stevenson's concern for texture is expressed in countless ways, not least in his writing for unusual and sonorous combinations, but also in his handling of chorus, organ, harp and guitar. It is scarcely surprising that the texture of the sound of the organ should have attracted him. Apart from the *Doubles on Rubbra's Cradle Hymn* (written as a Christmas greeting in 1976 for his friend Edmund Rubbra) and *Reflections on an Old Scots Psalm Tune* (written for Colin Scott-Sutherland), his first major work for organ is the *Prelude and Fugue on a 12-note Theme from Liszt's 'Faust Symphonie'.*

> Faust stands as the Western mythic archetype of the titanic ego out for itself at any cost, in league with the Evil One himself to attain an end which turns out to be illusory. Those immensely wise and many-sided guides of Ronald Stevenson, Goethe, Liszt and Busoni, allow Faust salvation, however: for in the end Faust realises that reality is infinitely bigger than he is and he identifies himself with the endless future. The *Prelude and Fugue,* written for the 150th anniversary of Liszt's birth treat the 12-note theme harmonically in the chorale-prelude and then in a strict five-part fugue. The counter-subject of the fugue is given an extraordinary *strettissimo maestralissimo* handling, where the parts are answering each other at the shortest possible distance of time (and the canon is going through all five parts) which Stevenson has described as a 'mountain range of sound – the Black Cuillinn of Skye'. In the final palindromic section the countersubject becomes the subject and the 12-note theme, like the evil to which Faust thought to have surrendered himself, is absorbed into the greater reality, becoming itself the countersubject. This typically Stevensonian gesture reflects his belief that the only just view of reality is the view that encompasses all reality.[15]

[15] James Reid Baxter, programme note for 'A Concert for Peace', Old St Pauls, Jeffrey Street, Edinburgh, 30 November 1988.

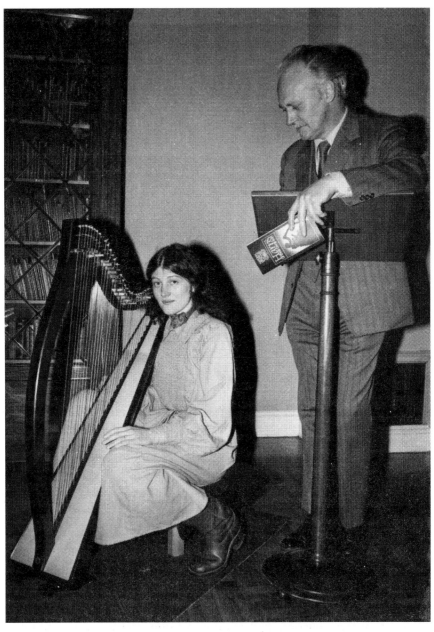

With his daughter Savourna, Edinburgh, 1981,
for the lecture-recital 'Harps of their own Sort'
given in the National Library of Scotland
(photograph courtesy of The Scotsman*)*

In 1981 Stevenson gave a lecture, 'Harps of their own Sort', accompanied on the clarsach by his daughter Savourna, for the opening of an exhibition at the National Library of Scotland. 'They delight very much in music, especially in harps of their own sort', wrote the sixteenth-century Scottish scholar, George Buchanan, of the inhabitants of the Western Isles.[16] Stevenson's meticulous research into Irish origins is impressive, but more so is his concern for the textural and harmonic possibilities of the clarsach:

> The clarsach has possibilities denied to the pedal harp. On the pedal harp, one pedal changes the pitch of every octave. On the clarsach, one single note can be changed by the blade without changing its octave. It can therefore play more complex harmonies than the pedal harp. The clarsach's harmonic vocabulary ranges from mediaeval to 20th-century bitonal or polyphonic dissonance.
>
> My miniature *Country Tune* (*Clarsair Annual,* No. 1, 1980)[17] [Ex. 77] exploits harmonies playable on the clarsach but not on the pedal harp.
>
> My album *Sounding Strings*, music from the six Celtic countries arranged for clarsach, (London, 1979),[18] utilises other possibilities (percussion on the soundbox, harmonics, etc.).[19]

Stevenson adds a 'Composer's note' to the score:

> Because I live in the country, in the delectable village of West Linton in the Borders; and – unlike some modern composers – I love tunes. My pen-pal Percy Grainger told me that he'd observed as a folksong collector that folksingers often sang a flattened 7th in the upper octave (it's easier to sing flatter higher up) and a sharpened leading-note in the lower octave. I've used this idea in my tune. Notice the unusual key-signature. Then in bar 3 I've written some harmonies playable on the clarsach but unplayable on the concert harp; because the clarsach can alter one blade at a time, whereas a pedal of the concert harp alters the same note in every octave. So my piece is also a small tribute to this glorious wee instrument, the Scottish clarsach.

Stevenson has written a number of important compositions for the pedal harp, too, the most important being the large-scale, two-movement *Duo Sonata* for harp and piano, and the *Fantasia Polifonica.* The first was commissioned by Ann Griffiths and first

---

[16] *Rerum Scoticarum Historia* (1582), trans. J. Gunn, *Enquiry*, 1807.

[17] The Clarsach Society, Edinburgh.

[18] United Music Publishers; Dwelly's *Gaelic Dictionary* (1st edn. 1901, 9th edn. 1977) gives the root of *clarsach* as 'a board or plank', referring to the soundbox. 'Sounding Strings', an expression used in old Gaelic poetry, also refers to the soundboard.

[19] Lecture series 1, National Library of Scotland, Edinburgh, March 1981.

Ex. 77

performed by her, with the composer, on Sunday, 28 February 1971 in the Purcell Room, London – a richly melodic work. The second, commissioned by the Finnish harpist Satu Salo, was given its premiere on 8 February 1984, also in the Purcell Room. In B flat minor, like the piano piece on which it is based,[20] it opens with a Prelude. The theme is treated in canon which, after a Kalevala-type song section, becomes a passacaglia. The work ends with a four-part fugue.

The variety of allusion in Stevenson's work is astonishing – and although many of these miscellaneous works have a noticeably

---

[20] 'The Harper', No. 8 of Sibelius' *Ten Pieces for Piano*, Op. 34 (1914–16).

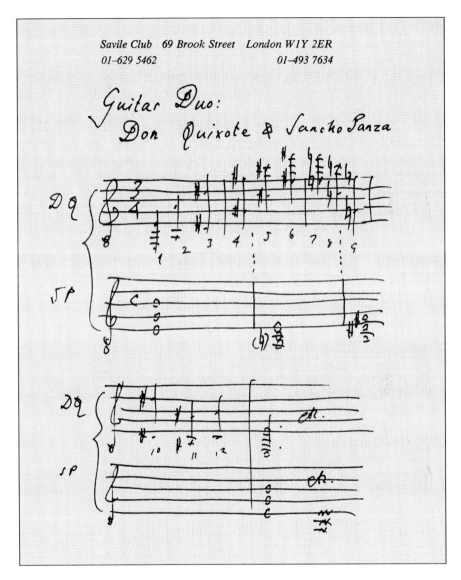

The beginning of the guitar duo Don Quixote and Sancho Panza –
*an explanatory sketch Stevenson made on a visit to London
to show the Don's high-flown thought in a twelve-note theme
and Panza's down-to-earth diatonic triads*

Scottish application,[21] two works in particular point to another influence in his music deriving from the more burlesque side of Busoni's aesthetic. They are the guitar duo *Don Quixote and Sancho Panza* – a colourful subject which had long attracted Stevenson – and *The Harlot's House* for percussion and free-bass accordion, based on a poem by Oscar Wilde.

The guitar duo depicts the two contrasting characters of Quixote and Sancho Panza, the one with a twelve-note theme and the other, its foil, the three primary triads, the whole woven into a kind of cycle of bagatelles (in the Beethovenian sense). The two themes amble harmoniously along at the outset, much dominated by the chattering Sancho Panza – and with the Don at prayer, his companion dances in derision. The two motifs, 'Quixote thinks and sighs' and 'Panza dances and laughs', are together embroiled in an accompanied fugue; and as the two characteristic identities interplay – idealist and realist – the music comes to a climax in the shout of 'Malancida canalla' ('evil guttersnipes') as Quixote falls in rage upon Master Peter's Puppet Show and destroys the pantomime. *Lento mesto*, with the twelve-note theme in drooping resignation, Quixote, the Knight of the Sorrowful Countenance, contemplates the wreckage – and not unexpectedly the true dénouement comes, 'not with a bang but a whimper', in the concluding pages.

This decorative work is almost outdone in extravagant imagery by the evocation, for free-bass accordion and percussion (written in 1988 for Owen Murray and Evelyn Glennie), of Wilde's poem, *The Harlot's House*. Subtitled a 'Dance Poem after Oscar Wilde', this burlesque composition was commissioned by The Lamp of Lothian (subsidised by the Scottish Arts Council). A grotesquerie, a *Totentanz*, mocking as if with cloven hoof on the xylophone keys, it is a vivid 25-minute piece culminating in the expressive 'love has entered into the house of lust'. A brilliant Sitwellian extravaganza, it gives expression to that mood and image that, Stevenson suggests, impelled him earlier to think in operatic terms of quite unusual subjects – and contemplate wholly original treatment.

---

[21] For example, the virtuosic *Scots Suite* for solo violin, a large and impassioned piece in four movements (the composer's own analysis is reproduced as Appendix Six, pp. 369–73, below); the film music for *Hammer and Thistle*, a TV documentary about Hugh MacDiarmid; and *Ballatis of Luve* – 'ballads of courtly love exploring the manic depressive nature of the amorous malady' end with an *Andante grave* based on the tuning of the lute, quoting cyclically from the four previous movements (*cf.* pp. 200–1).

*A recent photograph of Ronald Stevenson, at his desk
in 'The Den of Musiquity' (photograph by Colin Scott-Sutherland)*

To date Stevenson has not attempted opera, but he has considered several ideas – and in some measure the last two works discussed contain the expression of his dramatic sense, the surreal contrast to the reality of so much of his music. Yet he did conceive, in the 1950s of a television opera on the subject of the painter J. M. Turner. Of more immediate significance are the sketches, dating from 1987, for a fantastically colourful burlesque opera on the subject of Blake's *An Island in the Moon*. And around a decade earlier he expressed to me the idea that his main concern in opera would be to depersonalise the conventions of stage opera – to conceive a 'street' opera, to be staged in the open air, perhaps within a pedestrian precinct – with subjects such as the *Martyrdom of Red Clyde* (the subject being John MacLean, the Glasgow socialist activist) and on the trial of Georgi Dimitrov called *The Fire* (after Barbusse), both conceived as modern myths. In the autumn of 1990, too, Stevenson toyed with the idea of writing a libretto, in English and Italian, based on Mörike's novelle *Mozart auf der Reise nach Prague*.

But above all, the true stage of Stevenson's expression is to be found in a Scottish setting, the ultimate expression of a very real duality of personality, the Busonian/Latin and the Nordic/Celtic, which are quite often superimposed in his work, in what he sees as a world culture. But the apparent nationalism he expresses in his work is never parochial; and, as in his book *Western Music,* man is the core of his expression and concern.

The texture of *Bergstimmung* for horn and piano evokes

> The mystery of mountains
> Their gloom
> Their glory
> Their vortex
> Their peace[27]

whose echoing magic recalls the lonely slopes of the opening of the *Heroic Song.* This hill music echoes through the fastnesses of Stevenson's Gaelic choral triptych *Anns an Airde, as an Doimhne.*[28] The upthrusting company of mountains portrayed in the first of the set, 'Ceann Loch Aoineart' ('Kinloch Ainort') is depicted with uncanny sensitivity in the first vocal phrase.

This concern with the Gaelic and with the wild and craggy moorlands and hills of Scotland can be seen as a prelude to the epic choral work-in-progress, *Ben Dorain,* complete in sketch form.[29] This work, originally said to be a symphony, is conceived in one large movement, essentially a variation structure. The principal motif (Ex. 78) acts as the 'urlar or 'ground' of the richly tapestried variation structure.

This work promises to be the summation of Stevenson's music, incorporating the main thrust of his musical thought, based on the variation procedures of the classical *piobaireachd,* yet incorporating also fugue, and yet again the epitome of Busonian ideals. At one point (Ex. 79) this richness of texture and melodic decoration is very close to the music of Arnold Bax, for whom too Morar and the North were potent influences. Stevenson once quoted to me from Tennyson:

> [. . .] bright and fierce and fickle is the South
> And dark and true and tender is the North.[30]

And it is in this direction, northwards, that the magnetic mountain is drawing him.

---

[27] These are the composer's own lines, inscribed on the score.

[28] *Cf.* pp. 191–94.

[29] Cf. pp. 273–74.

[30] *The Princess: A Medley.*

Ex. 78

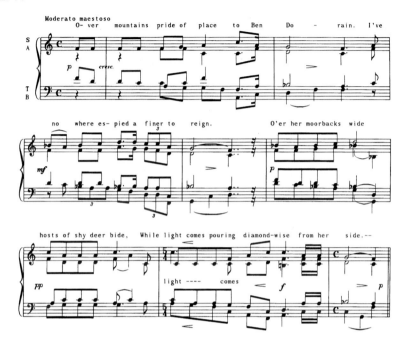

Ex. 79

Appendix One
STEVENSON'S
RECITAL PROGRAMMES
Colin Scott-Sutherland

Ronald Stevenson's capacity for large-scale, organised musical thought complements his exuberant enthusiasm for demonstration. These two elements characterise most of his highly original recital programmes, mingling the facets of renewed but always fresh experience, the delight of discovery, and the summation of achievement – and over all, a consummate sense of purpose which, allied to his persuasive advocacy, makes each of his recitals a unique, and always joyful, didactic experience.

I first experienced this kind of programme at Campbeltown in 1965 when, as my guest, Ronald Stevenson came to play to the Kintyre Music Society. The good folk of Kintyre were amazed and captivated. The programme consisted of Purcell, Bach and Mozart played on the spinet – with the Mozart (K397) repeated after the interval on the piano. I had found for him (avoiding the inevitable Town Hall upright) a magnificent and sonorous Scheidmayer grand – and the remainder of the programme, after Beethoven and Chopin, consisted of the exciting *Cracovienne Fantastique* of Paderewski, Szymanowski's *Étude*, Op. 4, No. 3, the *Three Pieces for the Young* of Lutosławski, three of the Grieg *Slåtter*, Grainger's *Scotch Strathspey and Reel*, and concluded with his own *Simple Variations on Purcell's 'New Scotch Tune'*. After the recital, we two alone in the hall, he gave a magisterial performance of the Bach/Busoni Chaconne.

> Everyone was so friendly in Campbeltown. Even as I stepped on the plane the coach driver shook my hand and thanked me for the concert. I showed him the two pages of MS notes for my musical celebration of Campbeltown[1] and he agreed that the Royal Burgh was worth something a bit better than the song [...].[2]

The element of virtuosity, even showmanship, in his playing, his enthusiastic didactic powers and passion for music that so often languishes for the lack of a persuasive and informed advocacy, all began to inform Stevenson's expression, both in composition and performance. The counterbalancing elements of emotional warmth and intellectual control are held in occasional equipoise – although quite frequently one or the other element predominates with quite characteristic results.

While ever a persuasive advocate of his own music Ronald Stevenson has devoted numerous recitals to the work of others – notably Grainger, Alan Bush, Ronald Center, Frank Merrick and Bernard Stevens. For the

---

[1] The first stirrings of *Fugue, Variations and Epilogue on a Theme of Bax*, the melody being from the second movement of the Second Symphony. On 8 October 1965 Ronald had written to me, after I had given him a copy of the full score, 'It is centuries since a man had such strange phantasmagoric dreams'.

[2] Letter to the author, dated 30 October 1965. The 'song', of course, was the popular 'Campbeltown Loch, I wish you were whisky'.

```
              KINTYRE MUSIC CLUB

            Tuesday September 28th 1965

       R O N A L D   S T E V E N S O N
             Spinet and Pianoforte

Spinet:
Suite No 1 in G   .............   PURCELL
The Queen's Dolour (realisation
by Ronald Stevenson)      ......
Ground in E minor         ......
Ground in D minor         ......
15 Two part Inventions ........   BACH
Menuet in D (K 355)   .........   MOZART
Fantasy in D minor (K 397) ....
              -0000000000-
Pianoforte:
Fantasy in D minor (K 397).....   MOZART
Sonata in F sharp major Op 78..   BEETHOVEN
3 Ecossaises Op 72 Nos 3-5  ...   CHOPIN
Cracovienne Fantastique  ......   PADEREWSKI
Chant du Voyageur       ........
Study in B flat minor  Op 4 (3)   SZYMANOWSKI
Three Mazurkas Op 50 (3,6,&14).
Three Popular Melodies ........   LITTOSLAWSKI
Three Slatter (Folk Dances)....   GRIEG
Scotch Strathspey and Reel ....   GRAINGER
Simple Variations on Purcell's
         Scotch Tune ..........   RONALD
                                  STEVENSON
```

The home-spun programme for Stevenson's
Kintyre recital in 1965

centenary of Frank Merrick's birth (30 April 1986), in a concert given together with the cellist Steven Isserlis and Mary Remnant (playing mediaeval instruments), he performed a number of pieces associated with Merrick, including Leschetizky's Toccata (Op. 46, No. 5), the Schubert *Impromptu* in B flat (D935, No. 3), the B flat *Nocturne* of Field, and Bax's *Paean* – as well as his own arrangement of the slow movement, 'Sea Scape', of Merrick's Second Piano Concerto.

At two recitals, on 3 and 5 May 1974, the first of these in Edinburgh's Reid Hall, the second in London's Wigmore, Stevenson played in aid of the 'Wat Tyler Fund' for his old friend the composer Alan Bush. Included in these recitals were pieces by Graham Whettam, Edmund Rubbra, Bernard Stevens, Havergal Brian and Robert Simpson – and the London premiere of Alan Bush's Piano Sonata in A flat, Op. 71 (composed in 1970, it is dedicated to Stevenson; he had previously played it in the 1972 Bath Festival and the Bromsgrove Festival of 1973). This was a big and challenging programme – as was his recital, 'The Transcendental Tradition', given on 21 April 1976 in the University of British Columbia, including, as the title implies, a variety of transcriptions for piano:

> The title of this programme is Peter Pears'. When he proposed it, I saw immediately how its three words suggested everything about the art of transcription. For that's what transcription is, or rather, should be: the transcendental tradition. An art based on tradition, but going beyond it; an art both old and new at the same time.
>
> Transcription, the art of re-working a composition in a performing medium different from the original, has the imprimatur of the centuries. It is not, as is

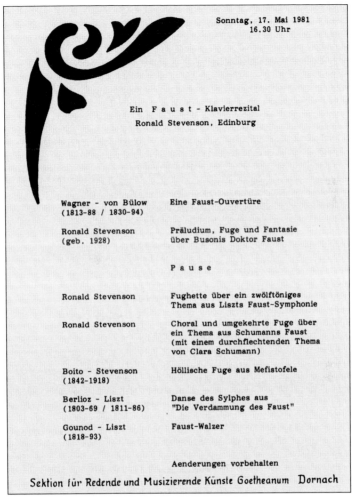

Sonntag, 17. Mai 1981
16.30 Uhr

Ein F a u s t - Klavierrezital
Ronald Stevenson, Edinburg

Wagner - von Bülow (1813-88 / 1830-94)	**Eine Faust-Ouvertüre**
Ronald Stevenson (geb. 1928)	**Präludium, Fuge und Fantasie** **über Busonis Doktor Faust**
	P a u s e
Ronald Stevenson	**Fughette über ein zwölftöniges** **Thema aus Liszts Faust-Symphonie**
Ronald Stevenson	**Choral und umgekehrte Fuge über** **ein Thema aus Schumanns Faust** **(mit einem durchflechtenden Thema** **von Clara Schumann)**
Boito - Stevenson (1842-1918)	**Höllische Fuge aus Mefistofele**
Berlioz - Liszt (1803-69 / 1811-86)	**Danse des Sylphes aus** **"Die Verdammung des Faust"**
Gounod - Liszt (1818-93)	**Faust-Walzer**

Aenderungen vorbehalten

Sektion für Redende und Musizierende Künste Goetheanum Dornach

Stevenson's 'Faust Recital', given in this instance
at the Goetheanum in Dornach, Switzerland, in May 1981

sometimes assumed, an aberration of the nineteenth century. To take an early example, Caccini's solo madrigal *Amarilli mia bella* was published in Florence in 1602; in London the following year, Peter Philips transcribed it for virginals – a transcription far more free than any of Liszt's transcriptions of Bach. True, in the nineteenth century the transcription sometimes degenerated into the cheap arrangement (or, more aptly, derangement). Unfortunately this brought the whole thing into undeserved odium. But the masters practised transcription, from Bach to Schoenberg. Bach, who transcribed Vivaldi, is himself the most frequently transcribed composer; his transcribers include Mendelssohn, Schumann, Liszt, Alkan, Brahms, Busoni, Godowsky, Grainger, Schoenberg, Segovia, Stokowski, Stravinsky and Walton. This list includes not only composers of transcriptions for piano, but also for other media; and it does not include the number of jazz-transcribers of Bach, whose number is legion.

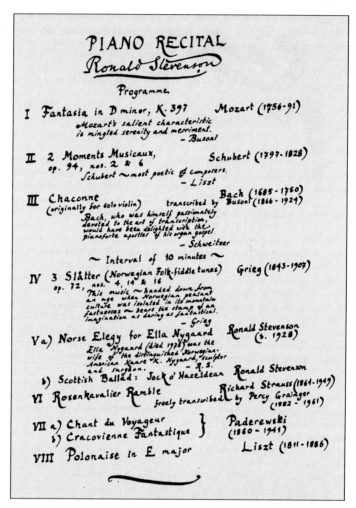

*Two programmes, in Stevenson's own hand, for recitals
given in Steiner Hall in Edinburgh, in March 1980
and November 1981 – the 'Year of the Disabled'*

The most prolific transcriber was Franz Liszt. If all nineteenth-century music were destroyed – heaven forbid! – with the exception of Liszt, nearly all the best of it would remain in Liszt's piano transcriptions, from the nine symphonies of Beethoven to the music of the Russian nationalists. Some of Liszt's finest transcriptions are of Schubert *Lieder*. After the early advocacy of the baritone Vogl, Schubert's songs fell into neglect. Liszt's transcriptions popularised them in the pre-gramophone era in a similar way to the growth in music appreciation effected by the gramophone. Some people think that the gramophone has invalidated transcription. Personally, I think the gramophone has given transcription a new validity. Too often, repeated listening to a favourite recording stereotypes one's view of a work. In this case a transcription, especially a free transcription, can shed light on familiar music.

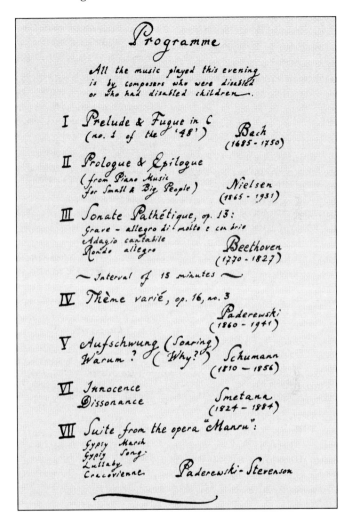

In his opuscule 'A New Aesthetic of Music' (1906) Busoni considers that the notation of music is, in itself, a transcription of an idea. From 'scription' to transcription is but a short step. Busoni adds that it's odd how variation-form is esteemed by *Urtext*-fetishists; while variation-form, when built on a borrowed theme, produces a whole series of transcriptions which, besides, are least faithful when most ingenious. So, to purists, the transcription is not good because it *varies* the original; while the variation is good, though it *transcribes* the original! The truth is that it is impossible to differentiate too finely between variation and transcription, or between transcription and composition. For every good transcription varies an original and is a composition in its own right.

Twentieth-century masters of transcription have all spoken out against irrational criticism and calumny. Godowsky wrote: 'Why should musicians be denied the privileges of comment, criticism, dissertation, discussion, and display of imaginative faculties when transcribing, arranging, or paraphrasing a standard work! Why should the literary men alone enjoy all the prerogatives!

Shakespeare built his plays on borrowed themes, and Molière said: *Je prends mon bien où je le trouve*. Grainger instanced the example of master musicians practising the art of transcription and commented: 'Why should the smaller flight, who really hardly know anything about anything at all, make such an uproar against arrangements and transcriptions?' But not all critics calumniate. Ernest Newman held that masterpieces of transcription are comparable to the work of great commentators, such as Scartazzini on the *Divina Commedia*, Conington on Virgil, Montague Summers on the Restoration dramatists. But the best appreciation comes from composers. In a letter to me, Benjamin Britten wrote: 'Transcription is a very serious form which has been much neglected recently'.

In a way, this essayette itself is a kind of transcription: random reflections on the opinions of other musicians ... and on Peter Pears' title.[3]

The items in that concert ranged from Liszt's transcription of Schubert's *Du bist die Ruh'* and Busoni's Bach Chaconne to Godowsky's reworking (for left hand alone) of Chopin's Op. 10, No. 9, Alkan's *Gavotte d'Orphée* of Gluck and Grainger's *Love Walked In* and *The Man I Love* of Gershwin.

Ronald Stevenson has frequently constructed recitals around a central theme or subject. At the St Andrews Festival in 1979 (20 February) his contribution was a performance entitled 'From the New World and the Old'. The recital included music by Chopin (the G minor *Ballade*) and the Bach-Busoni Chaconne, as well as Busoni's *Indian Diary*, Gershwin's *Three Preludes*, Grainger's paraphrase, *Ramble on the Love Duet*, from Strauss' *Der Rosenkavalier*, and items from Scott Joplin, Louis Chauvin and Eubie Blake.

On 17 November 1973, in aid of St Mary's Restoration, and the 'Lamp of Lothian' campaign, at St Mary's Church, Haddington, he played a programme ('Cathedrals in Sound') which followed Goethe's aphorism that 'Architecture is frozen music. Music, resounding architecture' This programme fittingly included Debussy's 'La Cathédrale Engloutie', the 'Carillon' from Liszt's *Weihnachtsbaum*, the *Prelude, Chorale and Fugue* of Franck – and also appropriately MacDowell's 'In Deep Woods' (*Ten Pieces*, Op. 65, No. 5; Stevenson had already noted its cathedral-like splendour in his song-cycle *Border Boyhood*) as well as his own 'Chorale-Pibroch' (from *A Scottish Triptych*).[4]

For the Georgian Theatre in Richmond (Yorkshire) on 5 October 1974, in a recital entitled 'The Piano's Tribute to the Stage', he played Chopin's Prelude in A and *Valse* in C sharp minor (both used in *Les Sylphides*). Alkan's *Gavotte d'Orphée*, the *Rigoletto* paraphrase of Liszt, Grünfeld's *Die Fledermaus* – and including his own *Prelude, Fugue and Fantasy on Themes from Busoni's 'Faust'* to complete the theatrical idea.

For Ella Grainger's 87th and 89th birthdays, in 1976 and 1978, he gave

[3] From Stevenson's programme notes.

[4] Stevenson has since made a recording embodying this idea: his *Cathedrals in Sound*, released on Altarus Records (AIR–CD–9043) in 1993, features music by Liszt, Chopin, Debussy, Marek, MacDowell, Sorabji, Bach-Busoni and Stevenson himself (*cf.* Appendix Nine: Discography, pp. 473–74).

various recitals in White Plains, New York, including – alongside, of course, music by Grainger himself – works by the other members of the 'Frankfurt Gang' (O'Neill, Scott, Quilter and Balfour Gardiner) as well as Percy's Scandinavian friends Sparre Olsen and Herman Sandby. He also played Dett's *Juba Dance* (with which Grainger was said on occasion to warm up before a performance). In these American recitals he also included pieces by Natalie Curtis-Burlin and Louis Ballard (Hunka No Zhe) – and quite characteristically, works of Grainger's Dutch friend Julius Röntgen.

At a Badenoch Arts Club recital on 29 October 1976, with the harpist Sancha Pielou, Ronald Stevenson echoed what he saw as 'Celtic Voices in Music', playing pieces by MacDowell, Francis George Scott, John Field – and giving the premiere of William Wordsworth's *Reflections*, Op. 101, for harp and piano, and his own *Duo Sonata* for harp and piano. And at Leeds Institute Gallery on 16 March 1980, not content with playing, *à propos* the Northern Muse, music by Grieg, Nielsen, Stenhammar, Delius, Baines and William Kinghorn, he delivered a lecture entitled 'The Northern Muse – an unknown quantity in British music, and a diatribe against fashion'.

Appendix Two
THE HARPSICHORD SONATA
Alan Cuckston

In 1968, as a young harpsichordist casting round for a composer to write me a big piece for performance in the Harrogate Festival, I picked out Ronald Stevenson as being most likely to provide a work sympathetic to my own style and programming. Although at that time I knew only the *Passacaglia on DSCH*, it seemed probable that Ronald's own command of virtuoso keyboard writing, coupled with his love of ancient musical forms, would be likely to produce a significant addition to the instrument's still abysmally poor representation in modern music. In the event the result was a really exciting challenge, providing the player with a four-movement work wholly suited to the instrument, within the mainstream traditions of melody, harmony and counterpoint.

My performance, on the Goble concert harpsichord equipped with pedals for rapid registration changes, elicited an enthusiastic review in *The Sunday Times*, under the headline 'A Sonata for the Sixties'. Prophetic words indeed, for within a year or two the movement towards historical 'authenticity' was the *dernier cri*, sweeping away those harpsichords built after Landowska's principles and replacing them with those built after the gospel according to Gustav Leonhardt. To keep up, players had to accustom themselves to articulating and phrasing on historic actions where changing registration was forbidden, except perhaps between movements. I was happy to find that Ronald's Sonata still 'worked' on such instruments and recall playing it on a (for me) most memorable night in January in the early 1970s in Kirkwall Cathedral to the *stillest* large audience I have ever had. They thought it was probably the first time a Baroque harpsichord had been heard on the Orkneys, a fact which *Punch* amusingly picked up some weeks later for 'This England'.[1]

The first movement, 'In heroic style', commences with a grand double-dotted pastiche of the seventeenth-century French overture manner, leading into a driving *Allegro deciso* sonata-movement with running contrapuntal figuration. The working-out includes some Scarlattian *capriccioso* hand-crossings, and Stevenson well understands the nature of the harpsichord's ability to communicate *crescendo* – and *decrescendo* – effects by thickening or thinning out the textural strands.

The following 'Dirge' movement introduces a chromatic ground bass after the Purcellian manner and the first episode, a wailing *Lachrymosa* in the treble juxtaposing the Lute and the Harp stops, is also built over a falling chromatic ground. An eloquent transition leads to a tunefully diatonic 'Sarabande' featuring arpeggiated common chords in the middle registers – those simple things at which the harpsichord sounds its most beautiful.

The next movement, a 'Dance' in triple time, again has common chords –

---

[1] *Sic!* –ED.

unrelated triads this time; and there's clever stuff where the right hand has to play on both manuals simultaneously as it spells out the tune and contributes to its accompaniment.

The last movement, an *Allegretto* rondo, is the most piquant melodically and harmonically, reminding one of early Poulenc and *Les Six*. It is the busiest, with bitonal overlappings on the two keyboards, and ends with a fantastic apotheosis recalling moments from all the previous movements in a grand summation.

Appendix Three
STEVENSON ON WRITING
FOR THE PIANO
A Documentary Record

The next six pages present extracts from two letters to Colin Scott-Sutherland from Ronald Stevenson, the first dated 9 March 1973 (pp. 314–16) and the second 12 November 1982 (pp. 317–19).

the evidence of Powishaoff's published music to hand, I can see that from his Russian background, he absorbed much of the French style that was always strong there (even in Tchaikovsky, who was half-French anyway). I remember now that Powishaoff used to play the earlier works of Chopin (another half-French Slav) with particular relish — such things as the Rondo in E flat. It is a certain neatness and crispness of style I mean. — No barn-storming! — That was another Russian style, exemplified by the Promethean, Jewish-Slav, Anton Rubinstein (who, incidentally, is the one pianist who fascinates me more than any other from eye-witness descriptions; there being no recordings, though there are rumours of an old Berliner cylinder.) Paderewski held in equipoise both the fastidious French style and the fiery Rubinstein style, sometimes being overcome by the fire and losing the fastidiousness!

After such reflections, to consider the contents of A Bach Book for Harriet Cohen is to descend to the nadir, which the dictionary says is the Aral opposite of the zenith. What a lot of bunglers these English composers are in piano-writing, as evinced in this album, which was a good idea spoilt!

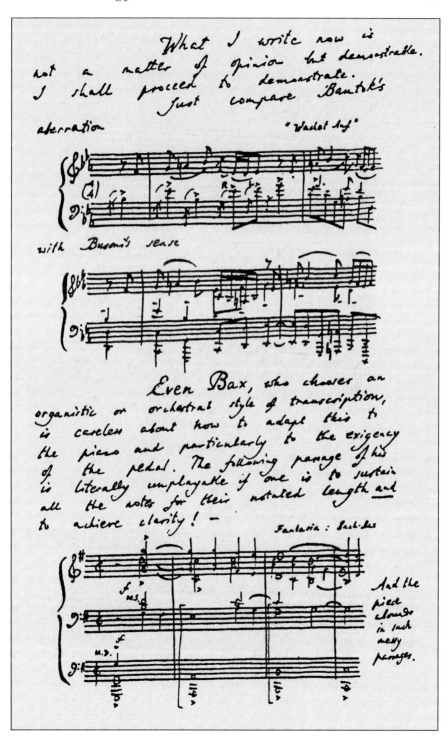

When I was about 20, I
made a similar mistake to Bax's in my
transcription of John Bull's <u>Galiard</u>:

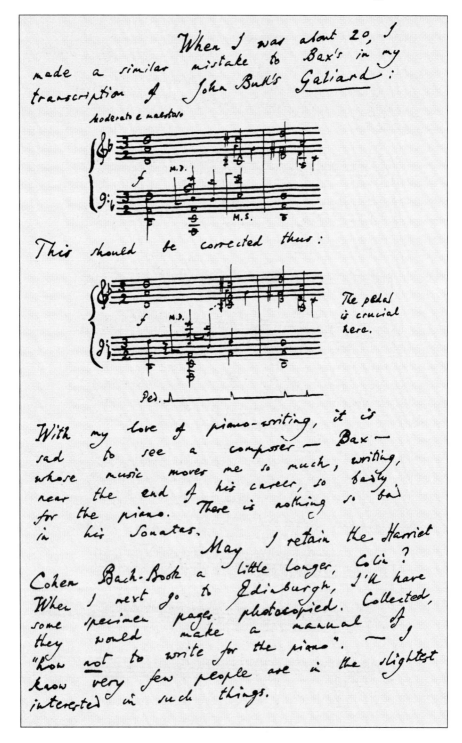

This should be corrected thus:

The pedal
is crucial
here.

With my love of piano-writing, it is
sad to see a composer — Bax —
whose music moves me so much, writing,
near the end of his career, so badly
for the piano. There is nothing so bad
in his Sonatas.
                    May I retain the Harriet
Cohen Bach-Book a little longer, Colin?
When I next go to Edinburgh, I'll have
some specimen pages photocopied. Collected,
they would make a manual of,
"how <u>not</u> to write for the piano". — I
know very few people are in the slightest
interested in such things.

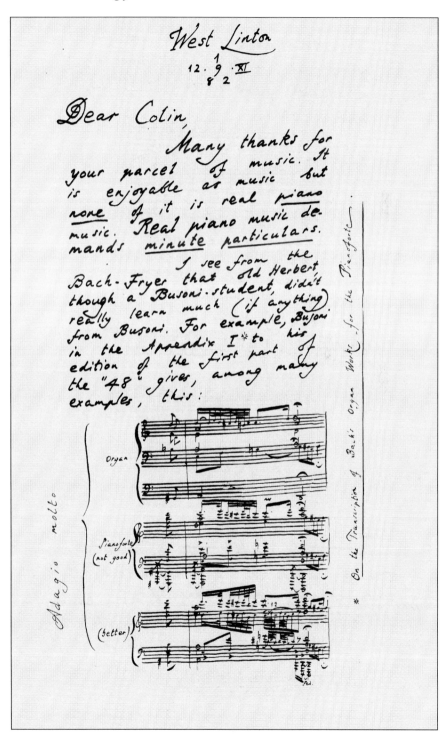

~ And what does ole Herb give us? Why, of course a "not good" version:

This style of writing was initiated by Schumann in an attempt to produce a quasi orchestral texture. It actually vitiates the sonority. For the above, Busoni would have written something like this:

(Also note the characteristically Busonian tenuti markings on the semiquavers in contradistinction to Fryer's genteel phrasing)

Also ~ pore ole Herb! ~ he gives us a gratuitous chromaticism straight out of Stainer's Crucifixion:

The G♭ is un-Bachian.

Percy, too, had his gratuitous chromaticisms: *cf.* *Blithe Bells*. But — *dio mio!* they are so Graingerously vulgar (truly) and are all over the place, so that they do have a consistency of their own.

The Holbrooke *looks* more pianistic than it is. It is not very inventive and really rather facile.

The Cooke is — or would be — not bad for fifth-rate Rachmaninov. — I'm meaning to be *objective*, not splenetic!

Altogether the English Georgians wrote some lovely music, but only York Bowen was a *master* piano-composer among the lot. I can demonstrate that. But it would need a book. And nobody would buy it. Besides, life is too short for *negative* subjects of study.

So, my dear Colin, I'm not ungrateful for your parcel: indeed grateful for the perspective it affords. Ever, Ronald.

P.S. Herbert Fryer was a charming, witty, kindly man (which has nothing to do with my comments above.)

Appendix Four
STEVENSON
AND THE CHILD
Colin Scott-Sutherland

When Ronald Stevenson was asked what he would wish to do on his sixtieth birthday (6 March 1988) his immediate response was 'spend it with the children, of course'. And spend it with the children he did – under the auspices of the European Piano Teachers' Association (EPTA),[1] in an upper room in St Mary's Music School in Edinburgh, in the company of a number of young players, pupils of Edinburgh teachers, with whom he conducted a master-class of enchanting warmth and sympathy. Concerned as much with approach, preparation and posture as with technique, he managed to enlarge Adam Carse's and Hilda Capp's little pieces – to say nothing of his own *A Wheen Tunes for Bairns tae Spiel* – into a series of object lessons that ranged far beyond the purely technical, interspersing his comments with hectic, excited and quite unpractised passages from Chopin, Bach and Grainger.

The inspiration of the young – indeed, of the ever-young – has the most profound effect upon him.

> His particular concern for the child, in the laments of the *Passacaglia* and the programme of the Second Piano Concerto, is expressed with the keen contrast of size and medium in the short pieces such as *A Wheen Tunes for Bairns tae Spiel, Three Scots Fairytales*, and in the Soutar song, *Day is Düne*. There are, too, the simple transcriptions of Delius; the careful editing and transcribing of *The Young Pianist's Grainger*; and the volume of harp arrangements *Sounding Strings* (composed for his younger daughter and published by United Music Publishers), which convey to the child, with the skill and touch of a born teacher, his own infectious delight in all that is music.[2]

His love of the child is exemplified in his connection with the Steiner-inspired Garvald School for the handicapped child (at Dolphinton, near his home) for whom he set for unison children's voices, descant recorder, violin, cello and guitar in 1965 the words of the Christian Morgenstern poem *One and All*, which became the school song and which he later transcribed as a *Meditation* for piano solo entitled *When the Morning Stars Sang Together*.

In 1961 he was teaching at Broughton School in Edinburgh. 'It bore no resemblance to being a musician, but I was in contact with the raw material of life.'[3] This kind of realism he evoked in the massive *Passacaglia on DSCH*. 'On the afternoon of the premiere I composed a new section of two pages based on the 17th-century Scottish pibroch *Lament for the Children* composed by Patrick Mór MacCrimmon as a lament for seven of his eight sons who died within a year. I recast his melody thinking of the child victims of

[1] Coincidentally, the tenth birthday of EPTA fell also on that date.

[2] Colin Scott-Sutherland, 'Ronald Stevenson', *British Music Now*, p. 36.

[3] *The Daily Mail*, 3 October 1966.

The first page of 'Shadow March'
from A Child's Garden of Verses
in Stevenson's manuscript

Nazism.'[4] It is no coincidence that this was sparked off in South Africa. And in September 1982, 'In Dandenong, Victoria, I composed, taught and recorded and broadcast (from Sydney) – all within a week – a little song for the mentally handicapped (over 100 of them between 2 and 60 years of age). Title – *Adam was a gardener*'.[5]

Nowhere is this insight reflected more poignantly than in the seventeen songs of *A Child's Garden of Verses* – a cycle to the words of his namesake, Robert Louis Stevenson. For all its apparently unpretentious nature, this cycle is perhaps one of the composer's most important and deepest creative expressions, enshrining a unique understanding of childhood experience – it can be compared with the most evocative pages of literature, such as the richly imagined opening introduction to Walter de la Mare's anthology *Come Hither* – and limns the poems with all the artistry of an illustrator, with decorative touches of acute perception, probing to the heart of the poet's vision. These are not in the truest sense poems for children – no more than de la Mare's 'Nod' would, except superficially, be a fit subject for a nursery wallpaper[6] – and Ronald Stevenson has chosen wisely the alternative, setting them as a kind of *Kinderszenen* rather than an *Album for the Young*.

Set for tenor, soprano and treble (the latter two being the voices of children), the cycle incorporates the dark element from which Ronald Stevenson's inspiration sprang (and which also inspired the poet): the feverish fears of the sick child, prey to his vivid imaginings with his wistful view from the sickroom window. The core of the work is the mysterious, even frightening, 'Shadow March' – 'All round the house is the jet black Night'[7] – which subtly combines the two voices of child and adult, casting its own baleful shadow into the sixth bar of the very first song of the cycle. From the tenor's opening exhortation (by the sick child 'now well and old'), to the faithful Nanny (Alison Cunningham or 'Cummy') to 'take Nurse, this little book you hold', to the wistful child's appeal 'and I would like so much to play' ('Bed in Summer') – and the poignancy of his plea, 'Leerie, see a little child and nod to him tonight' – it offers one of the most beautiful and most moving pieces of imaginative writing from the twentieth century that I have heard.

[4] *'Passacaglia on DSCH'*, *The Listener*, Vol. 82, No. 2115, 9 October 1969, p. 494; *cf.* pp. 63–64 and 85.

[5] Letter to the author, dated 16 September 1982.

[6] His subject, of course, is Death.

[7] This setting was made many years previously, and in many ways is the inspiration for the whole cycle.

Appendix Five
SOME STEVENSON
MINIATURES

Miniature is not a word which might readily be associated with Ronald Stevenson, whose *Passacaglia on DSCH* is one of the longest pieces of music in the literature of the piano. But this work is only one aspect of the composer whose concern as an artist has always been with essentials – and, after all, the massive framework of the *Passacaglia* is hung on the small basic and germinal fragment of DSCH: four notes. The source of his art is often enshrined in the miniature – though miniature only in the sense that a simple kernel concentrates both seed and essence of larger idea. Ronald Stevenson's smaller pieces – some no more than a page in length – represent a kind of distillation of his expression, some, like 'The Hushed Song' from the cycle *Border Boyhood*, concentrations of that mood of fierce joy which he so often sounds, others almost ingeniously simple melodic evocations, couched usually in a serpentine, quasi-Celtic canonic pattern. The Scots folk-music settings (scored for piano as well as other combinations of instrumental colour) and his realisations of Purcell are an ideal gateway through which to approach his music – and it will be quickly realised that those qualities which mark him as a teacher are similarly, in the music, those of directness, freshness of outlook and above all, conviction.

CS-S

PIANO

Retrospect	1945
The Queen's Dolour (Purcell)	1959
Simple Variations on Purcell's 'New Scotch Tune'	1964
'Song of the Crab-fisher', from *A Chinese Folk-song Suite*	1965
'From an Old Pibroch' (*Scottish Folk-music Settings*, No. 6)	1956/65
'Sailing Song' and 'A Little Mouth Music' from	
South Uist (Hebridean) Folk-song Suite	1965
'The Hushed Song' (No. 4, *Intermezzo*, from *Border Boyhood*)	1970
Doubles on Rubbra's Cradle Hymn	1974
Prelude and Chorale (An Easter Offering)	1978
'Hard is My Fate' (*Scottish Folk-music Settings*, No. 11)	1980
Preludette on the name George Gershwin	1981
Song without Words	1988

STRING QUARTET

'Canon in memoriam van Dieren' from *Four Meditations*	1964

(Small hands may omit inner notes played by thumb.)

Sonata for the Clavichord ~ Stevenson

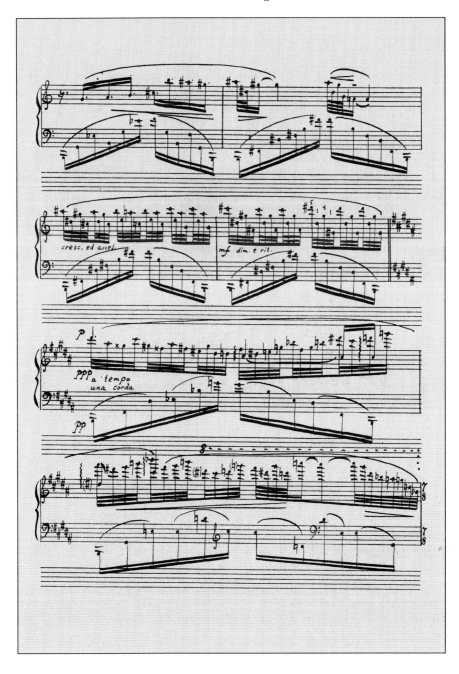

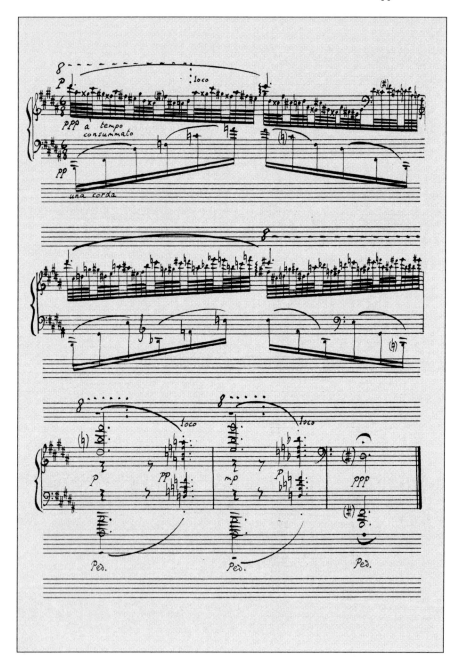

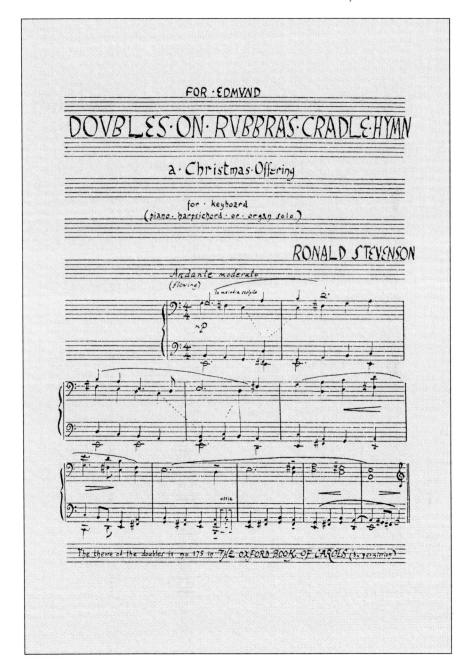

Prelude & Chorale - B

PRELUDETTE

on the name George Gershwin

Appendix Six
STEVENSON
ON HIS *SCOTS SUITE*

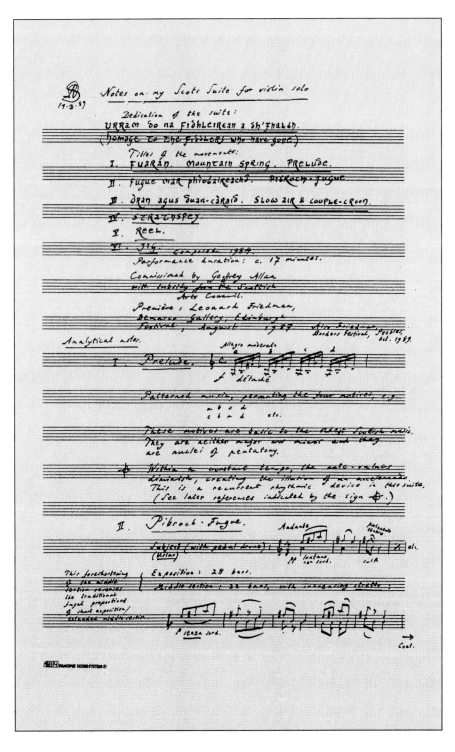

371

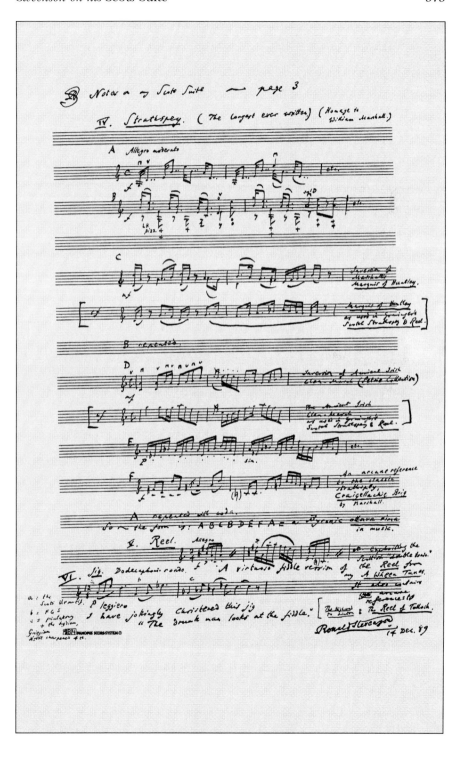

Appendix Seven
LIST OF WORKS
Martin Anderson

Introduction

Compiling a catalogue of the works of a composer such as Ronald
Stevenson can be done only by imposing a near-fictitious order on a creative
impulse that does not observe such niceties. His major works present no
difficulty to the cataloguer. But Stevenson shares Busoni's views on the
importance of transcription – that it is itself an act of composition – and in
Stevenson's own output a work may exist in several scorings, between which
it may (or may not) have changed in detail. It is occasionally hard to judge,
moreover, when a work is a transcription or paraphrase or contains so much
of Stevenson himself that it must be classed as an original composition. The
following catalogue endeavours to present Stevenson's vast output in a way
that may be of most practical help, both for performers and others.[1]

  Works are divided according to their scoring and are listed chronologically within each section (except for Stevenson's settings of texts by
MacDiarmid, Wilde and Soutar, which for convenience are grouped by
poet); Stevenson's transcriptions are likewise listed according to the forces
they employ. Dates may occasionally be approximate, and sometimes it has
proved impossible to establish them. Where available, timings and details
for first performances (FP), first public performances (FPP) and first
broadcast performances (FBP) are given. Works which are incomplete or
still in sketch form are listed separately after the main catalogue. Until the
mid-1960s Stevenson gave his works opus numbers but then abandoned the
practice and retrospectively removed them from earlier works.

---

[1] Its compilation would have been much more difficult without the thorough
groundwork of Malcolm MacDonald, Barry Ould and Colin Scott-Sutherland; I am
also considerably indebted to Michael Lister and to Ronald Stevenson himself.

A. ORIGINAL WORKS

The composer's comments on these works are generally taken from the scores; the more jocund come from his annotations on earlier drafts of this catalogue.

The Ronald Stevenson Society is well advanced on its ambitious project to publish the bulk of Stevenson's output; where no publisher is indicated in this worklist, it can reasonably be assumed that the publisher is – or will be – The Ronald Stevenson Society, from which a catalogue is available.

Duration

1. WORKS FOR LARGE ENSEMBLES

I. ORCHESTRA

Waltz in A major	3'

c. 1945
1111/0000/timp/piano/strings
Trio in D flat
Written for the Blackburn Ballet Club; lost
FP: Grand Theatre, Blackburn, 1945, cond. Fred Reidy

Fantasy (or *Fantasia*)	10'

1946
piano, strings
Exists also in an arrangement for two pianos

18 Variations on a Bach Chorale	10'

1946
strings
Exists also in a version for solo piano

Berceuse Symphonique	12'

April 1951
3222/4231/harp/timp./perc. (tgl., BD, cyms., susp. cyms., tubular bells)/strings
Introduzione: Andante – Largamente – Tranquillo – Doppio movimento
Dedicated to Gerda Busoni.
FP: Yorkshire Symphony Orchestra, cond. Maurice Miles, Leeds Town Hall, 24 June 1953

Waltzes: Tribute to Johann Strauss	7'

November 1952
2+1222/4321/timp./perc. (tgl., SD, BD, tamburino picc.)/strings
Moderato fantastico – Tempo di valse, elegamente – Fanfare *– Energico – Ritmico*
Exists also in a version for solo piano

Jamboree for Grainger   6'
1960, orch. 1961; dated '5 April 1961'
2 (II = picc.)222 (alto sax. *ad lib.*)/4230/timp./perc.(tgl., cym., xyl.)/harp/
piano/strings
Exists also in a version for two pianos

Keening Sang for a Makar: In Memoriam Francis George Scott   7'
January 1963
21(cor ang.)1(b. cl.)2(dbl bass.)/4231/timp./perc.(cym., BD)/harp/
piano/strings
Transcription for orchestra of No. 1 of *A Scottish Triptych* for piano solo

Scots Dance Toccata   10'
1965
2 (II = picc.)1cor angl. (= ob. II)2 (II = bass cl.)2 (II = dbl. bass.)/4330/
timp./ perc. (tgl., cyms., sus. cym., BD, SD, tubular bells in E flat, glsp.,
whip)/harp/piano/strings
FP: Scottish National Orchestra, cond. Alexander Gibson, Glasgow Proms,
Kelvin Hall, Glasgow, 4 July 1967
Publisher: Novello, London, 1970

Young Scotland Suite   15'
1976
3 (III = picc.)2cor angl. (= ob. III)33 (III = dbn.)/4331/timp., perc. (5: tgl.,
SD, glsp., tamb., cyms., susp. cym., BD, xyl., gong, tubular bells)/harp, 2
clarsachs/4 bagpipes/strings
1. 'Salute of the Pipers': *Moderato maestoso – Allegro – Camminando
accanitamente*
2. 'Sounding Strings': *Larghetto cantabile* (for harp, 2 clarsachs and strings
only)
3. 'Young Scotland March': *Allegro moderato ma con spirito*
FP: Lothian Region Combined Schools Orchestra, cond. Roderick Brydon,
Assembly Rooms, George St., Edinburgh, 23 October 1976

Recitative and Air on DSCH: In Memoriam Shostakovich   5'
Dated: '16 May 1980'
string orchestra
Exists also in versions for string quartet, violin and piano, viola and piano,
cello and piano, bassoon and piano, and solo piano

II. SOLO INSTRUMENT WITH ORCHESTRA

Piano Concerto No. 1, *Faust Triptych*   c. 32'
1959–60; dated 3 p.m., 7 April 1960
2 (II = picc.)2 (II = cor angl.)22/4230/timp./perc. (2: trgl., cym., susp.
cym.tam-t., tubular bells, SD, BD, glsp.)/strings
I. *Largo – Allegro*
II. *Fuga: Andante pensoso, tempo giusto*
III. *Adagio – Tempo di minuetto – Allegretto vivo –* Cadenza (In Memoriam N. S.
(23 Jan. 60)) *– Vivace – Adagio*

FP: Ronald Stevenson (piano), Scottish National Orchestra, cond. Alexander Gibson, Edinburgh, 8 January 1966
FBP: John Ogdon (piano), Scottish National Orchestra, cond. Franz-Paul Decker, BBC Radio 3, 22 January 1968
Publisher: Novello
Exists also in versions for solo piano and two pianos

Simple Variations on Purcell's 'New Scotch Tune'   6'
1964, orch. 1967
clarinet in B flat and strings
Expansion of the 1964 version for solo piano, later renamed *Little Jazz Variations on Purcell's 'Scotch Tune'*
Publisher: Scottish Music Information Centre

Piano Concerto No. 2, *The Continents*   40'
1970–72
2 (II = picc.)22/42 (I = D trpt)31/timp., perc. (4: tubular bells, tam-tam, tgl., SD, BD, cyms., susp. cym., Chinese wood-blocks, bongos, congas, glsp., xyl., bull-roarer, maracas, castanets, tamb.)/celesta/2 harps/strings
Allegro moderato – Moderato – Allegro con urgenza – Allegretto – Poco lento – Andante con moto – Allegro – Blues – Allegro ma non troppo, quasi di marcia – Allegro ritmico e commodo – Rag – Molto moderato
FP: Ronald Stevenson (piano), New Philharmonia Orchestra cond. Norman Del Mar, BBC Promenade Concert, Royal Albert Hall, London, 17 July 1972.
Publisher: Oxford University Press, 1972, withdrawn; now available from the Scottish Music Information Centre
A version for two pianos is in progress

Violin Concerto, *The Gypsy* (1977–79)   55'
2 (II = picc.).2 (II = cor ang.)22 (I = dbn)/2000/timp., perc. (3: tgl., tamb., SD, BD, xyl., tubular bells, vib., cyms.)/cimbalom, harp, piano, strings (10.8.6.6.4)
I. *Larghetto, calmo ed albeggiante – Allegretto (Danse Roumaine) – Tempo di Valse*
II. *Andante elegiaco – Adagietto – Cadenza in parte accompagnata – Tempo primo*
III. *Allegro cavalleresco –* Hardanger Wedding March – Wedding Dance – Norse Funeral March – Dance of Death – Blue Mountain Dance
FP: Hu Kun (violin), BBC Scottish Symphony Orchestra, cond. Sir Yehudi Menuhin, Royal Concert Hall, Glasgow, 21 May 1992
Commissioned by Sir Yehudi Menuhin
Publisher: Scottish Music Information Centre

Concerto for Cello and Orchestra, *The Solitary Singer* (1968–94)   40'
2(1)2(1)22/4221/perc. (3)/harp, piano, strings
I. 'Nocturne héroïque'
II. *Moderato – Allegro – Moderato – Lento ma con moto – Allegro festivo – Più mosso – Allegro*
III. 'Elegy': *Larghetto cantabile – Poco pi'u mosso – Moderato – Più mosso – Tempo primo – Poco più mosso*
Sketched January–September 1968, with further work in 1969, 1983, and

1992–4. Intended for Jacqueline Du Pré; resumed 1992 for Moray Welsh, in memoriam Jacqueline DuPré
Dedication: 'In memoriam Jackie Du Pré'
FP: Moray Welsh (cello), Royal Scottish National Orchestra cond. Walter Weller, Usher Hall, Edinburgh, 8 December 1995
Publisher: Scottish Music Information Centre

III. VOICE AND ORCHESTRA

Variations Vocalises sur deux thèmes de 'Les Troyens' (Vocalise Variations on Two Themes from 'The Trojans')   16'
1969
2222/3020/timp./perc. (BD)/strings/mezzo-soprano
Allegretto – Appassionato – Fugue: *Andante – Cadenza – Allegro appassionato*
Dedication: 'À l'ombre d'Hector et à sa Didon incomparable Mlle. Janet Baker'.

St Mary's May Songs   15'
1988–early April 1989
Soprano and strings
1. 'When that the month of May is cumen' (Chaucer, Prologue to The Legend of Good Women). *Allegro concitato*
Score dated: 'January 1989'
2. 'The May Queen' (Tennyson). *Allegretto*
3. 'Ommaggi a Maggio' (Rossetti, trans. into Italian by Ronald Stevenson; Rossetti's title was 'Fin di Maggio'). *Maestoso retorico (ma lirico)*
Dedication: 'Alla memoria del Maestro Ildebrando Pizzetti da Parma'
4. 'Winds of May' (Joyce). *Allegro con gaiezza*
Score dated: 'Jan. 1989'
Commissioned by St Mary's Music School, Edinburgh
FP: Caroline Coxon (soprano), St Mary's Music School, cond. Nigel Murray, Queen's Hall, Edinburgh, 17 June 1989
Nos. 1, 3 and 4 also exist in reductions for voice and piano, intended for use in rehearsal. No. 3 bears the dedication 'Alla gentilissima Signorina Susan Hamilton' and is dated 1989; that of No. 4 is dated: 'This copy made in Sent, Engadine, Switzerland, October 1988'.
Publisher: Scottish Music Information Centre

IV. WIND BAND

Corroborree for Grainger   12'
1960, rev. 1989 (completed late June, with subsequent revisions)
piano solo, wind band and percussion
Commissioned by Napier Polytechnic, Edinburgh
FP: Ronald Stevenson (piano), Napier Symphonic Wind Band, cond. Christopher Bell, Reid Concert Hall, Edinburgh, 24 June 1989
This work is a radical recomposition, with much new material, of the orchestral *Jamboree for Grainger*

V. MUSIC FOR BRASS

Brass Band

Strathclyde's Salute to Mandela   18'
1990–91
Commissioned by Largs Academy and Ayrshire Education Authority
FP: North Ayrshire Youth Brass Band, cond. Hugh Brennan, Barrfields
Pavilion, Largs, 8 October 1991.

Trumpets

Fanfare for Grainger   2'
1979
four trumpets in B flat with side-drum

2. CHAMBER MUSIC

I. STRING QUARTET

Allegro   4'
c. 1947

Four Meditations   10'
1964
1. *Preludio al corale: Molto moderato*   3½'
2. *Andante*   2'
3. *Canone: Andantino lagrimoso. In Memoriam Bernard van Dieren*[2]   2'
4. *Andante*   2½'
Transcriptions of Nos. 1, 5, 9 and 16 of *A 20th Century Music Diary* for solo
piano

Variations on a Theme by Manfred Gordon (Tema Ebraico)   5'
1978
Exists also in a version for piano

Ne'er Day Sang   3'
4 January 1963
Principal version is for piano

Recitative and Air: In memoriam Shostakovich   5'
Dated: 'York, 7 December 1987 finished at 1 a.m.'
Exists also in versions for string orchestra, bassoon and piano, violin and
piano, viola and piano, cello and piano, and solo piano

String Quartet, *Voces Vagabundae*   32'
spring–autumn 1990
I.   *Maestoso – Allegro ardente* ('. . . I take to the open road . . . the world
before me . . . leading wherever I choose . . .' – Walt Whitman)
II. *Scherzo: volante* (The Bird Path – Homage to Kenneth White)

---

[2] Reproduced in Appendix Five: Some Stevenson Miniatures, pp. 367–68.

III. *Adagietto cantabilissimo* ('A backward glance o'er travel'd roads' – Walt Whitman) –*continuando* –
IV. *Fuga alla Passeggiata (Andando moderato) – Fuga alla Strathspey (Allegro moderato) – Fuga alla Reel (Allegro con spirito) – Fuga doppia: alla Strathspey con Reel (nello stesso tempo che il Reel) – Fuga alla Giga ((♩. = 112) – Coda alla Quodlibet*
Commissioned by the Edinburgh String Quartet to mark their thirtieth anniversary
Score dated '8 August 1990'
FP: the Edinburgh String Quartet, St Bernard's Church, Edinburgh, 24 October 1990

II. PIANO QUARTET

Fantasy Quartet, 'Alma Alba'   15'
Dated: 'Finis 3 Feb. 1985'
Commissioned by the New Academy Concerts Society of Scotland with subsidy from the Scottish Arts Council.
FP: Naxos Ensemble, Glasgow, 1985

III. PIANO TRIO

Weihnachtsvariationen über Schoecks 'Agnes' für Familientrio   6'
December 1979

IV. WIND QUINTET

Pan-Celtic Wind Quintet   20'
2000
1. Early Morning Nocturne: Homage to the Irish John Field
2. The Sheep under the Snow – Manx Melody
3. A'e Gowden Lyric (One Golden Song) – Scots
4. Hal-an-Tow – Cornish Folkdance-Song
5. Contrapuntal Recollection
6. Dafydd y Gareg Wen a Clychau Aberdyfi (David of the White Rock & The Bells of Aberdovey) – Two Welsh Airs
Several of these movements rework material which appears elsewhere in Stevenson's *œuvre.* No. 1 develops the *Nocturne: Homage to John Field* for solo piano (and for flute/clarinet or piano); Nos. 2 and 4 are derived from Nos. 3 and 5 of *Sounding Strings* for clarsach or harp; and No. 3 is based on Stevenson's song (of which there is also a transcription for violin and piano).
FP: Flaxton Ensemble, Lecture Hall, Ayr Campus, Paisley University, 6 October 2001

V. RECORDER QUARTET

Chorale: On Another's Sorrow, for SATB recorder quartet   3'
1978

Principal form is as the final chorale in *19 Songs of Innocence* (1948), in a setting for SATB chorus (1965), and in a transcription for solo piano (1978)

VI. FLUTE AND CLARINET

Sérénade et Aubade   4′
1945

VII. FLUTE AND PIANO

Nocturne after John Field   6′
June/July 1952
Andante, B flat
Exists also in versions for clarinet and piano and for solo piano later renamed *Nocturne: Homage to John Field* to indicate that the music is original and not a transcription
FP: Tom Hay (clarinet), Alastair Chisholm (piano), Garvald School, Dolphinton, Peeblesshire, 19 July 1997 (Ronald Stevenson 70th-birthday concert)

VIII. OBOE AND PIANO

Minuet: Homage to Hindemith   5′
January 1947
Minuet: *Tempo di Minuetto*; and three Trios (*Poco Andante, Allegretto, Poco allegro*)

IX. CLARINET AND PIANO

Nocturne after John Field   6′
June/July 1952
Andante; B flat
Exists also in versions for flute and piano and for solo piano later renamed *Nocturne: Homage to John Field* to indicate that the music is original and not a transcription

X. BASSOON AND PIANO

Recitative and Air on DSCH: In memoriam Shostakovich   5′
1995
Exists also in versions for string orchestra, string quartet, violin and piano, viola and piano, cello and piano, and solo piano

XI. HORN AND PIANO

Bergstimmung (Mountain Mood/Beann-Fhonn)   10′
February 1986
Dedication: 'For Darryl Poulsen and Kenneth Weir to play in memory of Alban Berg, 50 years after the passing of the Austrian Master'
FP: Darryl Poulsen (horn), Kenneth Weir (piano), West Australian Conservatory, Perth, 4 March 1986

XII. HARP AND PIANO

Duo Sonata   15'
1970–71; score dated 30 January 1971
I. 'Celtic Sunlight': *Largo – Allegro*
II. 'Nocturne – The Midnight Sun': *Adagietto – Allegro vivace e vigoroso*
Commissioned by Ann Griffiths
Dedication: 'For Ann Griffiths'
FP: Ann Griffiths (harp), Ronald Stevenson (piano), Purcell Room,
London, 28 February 1971
The titles of the two movements were added after their composition.

Chiaroscuro: Homage to Rembrandt and his Biographer Van Loon   7'
1987
I. 'The Young Cavalier.' *Allegretto cavalleresco*
II. 'Saskia sleeps.' *Andante sognando*
III. 'A Little Night Watch.' *Alla Marcia notturnale*
Dedication: 'Epithalamium for Peter and Marian Kessel'
Exists also in versions for harp and harpsichord, clarsach and piano, and
clarsach and harpsichord

XIII. HARP OR CLARSACH AND HARPSICHORD OR PIANO

Chiaroscuro: Homage to Rembrandt and his Biographer Van Loon   7'
1987
Exists also in versions for harp and piano
FP: Savourna Stevenson (clarsach), Ronald Stevenson (piano), Grote Kerk,
Vera, Holland, 12 September 1987

XIV. VIOLIN AND PIANO

Sonata (original title *Sonatina Concertante*)   20'
1947, rev. 1952
Moderato maestoso – Agitato – Andante con variazione (4 variations and
Intermezzo) – *Reminiscenza – Allegro – Candenza – Passacaglia (Misurato) –
Fughetta (allegro umeristico)*
FP: Waldo Channon (violin), Ronald Stevenson (piano), Edinburgh, 1954

A'e Gowden Lyric (One Golden Song)   1½'
c. 1965
Adagio semplice, D major
Main version is for high voice and piano;[3] exists also in versions for solo
piano, and for violin and clarsach (as No. 10(a) of the score for the film
Hammer and Thistle)

---

[3] Reproduced on p. 183.

Melody on a Ground of Glazunov   6'
1970
Exists also in a version for solo piano; a second melody on a Glazunov
ground remains incomplete

Silberhochszeitsjahrestageswalzer   4'
1974
Dedication: 'Für Renate und Willi Amann'

Prelude for a Centenarian   1½'
June 1975 (composed in the interval of a concert)
Larghetto, A minor
Dedication: 'For Horace Fellowes at 100'
FP: Edna Arthur (violin), Ronald Stevenson (piano), Edinburgh Society of
Musicians, June 1975

Recitative and Air: In memoriam Shostakovich   5'
1987
Exists also in versions for solo piano, viola and piano, cello and piano,
bassoon and piano, string quartet and string orchestra

My Love is to the Light of Lights   3'
1996
Main version is for medium voice and piano

XV. VIOLIN AND GUITAR

Three Open-Air Dances   4'
c. 1973
Mainly on open strings for young players

XVI. VIOLIN OR CELLO AND PIANO

Jock o' Hazeldean: Scots Border Ballad   4'
1980
Originally composed for piano solo

XVII. VIOLA AND PIANO

Recitative and Air on DSCH: In memoriam Shostakovich
1987
Exists also in versions for solo piano, violin and piano, cello and piano,
bassoon and piano, string quartet and string orchestra

XVIII. CELLO AND PIANO

Suite   8'
1967
I.   Prelude
II. Strathspey
III. Reel
IV. Jig

Chorale and Fugue in Reverse on Two Themes by Robert and Clara Schumann 3′
1979
Exists also in a version for piano solo
Dedication: To Lawrence and Mabel Glover

Recitative and Air on DSCH: In Memoriam Shostakovich   5′
1976
Exists also in versions for string orchestra, string quartet, bassoon and
piano, violin and piano, viola and piano, and solo piano

Variations and Theme (The Bonnie Earl o' Moray)   15′
1974
Introduction: *Andante* – Var. I: *L'istesso tempo* – Var. II: *Andante grave* – Var.
III (cello solo): *Con moto fluente, quasi improvvisando* – Var. IV: *Alla marcia,
moderato ma fanfaronesco* (with swagger) – Var. V: *Fughetta alla giga, allegro ma
non troppo* – Var. VI: *Allegro* – Var. VII: *L'istesso tempo* – Var. VIII: *Marcia
funebre – Tema (L'istesso tempo)*
Dedication: 'For Moray Welsh'
FP: Moray Welsh (cello), Ronald Stevenson (piano), West Linton Musical
Society, West Linton, 16 March 1974

Wasserfall bei Nacht I   3′
Dated: 'In Wengen komponiert 19–21 Mai 1981'
Dedication: 'An Albert und Edith Wullschleger'
Exists also in versions for medium voice and piano (text: Christian
Morgenstern) and for cello and piano

Wasserfall bei Nacht II   4′
1983
Dedication: 'An Vreni und Heinz Lüscher'
Exists also as a song for baritone and piano (text: Christian Morgenstern)

XIX. TWO PIANOS

Fantasy   10′
1946
Originally for piano and strings, transcribed for two pianos on 30 September 1946

Fugue on a Fragment of Chopin   9′
1953, with later revisions
Dedication: 'To my friend Hugh Haggerty'
FP: Donna Amato and Alison Brewster, St John's, Smith Square, London,
6 June 1989.
Principal version is for solo piano

Piano Concerto No. 1, *Faust Triptych*   28′
1961
Transcription for two pianos – an expanded version of the *Prelude, Fugue
and Fantasy on Busoni's 'Faust'*
Publisher: Novello, 1973

Jamboree for Grainger 6'
1960
Exists also in a version for full orchestra, now replaced by *Corroboree for Grainger* for piano and wind band.

XX. TWO GUITARS

Don Quixote and Sancho Panza – A Bagatelle Cycle 25'
1982–83
Commissioned by Roger Quinn and Graham Cumberland with the assistance of the Scottish Arts Council.
Bagatelle Variations: 1: *Maestoso*; 2: *Passeggiata: Tempo comodo ma con moto*; 3. Pancho's Proverbs: *Tempo comodo parlando* – In Recort: *con paura*; 4. Quixote's Chorale: *Moderato*, 5. *Fuga*: Don Quixote thinks and sighs; Sancho Panza dances and laughs: *Allegro moderato*; 6. Sancho Panza's Pleasure: *Allegro alla danza*; 7. Don Quixote's Serenade: *Allegretto amoroso lusingando*; 8. Quixote's Lament (*Llanto*): *Lento*; 9. Don Quixote's Address to the Goatherds concerning the Age of Gold: *Pensoso in sogno* (*Valse lente*); 10. El Retablo de Maese Pedro: Pedro's Fanfare; 11. *La Oración de Peregrino*; 12. *Minuetto dei Marionetti*; 13. *Balada: 'Don Gaiferos y la Melisandra'*: *Allegretto quasi andantino*; 14. *Minuetto ritornello*; 15. *Los Moriscos* (Moorish Makhuri): *Allegro marziale*; 16. *Llanto (Homenaje a Barrios)*; 17. Coda: *Lento maestoso*
FP: The Scottish Guitar Duo (Phillip Thorne and Selena Madeley), Stevenson Hall, Royal Scottish Academy of Music and Drama, Glasgow, 20 November 1998.

XXI. FREE-BASS ACCORDION AND PERCUSSION

The Harlot's House (Dance Poem after Oscar Wilde): Duo for free-bass accordion, timpani and percussion 25'
Dated: 'June 1988'
Commissioned by the Lamp of Lothian Concert Society
Percussion (one player): tgl/cyms/susp. cym/SD/maracas/bongos/crotales/tubular bells/xyl/vibraphone (bowed)/ marimba/ BD/gong (*ad lib.*)
FP: Owen Murray (accordion) and Evelyn Glennie (timpani and percussion), Queen's Hall, Edinburgh (Festival), 30 August 1988 (this performance was heavily cut)

XXII. PIANO AND PERCUSSION

The Harlot's House (Dance Poem after Oscar Wilde): Duo for piano, timpani and percussion
Percussion (one player): as in XXI., above
Piano part transcribed from accordion part of XXI., above, by John Fritzell

XXIII. OTHER INSTRUMENTS

Ojala el nombre Casals resonase en las calles! (Let the name of Casals resound in the streets!) 4'
December 1976

Scored for cobla (Catalan street band of indigenous instruments)
Exists also in a version for solo piano

3. INSTRUMENTAL WORKS

I. PIANO

Ballad in A minor
c. 1944   4′
The manuscript was given to Stevenson's private mathematics tutor and is
probably lost.

Sonatina No. 1   7′
1945
I.   *Allegro moderato*
II. *Andante*
III. *Presto*
FP: Ronald Stevenson, Manchester, 1946

A Night Piece   2′
1945

Nocturne in D flat   3′
1945

Burlesque Dance   2′
c. 1945

Retrospect[4]   3′
c. 1945

18 Variations on a Bach Chorale   10′
1946
Exists also in a version for strings

Vox Stellarum   3′
1947

2 Studies   2′
1947
Dedicatee: Irving Wardle
One lost

Sonatina No. 2   6′
1947
I. *Adagietto*
II. Finale: *Allegro con moto*

Third Sonatina   15′
1948

---

[4] Reproduced in Appendix Five: Some Stevenson Miniatures, pp. 330–32.

I.   *In modo di marcia lenta*
II. Scherzo: *Allegro vivace*
III. *Veloce, leggiero e fantastico*

Chorale Prelude for Jean Sibelius   5′
1948
Moderato, velato e visionario
Sent to Sibelius in 1948 and acknowledged with a reply (in English) from
him.[5]

Fugue on a Fragment of Chopin   9′
1948 (for the centenary of Chopin's death)
FP: Ronald Stevenson, Blackburn, 1950
Exists also in a version for two pianos (1953)

Three Nativity Pieces   7′
April 1949
1. 'Gold' – Children's March: *Alla marcia*
2. 'Frankincense' – Arabesque: *Introduzione: Moderato – Grazioso, tempo di
valse*
3. 'Myrrh' – Elegiac Carol: *Prologo: Andante con angioscia soppresa* – Carol:
L'istesso tempo
The Carol is a piano transcription of an early carol for SATB unaccompanied chorus to words by J. H. ('Joe') Watson (a friend of D. H. Lawrence)

Fantasy on Doktor Faust   20′
1949
FP: Ronald Stevenson, Blackburn, 1949
Later (1959) incorporated into the *Prelude, Fugue and Fantasy on Busoni's
'Faust'*

Homage to William Shield ('The Ploughboy')   2′
c. 1949–50
Dedication: Benjamin Britten and Peter Pears

Andante Sereno   3½′
17 February 1950

Fugue on 'Clavis Astartis Magica'   4′
1950
Later (1959) incorporated into the *Prelude, Fugue and Fantasy on Busoni's
'Faust'*

Waltzes   7′
1950
Later (1952) orchestrated

Berceuse Symphonique   12′
1951

---

[5] Sibelius wrote one of his last letters to Stevenson: it was dated 29 August 1957, and
he died on 20 September.

The principal version is the orchestral one

Nocturne after John Field   6'
June/July 1952
Andante, B flat
Exists also in versions for flute and piano and for clarinet and piano; later
renamed *Nocturne: Homage to John Field* to indicate that the music is original,
not a transcription

Variations on a Theme of Pizzetti   11'
1955
As with the 1961 violin variations, the theme is the Sarabande from Pizzetti's
incidental music to D'Annunzio's drama *La Pisanella* (1913), but the two
sets of variations are otherwise entirely different

A 20th Century Music Diary   15'
1953–59
1. *Preludio al corale*
2. *Vivace scherzoso*
3. *Andante con moto*
4. *Allegro risoluto*
5. *Andante*
6. *Allegretto*
7. *Allegro scherzoso*
8. *Con moto amabile*
9. *Canone: Andantino lagrimoso. In Memoriam Bernard van Dieren*
10. *Motivo: Largo drammatico – Agitato volente (Cavalcata notturna)* [based on
BACH]
11. *Allegro moderato* (7 variations on the note-row in the Statue Scene of *Don
Giovanni*)
12. *Allegro moderato* (7 variations on a theme from Berlioz's *Damnation of
Faust*)
13. *Allegro molto* (fugue on a subject from Busoni's *Arlecchino*)
14. *Lento assai* (on the 12-note theme from Liszt's *Faust Symphony*)
15. *Lento*
16. *Andante*
FP: Ronald Stevenson, BBC Radio, Third Programme, 28 March 1967

Prelude, Fugue and Fantasy on Busoni's 'Faust'   28'
1959
Prelude: *Largo*
Fugue: *Tempo giusto –*
Fantasy: *Adagio*
FP: John Ogdon, Manchester Arts Festival, 1959
Publisher: Novello (ed. John Ogdon), 1968, as No. 4 in the series 'Virtuoso'
This work incorporates, in revised forms, the *Fugue on 'Clavis Astartis Magica'*
(1950) and *Fantasy on Doktor Faust* (1949), with a new preludial movement.
In its orchestral version (slightly expanded) it forms the First Piano
Concerto.

Six Pensées sur des Préludes de Chopin   12'
1959
FP: Harold Taylor, Edinburgh Society of Musicians, 22 February 1992

The Barren Fig: Blues Écossaise   2½'
1960–63
Dedication: 'In Memory of Kurt Weill'
Comodo; free tonality and bitonality
Piano transcription of a song

Passacaglia on DSCH   80–85'
1960–62; dated 'West Linton 24 December 1960–18 May 1962')
Pars Prima:
Sonata Allegro
Waltz in rondo-form
Episode
Suite (Prelude, Sarabande, Jig, Sarabande, Minuet, Jig, Gavotte, Polonaise)
Pibroch (Lament for the Children)
Episode: Arabesque Variations
Nocturne
Pars altera:
Reverie-Fantasy
Fanfare – Forebodings: Alarm – Glimpse of a War-Vision
Variations on 'Peace, Bread & the Land' (1917)
Symphonic March
Episode
Fandango
Pedal-point: 'To emergent Africa'
Central Episode: études
Variations in C minor
Pars tertia:
Adagio: Tribute to Bach
Triple Fugue over Ground Bass –
     Subject I: *Andamente*
     Subject II: B A C H
     Subject III: Dies Irae
Final Variations (*Adagissimo barocco*)
FP: Ronald Stevenson, Hiddingh Hall, Cape Town, 10 December 1963
FBP: John Ogdon, BBC Third Programme, 22 May 1966
Dedication: 'For Dimitri Shostakovich'
Publishers: Oxford University Press, 1967; Roberton, 1987; The Ronald
Stevenson Society, 1994
A telegram from Ronald Stevenson to John Ogdon of 1 April 1962
announces the completion of the work in a fair copy. The original version
lacked the section 'Lament for the Children' and the passages in 'To
Emergent Africa' that are played on the strings; both were added on the day
of the first performance. *Cumha na Cloinne (Lament for the Children)*, a
paraphrase of a seventeenth-century pibroch *ùrlar* by Patrick Mor
Macrimmon, was originally a separate piece.

A Wheen Tunes for Bairns tae Spiel: Four Scottish Pieces for Piano   3'
1964
1. 'Croon'
2. 'Drone'
3. 'Reel'
4. 'Spiel'
The title, in the Scots Doric dialect, means 'A Few Tunes for Youngsters to Play'.
Publisher: Schott, 1967

Simple Variations on Purcell's 'New Scotch Tune'   8'
1964, rev. 1975
The 1975 revision, undertaken at the instigation of Louis Kentner, entailed the addition of three variations in more virtuosic style and the renaming of the work *Little Jazz Variations on Purcell's 'New Scotch Tune'*
Publisher (revised version): The Ronald Stevenson Society, 1996[6]

A Scottish Triptych   17'
1959–68
1. 'Keening Sang for a Makar: In Memoriam Francis George Scott' (1959) 7'
FP: Ronald Stevenson, BBC Radio 3, 28 February 1968
Also orchestrated for large orchestra
2. 'Heroic Song for Hugh MacDiarmid' (July 1967)   5'
Libero – Maestoso irato
Commissioned by the BBC in honour of Hugh MacDiarmid's 75th birthday
FP: Ronald Stevenson, BBC Radio 3, 6 January 1969
3. 'Chorale Pibroch for Sorley MacLean' (1967)   5'
Molto moderato
Incorporates the *Pibroch: Calum Salum's Salute to the Seals* (original written for highland bagpipes). The original fair-copy manuscript (not identical with a later version) makes clear that the original title was simply *Chorale-Pibroch*, with the formal dedication 'To Sorley Maclean'; it also gives the tempo as *Moderato maestoso*. Formerly subtitled *From a Twentieth-Century Scottish Triptych*.
FP: Nos. 1–3, Joseph Banowetz, Altarus AIR-CD-9089 (CD)[7]

Valse Charlot and Valse Garbo: Two Children's Pieces for Solo Piano   3'
1965
Conceived as the first in a set of pieces 'like cigarette-cards of famous film-stars'
Published by The Ronald Stevenson Society as *Two Music Portraits*

So we'll go no more a-roving   4'
1965
Piano transcription of Stevenson's 1943 Byron setting, independent of

---

[6] The original version is reproduced in Appendix Five: Some Stevenson Miniatures, pp. 334–41.

[7] *Cf.* Appendix Nine, Discography, p. 475.

No. 9 of *L'Art Nouveau du Chant appliqué au Piano* ('So We'll Go No More A-Roving', after Maude Valérie White)

A'e Gowden lyric (One Golden Lyric)   3'
c. 1965
Principal version is as a song for high voice and piano;[8] exists also in versions for violin and piano, and for violin and clarsach (as No. 10(a) of the score for the film *Hammer and Thistle*)

Chime for Busoni's Centenary   1'
1966

Birthday Canon for Bill Kinghorn   2'
1966

Canonic Caprice (after Strauss' The Bat)   5'
End note: 'Composed. 15 Oct. 1966/24 Dec. 1966/28 Mar. 1967'
Dedication: 'To the memory of Moritz Rosenthal and to my friend Nicholas Davies who introduced me to Rosenthal's recordings'

Three Scots Fairytales   5'
1967
1. 'What the Fairy Piper told me' . . . March time
2. 'What the Fairy Harper told me' . . . *Andante*
3. 'What the Fairy Fiddler told me' . . . Jig time
Dedication: 'For Miss Jean Mackie'
No. 2 may be performed on clarsach.

Fughetta on a Theme by Dukas   2'
1967
Theme from *L'Apprenti sorcier*

Rondo   4'
1968

Melody on a Ground of Glazunov   6'
1970
Exists also in a version for violin and piano

Two Studies for Left Hand Alone on Preludes by Rachmaninov   5½'
1970

Minuet for Anna Katharina   2'
c. 1970

Mockingbird Fughetta   2'
c. 1970
On the American folksong

Peter Grimes Fantasy   7'
1971
Commissioned by BBC Television

---

[8] Reproduced on p. 183.

Dedication: 'To my young comrade-in-art, Graham Johnson'
FP: Ronald Stevenson, BBC Television (BBC2), Summer 1972
FPP: Ronald Stevenson, Wigmore Hall, London, 5 November 1973
Publisher: Boosey and Hawkes, 1972

A Little Hebridean Suite   4′
1971
1. 'Sheep on Shore'
2. 'Sun on Sea'
3. 'Stones and Sands'
Written for Stevenson's daughter Savourna

Hebridean Aeolian Harp: Study for piano   2′
1 March 1973
Allegro, G flat
Dedication: 'For Patrick [Douglas Hamilton] and in homage to Henry
Cowell'

Three Scottish Ballads   10′
1973
1. 'Lord Randal'. *Allegro moderato*; Strong, stark and steady.
Dedication: 'For Ailie Munro'
2. 'The Dowie Dens of Yarrow'. *Andante sostenuto*
Dedication: 'For Gerda'
3. 'Newhaven Fishwife's Cry'. *Moderato sostenuto – Allegro*
Dedication: 'For Marjorie (cheekily)'
FP: Nos. 2 and 3, Murray McLachlan, Olympia OCD 264 (CD); Nos. 1–3,
Ronald Brautigam (piano), Koch Schwann, 3-1590-2 H1 (CD)[9]

Promenade Pastorale   3′
Christmas 1973
'Hommage à Francis Poulenc et à Graham Johnson'

Recitative and Air: In memoriam Shostakovich   5′
1974
Commissioned for a 70th-birthday Festschrift; the subtitle was added when
Shostakovich died before his 70th birthday
Published: in Grigori Schneerson (ed.), *D. D. Shostakovich – Stati/Materyali*,
Sovyetski Kompozitor, Moscow, 1976
Exists also in versions for string orchestra, string quartet, bassoon and
piano, violin and piano, viola and piano, and cello and piano
FP: Joseph Banowetz, Altarus AIR-CD-9089 (CD)[10]

Kleine Doppelfuge   3′
1974
'Praeludium und Dopplefuge'

---

[9] *Cf.* Appendix Nine: Discography, p. 475.

[10] *Cf.* Appendix Nine: Discography, p. 475.

Doubles on Rubbra's 'Cradle Hymn': A Christmas Offering for Keyboard[11]   3′
December 1974
Allegro moderato, E minor
Dedication: 'For Edmund'
May also be performed on harpsichord or organ. The theme is No. 175 in
The Oxford Book of Carols, Oxford University Press, Oxford and London,
1928.

Eileen O'Malley's Jig & Air (or, The Pirate Queen's Jig & Air)   2′
June 1975
1. Quick jig (*Allegro alla giga*)
2. Slow air (*Aria – adagio*)
Dedication: 'To Eileen Machree'

Valsette et Musette Mignonettes: Occasional Waltz   3′
1975
Written for the Scottish Arts Club, Edinburgh, of which Stevenson is an
honorary member; the framed manuscript is displayed there, at the
entrance

A Book of Canons for Alan Bush on his 75th Birthday   7′
1975

Prelude for Alan Bush on his 75th Birthday   2′
1975

Prelude on a Theme of Busoni   3′
c. 1975

Ojala el nombre Casals resonase en las calles!   2′
Music for cobla (Catalan street band)
December 1976
Version for piano

Sonatina serenissima (In memoriam Benjamin Britten) (Sonatina No. 4)   5′
1973–77
I.   Barcaroletta (*Andante con moto*)
II. Fughetta (*Molto moderato, intimo*)
III. Chorale (*Lento*)
IV. Carol (*Allegretto*)
FP: Anthony Goldstone, *The Britten Connection*, Gamut CD 526 (recorded
27–28 March 1991)[12]

Variations on a Theme by Manfred Gordon (Tema Ebraico)   7′
1977
Exists also in a version for string quartet

---

[11] Reproduced in Appendix Five: Some Stevenson Miniatures, pp. 355–58.

[12] *Cf.* Appendix Nine: Discography, p. 475.

Prelude and Chorale (An Easter Offering)[13]   3′
1978
Dedication: 'For our very dearest Edith, Albert, Claudia and Christoph [Wullschleger]'

Chorale: *On Another's Sorrow*   3′
c. 1978
Exists primarily as the final chorale in *19 Songs of Innocence*, in a setting for SATB chorus with soli SATB; also scored for recorder quartet. As a piano solo it exists as an introduction to the chorale and is in the nature of an improvisation.

Norse Elegy for Ella Nygaard   4′
8 July 1976–15 June 1979
FP: Ronald Stevenson, Rudolf Steiner Hall, Edinburgh, 12 March 1980

Chorale and Fugue in Reverse on Two Themes by Robert and Clara Schumann   3′
1979
Dedication: Laurence, Mabel and Karen Glover
Exists also in a version for cello and piano

When the Morning Stars Sang Together (Meditation on a Morgenstern Song)   3′
March 1980
Based on the unison chorus *Eins und Alles (One and All)* of 1965

Barra Flyting Toccata   2′
April 1980
Allegro con spirito, F sharp major (Lydian)

Lyrical Fugue on a Theme of York Bowen   3½′
April 1980
'To John Lindsay (in tranquil recollection of a day when a young girl played York Bowen's A♭ Nocturne to its composer's delight)'

Ostinato macabre on the name Leopold Godowsky   1′
1980
For left hand only

Prelude for the Left Hand Alone   3′
c. 1980

Preludette on the name George Gershwin[14]   1′
March 1981
'For my very dear friend Harry [Winstanley] on his 50th birthday'

A Rosary of Variations on Seán Ó Riada's Irish Folk Mass   15′
21 January 1980

Welcoming Tune for Rachel
1981
A single-page miniature; Rachel is Stevenson's second granddaughter

---

[13] Reproduced in Appendix Five: Some Stevenson Miniatures, pp. 359–61.

[14] Reproduced in Appendix Five: Some Stevenson Miniatures, p. 366.

Three Twi-tunes
1. *Scots-Swedish Twi-tune* No. 1   ½′
Dated: 'Thought out at 31 Gayfield Square, Edinburgh, 9/9/79. Written out
at Townfoot House, West Linton: Yule 81'
Dedication: 'For my very dear friends Harry, Anna, Oscar and Leonora
[Winstanley]'
2. *Santa Lucia and the Star Boys (Italo-Swedish Twi-tune* No. 2 *)*   ½′
'A little polyphonic study for piano'
Dated: 'Composed Aberdeen to Edinburgh [drawing of train] 22 VI 82.
Writ out Townfoot House Yule 82 & March 83'
Dedication: 'For my dearest Harry, Anna, Oscar & Leonora'
3. *Scots-Swedish Twi-Tune* No. 3   1′
1980

Sneaky on Sixth. Rag-Blues   2′
1981
'For Dr Don Gillespie's moggy'. 'Sixth' is 6th Avenue, New York.

The Water of Tyne   6′
6 March 1982
'For my friend Bill Lynch. Ronald Stevenson on his 54th birthday (missing
M......)'

Dulas Courtly Dances   6′
1982
'For my friend Eileen O'Malley at Dulas Court'; Dulas Court was the
retirement home in Herefordshire maintained by the Musicians' Benevolent Fund.

Ragmaster   2′
April 1980–February 1984
Dedication: 'For Barry Ould and Don Gillespie in celebration and
commemoration of Eubie Blake'
Note on score: 'The A flat and D major sections were composed in April
1980; the C minor and C major sections were composed in February 1984'

Melody   3′
1985

Ein kleines Triptychon, 'In Memoriam Czesław Marek'   5′
1986
1. Prelude
2. *Mazurka alla fuga*
3. Chorale

Symphonic Elegy for Liszt   11′
1986
Note on score: 'Commissioned by Dr. Peter Hick, pianophile extraordinaire'
FP: Brian Davidson, St John's, Smith Square, London, 25 April 1989

Piccolo Niccolò Paganinesco   3'
1986
Dedication: 'To Laurenzio Guantaio' (i.e., Lawrence Glover)

Harlem (125th Street) Walkabout   2½'
1987
Bars 1–12 are a completion of a 1919 sketch by Percy Grainger. Grainger's
first title for his sketch was 'A Little March Air'. It was retitled by vote of the
audience at the first public performance.
FP: Ronald Stevenson, Public Library, White Plains, New York, 10 April 1987
Dedication: 'To Burnett Cross – from RS'

Ricordanza di San Romerio (A Pilgrimage for Piano)   2'
1987

Suitette: Hommage à Guex-Joris   3'
1987
Four pieces written on postcards, 'en 5 mouvements avec pastiche du
Menuet de Paderewski'. André Guex-Joris is Vice-President of the Société
Paderewski, Morges, Switzerland, and a famous phonothécaire.

A Threepenny Sonatina: Homage to Kurt Weill (Sonatina No. 5)   7'
1987–88
Moderato – Fughetta (poco allegro) – Tango
FP: Murray MacLachlan, Wigmore Hall, London, 4 January 2004

Motus Perpetuus (?) Temporibus Fatalibus   11'
1987–88
Large portions of this piece are reworked from No. 10, *Motivo: Largo
drammatico – Agitato volente (Cavalcata notturna),* of *A 20th Century Music
Diary.*
FP: Joseph Banowetz, Wigmore Hall, London, 7 November 1988
Dedication: 'For Joseph Banowitz' ('Omaggi a Bach Shostakovich Busoni
Schoenberg ... Dies illa, dies irae, calamitatis et miseriae . . .'
Note on manuscript: 'Commissioned by Joseph Banowetz. Begun New York,
April 1987. Completed W. Linton, July 1988'

Song without Words[15]   4'
January 1988
Commissioned by Martin Anderson

Dodecaphonic Bonfire (Falò Dodecafonico)   8'
1988
FP (partial, as 'work in progress'): Ronald Stevenson, improvised in the
Demarco Gallery, Edinburgh (during the Festival), August 1988 (this
version used material from *The Barren Fig: Blues Écossaise* of 1960/63 to
create an ending)

Variations-Study after Chopin's C sharp minor Waltz   2'
1988

---

[15] Reproduced in Appendix Five: Some Stevenson Miniatures, pp. 364–65.

Beltane Bonfire   8'
Commissioned by the Scottish International Piano Competition as test-
piece for Round 2 of the 1990 competition.
Dated: 'early summer 1989'
FP: Nigel Hutchison, Purcell Room, London, 6 February 1990

Fugue for Alan Bush at 90   2'
Dated: 'Late October to early November, 1990'

A Carlyle Suite   35'
1995
I.   Aubade – 'Here is dawning/Another blue day' (quoting from one of
       the few poems by Carlyle – *To-day*).
II.   Souvenir de Salon (Jane Welsh Carlyle listens to Chopin[16] Stevenson
       adds Jane Carlyle's comments from this meeting in 1848:): Introduct-
       ion – *Andante* – Prelude alla mazurka – Alla strathspey – *Andante* (Polish
       folk carol) – *Poco lento* (Souvenir of Scots psalm 'Martyrs') – Psalm and
       Mazurka combined – Postlude – Encore: *Valse à deux temps*
III.   Variations – Study in historical styles on Frederick the Great's Theme
       [as used by Bach in *A Musical Offering*, 1747]: *Maestoso barocco* – *Allegro
       rococo* [with Alberti bass] – *Allegro ardente, romantico* – *Modéré
       impressionistico* – Recitative and March – 12-note expressionist – *Calmo*:
       sketch for new classicality!
IV.   Jane Carlyle's Wit (scherzino)
V.   Serenade (referring to the Aubade)
Commissioned by Dumfries and Galloway Arts Association to commemorate
the bicentenary of the birth of Thomas Carlyle in 1795.
FP: Sheena Nicol, Church of Scotland, Ecclefechan, 2 December 1995.

Le festin d'Alkan   35'
1988–97
Concerto for solo piano, without orchestra: 'Petit concert en forme
d'études'
1. Free composition
2. Free transcription (of Alkan's Barcarolle in G minor, *Chants*, Book III,
Op. 65, No. 6)
3. Free multiple variations
Composer's note: 'This work encapsulates the composer's conviction that
composition, transcription and variation are all essentially one form'.
Commissioned by Dr Peter Hick
FP: Marc-André Hamelin, 'PianoWorks' festival, Blackheath Concert Halls,
London, 6 September 1998.

---

[16] 'Jane Welsh Carlyle on Chopin: I never heard the piano played before – could not
have believed the capabilities that be in it'; in a note to Ateş Orga (spring 1998)
Stevenson offers a gloss on his music: 'This variation comprises newly-composed
Polish dances and an old Polish carol which combine with the Scottish psalm-tune to
Psalm 23 (Martyrs)'.

Fugue, Variations and Epilogue on a Theme of Bax   19'
1982–83; 2003
The theme is the main one of the slow movement of Bax's Second
Symphony ('a beauty!', in Stevenson's estimation)
'For Colin Scott-Sutherland, premier Bax biographer'
FP: Jeremy Limb, Conway Hall, London, 4 May 2004

II. ORGAN

Prelude and Fugue on a 12-note Theme from Liszt's 'Faust-Symphonie'   11½'
Dated 'August 1961–February 1962'
Prelude: *Lento assai*
Fugue: *L'istesso tempo*
FBP: Nicholas Danby, BBC Radio 3, 2 February 1971
Publisher: Oxford University Press, 1971
The first thirteen bars of the fugue are a transcription of material from
No. 14 of *A 20th Century Music Diary*

Reflections on an Old Scots Psalm Tune   3'
12 March 1965
Adagietto; G minor
Dedication: 'For Colin'
The tune is 'Dundee' from Damon's Psalms, 1591.
FP: Thomas Lang-Reilly, Old St Paul's Church, Edinburgh, 30 November
1988 (Ronald Stevenson 60th-birthday concert)

Doubles on Rubbra's 'Cradle Hymn': A Christmas Offering for keyboard[17]   3'
December 1974
Dedication: 'For Edmund'
Allegro moderato, E minor
May also be performed on piano or harpsichord. The theme is No. 175 in
The Oxford Book of Carols, Oxford University Press, Oxford and London,
1928.

Organ Fugue on Themes from Wagner   6'
1984/86/94/98
'On the Shepherd's Air from Tristan'
Dedication: 'To Derek Watson, in gratitude for a memorable Liszt lecture'
Incorporated into the following work.

Chorale Prelude, Fugue and Chorale Postlude   c. 30'
1984/86/94/98/2000
The Chorale Postlude sets Tom Hubbard's Scots poem *Tristan and Isolde* for
contralto and tenor.
FP: Phillida Bannister (contralto), Christopher Ovenden (tenor), Jonathan
Scott (organ), Greyfriars Church, Edinburgh, 3 March 2003.

---

[17] Reproduced in Appendix Five: Some Stevenson Miniatures, pp. 355–58.

III. HARPSICHORD

Harpsichord Sonata   18'
1968
I.   'In heroic style' (*Largo maestoso – Allegro deciso*).
II. Dirge (Ground: *Andante – Lachrymosa: poco più lento* – Saraband: *Lento ma con moto* – Variation on Ground: *Andante*)
III. Dance (*Allegro vivace*)
IV. Rondo (*Allegretto*)
FP: Alan Cuckston, Harrogate Festival, 17 August 1968.
FBP: Alan Cuckston, BBC Radio 3, 11 June 1969

Doubles on Rubbra's 'Cradle Hymn': A Christmas Offering for Keyboard[18]   3'
December 1974
Dedication: 'For Edmund'
Allegro moderato, E minor
FP: Tim Mottershead, Garvald School, Dolphinton, Peeblesshire, July 1995
May also be performed on piano or organ. The theme is No. 175 in *The Oxford Book of Carols*, Oxford University Press, Oxford and London, 1928.

IV. VIOLIN

Variations on a Theme of Pizzetti   10'
1961
Tema; 1. *Andante;* 2. *Allegro;* 3. *L'istesso tempo: scherzando;* 4. *Allegro molto: perpetuum mobile;* 5. *Fughetta: tempo del tema*
FBP: Anthony Saltmarsh, BBC Third Programme, 18 January 1967.
As with the 1955 piano variations, the theme is the Saraband from Pizzetti's incidental music to D'Annunzio's drama *La Pisanella* (1913), but the two sets of variations are otherwise entirely different.

Scots Suite for solo fiddle   23'
1984
1. 'Fuaran' ('Mountain Spring'): Prelude. *Allegro molto*
2. 'Fugue mar Piobraireachd': Pibroch-Fugue. *Andante*
3. 'Oran agus duan-càraid': 'Slow Air and Couple-Croon'. ($\downarrow$ = 80)
4. Strathspey. *Allegro moderato*
5. Reel. Trescone. *Allegro*
6. Jig. *Vivace*
Commissioned by Geoffrey Allan
Dedication: 'Urram do na fidhleirean a dh'fhalbh/Homage to the fiddlers who have gone'
At the first performance Stevenson called the third movement 'Lone Song and Couple Croon' and the fourth 'The Drunk Man Looks at the Fiddle'.[19]
FP Leonard Friedman, Demarco Gallery, Edinburgh, 21 August 1988

---

[18] Reproduced in Appendix Five: Some Stevenson Miniatures, pp. 355–58.

[19] Stevenson's autograph observations on his *Scots Suite* are reproduced as Appendix Six on pp. 369–73.

V. GUITAR

Anger Dance   3'
1965
Allegro irato
Dedication: 'To Tim Clark'
Publisher: Schott, London, 1966 (Guitar Archive No. 222)
Original title: *Anti-Franco Dance*

Shy Geordie   4'
mid-1970s
Transcription of a song to a text by Helen Cruikshank; exists also in versions
for solo voice and voice and guitar

VI. PEDAL HARP

Two Cambrian Cantos
1965
1. 'In memory of my Welsh Gran who worked as a pit-child truck-pusher in
the 1860's'   3'
2. 'With memories of a childhood holiday in Wales'   2'
FBP: Ann Griffiths, BBC Third Programme, 18 January 1967
No. 1 exists in a version for clarsach.

Fantasia Polifonica   9½'
1983–84
1. Prelude. *Volante.*
2. Canon I, at the octave. *Moderato*
3. Canon II, at the ninth. *Un pocchis. più moto*
4. Canon III, at the tenth. *Allegretto*
5. *Aria con larghezza*
6. *Passacaglia maestosa*
7. *Ritornello funerio*
2. Ritornello No. 2
9. Ritornello No. 3
10. Canon IV, at the fourth. *Allegretto*
11. Canon V, at the fifth. *Allegro*
12. Canon VI, at the sixth. *Andante*
13. Canon VII, at the seventh. *Largo*
14. Canon VIII, at the octave. *Tranquillo*
15. *Corale a accordi giganteschi*
16. Fugue. *Andande pensoso*
FP: Satu Salo, 8 February 1984, Purcell Room, London

VII. CLARSACH

Cambrian Canto   3'
1965
'In memory of my Welsh Gran who worked as a pit-child truck-pusher in the
1860's'
Originally for pedal harp

Country Tune 2'
1979
Publisher: *Clarsair Annual*, No. 1, Clarsach Society, Edinburgh, 1980

What the Fairy Harper Told Me 2'
1967
No. 2 of *Three Scots Fairytales* for piano

VIII. FLUTE OR RECORDER

Three Improvisations on Themes of Emanuel Moór 4'
1986
I.   *Allegro moderato*
II. *Tempo di Minuetto grazioso*
III. *Andante*

IX. HIGHLAND BAGPIPE

Pibroch: Calum Salum's Salute to the Seals 12'
1967

X. FREE-BASS ACCORDION

Celtic Suite 8'
May 1984–December 1988
1. 'Celtic Lovesong' (dated 20–21 May 1984)
2. 'Celtic Lullaby'
3. 'Peaceful March of the Ever Young'
FP: Owen Murray, BBC Radio Scotland, 1986 (first movement only)

4. CHORAL MUSIC

1. *A CAPPELLA* CHORUS

I. SATB

Canticle to the Sun 3'
1955
Text: St Francis of Assisi, freely transl. Ronald Stevenson
For two female voices or two-part female chorus
Exists also in a version (1994) for SC

The Weyvers o' Blegburn 30'
1962
For chamber choir with young solo voice
Text: eight Lancashire dialect poems from 'The Poets of Blackburn',
published by *The Blackburn Times*, 1900

Chorale: On Another's Sorrow 3'
1965
Text: William Blake

With solo soprano
Principal version is as the final chorus in the *19 Songs of Innocence*, exists also in transcriptions for SATB recorder quartet and for piano solo

A Mediaeval Scottish Triptych 9'
1967
No. 1. 'Quhen Alexander oor Kynge was Dede'
Text: anon., c. 1300
Lento, lamentoso e lagrimoso
No. 2. 'Wallace's Lament for the Graham'
Text: Blin' Harry, *The Wallace*, c. 1490
Andante doloroso
No. 3, 'Fredome'
Text: John Barbour, *The Brus*, c. 1375
Allegro moderato e maestoso
FBP (No. 3 only): BBC Northern Singers, cond. Stephen Wilkinson, BBC Radio, Third Programme, 18 January 1967
FBP (complete): BBC Northern Singers, cond. Stephen Wilkinson, BBC Radio, Third Programme, 24 February 1969
FPP (complete): Cappella Nova, cond. Alan Taverner, Old St Paul's Church, Edinburgh, 30 November 1988 (Ronald Stevenson 60th-birthday concert)
Publisher (No. 3 only): Novello, London, 1969 (PSB 1624)
In No. 2 the chorus divides for some short passages up to SSAATTTBBBB.

Anns an Airde, as an Doimhne (*In the Heights, From the Depths*) 12'
1968
Texts: Sorley MacLean
1. 'Ceann Loch Aineart' (*Allegro*)
2. 'Calbharaigh' (*Moderato con moto – Andante*)
3. 'Lionmhoireachd anns na speuran' (*Adagio*)
Commissioned by the Greenock Gaelic Choir.
FP: The Orion Singers, cond. W. Grant Kidd (Isobel Dunlop Memorial Concert), St Cecilia's Hall, Edinburgh, 10 December 1976.
'Calbharaigh' exists also in a setting, in Scots (transl. Douglas Young), for tenor and piano in the song-cycle *The Infernal City*.

Amhran Talaidh (*Day is Düne*) 2'
1968
Text: Gaelic poem by Findlay McNeill from the Scots of William Soutar

Four Peace Motets 6/7'
1967
Texts: Bible
No. 1, 'Thou shalt not kill' (*Moderato con moto*)
No. 2, 'Put up again thy sword' (*Andante amabile*)
No. 3, 'They shall beat their swords into ploughshares' (*Allegro*)
No. 4, 'The Seventh Beatitude' (*Con pace*)
FP: Cappella Nova, cond. Alan Taverner, Old St Paul's Church, Edinburgh, 30 November 1988 (Ronald Stevenson 60th-birthday concert)
A version of No. 4, 'The Seventh Beatitude', exists also for tenor and piano

Choral Recitative and Psalm 23 15′
1990–92
Text: Gospel of St John in the Scots version by W. L. Lorimer; Recitative:
ch. 1, vv. 1–5; Psalm 23 in the Scots version by Alexander Montgomerie
Commissioned by R. L. C. Lorimer
Dated: 'Begun 6 June 1990 – completed 9 July 1992, West Linton; fair copy
completed 24 July'
FP: Cappella Nova, cond. Alan Taverner, 4 June 1993, St Mary's Cathedral,
Glasgow

Sunneplatz Magden 1½′
1979
Text: inscription on a Swiss house

Speak to Us of Children 1½′
1990
Text: Kahlil Gibran

Lines from Browning's 'Rabbi Ben Ezra' 1′
Date unknown
Dedication: To Betty and Grant Kidd

Villanelle de Noël: Carol 3′
Date unknown
Text: Tom Scott

II. SC

Canticle to the Sun 3′
1955
For two female voices or two-part female chorus
Text: St Francis of Assisi, freely transl. Ronald Stevenson
Exists also in a version for SATB chorus

III. SSAA/TTBB/SATB

Domino Roberto Carwor: In memoriam Robert Carver 25′
1987
Text: James Reid Baxter
Organ accompaniment *ad libitum* (*a cappella* preferred)
FP: Cappella Nova, cond. Alan Taverner, Old St Paul's Church, Edinburgh,
30 November 1988 (Ronald Stevenson 60th-birthday concert)
Commissioned by Cappella Nova, with funds provided by the Scottish Arts
Council

IV. TTBB

Dieses Hauses Schütz ist Reinlichkeit 2′
1979
Text: inscription on a Swiss house

V. SATB AND PIANO OR HARP

A Carol ('So she laid him in a manger') 2′

November 1948
Text: J. H. ('Joe') Watson
A piano transcription forms part of the third of the *Three Nativity Pieces* for
solo piano

3 Songs into Space   10′
1962
Texts: Walt Whitman

The Quiet Comes In   3′
1968 arr. 1976
For soprano solo, SATB chorus and harp or piano
Text: William Soutar
Dedication: Betty and Grant Kydd
Exists also in a version for voice and piano (1968)

A Wreath of Tunes for Percy Grainger   4′
For SATB and piano
before 1970
Text: Ronald Stevenson, to tunes by Grainger

The Linton Whipman Installation Song   2′
1976
Exists also in versions for voice and piano, unison voices and piano and for
unaccompanied children's chorus
Publisher: *The West Linton Whipman Play Handbook*, West Linton Whipman
Committee, 1976[20]

VI. SSAA

Sapphic Fragments   7½′
1963
For soprano solo, women's chorus and harp
Text: Sappho, in translation (probably that by Henry Thornton Wharton,
though unrecorded)

No Coward Soul is Mine   4½′
1966
For SSAA women's chorus and harp or piano
Text: Emily Brontë
Dedication: 'For Harrogate College Choir'
Commissioned by Harrogate College
Published: Novello, London, 1969 (supplement to *The Musical Times*,
February 1969)

[20] 'The Whipmen of Linton' is a benevolent society founded in West Linton in 1803;
Whipman Week takes place in the first week in June.

2. CHILDREN'S CHOIR

Eins und Alles (One and All) 5'
1960
Text: Christian Morgenstern transl. Ronald Stevenson
Andante semplice
Unison song for children's choir, descant recorder, violin, cello and guitar,
written as the school song for the Garvald School for children in need of
special care, Dolphinton, Peeblesshire; exists also in a version for high voice
and piano incorporated into the *Liederbüchlein für Regine Beate* (1966)

Hallowe'en Sang 2'
1963
Text: Ronald Stevenson
Round for children, for two or more solo voices

The Buckie Braes 2'
c. 1965
Text: William Soutar
For children's unison chorus and piano
Exists also in a version for voice and piano

Giftie-Sang 1½'
c. 1965
Text: Ronald Stevenson
For child's or children's voice(s) and piano with violin obbligato

Frogs and Toads and Newts 1'
1966
Text: Ronald Stevenson
Round for children

The Witches of Pendle: Pennine Pastorale 2½'
1968
Text: Margaret Greenhalgh (Lancashire dialect)
For children's chorus and piano; exists also in a version for high voice and
piano

Mocking-Bird Fughetta 1'
c. 1970
Text: folksong
Round for children's voices

On Cromshaw Chair 2'
c. 1970
Text: William Luker (Lancashire dialect verse)
For children's choir and piano

Musings by the Lyne Water 2'
1975
Text: Robert Sanderson (West Linton, 1888)
Andante

For children's voices and piano; exists also in a version for high voice and piano
Dedication: 'Tae the bairns o' Linton'
FP: The Linton Singers, cond. Murray Campbell, School Hall, West Linton, 1989

The Linton Whipman Installation Song   2'
1976
Exists also in versions for voice and piano, for SATB chorus and piano and for unison voices and piano

Hier ruht Heinrich Pestalozzi   2'
1978
Text: inscription on Pestalozzi's grave, Brugg, Switzerland
Set as a four-part round for high voices or children's choir

The Wallara Garden Song   1½'
August 1982
For unison chorus and accompaniment
Text: Ronald Stevenson
Dedication: 'For my friends at Wallara, Dandendong and District Mentally Retarded Children's Welfare Association – Victoria, Australia'

Adam was a gardener   2'
September 1982
Text: Ronald Stevenson
Composer's note: 'song for children in need of special care' (patients of Kevin Heinz Garden Centre, Dandenong, near Melbourne)
FBP: Melbourne, Australia, c. 1982

Karl Bellman's Little Swedish Song Book   5'
Date c. 1970
Text: Carl Bellman
'Simple setting' for voice(s) and piano

Two North Country Rhymes
1970
Canonic choruses for children's voices (SAA)
Text: traditional dialect verse
1. 'Little Lancashire Lad'   2'
2. 'Lancashire Fun'   2'

3. VOCAL DUET

Canticle to the Sun   3'
c. 1960
For soprano and contralto
Text: St Francis of Assisi, freely transl. Ronald Stevenson
Composed 'for my wife Marjorie to sing with a friend'

5. SONGS

1. SONG CYCLES

I. MEDIUM TO HIGH VOICE AND PIANO

Two Chinese Vocalises   3'
1982
1. 'Bird and Flower'
2. Untitled

Songs of Ancient China   6½'
1982–83
Texts: Anon., transl. Claire Clennell
1. 'Meng Chiang Nyu's Lament: Chinese Ballad' (Anon., c. 214BC). Slowly.
Dated: 'December 1982'
2. 'Lone Love's Longing (The Daughter-in-Law's Song): Chinese Folksong'.
Andante
Dated: 'November 1983'
3. 'Crab-Fisher's Song: Chinese Folk Dance-song'. *Allegro con spirito*
Dated: 'November 1983'
These are ancient Chinese melodies, described as 'arranged for piano
(including vocal melody and suitable accompaniment to it)'; Nos. 2 and 3
are stated to be arranged for harp as well. No. 3 is a free arrangement of
No. 5 of *A Chinese Folk-Song Suite* for solo piano

Song Diptych   4'
2003
1. 'Dawn Song in West Linton'
2. 'Evensong in West Linton'
Textx: Ronald Stevenson, Lowlands Scots
Dedication: Barbara Hall

Two Songs to Poems by David Betteridge   4'
2004
1. 'Nothing is Ever Really Lost'
2. 'Your Book Lies Open'
Text: David Betteridge

II. SOPRANO AND PIANO

Two Tagore Songs
1965
Texts: Rabindranath Tagore, from *Gitanjali*
1. 'The Source' (*Moderato semplice*; A minor)   4½'
2. 'When and Why?' (*Allegro corrente*; A minor)   5½'
Published by The Ronald Stevenson Society as *Diptych*

Liederbüchlein für Regine Beate   4½'
1966
Text: Christian Morgenstern
1. 'Reinkarnation' (transl. Ronald Stevenson)
2. 'O traure nicht' (transl. Ronald Stevenson)

3. 'Brüder' (transl. Ronald Stevenson)
4. 'Eins und Alles'
Dedication: 'In Memoriam Regina Wullschleger, †1966 aged eight'. The
first three songs were written for the funeral of Regine Beate Wullschleger;[21] 'Eins und Alles', written for children's chorus as the school song
for Garvald School, Dolphinton, was added because she was particularly
fond of it.

Two Songs   4′
c. 1958
Texts: R. L. Stevenson
1. 'The Shadow March'
2. 'The Lamplighter'
Later (1985) incorporated into *A Child's Garden of Verses*[22]

III. TENOR AND PIANO

Border Boyhood   24′
1970
Texts: Hugh MacDiarmid
Dedication: 'In memory of Tertia Liebenthal of Edinburgh, who loved the
Border Country'
1. 'The Joys I Knew' (*Allegro con nuovo ardore*)
2. 'Memories' (*Andante amabile*)
3. 'A Celebration of Colour' (*Molto moderato; autunnale*)
4. *Intermezzo*, for piano solo – 'Nocturne: The Hushed Song' (*Notturno:
Il Canto Calmato*) (*Andante calmissimo ed incantato*)[23]
5. 'The Nut Trees' (*Allegro*)
6. 'Fighting Spirit' (*Scherzo: giga alla marcia. Vivace misurato e spietato*) (*segue*) –
7. 'The Nook of the Night Paths' (*Fuga: piutosto grave*)
FP: Peter Pears (tenor), Ronald Stevenson (piano), Aldeburgh Festival,
Aldeburgh, 1971

The Infernal City   28′
1970–71
Texts: Hugh MacDiarmid and Sorley MacLean
1. 'Glasgow' (MacDiarmid) (*Piuttosto grave con passo ponderoso ed espressione
minacciosa*)
2. 'Auld Wife in High Spirits (in an Edinburgh Pub)' (MacDiarmid)
(*Comodo, a piacere, con fantasia*)
3. 'Glasgow 1960' (MacDiarmid) (*Allegro vivace, ritmico e narrante*)
4. Interlude, for piano solo (*Andante* (*segue*) –)
5. 'Calvary' (MacLean trans. Douglas Young) (*Andante, remoto, catalettico –
Moderato con moto (attacca)*)
6. 'Open Glasgow up!' (MacDiarmid) (*Moderato, solenne e con spazio*)

---

[21] *Cf.* Albert Wullschleger's essay, p. 244, above.

[22] *Cf.* p. 418.

[23] Reproduced in Appendix Five: Some Stevenson Miniatures, pp. 350–54.

7. 'The Aerial City' (MacDiarmid) (*Allegro albeggiante*)
Commissioned by Duncan Robertson
Dedication: 'For Duncan'; No. 5 bears an in memoriam individual
dedication to Erik Leslie Satie and No. 6 to Charles Rennie Mackintosh.
FP: Duncan Robertson (tenor), Ronald Stevenson (piano), Purcell Room,
London, 28 February 1971.
No. 5 is a re-working of 'Calbharaigh', No. 2 of *Anns an Airde, as an Doimhne*
for SATB chorus (1968) and exists also in a version for unaccompanied
voice, with alterations to allow the singing of either the Gaelic original or
the Douglas Young translation, and in another version for voice and
clarsach; published in Raymond Ross and Joy Hendry (eds.), *Sorley MacLean:*
Critical Essays, Scottish Academic Press, Edinburgh, 1986.

Lieder ohne Buchstaben (Unspelt Songs)   14'
1982
Texts: A. D. Hope
1. 'Such songs I would prepare...' (Slowly flowing in quiet rapture)
Dedication: 'For Richard Connolly'
2. 'When like the Sun...' (*Allegro gioioso*)
Dedication: 'For Judy & Adam Watson'
3. Chorale: 'Often had I found her fair'. (*Moderato con moto*)
Dedication: 'For Muriel and Neville Stanley'
4. 'The Gateway' (*Allegro estatico*) – Coda (only if sung as a cycle) (*Tranquillo*)

IV. BARITONE AND PIANO

Songs of Quest   20'
Spring–June 1974
Texts: John Davidson
1. 'The Boat is Chafing' (*Allegro barcarola, calmo*)
2. 'Vive la Vie' (*Allegro esultato e vivace*)
3. 'Vive la Mort' (*Allegro moderato*)
4. 'To the Generation Knocking at the Door' (*Moderato declamato – poco più*
mosso)
5. 'The Last Journey' (*Alla marcia, intrepido*)
Dedication: 'Dedicated to Francis Loring & the wandering spirit of Franz
Schubert'
FP: (semi-private) Francis Loring (baritone), Ronald Stevenson (piano),
The Hall Studio, London, 7 August 1974
FPP: Francis Loring (baritone), Ronald Stevenson (piano), Vienna,
12 August 1974
FPP (UK): Francis Loring (baritone), Ronald Stevenson (piano), St Cecilia's
Hall, Edinburgh, 20 November 1974 (recorded by the BBC but not
broadcast).

Hills of Home   12'
1974
Texts: R. L. Stevenson
1. 'Blows the Wind Today'. In memoriam Isobel Dunlop. (Slow march)
2. 'In the Highlands' (*Andante con moto*)

Dedication: 'For Frieda and William Wordsworth'
3. 'I Saw Rain Falling' (*Lento ma non troppo*)
Dedication: 'For Michael Oliver'
4. 'Requiem' (*Con moto sereno*)
FP: Ron Morrison (bass), Ronald Stevenson (piano), Isobel Dunlop
Memorial Concert, St Cecilia's Hall, Edinburgh, 10 December 1976

V. BASS-BARITONE AND PIANO

Songs from Factories and Fields   7'
1977
Text: Hugh MacDiarmid
1. 'Black in the Pit'
2. 'From Factories and Fields'
3. 'Och, it's Nonsense'

VI. HIGH VOICE AND HARP OR PIANO

Four Vietnamese Miniatures   9'
1965
Text: Ho Chi Minh, trans. David Halberstam
1. 'Song from Prison'
2. 'Evening'
3. 'Cock-crow'
4. 'Dawn'
FP: Duncan Robertson (tenor) and Ann Griffiths (harp), Purcell Room,
London, 28 February 1971

Nine Haiku, for soprano or tenor and harp or piano   12'
1971
Texts: Nos. 1–7, 9 – School of Bashō, words by Keith Bosley after the
       Japanese, from French translations in the *Trésor de la poésie universelle*
       (ed. Roger Caillois and Jean-Clarence Lambert, Gallimard, Paris,
       1958); No. 8 is by Keith Bosley himself
1.   'Dedication' (Kikaku, 1661–1707) (*Allegretto*)
2.   'The Fly' (Issa, 1763–1823) (*Allegro moderato*)
3.   'Gone Away' (Ransetsu, 1654–1707) (*Andante grave*)
4.   'Nocturne' (Bashō, 1644–94) (*Lento calmissimo*)
5.   'Master and Pupil' (Bashō and Kikaku) (*Recitativo: poco lento*)
6.   'Spring' (Kikaku) (*Allegretto*)
6(a). 'The Blossoming Cherry': aubade for harp (or piano) (*Allegro
       primaverile*)
7.   'Curfew' (Issa) (*Andante tranquillo*)
8.   'Hiroshima' (Keith Bosley) (*Moderato irato*)
9.   'Epilogue' (Bashō) (*Moderato*)
Composer's note: 'These songs fuse pentatony and dodecaphony; the first
and third lines of haiku have five syllables; the second line has seven
syllables. Each syllable in these R. S. songs has a different note of the
12-note sonic spectrum'.
Dedication: Norman Peterkin

FP: Duncan Robertson (tenor), Anne Griffiths (harp), Purcell Room, London, 28 February 1971

VII. MIXED VOICES AND PIANO

19 Songs of Innocence 45'
First version, for soprano, contralto, tenor and baritone soloists, final *a cappella* chorale and piano: 1947–48, 'finished May 1965'
Second version, for soprano, contralto, tenor and baritone soloists, final *a cappella* chorale, flute and string quintet (two violins, viola, cello and double-bass)
18 February–18 May 1966
Texts: William Blake
1. Introduction: 'Piping down the valleys wild' (soprano) (*Allegro*; D major)
2. 'The Shepherd (tenor) (*Allegretto pastorale*; F major)
3. 'The Echoing Green' (tenor) (*Allegro moderato e con spirito*; C major)
4. 'The Lamb' (soprano) (*Andante semplice*; F major)
5. 'The Little Black Boy' (bass) (*Moderato*; F minor)
6. 'The Blossom' (contralto) (*Allegretto*; E major)
7. 'The Chimney Sweeper' (bass) (Rondo in various tempi; A major)
8. 'The Little Boy Lost' (soprano) (*Allegretto*; C minor)
9. 'The Little Boy Found' (soprano) (*Allegretto*; A minor)
10. 'Laughing Song' (tenor) (*Allegro brillante*; B flat major)
11. 'A Cradle Song' (contralto) (*Andante semplice*; D flat major)
12. 'The Divine Image' (bass) (*Moderato*; G major)
13. 'Holy Thursday' (tenor) (*Alla marcia*; A minor)
14. 'Night' (contralto) (Various tempi, from *Andante* to *Allegro*; B major)
15. 'Infant Joy' (soprano) (*Moderato*; E major)
16. 'Spring' (soprano) (*Allegro primaverile*; B flat major)
17. 'Nurse's Song' (soprano) (Allegro; D minor)
18. 'A Dream' (tenor) (*Andante con moto sonnabulistico*; A minor)
19. Introduction and Chorale: 'On Another's Sorrow' (SATB) (*Moderato – Andante*; E major)
The order given here is that of the revised version, although there is a discrepancy between the manuscript and the published score, where No. 15, 'Infant Joy', renumbered, appears after No. 16, 'Spring'. Stevenson has stated in a programme note that the cycle was initially written 'for me to sing (or croak)' and that vocal compass was not realistically considered; it is in the second version that different songs were assigned to different voices. The keys of some of the songs were transposed between the two versions; those above are as in the second version. The finale, 'On Another's Sorrow', exists also in a setting for SATB chorus with solo soprano, soli SATB, and in transcriptions for SATB recorder quartet and for solo piano.
FP: The Artsong Collective (Moira Harris, soprano; Phillida Bannister, contralto; Wills Morgan, tenor; Jamieson Sutherland, baritone; Richard Black, piano), Conway Hall, London, 27 May 1998

Two Poe Songs 8'
October 1962
Texts: Edgar Allen Poe

1. 'Annabel Lee'   6'
For mezzo-soprano or contralto
Dedication: 'To Annabel Susan Ogdon, aet. 1'
Andante narrante, D minor/major
2. 'Eldorado'   8'
For tenor
FP: Peter Pears (tenor), Viola Tunnard (piano), Radio 3, c. 1975

Ballattis of Luve   25'
1972
For soprano, contralto, tenor, baritone and piano or lute or harpsichord
Texts: Alexander Scott (?1515–?1580)
1. 'It cumis you luvaris to be laill' (*Allegro molto*)
2. 'Luve preysis but comparesone' (*Moderato con amore*)
3. 'Lo, quhat it is to lufe!' (*Allegro e gagliardo*)
4. 'In June the jem of joy and geme' (*Allegretto sereno e con umore amabile*)
5. 'Fra raige of youth the rink has rune' (*Andante grave*)
Commissioned by the Saltire Singers
Dedication: 'For the Saltire Singers and Robert Spencer'
FP: Saltire Singers, Robert Spencer (lute), Leeds Music Society, 1972 (date unknown).

A Child's Garden of Verses   35'
1985
for soprano and/or tenor, with optional treble, young soprano and piano
Texts: Robert Louis Stevenson
1. 'Dedication' (*Moderato*)
2. 'Bed in Summer' (*Andando*)
3. 'The Land of Nod' (*Allegretto*)
4. 'Time to Rise' (*Allegro sciolto*)
5. 'Singing' (*Moderato con moto*)
6. 'Rain' (*Allegro*)
7. 'Windy Nights' (*Volante*)
8. 'Shadow March' (*Alla marcia, intrepida con paura*)
9. 'My Shadow' (*Allegretto corrente*)
10. 'Fairy Bread' (*Allegretto andando* – Daintily, simply, fey, strange, remote, strictly in time, with no rubato)
11. 'The Swing' (*Con moto quasi altalena e con slancio*)
12. 'Summer Sun' (*Moderato con moto*)
13. 'From a Railway Carriage' (*Allegro con urgenza*)
14. 'Autumn Fires' (*Moderato con moto tranquillo*)
15. 'When the Golden Day is Done' (*Andante tranquillo*)
16. 'The Lamplighter' (*Comodo*)
17. 'Envoy' (*Moderato narrante*)
FBP: Neil Mackie (tenor), Susan Hamilton (soprano), Richard Townhill (treble), Ronald Stevenson (piano), BBC Scotland, 30 December 1985, prefaced by a spoken introduction by the composer in conversation with Derek Watson.

2. INDIVIDUAL SONGS

All songs for medium to high voice unless otherwise indicated

I. UNACCOMPANIED VOICE

Little Lad (An Old Lancastrian Lullaby)   1½'
c. 1965
For unaccompanied soprano

Ninna-Nanna for Anna: Lullaby   1½'
1972
Text: Ronald Stevenson
For medium voice; written to greet his grand-daughter Anna-Wendy

Shy Geordie   1'
1973
Text: Helen Cruikshank
For medium unaccompanied voice
Published: *Chapman*, Nos. 27–28 (double issue), Summer 1980, Edinburgh,
p. 34 (facsimile).
Exists also in a version for voice and guitar and in a transcription for solo
guitar

Leaving Iona   3'
c. 1975
Text: Tom Fleming
Exists also in a version for voice and piano

Die Fusswaschung   2'
c. 1980
Text: Christian Morgenstern, transl. Ronald Stevenson

So Many Summers
November 1995
Text: Norman MacCaig
'Unaccompanied song for voice or fiddle'; 'Slow air, quietly'
Dedication: 'For Norman, my brother in C. M. G.'
Publisher: *Chapman*, Winter 1989 (MacCaig issue)

Calvary (Calbharaigh)
1968
Text: Sorley MacLean (Somhairle MacGill-Eain)
A re-working of 'Calbharaigh', No. 2 of *Anns an Airde, as an Doimhne* for
SATB chorus (1968); it exists also in a version for tenor and piano as No. 5
of *The Infernal City*; for unaccompanied voice, with alterations to allow the
singing of either the Gaelic original or the Douglas Young Lallans
translation; and in a further version for voice and clarsach

II. VOICE AND PIANO

The Rover   3'
1945
Text: Sir Walter Scott

SONGS TO POEMS BY WILLIAM SOUTAR
1965
All for medium-high voice and piano

Waggletail'

The Droll Wee Man

Dreepin Weather

Day is Düne
Published: *Child's Education Quarterly*, Spring 1968, and *Chapman*,
Nos. 89–90 (double-issue), Summer 1998, pp. 77–78; exists also (with
Gaelic and English texts) in versions for SATB chorus and for high voice
and guitar

The Lea

The Buckie Braes

Hill Sang

The Quiet Comes in
Exists also in a setting for soprano solo, SATB chorus and harp or piano
Dedication: Betty and W. Grant Kidd

The Plum Tree

To the Future
Published: *Chapman*, Nos. 89–90 (double-issue), Summer 1998, pp. 77–78
Exists also in a version for voice and guitar

A Lucky Chap

Ballad

Among High Hills

Hallowe'en Sang (*Andante molto misurato; Cauto e burlone* (Canny and
droll))
Dedication: Alastair Chisholm

There was a composer called Vlad   1'
7 March 1955
Text: Ronald Stevenson
Message of thanks to Roman Vlad, sent on a postcard, and described by the
composer as 'efemera!'

Come, Marjorie, Link Thi Arm i'Mine   2'
1966
Text: Edwin Waugh

Spring Song for a Dusky Chatelaine   2'
1966
Text: Alasdair Alldridge

SONGS TO POEMS BY JAMES JOYCE
1968
All for medium-high voice and piano or harp

A Flower Given to my Daughter

Silently She's Combing

In the Dark Pinewood

Lean out the Window Goldenhair

O Cool is my Valley Now

When the Shy Star Goes Forth

Who Goes Amid the Green Wood

Sleep Now, O Sleep Now

My Love is in a Light Attire

Winds of May' (Hommage to Roger Quilter)

Soft Sweet Music in the Air

Strings in the Earth and Air

Out by Donnycarney

I would in that Sweet Bosom Be
FP: Some of the above performed by Gerda Stevenson (soprano) and Ronald Stevenson (piano), Edinburgh Poetry Library, 1978 (date unknown)

To a Child Dancing in the Wind   3½′
1968
Text: W. B. Yeats
Exists also in a version for voice and guitar

Fiddler's Song   2′
1968
Text: George Mackay Brown
Composer's note: 'On a Tiree (Hebridean) holiday'

Titus Bronchitis   1½′
c. 1969
Text: Morris Kahn and Ronald Stevenson
Composer's note: 'efemera: fun-piece'

Wasserfall bei Nacht I   2′
1981
Text: Christian Morgenstern
Dated: 'In Wengen komponiert 19–21 Mai 1981'
Dedication: 'An Albert und Edith Wullschleger'
Exists also in a version for cello and piano, with or without voice

Herbst (Autumn)   2'
September 1983
Text: Christian Morgenstern, transl. Ronald Stevenson
Dedication: 'An Albert und Edith [Wullschleger], Heinz und Vreni
[Lüscher] in Herzensfreundschaft'

Wasserfall bei Nacht II   4'
1981–85
Text: Christian Morgenstern
Dated: 'Komponiert in Wengen bei Jungfrau: May 1981–Sept. 1983–May
1985'
Dedication: 'An Vreni and Heinz Lüscher in Dankbarkeit (1981–83–85)'

Farewell to the Farm   2'
'14 IV 89'
Text: Robert Louis Stevenson
Dedication: Patrick Cadell
Publisher: The Ronald Stevenson Society, as addendum to *A Child's Garden
of Verses*, 1994

The Linton Whipman Installation Song   2'
1967
Text: local rhyme
Written for the Borders festival; exists also in versions for unison voices and
piano, for solo children's chorus and for SATB chorus and piano

Welcome, Bonny Brid   2'
1968
Text: Samuel Laycock

The Carefree Highland Child   1½'
February 1981
Text: Byron

Scatter My Ashes   1'
1981
Text: John Galsworthy

Luv Sang
Text: Ellie McDonald
April 1992
Simply and fairly slowly
'Composed at Margaret's kind request. Dedicated to Margaret and Colin
Torrance on their silver wedding'

Wayfarer's Nocturne   3'
May 2002
Text: Goethe, *Wanderers Nachtlied II*; translation into Border Scots as
Gangrel's Nichtsang by Ronald Stevenson

Ae Year's Bairn   2'
2004

Text: Charles Murray
Dedication: Jamie Reid Baxter

MacDiarmid on Whalsay   2½'
August 2004
Text: Alan Riach

Zum Wilden Mann   2'
Date unknown
Text: anon., from a hotel registration book in Germany

Soprano and Piano

Full Fadum Five   2½'
c. 1955
Text: Shakespeare, from *The Tempest*

Mezzo-soprano and Piano

My Candle Burns at Both Ends   3'
1970
Text: Edna St Vincent Millay
Composer's note: 'study in cancrizans canon'
Exists also in a version for voice and string quartet

Christenmas Thochts o a Mither-tae-be   5'
1981
Text: Ronald Stevenson

The Seventh Beatitude
1985
This is an arrangement of the fourth of the *Peace Motets* for SATB chorus.
FP: Philip Langridge (tenor), Graham Johnson (piano), London Peace
Festival, August 1985.

Chanticleer   2'
1989
Text: Tessa Ransford
FP: Phillida Bannister (contralto), Ronald Stevenson (piano), St Cecilia's
Hall, Edinburgh, 16 February 1990

Gallowa Spring   2'
1989
Text: William Neill
FP: Phillida Bannister (contralto), Ronald Stevenson (piano), St Cecilia's
Hall, Edinburgh, 16 February 1990

Tenor and Piano

Eldorado   3'
before 1970
Text: Edgar Allan Poe
FP: Peter Pears (tenor), Viola Tunnard (piano), BBC Radio 3, Summer 1968

SONGS TO POEMS BY HUGH MACDIARMID

Soprano and Piano

The Robber   3'
1965

Tenor and Piano

The Bobbin Winder   2½'
10 February 1964
Corrente, fluido
FP: Peter Pears (tenor), Viola Tunnard (piano), BBC Radio 3, Summer 1968

O Wha's the Bride?   4'
1966

Tenor or High Baritone and Piano

Trompe l'œuil   2'
c. 1990
Andante con moto, semplice; A major

Baritone and Piano

Scots Steel and Irish Fire
1962
Dedication: 'To Norman Peterkin – on his 80th birthday, 21 December 1966'

The Skeleton of the Future   1'
11 February 1964
Andante con moto: quasi recitativo, drammatico e libero; free tonality
FP: Anthony Scales (baritone), John Humphreys (piano), Wigmore Hall, London, 25 March 1988.

Coronach for the End of the World   2'
12 February 1964
Allegro moderato, marziale; modal D

The Last Trump   2½'
late February 1964
Allegro assai – meno mosso, senza urgenza

At my Father's Grave
1967

The Fool   1'
March 1967
Dedication (added Christmas 1973): 'To M. M. =74'
Moderato irato; free tonality

My Love is to the Light of Lights   3'
c. 1970
Dedication: 'For Jean and Nigel [Murray] on 2 July 1977'

Lines from Buchanan's Epithalamium   2'
1977
Text: George Buchanan, transl. from the Latin by MacDiarmid

Lento ma non troppo, con grazia e dignità; G flat major

Weep and Wail No More
12 December 1978
Text: MacDiarmid 'from the Italian of Giuseppe Ungaretti'

High Voice and Piano

The Song of the Nightingale*   3'
1965

A'e Gowden Lyric**
1966
Adagio semplice; D major. Exists also in a version for violin and piano.
Dedication: 'For my son Gordon'

The Rose of All the World***   1½'
c. 1966

Medium Voice and Piano

The Gaelic Muse   2'
1964

Fairy Tales   2'
1966
Wi' a canny lilt (con moto amabile)

Bubblyjock
1966

Cophetua   2'
1966

In the Fall   6'
1968
Moderato; E flat

Low Voice and Piano

The Barren Fig: Blues Écossaise   2½'
1960–63)
Text: from *A Drunk Man Looks at the Thistle*
A note on the score says: 'Improvised: 23/I/60 Written out 7/7/53'.
Dedication: 'In memory of Kurt Weill'
Comodo; free tonality, with bitonal interlude. Exists also as a piece for solo
piano.

Unspecified Voice and Piano

The Bonnie Broukit Bairn
13–14 February 1964

Come Doon, Eagle
Date unknown

Age and the Hunter
Date unknown

* *Cf.* p. 164.
** Reproduced on p. 183.
*** Reproduced on p. 180.

To Music Sweet   2′
1975
Text: Stanley Herd
Andante
'Drawing-room ballad for tenor and piano'

Baritone and Piano

Voskhod over Edinburgh   2½′
1965
Text: Alan Bold
Exists also, in sketch form, in an orchestral version

O Death, Old Captain   3′
1965
Text: Alan Bold, from the French of Baudelaire

The Ballad of Sir Humphry Davy and Samuel Taylor Coleridge   3′
1965
Text: Alan Bold
Can be sung also by a mezzo-soprano or contralto

A Little Bit of Nietzsche   2′
1965
Text: Alan Bold
Can be sung also by a mezzo-soprano or contralto; exists also in a version for
voice and guitar

Shores (Tràighean)   2½′
1979
Text: Sorley Maclean
Dedication: 'Wedding Song for Jenny and Alasdair [Alldridge]'

Ballade of Good Whisky: Song for a Convivial Occasion   4′
c. 1958; lost, then rev. c. 1970
Text: Norman McCaig

A Slumber Did My Spirit Seal   2′
c. 1962
Text: William Wordsworth

The Old Familiar Faces   2′
c. 1965–95
Text: Charles Lamb

Small Cloud on the Horizon   2′
1980
Text: Aonghas MacNeacail

To my Wife   2′
1985
Text: Oscar Wilde

Magdalen Walks   2′
1985
Text: Oscar Wilde

Endymion   2′
1985
Text: Oscar Wilde

Requiescat   2′
1985
Text: Oscar Wilde

The Tree o' Libertie   2′
6 June 1989
Text: Robert Burns

Bass-baritone and Piano

War: A Dramatic Piece   5½′
1948
Text: William Blake
Moderato declamato – Allegro agitato – Adagio; C major

High Voice and Piano

Eins und Alles (One and All)   5′
1960
Text: Christian Morgenstern transl. Ronald Stevenson
Andante semplice
Exists also as unison song for children's choir, descant recorder, violin,
cello and guitar

The Witches of Pendle: Pennine Pastorale   2½′
1968
Text: Margaret Greenhalgh (Lancashire dialect)
Exists also in a version for children's chorus and piano

To my Mountain   1½′
Text: Kathleen Raine
1976

King and Queen o' the fower airts: A Ballant   c. 5′
Text: Sidney Goodsir Smith
High voice and piano
Dedicated to Charles King

High or Medium-high Voice and Piano

The Mezquita   2′
1977
Text: Sacheverell Sitwell
Lento

In Granada, in Granada: Llanto por García Lorca   c. 7′
1985–Spring 2002
Text: Sidney Goodsir Smith
For medium-high voice and piano or guitar

Medium Voice and Piano

The Violet   2′
1943
Text: Sir Walter Scott
Moderato teneramente, B major
Composer's note: 'My first composed song!'

So we'll go no more a roving   3′
1943
Text: Lord Byron
Andante, G major
Exists also in a later (1965) transcription for piano

The Light of Other Days   2′
1943
Text: Thomas Moore

Time's gane oot   3′
August 1977
Text: Duncan Glen
Dedication: 'For Margaret and Duncan'

The Moon   2½′
1977
Text: Sacheverell Sitwell
'Nocturne for medium-high voice and piano'
Andante notturnale

Music
1985
Text: Walter de la Mare

Triad   1′
July 1987
Text: Kathleen Raine

The Aran Islands   c. 4′
1980–20 May 1999
Medium voice and piano
Text: Dermot O'Byrne (pseudonym of Arnold Bax)
The music is ascribed to 'Raghnall MacStefaian', the Gaelic form of 'Ronald
Stevenson'
Lento ma con moto
'For Colin, for his book on Bax'

Medium or Low Voice and Piano

Berceuse   3′
6 August 1989
Text: Busoni and Oehlenschlager, transl. Ronald Stevenson
Music adapted from the piano version of Busoni's *Berceuse Élégiaque*
Dedication: 'Busoni dedicated the orchestral version to his mother, as I do

in memory of mine in the present new version (6 August 1989). This fair copy was writ in London, 7 August 1989, on the day of John Ogdon's funeral. This copy finished in the cabin studio, Townfoot House, W. Linton Peeblesshire, Scotland, 9 August 1989'
Exists also in versions for medium voice and harp and for contralto and guitar

Song of an Indomitable Heroine   2'
1967
Text: Nouven Thi Chau
Described by the composer as a 'footnote to *9 Haiku*'

The Princess of Scotland   1½'
Date unknown
Text: Rachel Annand Taylor
Published: *Chapman*, Nos. 89–90 (double-issue), Summer 1998, pp. 25–27 (facsimile)

III. VOICE AND OTHER INSTRUMENTS

High Voice and Guitar

To a Child Dancing in the Wind   2'
c. 1968
Text: W. B. Yeats
Exists also in a version for voice and piano

Shy Geordie   1'
mid-1970s
Text: Helen Cruikshank
Exists also in a version for solo voice and a transcription for solo guitar

Day is Düne   2½'
late 1989
Text: William Soutar
Exists also in versions for SATB chorus and for voice and piano

A Little Bit of Nietzsche   2'
Date unknown
Text: Alan Bold
Exists also for baritone and piano

Contralto and Guitar

Berceuse   3'
August 1989
Text: Busoni and Oehlenschlager, transl. Ronald Stevenson
Music adapted from the piano version of Busoni's *Berceuse Élégiaque*
Dedication: 'Alla memoria delle due madri'
FP: Phillida Bannister (contralto), Alpin Smart (guitar), National Library of Scotland, Edinburgh, 8 December 1989
Exists also in a version for medium voice and piano or harp

Voice and Violin

A Year Owre Young   3′
For mezzo-soprano and violin
4–5 May 1987
Text: James Hogg
Composer's note: 'played by Leonard Friedman on the restored authentic James Hogg fiddle (restored by the composer's son, the luthier Gordon Stevenson)'

The Female Maniac Billy's Song   2′
1987
Melody by James Hogg, 'the Ettrick Shepherd'
FP: Gerda Stevenson (mezzo-soprano), Leonard Friedman (violin), Border Festival, Yarrow Kirk, Yarrow, Selkirkshire, 27 September 1988

Voice, Piano and Violin

The Gangrel Fiddler, for baritone or mezzo-soprano, violin obbligato and piano   12′
1987
Texts (in Aberdonian Doric): Donald Gordon
1. 'The Gangrel Fiddler' (*Moderato*)
2. 'Bairnsang' (*Allegretto quasi giga*)
3. 'Lang Journey Back' (*Allegro con slancio*)
Dedication: 'To Molly Gordon & Charles & Vera King'
FP: Aberdeen Art College, 1987; performers and date unknown

Voice and String Quartet

My Candle Burns at Both Ends   2½′
1970
Text: Edna St Vincent Millay
Composer's note: 'study in cancrizans canon'
Exists also in a version for voice and piano

High Voice and Harp

Nine Haiku, for soprano or tenor and harp   12′
1971
Texts: School of Bashō, transl. Keith Bosley[24]

Medium Voice and Harp

Berceuse   3′
6 August 1989
Text: Busoni and Oehlenschlager, transl. Ronald Stevenson
Music adapted from the piano version of Busoni's *Berceuse Élégiaque*[25]
Exists also in versions for medium voice and piano and for contralto and guitar

[24] For details, *cf.* p. 416.

[25] For details, *cf.* p. 428.

Voice and Clarsach

Calbharaigh (Calvary) 3'
Text: Sorley MacLean (Somhairle MacGill-Eain)
A re-working of 'Calbharaigh', No. 2 of *Anns an Airde, as an Doimhne* for
SATB chorus; it exists also in a version for tenor and piano as No. 5 of *The
Infernal City*; and for unaccompanied voice, with alterations to allow the
singing of either the Gaelic original or the Douglas Young translation into
Lowland Scots (Lallans).

Voice and Recorder

To Autumn 2'
Summer 1967
Text: William Blake
For soprano and tenor recorder

6. MUSIC FOR STAGE AND SCREEN

I. BALLET

Peter and the Wolf
1944?
Written for Blackburn Ballet Club; lost. Stevenson observes that the score
comprised 'c. ½ an hour's music – juvenilia but good experience'.
FP: Blackburn Ballet Club Orchestra, Ronald Stevenson (piano), cond. Fred
Reidy, Queen's Hall, Blackburn, ?1944

II. TELEVISION SCORE

Hammer and Thistle 20'
Music for a television documentary (Independent TV, Manchester) on BBC
Scotland on the life of Hugh MacDiarmid, for chamber ensemble (piano,
clarsach, violin, guitar, bagpipes, shepherd's pipe, Jew's harp, German
melodeon)
1. Opening sequence (clarsach, Lowland bagpipe, violin and piano)
2. 'Crowdieknowe' (clarsach, violin and piano)
2 (a). 'I would creep up' (clarsach, violin, piano; also piano solo)
3. 'Drums in the Walligate' (clarsach, Lowland bagpipe, violin and piano)
3 (a). 'The English across the Border'
4. 'At my Father's Grave' (clarsach, violin and piano)
4 (a). 'Cakewalk' (clarsach, Lowland bagpipe, violin and piano)
5. 'Flooers o' the Forest' (Highland bagpipe)
5 (a). 'The Revolutionary Wave' (piano solo)
5 (b). 'MacLean's End' (piano solo)
6. 'A Rose Loupt Oot' (clarsach and piano)
7. Playing-out Music (clarsach, Lowland bagpipe, violin and piano; also for
piano solo)
8. Introduction to Part 2 (violin and piano)
9. 'The Jungian Uphellya' (violin and piano)

10. 'The Siren Sang' (voice, clarsach, shepherd's pipe and piano)

10 (a). 'A'e Gowden Lyric' (violin and clarsach)

10 (b). 'Oriental Provenance' (Bulgarian bagpipe, clarsach, violin and piano)

11. 'Pibroch: MacDiarmid's Ancient Conflict' (Highland bagpipe)

11 (a). 'The Waters of Shetland' (clarsach)

11 (b). 'Trow Tune' (guitar; also violin solo)

11 (c) 'We Must be Humble' (piano solo)

11 (d). 'Here a Man Must Shed the Encumbrances' (piano solo)

12. 'Lenin's Tomb' (clarsach, violin and piano)

13. 'Mussolini Sequence' (violin and piano)

14 (a). Play-out Music to Part 2 (piano solo)

14 (b). 'Tartan-Red Patch-Kilt' (Lowland bagpipe, violin and piano)

15. 'War Music' (Highland bagpipe and piano)

16. 'Slum Music' (violin and piano)

17. 'Improvisation' (Jew's harp and German melodeon)

17(a). 'The Barren Fig' (voice, violin and piano)

18. 'Moon Music' (violin and piano)

19. Finale to Part 3 (voice, Lowland bagpipe, clarsach, violin and piano)

Exeunt (piano solo)

B. TRANSCRIPTIONS, ARRANGEMENTS, CADENZAS AND EDITIONS

I. ORCHESTRA

BRITTEN, Walzt [*sic*: 'Britten's childhood misspelling'], Op. 3, No. 2, transcribed for chamber orchestra, c. 1980   3'

BULL, *Spanish Pavan*, as *Pavan* for chamber orchestra: 1.1.1.1/1.0.0.0/ strings) (1955)   4'
Bull's original is the same work as that transcribed for solo piano, here rethought and reworked; incorporated (2004) into the *John Bull Suite*
FP: RTE Orchestra, cond. Francesco Mander, 1960 (date unknown), Radio Eireann, Dublin
——, *John Bull Suite* (2004)   c. 12'
1. Pavan (scoring as above)
2. Galliard (strings)
3. Jig, 'The King's Hunt' (3.3.3.3/4.2.1.0/timp./perc. (tgl., cym., BD)/ harp/strings)

VAN DIEREN, 'Weep you no more, Sad Fountains', transcribed as a 'Consolation for small orchestra' (2.1.2.2/1.0.0.0/celeste/harp/strings) (1951)   3'

II. BRASS BAND AND PIANO[26]

SOUSA, *The Washington Post*, arranged for the band of Boldon Colliery School (1951; lost)
——, *The Stars and Stripes for Ever*, arranged for the band of Boldon Colliery School (1951; lost)

III. INSTRUMENTAL ENSEMBLE

DELIUS, *Dance Rhapsody* No. 1, excerpts arranged for oboe, bassoon, violin and piano duet (c. 1966)   2'

GERSHWIN, 'Summertime', from *Porgy and Bess*, transcribed for flute, clarinet, bassoon, solo violin and string quartet (20 October 1988)   2½'

GRAINGER, *Over the Hills and Far Away (Children's March)*, arranged for oboe, bassoon, violin and piano 3-some (c. 1966)   2'
——, *Shepherd's Hey*, arranged for violin, treble (or tenor) recorder and

---

[26] Stevenson left these arrangements behind when he left his job teaching at Boldon Colliery School to move to Edinburgh in 1952. The Colliery has since closed, and it is doubtful that any of these scores have survived; although the school is still in existence, enquiries have been abortive.

anglo-concertina (c. 1966); 'Arranged for my son Gordon to try out with his local folk group'   2½'

IV. PIANO

ANON., *Sumer is icumen in* as No. 1 of *Two Eclogues*[27] (1951)
——, *African Twi-Tune: The Bantu and Akrikaaner National Hymns Combined* (1964)

——, 'Fenesta Vascia' (Neapolitan song), included in *L'Art Nouveau du Chant Appliqué au Piano*[28]

BACH, *Preludio con Fuga* in A minor, BWV551 (1948); Stevenson notes that this was his 'first study in Busonian transcription. – Good!'

BACH/STOKOWSKI, *Komm, süsser Tod,* BWV478 (1 April 1991)   3'

---

[27] No. 2 is a transcription of Shields' *The Ploughboy* from 1956; *cf.* p. 442.

[28] The final form of *L'Art Nouveau du Chant Appliqué au Piano* – described by Stevenson as 'an appendix to Thalberg' and bearing the explanatory subtitle 'Piano Transcriptions of Victorian and Edwardian Songs being Études in the Lost Art of bel canto piano-playing by Ronald Stevenson' – has yet to be established but will probably include:
  ANON., 'Fenesta Vascia' (Neapolitan Song)
  BALFE, 'When Other Lips'
  BAX 'The White Peace'
  BRIDGE, 'Go Not, Happy Day'*
  CADMAN, 'At Dawning'
  COLERIDGE-TAYLOR, 'Eléanore'*
  ——, 'Demande et Réponse' (*Petite Suite de Concert*)*
  J. NICHOLLS CROUCH, 'Kathleen Mavourneen'
  STEPHEN FOSTER, 'Beautiful Dreamer'*
  ——, 'Come where my Love Lies Dreaming'*
  ——, 'Jeannie with the Light Brown Hair'*
  ——, 'Where My Heart Lies'*
  REYNALDO HAHN, 'Si mes vers avaient des ailes! ('If my rhymes were only wingèd!')
  HAMILTON HARTY, 'My Làgan Love'
  LEONCAVALLO, 'La Mattinata'
  MEYERBEER, 'Plus blanche que la blanche hermine' (*Les Huguenots*)
  NOVELLO, 'Fly Home, Little Heart'*
  ——, 'We'll Gather Lilacs'*
  RACHMANINOV, 'In the Silence of the Secret Night'*
  ——, 'Spring Waters'
  ROMBERG, 'Will you remember (Sweethearts)' (*Maytime*)*
  OLEY SPEAKS, 'Sylvia'
  W. VINCENT WALLACE, 'In Happy Moments Day by Day', for left-hand solo
  ——, 'Scenes that are Brightest', for left-hand solo
  MAUDE VALÉRIE WHITE, 'So We'll Go No More A-Roving'*
*Published by The Ronald Stevenson Society

BALFE, 'When Other Lips', included in *L'Art Nouveau du Chant Appliqué au Piano*[29] (June 1980)

BARRIOS, *Romanza quasi cello* (c. 1980)   2'

BAX, 'The White Peace', included in *L'Art Nouveau du Chant Appliqué au Piano*[30] (1984); dedicated 'To my dear friend CS-S as a small token of gratitude for the many hours of pleasure his book on Bax has given – read in the open air, often on the machair of Gott Bay, Tiree'   2½'

BERG, 'Wiegenlied' from *Wozzeck*, transcribed as *Wiegenlied aus Wozzeck* (1953); dedicated to Luigi Dallapiccola, who expressed his approval when Stevenson played him the work in 1955.   4½'
——, *Kinderspiel: Schluss-Szene aus 'Wozzeck'*, free transcription for piano (1985/88) – 'coda added to the *Wiegenlied'*. Drafted in Perth, Australia, November 1985; completed in Sent, Unter Engadin, Switzerland, October 1988. Dated '8–9.X.1988'. Dedication: 'An Malcolm' (MacDonald)   4½'

BOCCHERINI, Minuet from String Quintet in E, Op. 13, No. 5 (G275), transcribed as *Menuetto Celebre del Boccherini in forma d'uno studio polifonico*
——, Minuet from String Quintet in E, transcribed for left hand (1970)
——, Minuet from String Quintet in E, transcribed for right hand (1970)

BOITO, 'Fuga Infernale' from *Mefistofele*, Act II, scene 2, transcribed as *Infernal Fugue* (Dornach, 17 May 1981)

BOUGHTON, 'Luring Song' from *The Immortal Hour* (1980)

BRAHMS, 'Edward', No. 1, duet for alto, tenor and piano, of the *Balladen und Romanzen*, Op. 75 (late 1992)

BRIDGE, 'Go Not, Happy Day', included in *L'Art Nouveau du Chant Appliqué au Piano*[31] (June 1980)   2½'

BULL, Pavan, Galliard and Jig, transcribed as *Three Elizabethan Pieces after John Bull* (1950)   15'

BURNS, *Auld Lang Syne*, transcribed as No. 1 of *Songs for a Burns Supper* (1968); exists also in a version for clarsach
——, *Ae fond kiss*, transcribed as No. 2 of *Songs for a Burns Supper* (1968); exists also in versions for two cellos and for clarsach

BUSH, 'The Minstrel's Lay' from *Wat Tyler* (April 1974). Dedication: 'For Nancy [Bush] from the transcriber'. FP: Ronald Stevenson, Wigmore Hall, London, 5 May 1974   5½'

BUSONI, Polonaise from the *Sonatina ad usum infantis*, simplified transcription (c. 1975). Dedication: 'For Harry Winstanley'.   2'
——, Three Marches from *Turandot* (1948)

---

[29] *Cf.* note 28 on p. 434.

[30] *Cf.* note 28 on p. 434.

[31] *Cf.* note 28 on p. 434.

CADMAN, 'L'aurore', transcribed as 'At Dawning', included in *L'Art Nouveau du Chant Appliqué au Piano*[32] (1985). Dated: 'New York, March 1985'

CARREÑO, *A Little Waltz* (c. 1980)

CASALS, *O Vos Omnes* (1975)
———, *Recordare Virgo Mater* (1975)
———, *Sant Mari de Canigo* (1975)
———, *Song of the Birds* (1975)
———, *Tres Estofas de amor* (1975)

CHARPENTIER, Romance from *Louise* (c. 1970)

CHOPIN, *Étude* in A minor, Op. 10, No. 2 combined with Rimsky-Korsakov, 'The Flight of the Bumble-bee' from *The Tale of Tsar Saltan*, as *Étudette: Hommage à Korsakov et Chopin* (6 June 1987). Subtitle: 'Spectre d'Alkan' FP: Murray McLachlan, Queen's Hall, Edinburgh, June 1988 (BBC recital) 3′
A Little Chopin Notebook (1984): 'Prelude no. 2 as a canon/Étude op. 25, no. 1/About 3 others mislaid (!) – for young pianists, based on Chopin's own method for beginners'
3 Contrapuntal Studies on Chopin Waltzes (begun c. 1955; completed 2003)
  1. Waltz in A flat, Op. 34, No. 1, transcribed for right hand alone
  2. Waltz in A flat, Op. 42, transcribed for left hand alone
  3. Nos. 1 and 2 combined for two hands

COLERIDGE-TAYLOR, 'Demande et Réponse' (from *Petite Suite de Concert*) included in *L'Art Nouveau du Chant Appliqué au Piano*[33] (18 August 1981: 'For Marjorie on our anniversary')
———, 'Eléanore', included in *L'Art Nouveau du Chant Appliqué au Piano*[34] (June 1980)

CROUCH, J. NICHOLLS, 'Kathleen Mavourneen', included in *L'Art Nouveau du Chant Appliqué au Piano*[35] (June 1985)

DELIUS, *Brigg Fair*, arranged as No. 2 of *Eight Children's Pieces* (1962)
———, *Dance Rhapsody* No. 1, arranged as 'Dance', No. 1 of *Eight Children's Pieces* (1962)
———, 'Intermezzo' from *Brigg Fair*, arranged as No. 7 of *Eight Children's Pieces* (1962)
———, 'La Calinda' from *Koanga*, arranged as No. 3 of *Eight Children's Pieces* (1962)
———, 'Late Swallows' (Eric Fenby's title of his string-orchestral arrangement of the slow movement of Delius' String Quartet), arranged as No. 6 of *Eight Children's Pieces* (1962)

---

[32] *Cf.* note 28 on p. 434.

[33] *Cf.* note 28 on p. 434.

[34] *Cf.* note 28 on p. 434.

[35] *Cf.* note 28 on p. 434.

——, 'Love's Philosophy', No. 2 of *3 Songs* (1891) (27 December 1991); 'For Colin'

——, *On Hearing the First Cuckoo in Spring*, arranged as 'The Cuckoo', No. 5 of *Eight Children's Pieces* (1962)

——, 'Serenade' from *Hassan*, arranged as No. 4 of *Eight Children's Pieces* (1962)

——, *Song of the High Hills*, arranged as No. 8 of *Eight Children's Pieces* (1962)

——, 'Wiegenlied der Ewigkeit' ('Eternity's Cradle-song') from *A Mass of Life* (1980)

ELLINGTON, *Mood Indigo*, contrapuntal reworking (1988)

FIELD, *Rêverie-Nocturne* (1965)

FOSTER, 'Beautiful Dreamer', included in *L'Art Nouveau du Chant Appliqué au Piano*[36] (April 1980)

——, 'Come Where My Love Lies Dreaming', included in *L'Art Nouveau du Chant Appliqué au Piano*[37] (April 1980)

——, 'Jeannie with the Light Brown Hair', included in *L'Art Nouveau du Chant Appliqué au Piano*[38] (April 1980)

——, 'Where My Heart Lies', included in *L'Art Nouveau du Chant Appliqué au Piano*[39]

FOULDS, 'Eileen Aroon', sketches, dated 'Good Friday 1989 [23 March]'

GLUCK, 'Dance of the Blessed Spirits' from *Orfeo ed Euridice* (1965)

GOUNOD, 'Mephistopheles' Serenade' from *Faust* (1980s)

GRAINGER, ELLA, *Love at First Sight*, 'For Ella on May Day 1976'
——, *Poetry, Song and Picture Book* (c. 1980)

GRAINGER, PERCY, *Hill Song* No. 1 (1960)   20'
——, *Green Bushes* (1963)   8'
——, 'Northern March' from *Youthful Suite* (1983)
——, *The Power of Rome and the Christian Heart* (1981)   15'
——, *Three Scotch Folk-Songs* (1983)
    1. 'Will ye gang to the Hielands, Leezie Lindsay?'
    2. 'Mo Nighean Dubh'
    3(a). 'O gin I were where Gadie Rins' (performing edition)
    3(b). 'O gin I were where Gadie Rins' (simplified arrangement)
Published: C. F. Peters, Frankfurt, London and New York, 1984 (dated 1983)

---

[36] *Cf.* note 28 on p. 434.

[37] *Cf.* note 28 on p. 434.

[38] *Cf.* note 28 on p. 434.

[39] *Cf.* note 28 on p. 434.

——, *The Young Pianist's Grainger*[40] (1966). Publisher: Schott (Edn. 11005), London, 1967

GRIEG, *Den bergtekne*, (early November 1990; final version of a transcription begun many years earlier)

GRUBER, *Stille Nacht* (1965)

HAHN, *Si mes vers avaient des ailes!*, included in *L'Art Nouveau du Chant Appliqué au Piano*[41] (1980)

HANDY, W. C., *St Louis Blues*, transcribed as No. 1 of *Children's Anthology of Blues and Ragtime* (c. 1970)   1'
——, *St Louis Blues*, 'in canonic form' (1978)

HARTY, 'My Làgan Love', included in *L'Art Nouveau du Chant Appliqué au Piano*[42] (1982). Dated: West Linton 18-III-1982'. Dedication: 'For Lawrence [Glover] from the transcriber'

JOPLIN, *Maple Leaf Rag*, transcribed as No. 2 of *Children's Anthology of Blues and Ragtime* (c. 1970)   1'

KILPINEN, 'Kehtolaulu' ('Lullaby'), *Songs to Poems by V. A. Koskenniemi*, Op. 23, No. 4, transcribed as No. 3 of *Four Songs of Yrjö Kilpinen* (1970)
——, 'Kesäyö' ('Summer Night'), *Songs to Poems by V. A. Koskenniemi*, Op. 23, No. 3, transcribed as No. 2 of *Four Songs of Yrjö Kilpinen* (1970)
——, 'Der Zugvogel' ('The Migrating Bird'), *Tunturilauluja*, Op. 53, No. 3, transcribed as No. 1 of *Four Songs of Yrjö Kilpinen* (1970)
——, 'Vöglein Schwermut' ('Little Bird Despair'), *Lieder um den Tod*, Op. 62, No. 1, transcribed as No. 4 of *Four Songs of Yrjö Kilpinen* (1970)

---

[40] The Young Person's Grainger is an album containing:

Country Gardens	Simplified edition by Percy Grainger
Shepherd's Hey	Simplified edition by Percy Grainger
Molly on the Shore	Abridged by Ronald Stevenson
Mock Morris	Easy arrangement by Ronald Stevenson
Beautiful Fresh Flower	Easy arrangement by Ronald Stevenson
Australian Up-Country Song	Edited by Ronald Stevenson
Irish Tune from Country Derry	Edited by Ronald Stevenson
Walking Tune	Easy arrangement by Ronald Stevenson
Hill Song No. 1	Easy arrangement by Ronald Stevenson
To a Nordic Princess	Easy arrangement by Ronald Stevenson
One More Day my John	Edited by Ronald Stevenson
Spoon River	Easy arrangement by Ronald Stevenson
Blithe Bells	Easy version by Percy Grainger
Over the Hills and Far Away	Easy arrangement by Ronald Stevenson
Now o now I needs must part	Freely set for piano by Percy Grainger.

Stevenson also supplied an introductory note on Percy Grainger and notes on the music (both dated 8 July 1966).

[41] *Cf.* note 28 on p. 434.

[42] *Cf.* note 28 on p. 434.

LEONCAVALLO, 'La Mattinata', included in *L'Art Nouveau du Chant Appliqué au Piano* (1981).[43] Dated: 'La Mattinata del 28 Ottobre 1981'. Dedication: 'For Nick Davies, at his request'   3½'

MAHLER, Symphony No. 10: *Adagio* (1987); 'Finished in the Swiss Alps'. FP: Alton Chung Ming Chan, Vysočina Music Festival, Jihlava, Czech Republic, 15 July 2002.   c. 30'

MERRICK, 'Seascape' (second movement of Piano Concerto No. 2), transcribed as *Hebridean Seascape* (early 1986). FP: Ronald Stevenson, Merrick Centenary Concert, Purcell Room, London, 30 April 1986. Publisher: Roberton, 1988 ('facsimile of the transcriber's MS – in his opinion one of the best examples of his calligraphy').   7'

MEYER, ERNST HERMANN, 'A Man's a Man for a' that'

MEYERBEER, 'Plus blanche que la plus blanche ermine' from *Les Huguenots* (1975)   3'

MORRISON, *Rory Dall Morrison's Harp Book*, realisations (1978)
  1. 'Oran do Iain Breac MacLeoid (Song for John MacLeod of Dunvegan)'   2'
  2. 'Feill nan Crann (Fair Harp Key or Lament for the Lost Harp Key)'3'
  3. 'A'cheud di-luain de'n raithe (The First Monday of the Quarter)'   2'
  4. 'Creach na ciadoin (Wednesday's Bereavement)'   2½'
  5. 'Oran do MhacLeoid Dhun Bheagan (Song to the MacLeod of Dunvegan)'   2'
  6. 'Fuath nan Fidhleirean (The Fiddler's Contempt, or Rory's Reply to the Fiddler)'   3'
  7. 'Cumha Peathar Ruadri (Lament for Rory's Sister)'   3'
  8. 'Suipear Tighearna Leoid (Lude's Supper)'   2'

MOZART, 'Einleitungen' from the *Larghetto* of the Piano Concerto No. 24 in C minor, K491 (date unknown)
——, *Fantasy* in F minor, K608 (1952)

NIELSEN, *Commotio*, Op. 58/FS155 (1966)

NOVELLO, 'We'll Gather Lilacs', transcribed with Rachmaninov, *Lilacs*, as accompaniment (1980)
——, 'Fly Home, Little Heart', included in *L'Art Nouveau du Chant Appliqué au Piano*[44]
——, 'We'll Gather Lilacs', included in *L'Art Nouveau du Chant Appliqué au Piano*[45]

O'CAROLAN, *Carolan's Dream* (1975)
——, *Carolan's Maggot* (1975)

[43] *Cf.* note 28 on p. 434.

[44] *Cf.* note 28 on p. 434.

[45] *Cf.* note 28 on p. 434.

——, *Carolan's Quarrel with the Landlady* (1975)
——, *Lord Inchiquin* (1975)

PADEREWSKI, 'Dans la forêt' from *Four Songs* (1966)
——, 'L'amour fatal' from *Four Songs* (1966)
——, Suite from *Manru* (November–December 1961)   12½'
  1. 'Introduction and Gypsy March'
  2. 'Gypsy Song'
  3. Lullaby' (dated '10/11/61')
  4. 'Cracovienne'

PURCELL, Ground in C minor (1955)
——, Ground in E minor, transcribed as Ground in E flat minor (1957)
——, Ground in D minor (1958)
——, *The Queen's Dolour – A Farewell*: 'harmonised realisation from treble and bass lines only', 'arranged in my language in an (almost) apologetic derangement! "Transcription" is a creative re-working!' (1959).[46] Exists also in a version for guitar.   3'
——, Toccata (1955) – in Stevenson's view, 'a very fine transcription (self-critique!) which is both respectful and newly individual; traditional and exploratory (!!) musicological (heu!!!) and inventive – Yes!'
——, Hornpipe (1995)   3'

RACHMANINOV, Prelude in E flat, Op. 23, No. 6 (transcribed for left hand)
——, 'In the Silence of the Secret Night', Op. 4, No. 3, included in *L'Art Nouveau du Chant Appliqué au Piano*[47] (1982)
——, 'Lilacs', Op. 21, No. 5, transcribed as accompaniment to Novello, 'We'll Gather Lilacs') (1980)
——, 'Spring Waters', Op. 14, No. 11, included in *L'Art Nouveau du Chant Appliqué au Piano*[48] (August 1986)
——, *Eighteenth Variation from the Rhapsody on a Theme of Paganini*; exists in two versions – concert and simplified – both intended for schoolchildren (c. 1980)

RIMSKY-KORSAKOV, 'The Flight of the Bumble-bee' from *The Tale of Tsar Saltan*, combined with Chopin, *Étude* in A minor, Op. 10, No. 2, as *Étudette: Hommage à Korsakov et Chopin* (1986). FP: Murray McLachlan, Queen's Hall, Edinburgh, June 1988 (BBC recital)   2'

ROMBERG, 'Sweetheart's Waltz after Sigmund Romberg', No. 1 of *Deux Esquisses Exquises en formes de canons*, 'Miniature Waltz in Canon Form' (1980)
——, 'Will You Remember (Sweethearts)' from *Maytime*, transcribed as No. 2 of *Deux Esquisses Exquises en formes de canons*, 'Waltz in canon-form' (1988)

---

[46] Reproduced in Appendix Five: Some Stevenson Miniatures, p. 333.

[47] *Cf.* note 28 on p. 434.

[48] *Cf.* note 28 on p. 434.

Rubbra, Fugue from *Introduction, Aria and Fugue*, 'rewritten in a loyal semi-transcription', with the approval of the composer (c. 1965)

Schubert, *Écossaises* (1974); 'For my friend Gilbert Cole'. fp: Ronald Stevenson, St Cecilia's Hall, Edinburgh, 20 November 1974

——, *Sechs Ländler* in B flat, D374, realised as *Ländler für Klavier*: 'the Schubert MS has only the melody line' (1974)   4′

Scott, F. G., 'There's news, lassies, news' (*Thirty-Five Scottish Lyrics*, 1949), transcribed as No. 1 of *Nine Songs of Francis George Scott* (January 1961; revised April 1977).   2′

——, 'Ay waulkin, O' (*Scottish Lyrics*, 1922) transcribed as No. 2 of *Nine Songs of Francis George Scott* (19 January 1963; revised 1977).   4½′

——, 'Border Riding Rhythm', unpublished manuscript supplied by George Scott, son of the composer

——, 'Crowdieknowe', (*Scottish Lyrics*, 1934) transcribed as No. 7 of *Nine Songs of Francis George Scott* (1963). Manuscript marked: 'Transcribed: 3 Febr. 1963. Revised: 1971. Re-revised with extended coda: early July 1989. Twenty-six years of devotion to a masterpiece of Mephistophelian balladry, worthy of Busoni's *Doktor Faust* and linking the eldritch Scottish borders with the Faust legend'.   3′

——, 'Deil's Dance' (a combination of two *Intuitions* for piano), transcribed as No. 9 of *Nine Songs of Francis George Scott* (date unknown).

——, 'Milkwort and Bog-cotton', (*Scottish Lyrics*, 1934), transcribed as No. 6 of *Nine Songs of Francis George Scott* (9 February 1963).   3′

——, 'O were my love yon lilac fair' (*Scottish Lyrics*, 1922) transcribed as No. 3 of *Nine Songs of Francis George Scott* (2 February 1963; revised September 1988).   4′

——, 'Since All thy Vows, False Maid, are Blown to Air' (*Scottish Lyrics*, 1939), transcribed as No. 8 of *Nine Songs of Francis George Scott*. Dated: '28 September 1982'. Dedication: 'Dedicated to the composer's son, George N. Scott, from the transcriber'. Note on score: 'Transcribed on returning home from a 3 months' Australian concert tour, and finding a gift awaiting me: F. G. Scott's copy of Busoni's *Von der Einheit der Musik*, very kindly presented by the composer's son George: for me a symbolic gift of a communion of minds. –R. S.'   4′

——, 'Wee Willie Gray', (*Scottish Lyrics*, 1939), transcribed as No. 4 of *Nine Songs of Francis George Scott* (8 February 1963; revised 1979; revised 5–6 July 1989).   1½′

——, 'Wha is that at my bower-door?', (*Scottish Lyrics*, 1939) transcribed as No. 5 of *Nine Songs of Francis George Scott* (15 February 1963).   2½′

Stevenson's transcription of Scott's songs were originally seven in number; 'Since All Thy Vows' and 'Deil's Dance' were added in 1982 and 1983 respectively. Published by Roberton, Aylesbury, forthcoming. fp: Nos. 1–7 and 9, Murray McLachlan, Olympia ocd 264 (CD)[49]

---

[49] *Cf.* Appendix Nine: Discography, pp. 475–76.

SHIELD, *The Ploughboy*, as No. 2 of *Two Eclogues*[50] (1956)

SIBELIUS, *Two Songs from Shakespeare's 'Twelfth Night'*, Op. 60, transcribed as *Two Pieces from the Incidental Music to Twelfth Night* (1966)
1. 'Come Away, Death'
2. 'Hey ho, the Wind and the Rain'

SORABJI; 'Dans la grotte' (*Trois Fêtes Galantes de Verlaine*, No. 3, c. 1919) 3' 1986
Dedication: Alistair Hinton

SPEAKS, OLEY, *Sylvia*, included in *L'Art Nouveau du Chant Appliqué au Piano*[51] (August 1986)

STEVENS, BERNARD, *A Birthday Song*, 'transcribed from B. S.'s piano duet to piano solo' as *Canto di compleanno* (1974)

STEVENSON, SAVOURNA, *Nocturne-Lullaby* for clarsach (c. 1966). Exists also in a version for clarinet and piano.

STEVENSON (NORRIS), SAVOURNA, *Lament for a Blind Harper*, transcribed for left hand alone ('Yule 1986')

TAUBER, 'My Heart and I', transcribed as *Tauberiana*; 'For Anne Scott in mutual love of Richard of the singing heart' (1980)

TCHAIKOVSKY, 'Love Theme' from *Romeo and Juliet*; 'Loving wedding gift to Nick & Valery' (11 July 1968)
——, Main theme of the *Allegro non troppo* (first movement) of Symphony No. 6 (1970)

VAN DIEREN, String Quartet No. 5, 'transcribed as a piano sonata (which B. v. D. never composed)' (1987)
——, *Spring Song of the Birds* (text by King James I of Scotland) (1987)
——, *Weep you no more, Sad Fountains* (1951)   3'

VERDI/LISZT, *Rigoletto Paraphrase*, as *Rigolet Rag*. Dated: 'Christmas 1973'. Dedication: 'For Jimmy and Betty Blair [neighbours] – Chistmas 1973'. Exists also in a version for viola and piano

VILLA-LOBOS, *Bachianas Brasileiras* No. 5
——, Prelude No. 3 (from the *Twelve Preludes* for guiter) (before 1970)

WAGNER/WITTGENSTEIN, Quintet from *Die Meistersinger*, 'elaborated for left hand alone' – Stevenson's is a reworking of Wittgenstein's arrangement (1980)

WALLACE, W. VINCENT, 'In Happy Moments Day by Day', transcribed for left hand in *L'Art Nouveau du Chant Appliqué au Piano*[52] (March–April 1980)

---

[50] No. 1 is a transcription of *Sumer is icumen in* from 1951; *cf.* p. 434.

[51] *Cf.* note 28 on p. 434.

[52] *Cf.* note 28 on p. 434.

——, 'Scenes that are Brightest', transcribed for left hand in *L'Art Nouveau du Chant Appliqué au Piano*[53] (March–April 1980)

WHITE, MAUD VALÉRIE, 'So We'll Go No More a-Roving', included in *L'Art Nouveau du Chant Appliqué au Piano*[54] (July 1980)

YSAŸE, Six Sonatas for solo violin, Op. 27, transcribed as six piano sonatas (November 1981–January 1982: the *Preludio* of No. 1 is dated 'West Linton 29.XII.81')   60′

V. ORGAN

BUSONI, *Sonatina brevis* (*Sonatina* No. 5), transcribed for organ with Baroque registration (1997)   5′

VI. HARPSICHORD

PURCELL, *The Queen's Dolour* (1959)[55]   3′

VII. TWO PIANOS

BURNS, *Auld Lang Syne*   2′

ROSSINI, Galop from *William Tell*, arranged for child pianists (1980)   3′

STRAUSS, JOHANN, II, *Pizzicato Polka* (c. 1980)   2′

VIII. VIOLIN

CHOPIN, *Étude* in E major, Op. 10, No. 3, transcribed as *Studio Lirico* (1981)
——, *Étude* in A minor, Op. 25, No. 4, as *Studio Paganinesco* (1981)

PURCELL, Ground in C minor, transcribed in G minor as No. 1 of *Three Transcriptions from Purcell*; in the repertoire of the late Leonard Friedman (1958). Dedicated to Yehudi Menuhin
——, Ground in D minor, transcribed as No. 3 of *Three Transcriptions from Purcell*; in the repertoire of the late Leonard Friedman (1958). Dedicated to Yehudi Menuhin
——, Ground in E minor, transcribed in D minor as No. 2 of *Three Transcriptions from Purcell*; in the repertoire of the late Leonard Friedman (1958). Dedicated to Yehudi Menuhin   2½′

IX. VIOLIN AND PIANO

ANON., 'Hard is my Fate', from *The Simon Fraser of Knockie Collection*, transcribed for the BBC Scotland broadcast *Maisters o' the Bow* (1970). FP: Aly Bain (violin), Ronald Stevenson (piano), BBC Radio Scotland, 1970   2½′

---

[53] *Cf.* note 28 on p. 434.

[54] *Cf.* note 28 on p. 434.

[55] Reproduced in Appendix Five: Some Stevenson Miniatures, p. 333.

B<small>LAKE</small>, *The Chevy Chase Rag* (1980). Exists also in a version for two recorders and piano   1½′

Gow, 'John Gow's Compliments to the Minstrels o Scotland' transcribed for the BBC Scotland broadcast *Maisters o' the Bow* (1970). F<small>P</small>: Aly Bain (violin), Ronald Stevenson (piano), BBC Radio Scotland, 1970   3′

M<small>ACKINTOSH</small>, R<small>OB</small>, 'Lady Charlotte Campbell' (Strathspey), transcribed for the BBC Scotland broadcast *Maisters o' the Bow* (1970). F<small>P</small>: Aly Bain (violin), Ronald Stevenson (piano), BBC Radio Scotland, 1970   2½′
——, 'Lady Charlotte Campbell' (Reel), transcribed for the BBC Scotland broadcast *Maisters o' the Bow* (1970). F<small>P</small>: Aly Bain (violin), Ronald Stevenson (piano), BBC Radio Scotland, 1970   2′
——, 'Miss Campbell of Sadell', transcribed for the BBC Scotland broadcast *Maisters o' the Bow* (1970). F<small>P</small>: Aly Bain (violin), Ronald Stevenson (piano), BBC Radio Scotland, 1970

M<small>ARSHALL</small>, W<small>ILLIAM</small>, 'Craigellachie Brig' (Strathspey), transcribed for the BBC Scotland broadcast *Maisters o' the Bow* (1970). F<small>P</small>: Aly Bain (violin), Ronald Stevenson (piano), BBC Radio Scotland, 1970
——, 'Keithmore' (Strathspey), transcribed for the BBC Scotland broadcast *Maisters o' the Bow* (1970). F<small>P</small>: Aly Bain (violin), Ronald Stevenson (piano), BBC Radio Scotland, 1970
——, 'Miss Catharine Stuart of Pettyvaich' (Jig), transcribed for the BBC Scotland broadcast *Maisters o' the Bow* (1970). F<small>P</small>: Aly Bain (violin), Ronald Stevenson (piano), BBC Radio Scotland, 1970
——, 'Mr Marshall's Complaint to Neil Gow' (Slow Air), transcribed for the BBC Scotland broadcast *Maisters o' the Bow* (1970). F<small>P</small>: Aly Bain (violin), Ronald Stevenson (piano), BBC Radio Scotland, 1970
——, 'Mrs Hamilton of Wishaw's Strathspey', transcribed for the BBC Scotland broadcast *Maisters o' the Bow* (1970). F<small>P</small>: Aly Bain (violin), Ronald Stevenson (piano), BBC Radio Scotland, 1970
——, 'Sir Walter Scott, Bart.' (slow air) transcribed for the BBC Scotland broadcast *Maisters o' the Bow* (1970). F<small>P</small>: Aly Bain (violin), Ronald Stevenson (piano), BBC Radio Scotland, 1970

X. VIOLA AND PIANO

B<small>LAKE</small>, *The Chevy Chase Rag*. Exists also in versions for two recorders and piano and for violin and piano

V<small>ERDI</small>/L<small>ISZT</small>, *Rigoletto Paraphrase*, as *Rigolet Rag*. Exists also in a version for solo piano

XI. CELLO AND PIANO

B<small>USONI</small>, *Drei Albumblätter* (1980)
——, 'Epilogo' from *An die Jugend* (1974). F<small>P</small>: Moray Welsh (cello), Ronald Stevenson (piano), Bromsgrove Festival, 1974 (for the fiftieth anniversary of Busoni's death)

XII. TWO CELLOS

BURNS, *Ae fond kiss*, transcribed as No. 2 of *Songs for a Burns Supper* (1968). The three *Songs for a Burns Supper* are for clarsach; No. 2 exists also in a version for solo piano

XIII. CLARINET AND PIANO

STEVENSON, SAVOURNA, *Nocturne-Lullaby* for clarsach (c. 1966). Exists also in a version for piano.

XIV. BASSOON

MOZART, *Due Allegri*, KK1B and 1C arranged as *Doubly Happy Mozart* (c. 1960)   2½′

XV. GUITAR

BACH, Praeludium VII from *The Well-tempered Clavier*, BWV858   3′

BUSONI, *Albumblatt* No. 1 (1970)

GRANADOS, 'Balada: El Amor y la Muerte', No. 5 of *Goyescas* transcribed as *Ballad of Love and Death* (1970)   3′

PURCELL, Ground in D minor, transcribed in B minor as No. 3 *of Three Transcriptions from Purcell* (1958)
——, Ground in E minor, transcribed as No. 2 of *Three Transcriptions from Purcell* (1958)   2½′
——, *The Queen's Dolour – A Farewell*, transcribed as No. 1 of *Three Transcriptions from Purcell* (1959)   3′

XVI. HARP

FIELD, *Nocturne* No. 1 in E flat (concert version) (date unknown)
——, *Nocturne* No. 1 in E flat (abridged version) (date unknown)
——, *Nocturne* No. 17 in E major (*Nocturne-Pastorale*) (concert version) (date unknown)
——, *Nocturne* No. 17 in E major (*Nocturne-Pastorale*) (abridged version) (date unknown)

GOW, JOHN, *The Cries of Edinburgh* (1970)

MORRISON, *Rory Dall Morrison's Harp Book*, realisations (1970)[56]

RAVEL, *Pavane pour une Infante Défunte* (1968)

SAINT-SAËNS, 'Le cygne' from *Le carnaval des animaux* (1968)

XVII. CLARSACH

BANTOCK, 'Song to the Seals', No. 1 of *Songs of the Western Isles* for voice and

---

[56] For details, *cf.* p. 439.

orchestra or piano (melody from Marjorie Kennedy-Fraser's *Songs of the Hebrides*), 'For Savourna and Mark' (Christmas 1982)

BOUGHTON, 'Fairy Song' from *The Immortal Hour* (1970)

BURNS, *Ae fond kiss*, transcribed as No. 2 of *Songs for a Burns Supper* (1968); exists also in versions for piano and for two cellos   3'
——, *Auld Lang Syne*, transcribed as No. 1 of *Songs for a Burns Supper* (1968)   2'
——, *Flow Gently, Sweet Afton*, transcribed as No. 3 of *Songs for a Burns Supper* (1968)   3'

MORRISON, *Rory Dall Morrison's Harp Book*, realisations (1970)[57]

O'CAROLAN, *Carolan's Dream* (1970)
——, *Carolan's Maggot* (1970)
——, *Carolan's Quarrel* (1970)
——, *Lord Inchiquin* (1970)

XVIII. CLARSACH AND VIOLIN

MACKINTOSH, 'Lady Charlotte Campbell' (Reel), transcribed for the BBC Scotland broadcast *Maisters o' the Bow* (1970)
——, 'Lady Charlotte Campbell' (Strathspey), transcribed for the BBC Scotland broadcast *Maisters o' the Bow* (1970)
——, 'Miss Campbell of Sadell', transcribed for the BBC Scotland broadcast *Maisters o' the Bow* (1970)

XIX. CLARSACH AND PIANO

CHOPIN, *Cantabile* (without opus number; printed in Vol. XVIII, p. 40, of the Paderewski edition of Chopin's music, PWM, Cracow, 1985) (1985)

XX. PIANO TRIO

SCHUBERT, *Sechs Ländler* in B flat, D374 (1977)   4'

XXI. FLUTE AND CELLO

GRAINGER, *Molly on the Shore* (1970)
——, *Spoon River* (1970)
——, 'The Reel of Tulloch' from *Scotch Strathspey and Reel* (1970)

XXII. STRING QUARTET

BUSONI, *Sonatina ad usum infantis* transcribed as *Quartettino* (20–26 November 1965)   7'

---

[57] For details, *cf.* p. 439.

XXIII. TWO CELLOS

BURNS, *Ae fond Kiss* (1970); exists also in versions for clarsach, as No. 2 of *Songs for a Burns Supper*, and for solo piano

XXIV. TWO RECORDERS AND PIANO

BLAKE, *The Chevy Chase Rag* (1981); exists also in versions for violin and piano and for viola and piano

GRAINGER, *Australian Up-Country Song* (1965)

———, *Over the Hills and Far Away (Children's March)* (1965)

XXV. VOICE AND PIANO

BEETHOVEN, 'Ode to Joy', from Symphony No. 9; text: Burns ('"A man's a man for a' that" fits the Beethoven *Ode to Joy* perfectly – like a glove – *An R. S. discovery!'*)

BUSONI, *A Political Panel*; music by Busoni, adapted by Stevenson (date unknown) to poems in the languages of the four principal combatants of World War I:
1. 'Erinnerungen und Vorerinnerungen'
Text: Busoni, 1925; music from his Violin Sonata No. 2
2. 'Noël à la fin de la guerre'
Text: Jean Cocteau; music from the *Sonata in diem nativitatis Christi*
3. 'A Dante'
Text: Gabriele d'Annunzio; music from *Doktor Faust*
4. 'By Babylon's Waters'
Text: Lord Byron; music from Busoni's German setting of the same poem

GRIEG, *Den Bergtekne*; the score is prefaced by Stevenson's Scots translation of the Norwegian folk ballad which Grieg sets (1990)

XXVI. VOICE AND CLARSACH

RUBBRA, *A Duan of Barra*; text: Murdo Maclean (1970)

XXVII. VOICE AND HARP

GRAINGER, *The Power of Rome and the Christian Heart*, arranged for tenor and harp; text: Rudyard Kipling (1975)

XXVIII. CHORUS

DELIUS, 'Serenade' from *Hassan*, for SATB chorus and piano (1960); text: Ronald Stevenson

SORABJI, *Bell-Chorale for the Carillon of St Luke's, Germantown, Pa.*, harmonised for *a cappella* SATB chorus as *Hymnus in Memoriam KSS* (29 August 1990). Text: Rumi, transl. Reynold Nicolson, 'The Song of the Reeds'. Dedication: 'To celebrate the nuptials of Terry and Alistair'

VILLA-LOBOS, Vocalise from *Bachianas Brasileiras* No. 5, transcribed for female voices (SSAA) (1975)

2. FOLKSONG ARRANGEMENTS

I. ORCHESTRA

Three Scottish Folk-Music Settings 6'
1965
1. 'Waly, waly'
2. 'A Rosebud by my Early Walk'
3. 'Hielan' Lament'
strings
FBP: BBC Scottish Symphony Orchestra, cond. R. Smellie, BBC Radio
Scotland, c. 1966

II. SATB CHORUS AND PIANO

The Christ Child's Carol 7'
September 1969
Text: Ranald Rankin
Hebridean folksong arranged for the Peebles Music Club.
Exists also in versions for baritone solo and SATB chorus and for solo piano
as No. 7 of *South Uist (Hebridean) Folk-Song Suite*

III. VOICE AND PIANO

The Royal Mile: A Sequence of Scottish Folksongs (1956)

Scottish Folk-Music Settings, for baritone (1957)
'Lang Hae We Pairted Been'

IV. PIANO

Skye Boat Song (after the arrangement by Percy Grainger)

Scottish Folk-Music Settings
'Lang Hae We Pairted Been' (*Andante*; C minor) (1961)
'Waly, Waly' (*Andante*) (1959)
'A Rosebud by my Early Walk' (*Allegretto*) (1961)
'John Anderson, my Jo' (*Lento con moto*) (1961)
'Ne'erday Sang' (*Andante ardente*; E flat) (1962, revised 1963; further
retouched 28 June 1966). Source: William Sterling, Cantus Part-book, 1639.
'From an Old Pibroch' (*Allegretto/Andante*; A major) (1956, rev. 1965)
'Ca' the Yowes' (*Andante*) (1965)
'Hielan' Lament' (*Lento con moto*) (1965)
'The Birks o' Aberfeldy' (*Allegretto*) (1965)
'Jock o Hazeldean' (*Andante fluente*) (date unknown); exists also in an
arrangement for two pianos
'Hard is My Fate' (*Moderato stoico*) (19 February 1980). Melody from *Simon
Fraser of Knockie Collection*, No. 125; Inscription: 'Set at my son Gordon's
request'. Exists also in a version for violin and piano.
'Wo betyd thy Wearie Bodie' (*Andante mesto*) (date unknown)
'The Queen's Maries' (*Lento con moto*) (date unknown)

The publication by The Ronald Stevenson Society omits 'The Birks o' Aberfeldy', 'Wo betyd thy Wearie Bodie' and 'The Queen's Monies'; it is intended that they should be included in a later edition.

Willy's Drooned in Yarrow (*Willy's Rare*) 2′

Sounding Strings
1979
14 arrangements of folktunes from six Celtic countries
Intended primarily for the clarsach; performable also on pedal harp[58]
Publisher: United Music Publishers, London, 1979

Ten Airs from the Abbotsford Collection 15′
1984
1. 'Brown Robin' (*Moderato*)
2. 'The Cruel Sister' (*Andante*)
3. 'Clerk Colvin' (*Allegretto*)
4. 'John the Scot' (*Allegro stoico*)
5. 'Lady Elspat' (*Andante*)
6. 'Erlington' (*Moderato*)
7. 'Hobbie Noble' (*Allegro*)
8. 'Jamie Telfer' (*Andante*)
9. 'Outlaw Murray' (*Allegro*)
10. 'The Laidly Worm' (*Lento con moto*)

Clapping Song from South Uist 'arranged for easy piano' (*Allegro*) (1968). Exists also in an arrangement for two pianos.

Irish Folk-Song Suite 10′
1965
1. 'The Mantle so green' (*Andante*)
2. 'Luvlie Willie' (*Andante con moto*)
3. 'Gra'geal mo chroi' ('Lilywhite love o' my heart') (*Allegro corrente*)
4. 'Mary from Dungloe' (Slow)
Exists also in a version for piano duet

Chinese Folk-Song Suite 10′
May 1965
1. 'The Washer-woman and the Flower-girl' (*Con moto tranquillo*)
2. 'A Song for New Year's Day' (*Andante*)
3. 'War-widow's Lament' (*Lento*)
4. 'Beautiful Fresh Flower' (*Allegretto*)
5. 'Song of the Crab-fisher' (*Allegro con spirito*)[59]
Nos. 2 and 5 also exist in versions for piano duet
Dedication: 'To Chiu Shou Ping'

Ghanaian Folk-Song Suite 7′
1965

---

[58] For details, *cf.* Folksong Arrangements, VIII: Clarsach, p. 451.

[59] Reproduced in Appendix Five: Some Stevenson Miniatures, pp. 342–45.

1. 'Song of Valour'
2. 'Consolation'
3. 'Leopard Dance'

South Uist (Hebridean) Folk-Song Suite   7'
1969
1. 'Sailing Song' (Lively, jolly, robust)
2. 'A Witching Song for the Milking' (*Allegretto*)
3. 'A Little Mouth Music' (*Allegro alla danza*)
4. 'Waulking Song' (*Moderato*)
5. 'Spinning Song' (*Allegro corrente*)
6. 'A Tired Mother's Lullaby' (*Andante stanco*)
7. 'The Child Christ's Lullaby' (*Andante semplice*)
FP: Ronald Brautigam (piano), Koch Schwann, 3-1590-2 H1 (CD)[60]

Australian Log-Book (Australian Folk-Song Suite)   5'
July 1980
1. 'Bound for South Australia (Capstan and Halyard Shanties)' (Slow)
2. 'Waltzing Mathilde' (Brisk)
3. 'Ned Kelly's Ballad' (Moderately quick)
Inscription: 'Composed fresh from my concert tour in Victoria, Australia,
and my ever-to-be-remembered visit to the Grainger Museum, Univ. of
Melbourne. Writ in fair copy, Christmas – Yule 1980'
Dedication: 'For Felix Maegher'

Le Clerc de Tremolo (Breton Folksong)

Meng Chiang Nyu's Lament (Chinese Ballad; No. 2 of the *Songs of Ancient
China* for voice and piano) (1983/84)   2'

The Poor Irish Boy, Irish Folk-tune notated by G. F. Handel in Dublin in 1742,
harmonised (1980)   2'

Fenesta Vascia (Neapolitan folksong), included in *L'Art Nouveau du Chant
Appliqué au Piano*[61] (February 1986)   3'
Dedication: Richard Connolly in Australia

V. PIANO DUET

Irish Folk-Song Suite   10'
1965
Exists also in a version for solo piano

Two Chinese Folk-songs   4'
May 1965
1. 'A Song for New Year's Day' (*Andante*)
2. 'Song of the Crab-fisher' (*Allegro con spirito*)

---

[60] *Cf.* Appendix Nine: Discography, p. 475; Nos. 1 and 3 are reproduced in
Appendix Five: Some Stevenson Miniatures, pp. 347–49, above.

[61] *Cf.* note 28 on p. 434.

These two pieces also exist as Nos. 2 and 5 for solo piano as part of the *Chinese Folk-song Suite.*

VI. TWO PIANOS

'Bonnie Dundee' (1980)
'Clapping Song from South Uist' (1980); exists also in an arrangement 'for easy piano'
'Coulter's Candy' (1980)
'Flow Gently, Sweet Afton' (1982)
'Jock o Hazeldean' (1975)
'The High Road to Linton' (1980)
'Ye Banks and Braes' (1980)

VII. VIOLIN AND PIANO

'La Basse-Breton' (1980)
'Hard is My Fate' (date unknown). Melody from *Simon Fraser of Knockie Collection*, No. 125; inscription: 'Set at my son Gordon's request'. Exists also in a version for solo piano as No. 11 of *Scottish Folk-Music Settings*

VIII. CLARSACH

Sounding Strings
1979
14 arrangements of folktunes from six Celtic countries
1. 'Harp of Gold (Y Delyn Aur): Welsh Air' (Broad, bardic)
2. 'The Ash Grove (Lwyn On): Welsh Air' (*Allegretto*)
3. 'Hal-an-tow: The Floral Dance from Helston, Cornwall' (*Allegro*)
4. 'A Fairy's Love Song: Hebridean Air' (*Moderato*)
5. 'The Sheep under the Snow: Manx Air' (*Andante*)
6. 'Savourneen Deelish: Irish Gaelic Air' (Fairly slowly)
7. 'The Cockle-gatherer: Hebridean Dance-song' (*Allegretto*)
8. 'Tune from County Derry: Irish Air' (Slowly)
9. 'Eriskay Love-Lilt: Hebridean Air'. (*Andante, accarezzante* (caressingly))
10. 'Ben Dorain: Scottish Gaelic Air' (*Moderato maestoso*)
11. 'La Basse-Breton: Folk Dance from Brittany' (*Allegro*)
12. 'The Old Woman's Reel: Folk Dance from Barra, Outer Hebrides' ('Not fast but fairly sprightly (remember it's an *old* woman's dance)')
13. 'L'Angelus Breton: Folksong from Brittany' (*Andante amabile* (gently))
14. 'The Child Christ's Lullaby: Hebridean Carol from South Uist' (*Andante*)
Publisher: United Music Publishers, London, 1979
Dedication: Savourna Stevenson
May be performed also on pedal harp or piano

IX. CLARSACH ENSEMBLE

Eilead's na huraibh o ho! (Walking Song from South Uist), for three or four clarsachs

X. HARP

Sounding Strings[62]
1979
Publisher: United Music Publishers, London, 1979

XI. HIGHLAND BAGPIPE

GRAINGER, *Kintra Gairdens* (1980)

CADENZAS

BEETHOVEN, two cadenzas for first movement of the Violin Sonata No. 9 in A major, Op. 47, 'Kreutzer'

MOZART, three cadenzas for the Piano Concerto No. 20 in D minor, K466 (before 1961)
——, cadenza for the Piano Concerto No. 24 in C minor, K491 (1972)

SCHUBERT/LISZT, cadenza for the 'Wanderer' Fantasy, D760 (1966)

EDITIONS

D'ALBERT, *Gavotte and Musette*, Op. 1 (March 1988)

BRIAN, transcr. MACDONALD, March from *Turandot*, revision (1979). Dedication: 'In high regard for the genius of Havergal Brian and for efforts in his cause by Malcolm MacDonald and Graham Hatton. 20.VII.79'.

BUSONI, 'Polonaise' from *Sonatina ad usum infantis*: simplified version 'for Harry and Anna' (c. 1980)

CENTER, Piano Sonata, performing edition (1970)

DORWARD, Piano Concerto, performing edition (1970)

GRAINGER, *The Young Person's Grainger*[63] (1966)
——, *In Dahomey (Calkwalk Smasher)* (date unknown) Publisher: Edition Peters, 1987
——, *Three Scotch Folksongs* (from *Songs of the North*) (date unknown). Publisher: Edition Peters, 1983
——, *Bridal Lullaby* (1987–summer 1989). Publisher Bardic Edition, Aylesbury, c. 1990.

HINTON, *Scottish Ballad*, performing edition (1980)

SCOTT, F. G., *Border Riding Rhythm* (date unknown)

---

[62] For details, *cf.* p. 451.

[63] *Cf.* note 39 on p. 438.

SORABJI, *Fantasiettina sul nome illustre dell'egregio poeta Hugh MacDiarmid ossia Christopher Grieve* (1961) performing edition (date unknown). FP: Ronald Stevenson (piano), Edinburgh, 23 August 1981. Publisher: Bardic Edition, 1989

VAN DIEREN, *Piccolo Pralinudettino Fridato,* performing edition (1988). Publisher: Bardic Edition, 1988

WORDSWORTH, *Valediction,* performing edition (1988)

C. WORKS IN PROGRESS

I. ORCHESTRA

Suite for Isadora Duncan
c. 1952–54
orchestra
Unfinished; extensive drafts in short score

Variations round a Childhood Tune of Carl Nielsen   12′
Sketched August–September 1965, with further work in 1967 and 1968
Dedicatee: Robert Simpson
Exists also in a version for solo piano, similarly incomplete

Elegy for Kathleen Ferrier
1968–69
chamber orchestra
Exists also in a version (similarly incomplete) for piano solo

II. CHORUS AND ORCHESTRA

Ben Dorain
1962–
Double chorus (large and chamber), two orchestras (large and chamber)
Text: Duncan ban MacIntyre, trans. Hugh MacDiarmid
Many sketches

III. TWO PIANOS

Piano Concerto No. 2, *The Continents* (1970–72)   40′
1973
Transcription for two pianos

IV. PIANO

Variations round a Childhood Tune of Carl Nielsen   12′
Sketched August–September 1965, with further work in 1967 and 1968.
Dedicatee: Robert Simpson
Exists also as an orchestral piece, similarly incomplete.

Elegy for Kathleen Ferrier
1968–69
Exists also in a similarly incomplete version for chamber orchestra

V. VOICE(S) AND PIANO

Songs and Verses from Blake's 'An Island in the Moon'   8′ to date
Begun 1985–86

Text: William Blake
Unfinished; includes 'Lo, the bat with leathern wing' ('Scena for bass and piano', 30 June 1987, *Allegretto quasi polka*; dedication: 'For Geoffrey')

Borrovian Characters
Date unknown
For soprano, baritone and piano
Text: George Borrow
'Work in progress'

D. WORKS INCOMPLETE OR IN SKETCH FORM

I. ORCHESTRA

Variations on an Old Welsh Hymn (Aberystwyth)
c. 1960
double string orchestra
Sketches exist also for a version for two pianos

II. INSTRUMENT WITH ORCHESTRA
Concertino for bassoon and orchestra
early 1950s
Only two themes sketched

Rhapsody in memoriam Ernest Bloch
c. 1993
violin and strings
Sketches only

III. PIANO TRIO

Piano Trio
1979

IV. TWO PIANOS

Variations on an Old Welsh Hymn (Aberystwyth)
c. 1960
Exists also, in sketch form, in a version for double string orchestra

V. PIANO

Overture for Piano
1945

Allegro Barocco
1948

Pavan alla Stokowski
c. 1948
'1 page sketch inspired by Stokowski's orchestration'

Poetic Strathspey
c. 1960
Sketch, 'suggested by Smetana's Polkas Poétiques'

Étudiette 'Quasi pedale tonale'
1966

Birthday Prelude for Ernst Herrmann Meyer
1966

Scots Dances
c. 1967
Sketches for the orchestral *Scots Dance Toccata*

Beyond the Sunset (In memoriam Lewis Grassic Gibbon)
c. 1970
Sketch only

(Second) *Melody on a Ground of Glazunov*
c. 1970
Sketch only

Rebel March
1972
For Bernadette Devlin

Variations on 'Sally': Homage to Gracie Fields
c. 1980–
Extended sketches

Sonatina in Diem anni novi
1985
Sketches only

Fugue on a 12-note Theme from Cecil Gray's 'The Temptation of St Anthony'
mid-1993
Planned but not written

Sonatina nach Offenbach
1950–97
Still in sketch form

Variations on a Theme by Brahms
Date unknown
Sketches only; the theme is from the slow movement of the Piano Sonata
No. 3 in F minor, Op. 5

VI. CELLO

Suite of Scots Airs and Dances   3′
1968
Two movements completed

VII. VOICE(S) AND PIANO

Baritone and Piano

Skald's Death
Date unknown
Text: Hugh MacDiarmid

Address from the Dock: Monologue
Date unknown
Text: John MacLean

West Wind   3′
Date unknown
Text: John Masefield

Medium or Low Voice and Piano

At Robert Ferguson's Grave
Date unknown
Text: Robert Garioch

The Scarlet Woman
c. 1966
Text: Hugh MacDiarmid

Unspecified Voice and Piano

The Marmoreal Boy
late 1990
Text: Conrad Ferdinand Mayer, transl. Ronald Stevenson

A Boy's Song
Date unknown
Text: James Hogg

Song of the Wandering Jew
1966
Text: William Wordsworth
Incorporated (without text) into *Le festin d'Alkan* for solo piano

O Swallow
Date unknown
Text: Tennyson

Thoughts from Thoreau
Date unknown
Text: Thoreau

VIII. VOICE AND GUITAR

A Boy's Song
Date unknown
Text: James Hogg
Exists also in a similarly incomplete version for voice and piano

IX. OPERA

William Turner (mid-1950s)
One-act opera for television on episodes from the life of the painter J. W. M. Turner
Libretto: James Ritchie (Stevenson notes that it is 'an *excellent* libretto' – and yet it was withdrawn by the librettist)

Incomplete – 'Very few pages of MS (in vocal score) extant'

The Road to Prague (begun late September/early October 1990)
Chamber opera
Libretto: Ronald Stevenson, after Mörike's novella *Mozart auf der Reise nach Prag*

X. TRANSCRIPTIONS

Orchestra or Two Pianos

PURCELL, *Prelude, Fugue and Figured Fugue,* for two pianos or piano (harpsichord) and string orchestra

Piano

BACH, 'Das alte Jahr vergangen ist', from the *Orgelbüchlein*, BWV614: sketches for a sonatina

Appendix Eight
BIBLIOGRAPHY

1. Writings by Ronald Stevenson

1. Books

Western Music – An Introduction, Kahn & Averill, London, 1971 (2nd edn. in preparation).

The Paderewski Paradox, The Klavar Foundation of Great Britain, Lincoln/La Société Paderewski, Morges, Switzerland, 1992.

Ronald Stevenson on Music, Vol. One, *Busoni: Aspects of a Genius*, Toccata Press, London, forthcoming.[1]

2. Contributions to Books

'Holst', in *Enciclopedio dello Spettacolo*, Vol. vi, 1959, pp. 371–72.

'MacDiarmid, Joyce and Busoni', in K. D. Duval and Sydney Goodsir Smith (eds.), *MacDiarmid: A Festschrift*, Duval, Edinburgh, 1962, pp. 141–54.

'The Emergence of a Scottish Music', in Karl Miller (ed.), *Memories of a Modern Scotland*, Faber, London, 1971, pp. 189–97.

'Concerted Works', in Lewis Foreman (ed.), *Edmund Rubbra*, Triad Press, Rickmansworth, 1977, pp. 43–51.

'Introduction' and 'Bush's Piano Music', in *Time Remembered: An 80th Birthday Symposium*, Bravura Publications, Kidderminster, 1981, pp. 7–8 and 36–44.

'Grainger and the Piano', in Lewis Foreman (ed.), *The Percy Grainger Companion*, Thames Publishing, London, 1981, pp. 113–22.

'Grainger's Transcriptions', *Studies in Music* (Grainger Centennial Volume, University of Western Australia), No. 16, 1982, pp. 84–89.

'The Piano Music', in Christopher Norris (ed.), *Shostakovich: The Man and his Music*, Lawrence & Wishart, London, 1982, pp. 81–103.

'MacLean: Musician Manqué (and a Composer's Collaboration)', in Raymond J. Ross and Joy Hendry (eds.), *Sorley MacLean: Critical Essays*, Edinburgh Academic Press, Edinburgh, 1988, pp. 176–83.

3. Contributions to Periodicals

I. ARTICLES

'Busoni and Mozart', *The Score*, No. 13, September 1955, pp. 25–38.

---

[1] *Cf.* note 5 on p. 23, above.

'Busoni: The Legend of a Prodigal', *The Score*, No. 15, March 1956, pp. 15–30.

'Busoni e la Gran Bretagna', *Bolletino Storico Empolese*, Vol. 1, anno II, No. 4, 1958, pp. 303–13.

'Maurice Emmanuel: A Belated Apologia', *Music and Letters*, Vol. 40, April 1959, pp. 154–65.

'An Introduction to the Music of Roman Vlad', *The Music Review*, Vol. 22, No. 2, May 1961, pp. 124–35.

'Alan Bush: Committed Composer', *Music Review*, Vol. 25, No. 4, November 1964, pp. 323–42.

'Alan Bush az elkotelezett zeneszerso. Bushzenezzerzoi palyayanak vazlata', *Magyar Zene*, No. 3, June 1965, pp. 270–88.

'Busoni Centenary Concerts', *The Listener*, Vol. LXXVI, No. 1959, 13 October 1966, p. 548.

'Britten "War Requiem" ', *The Listener*, Vol. 78, No. 2014, 2 November 1967, p. 581.

'Bernard Stevens', *The Musical Times*, cix, June 1968, pp. 525–27.

'André Previn', *The Listener*, Vol. 81, No. 2090, 17 April 1969, p. 542.

'Tovey', *The Listener*, Vol. 81, No. 2095, 22 May 1969, pp. 725–26.

'*Passacaglia on DSCH*', *The Listener*, Vol. 82, No. 2115, 9 October 1969, p. 494.

'Heifetz in Tartan: Scots Fiddle Competition', *The Listener*, Vol. 82, No. 2131, 29 January 1970, p. 158.

'Alan Bush in the '70s', *The Musical Times*, cxiii, July 1972, pp. 66–163.

'Busoni's Great Fugue', *The Listener*, Vol. 87, No. 2236, 3 February 1972, p. 157.

'Mefausto', *The Listener*, Vol. 89, No. 2284, 4 January 1973, p. 25.

'The Composer and Scottish Folk Music', *Scottish International*, April 1973, pp. 14–15.

'Music's Mowgli', *Books and Bookmen*, Vol. 22, No. 6, March 1977, pp. 18–19.

'Random Relics of Percy Grainger', *Grainger Journal*, Vol. 1, No. 2, 1978, pp. 12–13.

'Busoni – Doktor Faust of the Keyboard', *EPTA Piano Journal*, Vol. 1, No. 1, undated (c. February 1980), pp. 14–15.

'Bach and Wagner: A Journey in Music', *Grainger Journal*, Vol. 3, No. 1, 1980, pp. 10–13.

'Busoni – Necromancer of the Keyboard', *The Listener*, Vol. 103, No. 2656, 3 April 1980, p. 443.

'The Buddha's Fire Sermon', *Godowsky Society Newsletter*, Vol. 1, No. 1, 1980, p. 15.

Harps of their own Sort, Lecture Series 1, National Library of Scotland, March 1981.

'Alan Bush – Marxist Composer', *Performance*, Spring 1981, pp. 44–45.

'Enescu, the Aeneas of Our Days', *Performance*, February/March 1982, pp. 11–12.

'Szymanowski at the Piano', *Godowsky Society Newsletter*, Vol. 3. No. 1, 1983, pp. 3–6.

'Bernard Stevens', *Tempo*, No. 145, June 1983, p. 27.

'The Truth about Bax', *3 Magazine*, Vol. 2, No. 11, November 1983, pp. 2–3.

'Leopold Godowsky' (transcription of BBC Radio 3 broadcast of 28 December 1970), *Godowsky Society Newsletter*, Vol. 4, No. 2, 1984, pp. 7–11.

'Delius's Sources', *Tempo*, No. 151, December 1984, pp. 24–27.

'Notes on Aspects of Godowsky as Composer', *Godowsky Society Newsletter*, Vol. 5, No. 1, 1985, p. 2b.

'Peter Grimes Fantasy: A Lesson given by the Composer to Mao Weo Hui at Shanghai Conservatory', *EPTA Piano Journal*, Vol. 8, No. 24, October 1987, pp. 15–16.

'Obituary Notice: K. S. Sorabji', *Classical Music*, No. 364, 12 November 1988, p. 11.

'Composing a Song-Cycle, *Chapman*, Nos. 89–90 (double issue), Summer 1998, pp. 33–36.

'Busoni and Melody', *Chapman*, Nos. 89–90 (double issue), Summer 1998, pp. 81–86.

'Summer Sensation', *International Piano*, Vol. 5, No. 19, January/February 2002, pp. 48–49.

II. Reviews of Books

Alfredo Casella, *Music in my Time*, in *The Chesterian*, Vol. XXX, No. 183, July 1955, pp. 24–26.

Ferruccio Busoni, *Wesen und Einheit der Musik*, in *The Chesterian*, Vol. XXXI, No. 187, Summer 1956, pp. 31–33.

Roman Vlad, *Modernità e Tradizione*, in *The Chesterian*, Vol. XXXI, No. 190, Spring 1957, pp. 131–33.

Mabel Dolmetsch, *A Personal Recollection of Arnold Dolmetsch*, in *The Chesterian*, Vol. XXXII, No. 194, Spring 1958, pp. 121–23.

Lady Mayer, *The Forgotten Master: The Life and Times of Louis Spohr*, in *The Chesterian*, Vol. XXXIV, No. 199, Summer 1959, pp. 29–31.

Thomas Beecham, *Delius*, in *The Chesterian*, Vol. XXXIV, No. 202, Spring 1960, pp. 132–35.

Judith Litante, *A Natural Approach to Singing*, in *The Chesterian*, Vol. XXXV, No. 203, Summer 1960, pp. 226–29.

Reginald Nettel, *Havergal Brian: The Man and his Music*, Kenneth Eastaugh, *Havergal Brian: The Making of a Composer*, and Lewis Foreman, *Havergal Brian and the Performance of his Orchestral Music*, in *Books and Bookmen*, Vol. 22, No. 3, December 1976, pp. 62–63.

Theodore Ethel, *Piano Music for the Left Hand*, in *The Godowsky Society Newsletter*, Vol. 3, No. 2, 1983, pp. 8–11.

Antony Beaumont, *Busoni the Composer*, in *The Times Literary Supplement*, 6 December 1985, p. 1398.

Joseph Banowetz, *The Pianist's Guide to Pedalling*, in *The Godowsky Society Newsletter*, Vol. 5, No. 2, 1986, pp. 18–20.

Antony Beaumont (ed.), *Ferruccio Busoni – Selected Letters*, in *Tempo*, No. 163, December 1987, pp. 27–29.

Michael Davidson, *Mozart and the Pianist*, in *International Piano*, Vol. 5, No. 18, November/December 2001, p. 85.

Arnold Bax, *Ideala*, ed. Colin Scott-Sutherland, in *International Piano*, Vol. 7, No. 25, January/February 2003, pp. 84–85.

III. Reviews of Broadcasts

All of these items were published in The Listener, *in the column 'Last Week's Music'.*

Bush, Gerhard, Simpson, Wilson, Vol. 78, No. 2005, 31 August 1967, pp. 413–14.

Pfitzner, Shostakovich, Vol. 78, No. 2009, 28 September 1967, pp. 283–84.

Hindemith, Wordsworth, Vol. 78, No. 2016, 16 November 1967, p. 646.

Walton, Wellesz, Maconchy, Vol. 79, No. 2024, 11 January 1968, p. 58.

F. G. Scott, Alkan, Vol. 79, No. 2028, 8 February 1968, p. 186.

Reger, Messiaen, Brian, Vol. 79, No. 2034, 21 March 1968, p. 386.

Indian Music, Vol. 79, No. 2039, 25 April 1968, p. 531.

Style and Interpretation, Vol. 79, No. 2044, 30 May 1968, p. 710.

Britten (Aldeburgh Festival), Vol. 80, No. 2049, 4 July 1968, p. 26.

Elgar, Vol. 80, No. 2052, 25 July 1968, pp. 122–23.

Bernstein, Stravinsky, Lutosławski, Vol. 80, No. 2054, 8 August 1968, pp. 185–86.

Delius (Requiem), Vol. 80, No. 2059, 12 September 1968, p. 346.

Schubert, Vol. 80, No. 2063, 10 October 1968, p. 482.

Rossini, Vol. 80, No. 2069, 21 November 1968, p. 692–93.

Menotti, Vol. 81, No. 2079, 2 January 1969, p. 39.

Jazz, Vol. 81, No. 2084, 6 February 1969, pp. 185–86.

Dallapiccola, Vol. 81, No. 2087, 22 March 1969, p. 135.

Duke Ellington, Vol. 81, No. 2093, 8 May 1969, pp. 658–59.

Stokowski, Vol. 81, No. 2100, 26 June 1969, p. 793.

Szeryng, Bush, Vol. 82, No. 2105, 31 July 1969, pp. 161–62.

Folk Music, Vol. 82, No. 2113, 25 September 1969, p. 429.

Schumann, Vol. 82, No. 2121, 20 November 1969, p. 711.

Gershwin, Vol. 83, No. 2128, 8 January 1970, p. 58.

Grainger, Vol. 83, No. 2137, 12 March 1970, p. 353.

Lehár, Vol. 83, No. 2145, 7 May 1970, pp. 625–26.

4. Editions

Bernhard Ziehn, *Canonic Studies*, Kahn & Averill, London, 1976.

2. Writings on Ronald Stevenson

A special edition of the Scottish poetry magazine *Chapman*, Nos. 89–90 (double issue), was published in 1998 to celebrate Stevenson's seventieth birthday. A number of his friends and associates contributed essays, which are listed here by author; Stevenson's own contributions are listed under 'Writings by Ronald Stevenson'.[2]

ANDERSON, MARTIN, 'A Composer Loyal to His Principles' (interview), *Fanfare*, Vol. 18, No. 5, May/June 1995, pp. 100–7.
——, 'Ronald Stevenson's Cello Concerto', *Tempo*, No. 196, April 1996, pp. 47–49.
——, 'An Age of Enlightenment', *Chapman*, Nos. 89–90 (double issue), Summer 1998, pp. 67–70.
——, 'The Meaning of Life in 80 Minutes', *The Independent*, 16 February 2001, p. 16.
——, review of first performance of *Fugue, Variations and Epilogue on a Theme of Bax*, *Tempo*, No. 231, January 2005, p. 54.

BAXTER, JAMES REID, ' "The Gypsy" – Ronald Stevenson's Violin Concerto', *Tempo*, No. 183, December 1992.

---

[2] *Cf.* p. 463.

——, 'Ronald Stevenson and the Choral Voice', *Chapman*, Nos. 89–90 (double issue), Summer 1998, pp. 40–45.

CHISHOLM, ALASTAIR, 'Stevenson's Soutar Settings in the Context of Some Personal Memories', *Chapman*, Nos. 89–90 (double issue), Summer 1998, pp. 74–76.

CORLEONIS, ADRIAN, 'A Caledonian Orpheus', *Fanfare*, Vol. 12, No. 5, May/ June 1989, pp. 520–27.

CROWE, VICTORIA, 'Tribute to Ronald Stevenson', *Chapman*, Nos. 89–90 (double issue), Summer 1998, *Chapman*, Nos. 89–90 (double issue), Summer 1998, pp. 48–50.

ELBORN, GEOFFREY, 'Ronald Stevenson the Man', *Chapman*, Nos. 89–90 (double issue), Summer 1998, pp. 60–62.

HARRY, MARTYN, 'Ronald Stevenson Sixtieth Birthday Celebrations', *Music and Musicians*, October 1988, pp. 46–7.

HARRIS, T. J. G., 'A Stupendous Unity', *Quadrant*, Melbourne, April 1991.

HUGHES, LAURENCE, 'Ronald Stevenson: a 70th birthday tribute', *The Independent*, Eye on Friday, 6 March 1998, p. 19.

HUTTON, PHILLIP, 'The Stevenson Scandal', *Chapman*, Nos. 89–90 (double issue), Summer 1998, pp. 88–90.

LAMBTON, CHRISTOPHER, 'Dear Ronald Stevenson', *BBC Music Magazine*, Vol. 7, No. 5, January 1999, pp. 26–28.
——, 'Collecting Key Signatures', *The Daily Telegraph*, 2 January 1999.

MACDONALD, CALUM, 'Last Week's Broadcast Music' (review of the premiere of the Piano Concerto No. 2), *The Listener*, Vol. 88, No. 2245, 24 August 1972.
——, 'Stevenson: *Passacaglia on DSCH*' and 'Twentieth Century Operatic Fantasies', *Tempo*, No. 166, September 1988, pp. 56–58.
——, 'Edinburgh Festival and After – Ronald Stevenson', *Tempo*, No. 167, December 1988, pp. 54–56.
——, 'Discovering Ronald Stevenson', *CD Review*, No. 50, December 1990, pp. 34–35.
——, 'Stevenson's *Voces Vagabundae*', *Tempo*, No. 175, December 1990, p.
——, 'Piano Music from Scotland', *CD Review*, March 1991, p. 72.

MACDONALD, MALCOLM, 'Ronald Stevenson', *Music Events*, July 1972, pp. 10–11.
——, *Ronald Stevenson: A Musical Biography*, National Library of Scotland, Edinburgh, 1989.
——, 'Aspects of Scottish Musical Nationalism in the 20th century, with special reference to the music of F. G. Scott, Ronald Center and Ronald Stevenson', in Tomi Mäkelä (ed.), *Music and Nationalism in 20th-Century Great Britain and Finland*, Von Böckel Verlag, Hamburg, 1998, pp. 111–32.
——, 'A Plaited Music: Ronald Stevenson at Seventy', *Chapman*, Nos. 89–90 (double issue), Summer 1998, pp. 13–21.

MacNeacail, Rob, 'Interview', *Chapman*, Nos. 89–90 (double issue), Summer 1998, pp. 5–8.

MacNeacail, Angus, 'Meeting Ronald', *Chapman*, Nos. 89–90 (double issue), Summer 1998, pp. 9–12.

McGuire, Eddie, 'Stevenson, Music and Marxism', *Chapman*, Nos. 89–90 (double issue), Summer 1998, pp. 28–32.

McLachlan, Murray, 'Unsung Heroes: Ronald Stevenson', *Piano Magazine*, Vol. 11, No. 2, March/April 2003, pp. 38–39.

McManus, Tony, 'Innocence and Experience – Ronald Stevenson at Seventy', *Cencrastus*, No. 61, pp. 27–32.

Moffat, Alexander, 'Comrades-in-art', *Chapman*, Nos. 89–90 (double issue), Summer 1998, pp. 71–74.

Orga, Ateş, 'Ronald Stevenson', *Music and Musicians*, Vol. 27, October 1968, pp. 178–80.
——, 'The Piano Music of Ronald Stevenson', *Musical Opinion*, Vol. 92, No. 1098, March 1969, pp. 292–95.

——, 'Master of Invention', *International Piano Quarterly*, summer 1998, pp. 73–76.

John Purser, *Scotland's Music*, Mainstream Publishing, Edinburgh and London, 1992, pp. 244, 251, 257–58 and 276–77.
——, 'A Filter in the Stream', *Chapman*, Nos. 89–90 (double issue), Summer 1998, pp. 63–64.

Rumson, Gordon, 'Radical Traditionalist', *International Piano*, Vol. 6, No. 21, May–June 2002, pp. 38–41.

Scott-Sutherland, Colin, 'The Music of Ronald Stevenson', *The Music Review*, Vol. 26, No. 2, May 1965, pp. 118–28.
——, Review of *The Young Person's Grainger* and *A Wheen Tunes for Bairns tae Spiel*, in *The Music Review*, Vol. 31, No. 2, May 1970, pp. 172–73.
——, 'Ronald Stevenson', in Lewis Foreman (ed.), *British Music Now*, Paul Elek, London, 1977, pp. 32–40.
——, 'Ronald Stevenson', *The New Grove Dictionary of Music and Musicians*, Vol. 18, Macmillan, London, 1980, pp. 137–38.
——, 'Thoughts on Ronald Stevenson's MacDiarmid Songs', *Tempo*, No. 188, March 1994.
——, 'Ronald Stevenson at Seventy', *Music Current* (newsletter of the Scottish Music Information Centre), No. 87, Spring 1998, pp. 1 and 6.
——, 'Stevenson and the Child', *Chapman*, Nos. 89–90 (double issue), Summer 1998, pp. 37–39.
——, 'The Shorter Piano Works of Ronald Stevenson', *EPTA Piano Journal*, Vol. 19, No. 56, Summer 1998, pp. 21–23.
——, 'Ronald Stevenson Celebrating his 75th year', *Piano Professional*, No. 3, September 2003, pp. 8–10.

——, '"What the Minstrel told us"': Ronald Stevenson, Bax and the North', *British Music*, Vol. 26 (2004), pp. 76–79.

SMITH, HARRIET, 'Playing with Words', *International Piano Quarterly*, Summer 1998, pp. 70–72.

STEEL, JUDY, 'Ronald Stevenson and the Early Borders Festivals', *Chapman*, Nos. 89–90 (double issue), Summer 1998, pp. 46–47.

WALTON, CHRIS, 'Composer in Interview: Ronald Stevenson – A Scot in "Emergent Africa"', *Tempo*, No. 225, July 2003, pp. 23–31.

WATSON, DEREK, 'The Contrapuntal Muse', *Chapman*, Nos. 89–90 (double issue), Summer 1998, pp. 51–54.

WHITE, KENNETH, 'The Atlantic Cantata', *Chapman*, Nos. 89–90 (double issue), Summer 1998, pp. 57–59.

WILSON, COLIN, *The Brandy of the Damned*, John Baker, 1964, republished as *Colin Wilson on Music*, Pan Books, London, 1967, pp. 178–80.

WOOD, RUZENA, 'The Man in the Fedora', *Chapman*, Nos. 89–90 (double issue), Summer 1998, pp. 22–24.

WRIGHT, GORDON, *MacDiarmid: An Illustrated Biography*, Gordon Wright, Edinburgh, 1977, p. 137.

Appendix Nine
DISCOGRAPHY

1. RECORDINGS BY RONALD STEVENSON

I. Commercial Recordings

All recordings are on compact disc unless otherwise indicated.

BACH arr. BUSONI, Partita in D minor, BWV1004: Chaconne, Altarus, AIR-CD-9043.

BERG arr. STEVENSON, *Wiegenlied aus Wozzeck*, Altarus, AIR-CD-9042.

BUSH arr. STEVENSON, 'The Minstrel's Lay' from *Wat Tyler*, Altarus, AIR-CD-9042.

BUSONI, *An die Jugend*: Epilogue, Altarus, AIR-CD-9041.

——, *Prélude et Étude en Arpèges*, Altarus, AIR-CD-9041.

——, *Tanzwalzer*, Altarus, AIR-CD-9041.

——, Toccata, Altarus, AIR-CD-9041.

——, *Zehn Variationen über ein Präludium von Chopin* (1922 version[1]), Altarus, AIR-CD-9041.

——, *Fantasia Contrappuntistica* (1921 version), with Joseph Banowetz (piano), Altarus AIR-CD-9044.

——, *Finnländische Volksweisen*, with Joseph Banowetz (piano), Altarus AIR-CD-9044.

——, *Fuge über das Volkslied 'O, du mein lieber Augustin'*, with Joseph Banowetz (pianos), Altarus AIR-CD-9044.

——, *Improvisation über das Bachsche Chorallied 'Wie wohl ist mir, o Freund der Seele'*, with Joseph Banowetz (piano), Altarus AIR-CD-9044.

CENTER, *Dona Nobis Pacem*, with Kathleen Livingstone (soprano), Neil Mackie (tenor), William Watson (baritone), Ronald Leith (organ), Ronald Forbes (timpani), Susan Main (side-drum), Queen's Cross Chamber Chorus, cond. Geoffrey Atkinson, Altarus, AIR-2-9100 (LP).

——, Piano Sonata, Altarus, AIR-2-9100 (LP).

CHOPIN, *Nocturne* in C minor, Op. 48, No. 1, Altarus, AIR-CD-9043.

——, *Prelude* in C minor, Op. 28, No. , Altarus, AIR-CD-9043.

DEBUSSY, *Préludes*, Book 1: No. 10, '*La Cathédrale Engloutie*', Altarus, AIR-CD-9043.

GRAINGER, *Rosenkavalier Ramble*, Altarus, AIR-CD-9042.

——, *Scotch Strathspey and Reel*, Altarus, AIR-CD-9040.

——, arr. STEVENSON, *Hill Song* No. 1, Altarus, AIR-CD-9040.

——, arr. STEVENSON, *Three Scotch Folksongs*, Altarus, AIR-CD-9040.

LISZT, *Weihnachtsbaum*: Nos. 6, '*Carillon*', and 9, '*Abendglocken*', Altarus, AIR-CD-9043.

---

[1] This recording includes a previously unpublished variation; it had remained in manuscript until its publication in 1991 by Bardic Edition, Aylesbury.

MacDowell, *New England Idylls*: No. 5, 'In Deep Woods', Altarus, AIR-CD-9043.

Marek, *Triptychon*, Op. 8, Altarus, AIR-CD-9043.

Mozart arr. Busoni, *Fantasy* in F minor, K608, with Joseph Banowetz (piano), Altarus AIR-CD-9044.

Sorabji, *Fantasiettina sul nome illustre dell'egregio poeta Hugh MacDiarmid ossia Christopher Grieve*, Altarus, AIR-CD-9043.

Stevenson, *Heroic Song for Hugh MacDiarmid*, Altarus, AIR-CD-9043.

——, *Passacaglia on DSCH*, Altarus, AIR-CD-9091(2).

——, *Peter Grimes Fantasy*, Altarus, AIR-CD-9042.

——, *Prelude, Fugue and Fantasy on Themes from Busoni's 'Faust'*, Altarus, AIR-CD-9091(2) and AIR-CD-9042.

——, *Recitative and Air*, Altarus, AIR-CD-9091(2).

Trad. arr Grainger, *Songs of the North*, Altarus, AIR-CD-9040.

2. Broadcast Recordings

The National Sound Archive of The British Library maintains a collection of Ronald Stevenson's recordings for BBC Radio, of his own music and of that of other composers, as well as recordings of performances of Stevenson's music by other musicians. It also holds commercial Stevenson recordings. The National Sound Archive (formerly the British Institute of Recorded Sound) has access to BBC Sound Archive recordings, which likewise contain a number of Stevenson recordings. Both Archives also hold several talks by Ronald Stevenson, broadcast or otherwise.

Issue No. 42/43 of *Recorded Sound* (the journal formerly published by the BIRS) for April–July 1971 contains (p. 755) a complete list of recordings of Stevenson's music up to that time. The NSA can supply further details upon request. Enquiries should be addressed to the Library and Information Service, National Sound Archive, British Library, 96 Euston Road, London NW1 2DB; telephone 0207 412 7432; fax: 0207 412 7441; Web: http://www/bl.uk/collections/sound-archive/wam.html; e-mail: NSA-wam@bl.uk

2. RECORDINGS BY OTHERS OF MUSIC BY RONALD STEVENSON

I. Orchestral Music

Piano Concerto No. 1, *A Faust Triptych*, Murray McLachlan (piano), Chetham's Symphony Orchestra, cond. Julian Clayton, Olympia, OCD 429.

Piano Concerto No. 2, *The Continents*, Murray McLachlan (piano), Chetham's Symphony Orchestra, cond. Julian Clayton, Olympia, OCD 429.

II. Chamber Music

A. String Quartet

Four Meditations, rec. Jan Becher String Quartet, Alain Van Kerckhoven Éditeur, AVK 005

Recitative and Air: In memoriam Shostakovich, rec. Jan Becher String Quartet, Alain Van Kerckhoven Éditeur, AVK 005.

String Quartet, *Voces Vagabundae,* rec. Martinů Quartet, Arco Diva UP0052–2.

B. Piano Duet

Two Chinese Folk Songs, rec. Goldstone and Clemmow, The Divine Art, 25024

III. Instrumental Music

A. Music for Piano

1. Original Works

Beltane Bonfire, rec. Donna Amato, Altarus AIR-CD-9021.

——, rec. Murray McLachlan, Olympia, OCD 264.

Den Bergtekne, Donna Amato, Altarus, AIR-CD-9022.

Fugue on a Fragment of Chopin, rec. Joseph Banowetz, Altarus, AIR-CD-9089.

Motus Perpetuus (?) Temporibus Fatalibus, rec. Joseph Banowetz, Altarus, AIR-CD-9089.

Norse Elegy for Ella Nygaard, Donna Amato, Altarus, AIR-CD-9022.

Passacaglia on DSCH, rec. John Ogdon, HMV ASP 2321-220 (LP).

——, Murray MacLachan, The Divine Art 25013.

——, rec. Raymond Clarke, Marco Polo 8.223545.

——, rec. Murray McLachlan, The Divine Art, 25013.

Recitative and Air, rec. Joseph Banowetz, Altarus, AIR-CD-9089.

Scottish Triptych, A, rec. Joseph Banowetz, Altarus, AIR-CD-9089.

Sonatina No. 1, John Ogdon, Altarus, AIR-CD-9063.

Sonatina Serenissima, rec. Anthony Goldstone, Gamut, GAM CD 526.

South Uist (Hebridean) Folk-Song Suite, rec. Ronald Brautigam, Koch Schwann, 3-1590-2 H1

Symphonic Elegy for Liszt, rec. Joseph Banowetz, Altarus, AIR-CD-9089.

Three Scottish Ballads, rec. Ronald Brautigam, Koch Schwann, 3-1590-2 H1

Three Scottish Ballads: No. 2, 'The Dowie Dens o' Yarrow', and No. 3, 'Newhaven Fishwife's Cry', rec. Murray McLachlan, Olympia, OCD 264.

20th Century Music Diary, A, rec. Joseph Banowetz, Altarus, AIR-CD-9089.

Wheen Tunes for Bairns tae Spiel, A, rec. Ronald Brautigam, Koch Schwann, 3-1590-2 H1.

2. Transcriptions

SCOTT, F. G. 'Since all thy vows, false maid, are blown to air', rec. Murray McLachlan, Olympia, OCD 264.

——, 'Wha is that at my bower-door', rec. Murray McLachlan, Olympia, OCD 264.

——, 'O were my love yon lilac fare', rec. Murray McLachlan, Olympia, OCD 264.

——, 'Wee Willie Gray', rec. Murray McLachlan, Olympia OCD 264.

——, 'Milkwort and Bog-cotton', rec. Murray McLachlan, Olympia, OCD 264.
——, 'Crowdieknowe', rec. Murray McLachlan, Olympia, OCD 264.
——, 'Aye waukin, O', rec. Murray McLachlan, Olympia, OCD 264.
——, 'There's news, lasses, news', rec. Murray McLachlan, Olympia, OCD 264.

B. Music for Organ
Prelude and Fugue on a Theme of Liszt, rec. Kevin Bowyer, Altarus, AIR-CD-9063(2).
Fugue on a Shepherd's Air from 'Tristan and Isolde', rec. Jonathan Scott, ASC Records, ASC CD 42.
Reflections on an Old Scots Psalm Tune, rec. Jonathan Scott, ASC Records, ASC CD 42.

C. Music for Violin
Scots Suite for solo violin, rec. Petr Maceček, Waldmann, JW014-2.

IV. Choral Music
'Calbharaigh' ('Calvary') from *Anns an Airde, as an Doimnhe*, rec. Section Art Vocal du Cercle Culturel des Communautés Européennes à Luxembourg, dir. Dafydd Bullock, in *Eurocantica*, SAIN SCD 2047.
Domino Roberto Carwor: In Memoriam Robert Carver, rec. Cappella Nova, dir. Alan Tavener, Linn Records, CKD 014.

V. Songs
Border Boyhood, rec. The Artsong Collective (Wills Morgan, tenor; Richard Black, piano), Musaeus MZCD100.
Child's Garden of Verses, A, rec. The Artsong Collective (Moira Harris, soprano; Wills Morgan, tenor; Richard Black, piano), Musaeus MZCD100.
Nine Haiku, rec. The Artsong Collective (Moira Harris, soprano; Richard Black, piano), Musaeus MZCD100.
A'e Gowden Lyric – Songs by Ronald Stevenson: Tràighean (Shores), The Gaelic Muse, The Bobbin-winder, The Robber, O Wha's the Bride?, Trompe L'Oeuil, Hill Sang, Plum Tree, To the Future, Buckie Braes, Halloween Sang, The Droll Wee Man, The Quiet Comes In, Day is Dune, The Rose of all the World, The Bonnie Broukit Bairn, Fairytales, A'e Gowden Lyric, A Child's Garden of Verses (cycle), Susan Hamilton (soprano), John Cameron (piano), Delphian DCD34006.

Index
of Ronald Stevenson's Music

Numbers in italics refer to illustrations

477

General
Index

Numbers in italics refer to illustrations

The Ronald Stevenson Society

The Ronald Stevenson Society, Scotland, was founded in 1993 to spread awareness of the composer, his music and his music-making. The Society has already published a substantial part of Stevenson's output and adds regularly to the pieces available; it publishes a catalogue which is updated annually.

Membership of the Ronald Stevenson Society is open to all. The benefits include a newsletter three times a year and an annual summer school. For more information or to join please contact the Secretary at the address shown below, or by fax or e-mail.

Patrons: Joseph Banowetz, Lord Patrick Douglas Hamilton, Graham Johnson OBE

The Ronald Stevenson Society, 3 Chamberlain Road, Edinburgh, EH10 4DL
Fax +44 (0)131 229 9298
E-mail: info@rssoc.org.uk
www.rssoc.org.uk